The Age of Dürer and Holbein
German Drawings 1400-1550

Hans Holbein the Younger *A Wildman brandishing an uprooted tree trunk* (no. 195)

The Age of
Dürer and Holbein

German Drawings 1400-1550

John Rowlands

With the assistance
of Giulia Bartrum

Published for the Trustees of the British Museum
by British Museum Publications

© 1988 The Trustees of the British Museum

Published by British Museum Publications Ltd
46 Bloomsbury Street, London WC1B 3QQ

British Library Cataloguing in Publication Data

Rowlands, John
    The age of Dürer and Holbein: German drawings
    1400–1550.
    1. German drawings 1400–1550. Catalogues,
    indexes
    I. Title   II. British Museum
    741.943'074

    ISBN 0-7141-1639-4

FRONT COVER Albrecht Dürer: Detail from
A 'weierhaus' (no.42)
BACK COVER Master of the Votive Painting of
St Lambrecht: *Lamentation over the Dead Christ*
(no.3 verso)

Designed by James Shurmer

Set in Baskerville and printed in Great Britain by
Jolly & Barber Ltd, Rugby

il from Dürer's Head of the Dead Christ

a, not famous
must have de-
geoning white
lling out" Na-
in the run-up
lections for all
in October. He
it Cuba's with-
by its Soviet
aste for distant
s decisive vic-
onslaught" on
national Com-
lso argue that
th Africa's eco-
n pose no real

ss conferences
the UN Secre-
y build up an
al superpower
game involving
Moscow. Hav-
ative by being
e, South Africa
accuse anyone
rd of foot-drag-
rint of the Gen-
ls there is still
metable for Cu-
only a schedule
by September 1
or after August
.
ne South Africa
free Namibia.
npteenth with-
ace the first SA
n 1975, and the
aka Accord be-
Angola's Marx-
nt in 1984. Link-
e ceased to be
triangular. The
want the anti-
led from its An-
turn for ceasing
vil war with the
h Africa breaks
nouring such an
is irrelevant be-
y on an alterna-
cently built up

with US help, from Zaire, Angola's
hostile neighbour to the north-east.
This is presumably why Unita left
the southern front near Namibia
this year to return to guerrilla-fight-
ing further north. Unita, alone of all
the parties involved, has rejected
the ceasefire, which is rather a large
loose end to leave lying about as
everyone else rides off into the
sunset.

Limited appeal

WHAT did you do at work
today ? The televised recruitment advertisement, which starts to
run tomorrow night, shows one girl
putting tea bags into cups while another places an oxygen mask over a
patient's mouth. At a cost of £700,000
the Department of Health hopes to
persuade several thousand girls to
switch from secretarial work to
nursing. The advertisement — the
first recruitment campaign the NHS
has ever run on television — is a
slick professional job. There is only
one problem: it is aimed at the
wrong target.

Five months ago Mr Len Peach,
the NHS chief executive, described
to a national conference on nursing
the problems which the shrinking
pool of female school leavers presented to the health service. Unless
present recruitment policies were
changed, he explained, the NHS
would have to sign up more than
half of all girls leaving school with
five 'O' levels and one 'A' level by
1992. He went on: "It is self evident
that recruitment of this group on
this scale is impossible. It can't be
done." Instead, he urged district
health authorities to widen the
entry gate. There was a large pool of

potential recruits the NH
leaving untapped: older e
cluding former nurses wh
to raise families, ethnic
and most radical of all
Peach said he would not
until every district health
had tested this market.

Mr Peach needs to ha
with head office, which
not picked up his mess
proudly invited health
dents to a preview of
recruitment campaign.
about the target audien
partment explained th
women were "the most i
available recruitment
Other groups were to
later. But if the Depart
break down the widesp
dice that nursing is won
then it has to start now.
opportunity than its firs
recuitment campaign ?
has reinforced the stere
is a serious reverse for
recruitment strategy.

There are two other pr
ing NHS recruiting team
is pay. Many girls — let
men — are not going to
to the profession until th
over the pay deal is clea
last review did promise
proper career structure
aries that could suppo
The Prime Minister p
fund the reward compl
the regrading process
ever, confusion has re
putes over grades and
the Prime Minister's c
as the estimated cost ha
continue to grow. An
Prime Ministerial cc
would be welcome.

The second problem
surd. Free brochures or
sion will be sent to any
plies but school leavers,
they want to start traini
to pay £6 just for the

missal (Comment, August 6) of
"armed struggle" as an accurate description of a people's
last resort against colonial rule
— you term it "woolly" and al-
lege that the Bishops got their

Banging to rights an out-dated a

HOLLOWAY prison, where
the current Prison Officers'
Association dispute began, has

LOVELY, JUST

form. Is anyone at HQ living in the real world ? When banks, building societies and computer companies are offering all sorts of inducements, the department seems intent on deterring recruits.

Playing it by the clock

ON THE one hand, an athlete of brilliance, even of genius, who has brought home from previous Olympics two gold medals and two silver; on the other, a crude rulebook. Seen in this light it is really no contest. Just as in 1984, when Sebastian Coe was beaten by Peter Elliott in the trials at Crystal Palace but was selected for the 1500 metres at Los Angeles even so, and won it, both sentiment and tradition demand that Coe should again be given the third, discretionary place in the British team for Seoul. The selectors wanted to keep that option open so that Coe could have a further chance to prove himself at forthcoming meetings in Zurich, Cologne and Berne. But the British Amateur Athletics Board, on a majority vote of 11 to 10, has over-ruled them. It has rejected the defence put forward on Coe's behalf that he misjudged his preparations, returning too late from altitude training in Switzerland. Coe has failed to meet the requirements which the rulebook laid down, and that is the end of the matter.

But is sentiment the most reliable guide in these matters ? Had the Board, once the rule-book was established, any real choice ? Sebastian Coe is 31. There was absolutely no way of telling whether his disastrous performance at Birmingham was a one-off failure or a sign that Coe is now in the twilight of his outstanding athletic career. Certainly they will be vilified for having rejected him. But suppose they had turned a blind eye to the rules (and also to the legitimate aspirations of Peter Elliott, a performer of much less glamour but indisputable recent success) only for Seb to fail when he got to Seoul: how the howls would have gone up against them for bending the rules, for succumbing to sentiment, for responding to history rather than 1988 realities.

That, it should be said, is a more charitable view of the Board's motives for Coe's rejection than many will take. His father and coach, Peter Coe, thinks the true explanation is political. The athlete's exclusion, it is argued, has less to do with his form on the track than his record as vice-chairman of the Sports Council, which in 1985, at a meeting he chaired, excluded athletics from a list of recipients for £5.25 million of official largesse. But again the majority on the Board have a solid defence. Like it or not (and Sebastian didn't: he attacked it and tried to get it changed) a selection system had been agreed. Once agreed, it had to be honoured.

So the real dispute in the matter of Coe's exclusion is whether rigid rule-books are right. In all major sports, routine performance is at best a patchy guide to the outcome of great events. The England cricket selectors might escape their present obloquy if they chose their teams by a rule-book, confining their choice, for example, to those at the head of the averages — on which basis, such players as Holmes of Glamorgan and Fletcher of Yorkshire would have been in the England side at the Oval. The real skill in team selection is in knowing when to take risks, when to back a hunch against the statistics. Having rule-books is clearly a comfort: but it may also, in the end, be a kind of abdication.

ical system for prisoners

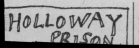

that many women prison officers would welcome). They are assigned to a role of being little more than turnkeys with a poor

Border cheques

WAS intrigued at Gordon Brown's comments (Guard-

Nuremberg trails

Tim Hilton on a handsome survey of the golden age of German art at the British Museum

SUPPOSE that the embitterment of two world wars is mostly responsible for our neglect of the forested, obscure, dark-to-golden classic age of German art. Who thinks of Nuremberg as a Renaissance city, where art and learning flourished?

The Age of Dürer and Holbein, the British Museum's handsome survey of German drawing between 1400 and 1550, is the sort of exhibition that ought to help to reunite us with a culture that now seems remote. It's fascinating, and quite big, so one does not at first realise how much must be missing. Yet the show is borrowed only from British collections, and while we are shown numerous artists we have only a glimpse of any of them.

It's good, though, to be given an indication of the range and diversity of art at the turn of the fourteenth century. It is the period at the end of the "international gothic" when we first find individual drawings on separate sheets of paper (as opposed to illuminated manuscripts and the like), and the growth of personal style is perhaps the great theme of the earlier part of the installation.

John Rowlands, whose exhibition it is, has brought much scholarship to support his connoiseur's eye in separating artists and giving them an identity. So now we can meet, for instance, The Master of the Votive Painting of St Lambrecht — whom Rowlands takes to be a pupil of The Master of the Vienna Adoration — and then Rueland Frueauf the Younger, Stefan Lochner, Bernhard Strigel (who has a lovely, calm drawing of St Vitus, patron saint of dancers and actors) and The Master of the Drapery Studies, also known to those who know about such things as The Master of the Coburg Roundels.

None of these minor artists is more tantalising than Martin Schongauer, active in the upper Rhineland in the later fifteenth century. He provides one of the first secular images of the exhibition. It is a pen and brown ink study of a girl who is holding up her skirts with one hand, while with the other she holds a bird's wing, and fans the flame of a fire with it. These may be the flames of desire, Rowlands comments, before quickly passing to more serious matters. But here, surely, is a touch of late medieval genius — the sight of someone innocent, wondering, exploring the self and natural world of creation.

A century ago, cultural critics and historians (a class who are notably absent from Rowlands thoughts) liked to think of "moments" or turning-points when the Renaissance began, or, later, entered its decline. A person who wished to find such a symbolic moment for the German new age might choose Dürer's first travels after his apprenticeship, when he hoped to meet his admired Schongauer and probably purchased this mysterious poetic little drawing.

This is Dürer's exhibition. Immediately one enters the galleries given to his drawing, one feels the freshness of his art. It is one of those times when a sudden access of technical accomplishment goes hand in hand with an enlargement of spirit. Dürer seems master~ as the earlier masters were~ Still full of the medieval, he~ a new love of beauty, and q~ nature. Proud and self-conscious, his ruling passion seems none the less to be a~ magnificent curiosity.

After his *wanderjahre* of~ early 1940s, Dürer went to~ ice — this was 20 years bef~ Holbein went to England —~ encountered the leading pa~ ers of the day, including Be~ lini, one of the oldest of the~ then in his eightieth year.~ especially pleasurable and~ clusively personal drawing~ of Three Orientals, taken f~ a Bellini painting. Even wh~ he copied, Bellini was his co~ man.

His admiration for other~ painters is a complicated a~ yet is essential to his posit~ as a great artist and his co~ quest of provincialism. I a~ retical in finding his water~ ours of the country aroun~ Nuremburg too bland. The~ certainly innovative, some~ the first of all pure landsca~ studies. Yet I prefer the lea~ drawings and engravings,~ which crackled with techn~ and emotion.

Why does this exhibitio~ no note of the Melancolia,~ The Knight, Death and the~ Devil, Dürer's consummat~ legories? Perhaps their te~ and tragic iconography, so~ meaningful to the 19th cen~ mind, fails to excite the m~ connoisseur? However, th~ may be, one reflects that s~ conceptions are very far~ removed from court art.

Holbein's achievements~ pecially in portraiture, ar~ in dispute and scarcely ne~ praise. Nonetheless he dis~ points. He is a court artist~ cannot sense that human~ and destiny is less than co~

● *British Museum until O~ ber 16.*

Contents

Foreword

The drawings included in this exhibition have been drawn entirely from collections in the United Kingdom, principally from that in this Museum. The richness of the British Museum's collection is based on two main sources: the benefaction of its founder, Sir Hans Sloane (from whom came many of the drawings by Dürer and his followers, and the applied art designs by Holbein), and the purchase of the collection of John Malcolm of Poltalloch. The works have been chosen to give as varied a picture as possible of the draughtsmanship of the German masters at the time of that school's preeminence. My study of them has been carried on, more often than not intermittently, over many years, and frequently has had to be sacrificed to other priorities. The catalogue is founded on this research, and the entries are often a revision of those for the comprehensive work still in hand, covering all the drawings of the German school until the middle of the sixteenth century in the British Museum. It will soon be apparent that my debt to previous generations of connoisseurs and scholars is very considerable. Even though one may at times regret, perhaps somewhat ungraciously, that so much has already been written on certain drawings, especially when trying to disentangle the various opinions and their subtleties from one another, this can be a useful spur to uncovering new insights.

First, I should mention Campbell Dodgson, a former Keeper of the Department of Prints and Drawings (1912–32), who was a leading authority and writer on German art in his day, and a very considerable benefactor of the Museum. Similarly Sir Karl Parker who, at the beginning of his career, was an assistant keeper in the Department and made a valuable contribution in the field. Among the leading continental scholars of the past, Friedrich Winkler, Elfried Bock and Otto Benesch have made substantial contributions, and I must also mention the diligent work of Hans and Erica Tietze, even though my disagreements with them are legion.

Amongst my colleagues it is my pleasure to pay the warmest tribute to their contribution as fellow 'labourers in the vineyard' as well as the encouragement they and their work have given me. Of these my debt is owed, particularly amongst my senior colleagues, to Edmund Schilling, Peter Halm, Fedja Anzelewsky, Bruno Bushart, Hanspeter Landolt, Peter Strieder and Franz Winzinger; and among my contemporaries, Dieter Koepplin, Tilman Falk, Dieter Kuhrmann, Fritz Koreny, Hans Mielke, Edeltraud Rettich, Gisela Goldberg and Charita Mesenseva.

Without the great generosity of lenders this survey would have lacked many key works and certain important masters would not have been properly represented. The Trustees are most grateful to them for agreeing to be temporarily parted from their treasures, and for granting permission for their works to be reproduced in the catalogue:

The Visitors of the Ashmolean Museum, Oxford, and the Director, Dr Christopher White; Dr Nicholas Penny, Keeper, the Department of Western Art, and Miss Emma Chambers, the Print Room Supervisor; Mrs Noelle Brown (nos.24, 92, 101, 119, 181, 184, 189, 190).

The Trustees of the Barber Institute of Fine Arts, the University of Birmingham, and the Director, Professor Hamish Miles (no.192).

The British Library Board, and the Director, Special Collections, Mrs Sarah Tyacke; Ms Jane Carr, Miss Janet Backhouse and Miss Pamela Porter (nos.1, 20, 30, 67, 87, 120, 153).

The Governing Body of Christ Church, Oxford, and the Dean, the Very Reverend Eric Heaton; the Assistant Curator, Dr Catherine Whistler (nos.59, 106, 122).

The Provost, the Lord Charteris of Amisfield, GCVO, and the Fellows of Eton College; the College Librarian, Mr Paul Quarrie (no.155).

The Syndics of the Fitzwilliam Museum, Cambridge, and the Director, Professor Michael Jaffé; the Keeper of Paintings, Drawings and Prints, Mr David Scrase (no.141).

The Guildhall Library, the Corporation of the City of London, and the Director of Libraries and Art Galleries, Mr Melvyn Barnes; the Keeper of Prints and Maps, Mr Ralph Hyde (no.132).

The Trustees of the National Gallery of Scotland, Edinburgh and the Director, Mr Timothy Clifford; the Keeper of the Department of Prints and Drawings, Mr Hugh Macandrew (nos.86, 88).

The Trustees of the National Portrait Gallery, London, and the Director, Dr John Hayes; the Registrar, Mr Kai Kin Yung (no.213).

The Collection of the Earl of Pembroke and Montgomery, Wilton House (no.199).

The Board of Trustees of the Royal Armouries, HM Tower of London, and the Master Armourer, Mr A.V.G.Norman; the Librarian, Mrs Sarah B. Bailey (no.5).

Private Collections (nos.2, 7, 8, 32, 89, 121, 126, 142, 145, 151, 152, 159, 164, 176).

University College, London, and the Curator of the College Collections, Mrs Mary Lightbown; Mr Nicholas Dawton (nos.105, 137, 149, 150, 166).

The Board of Trustees of the Victoria & Albert Museum, London, the former and present Directors, Dr Sir Roy C. Strong, and Ms E. Esteve-Coll; the Keeper of Designs, Prints and Drawings, Mr John Murdoch; Curator of Object Movement, Mrs Liz Miller (nos.11, 12, 13, 148, 201).

The Trustees of the Wernher Collection, Luton Hoo, Bedfordshire (no.162).

I am very grateful also to those colleagues who have assisted me over particular questions discussed within the catalogue: Dr Barbara Butts, concerning her study of Hans von Kulmbach; Dr Elizabeth Carmichael, Dr Christian Feest, and Mr William C. Sturtevant, concerning the Indians of Central and South America; Mr Peter Hogg, for his help with the Danish language; Dr Pagitz, and Dr Andrew S. Ciechanowiecki for their assistance with no.177; Dr Andrew Prescott, for assistance over the reading of an inscription; Mr Graham Rimer, for explaining about the workings of the crossbow; Dr Michael Rogers, for his advice about Turkish costume books; Dr Evelyn Silber, for sharing her knowledge of Sibilla von Bondorf; Mr Cyril Titus of the Research Laboratory, the British Library, for help with reading the faint drawing on the shield on no.192. I would also like to thank Mrs Rosi Schilling who has been most helpful at every stage and given much valuable support.

Within the Museum itself we have received immediate assistance from all sides, whenever required. The staff of British Museum Publications, especially Miss Suzannah Gough, have spared no effort in the production of the catalogue, and the creative energies of the Design Office under Miss Margaret Hall, especially Mrs Andy Creed-Miles, and Mr Gordon Barber, have readily produced a worthy solution to every difficulty.

Within the Department I am much beholden to all my colleagues for their forebearance and active support during all the months of preparation, in particular, Miss Janice Reading for her efficient handling of the administrative details, and Miss Geraldine Miles, who has typed everything with her customary enthusiasm. Finally I must express my warmest appreciation to Giulia Bartrum for working with such devoted dedication on the preparation of the catalogue and on every aspect of the exhibition and its assemblage.

John Rowlands, *Keeper*

Introduction

To describe in a few words the complex development and achievement of the artists working in central Europe at the end of the Middle Ages is not an easy task. For the connoisseur of drawings, however, it is always pleasurable to study what survives from that period. While one can marvel at the continuity of a great tradition which was shared with other parts of Europe, the diversity of artistic personalities and the rich pageant of their work gives us a remarkable insight into the period and the way in which these artists executed their commissions.

As the title of this exhibition catalogue suggests, two great geniuses came to dominate the artistic world north of the Alps, but it should be understood that there were many other German artists of considerable worth during the same period. Even the lesser lights showed themselves to be artists of distinct originality. All this is vividly expressed in the drawings which they produced, even in the case of those artists for whom draughtsmanship appears not to have been a particularly vital part of the creative process.

I shall not attempt here to describe art historians' analyses of the artistic developments in the German-speaking world in the fifteenth and early sixteenth centuries. This does not mean to say that such analysis is profitless but as it has been done so often and with such a variety of results it could cloud rather than illumine the face of knowledge. One must be aware, however, that the artists of this period belonged to a culture in which traditional practices and modes of expression held sway and that this tradition spread far wider across Europe than just the German-speaking regions. An underlying mode of accepted artistic behaviour brought about a continuity which in turn nurtured a rich cornucopia of invention. To appreciate this continuity, the period embraced by the exhibition has been extended well before the birth of Albrecht Dürer in 1471, to outline various regional styles in draughtsmanship from the earlier parts of the fifteenth century, including drawings akin to certain leading artists. The early years of the century also happen to be a good moment to begin, since it is from this time that the first drawings on paper (apart from those on manuscripts), executed north of the Alps survive in any quantity. From this pre-Dürer period we can make out the main characteristics of late Gothic art. In general, the uses for which drawings were executed persisted throughout the whole period, although some new uses came to be added through either the coming of a new invention, like printing from movable type, or the emergence of new interests and means of expression, such as the artists' study of nature, and draughtsmen's portrayal of the human sitter.

The period from 1370 until about 1420 is known as the *International Gothic Style*. This term, first coined by the French scholar Louis Courajod (in his lectures at L'Ecole du Louvre from 1887–96), described the art at the end of the fourteenth century and beginning of the fifteenth as *l'art international*. Not unexpectedly, he saw this *Gothicité universelle* as an all-pervading style, whose origins and prime examples were to be found in France, a country whose leadership, he thought, provided the spur to developments elsewhere in Europe during the early fifteenth century. Since Courajod's day, a rather different picture of the art of that time has emerged (despite the distortions of chauvinism, however unconscious they may have been). Because of Courajod's concept of a ubiquitous style stretching from the Ile de France to Bohemia and beyond, scholars were prompted to annex whole groups of works and move them from one region to another, usually to their own country. Although this form of nationalistic ex-appropriation is not so common nowadays, one cannot discount this trait entirely from the present-day study of late Medieval art. Fortunately, we are now able to distinguish regional differences more clearly and, in some cases, to identify the works of particular artists, whose place of activity is also often known to us. This is not to say that there is still not plenty of room for continuing debate and speculation. A general picture has arisen of similar styles from western Europe from about 1400 onwards which are distinguished by various regional characteristics. An atmosphere of elegant opulence and aristocratic exclusiveness pervaded the art of the time, whether it was produced in Spain, Lombardy, England, France, Bohemia or South Germany. More appropriate here, perhaps, is the German term applied especially to German sculpture of the period, *Weiche Stil* (the soft style). Many of the finest examples of this style came from Bohemia and Austria as well as South Germany, and it is from these areas that the earliest examples of draughtsmanship in the exhibition come. The illustrations from Bohemia to the Travels of Sir John Mandeville of 1410–20 (no.1) are excellent examples of the rich deluxe quality of the best art: that produced for the most cultured and frequently the wealthiest patrons in both Church and State. These drawings reflect a time of ostentation in both religious and secular art, perhaps best typified by the bejewelled reliquary. The tendency to cloak everything with exquisite courtliness, as though the Kingdom of Heaven was a court of the Virgin, according to the latest Burgundian nouveau riche fashion, was particularly intense during the first half of the fifteenth century, and is present in the works of the great Flemish Masters led by Jan van Eyck (active 1422–41). This trait of elegance persisted in one form or another throughout the century being still a potent force in the works of Martin Schongauer (q.v.) and the youthful Dürer (q.v.).

There is a continuous link between the art forms of the last quarter of the fifteenth century and those of preceding generations. The syntax and vocabulary used is common to both, and the later forms are clearly evolved from what had gone before. Although this is evident in every aspect of artistic practice, it is most immediately noticeable in the persistence of decorative elements into the early decades of the sixteenth century, such as the design of tabernacle-pinnacles, choir-stalls, sacrament-houses, and the use of foliage and branches as widely scattered ornamental motifs. The uses of drawings show the same continuity: the production by artists of model – or pattern-books – of drawings was a constant feature of Medieval art. With such collections of sheets of drawings, later often mistakenly called sketchbooks, artists gathered their *memoranda* – sources of various designs for further use by the studio. They might be collections of characteristic heads, animals and birds in appropriate poses, records of figures either individual or in groups, and compositions, either partial or complete, with colour notes or with the colours themselves added with wash. Such handbooks were highly prized and one of the chief treasures of any artist's studio, enabling his work to be perpetuated by his heir or successor after his death. This practice continued well into the Renaissance in Germany, and one can cite the Cranach studio as an outstanding example (see no.144).

If we exclude the pen illustrations in manuscripts, such as chronicles and books of devotion, the vast majority of the drawings that survive, until we reach the last quarter of the fifteenth century, are either sheets from pattern-books, or individual subjects later cut from them to make seemingly independent drawings in the modern sense. A fine example is *The Mocking of Christ* by the Master of the 'Worcester Christ Carrying the Cross' (no.4) from the second quarter of the fifteenth century. This drawing's function as a record is demonstrated by the reappearance of the subject, with minor variations, on a panel of the great altarpiece in the Cathedral at Kassa, formerly in Hungary (now Košice, Czechoslovakia). The drawing, or one similar to it, was evidently also the source for details in a drawing from the workshop of Hans Holbein the Elder of c.1500. This illustrates a common practice, which we would see repeated again and again if the drawings of this kind had survived more abundantly.

This transmission and persistence of artistic formulas and designs which we find throughout the whole period up to and after 1500 would have been impracticable without such pattern-books. It is merely the chance of fate that one of the largest corpus of such drawings from a particular source should be the large number of sheets now attributed to the Master of the Drapery Studies (q.v.) from the Upper Rhineland. Because of such vagaries, too, drawings by a number of the leading German masters prior to Dürer are not known to have survived. Where they do appear, it is more likely that they are records of works by the Master produced in his studio, but not necessarily by the Master himself. For instance, Konrad Witz (1400/10–44/6), the leading artist active in Switzerland and the Upper Rhineland in the first half of the fifteenth century, has only a small group of drawings associated with his name; these are now usually regarded as records from his studio or thought to be by followers working under his influence (see no.18). Some other artists' drawings have no record from their studios. For instance, there are no drawings known by Lucas Moser, the painter of the Magdalen altarpiece of 1431 at Tiefbronn, and there are only relatively few designs for carved altarpieces, considering the large number of workshops producing them. They were after all the commonest feature of the German church interior until the Reformation. No drawings can be firmly attributed to Hans Multscher (c.1400–67), the great sculptor from Ulm, Likewise, nothing can be safely attributed to such important sculptors as Michael Pacher (active c.1465?–98) and Michael Erhart (c.1440–after 1522) and Georg Erhart, his son (c.1460–1540). Later still, only a few drawings by Veit Stoss (active c.1477–1533) have come down to us, along with those few designs recorded in his engravings; but there are none from Tilman Riemenschneider and his workshop. Before Martin Schongauer (q.v.) the same is the case with the earliest engravers; only a small handful of drawings attributed to the Master E.S. (active before 1450–67) is known.

The position is quite different with architecture, since a large number of drawings, accumulated by successive generations of architects have survived due to the fact that their workshops often functioned until long after the end of the Middle Ages. The continued establishment of the masons on the site maintaining a large Gothic building, has meant that the plans and elevations for the building were, for the most part, kept together for a long time (see nos.11–13). Because of this the completion of Gothic buildings such as the tower and spire of Ulm cathedral, were possible, and also work outstanding to Cologne Cathedral in the nineteenth century.

One of the notable characteristics of German art of the period is the richness of regional variations. Each region's special character often enables us to place a particular drawing, which is especially useful when the artist cannot be identified for want of sufficient clues. Local patronage and municipal pride stimulated and sustained local effort in a way not found in nations like France and England, which were more centrally organised. This regional spice flavoured the whole of German art, but could, at the same time, promote a provincialism and a conservatism that preferred the well-trodden paths and shunned the novel. Against this tendency, there were the opportunities and experiences that travel provided, especially from the artist's years as a journeyman, when he completed his apprenticeship and left his native town to offer his services to masters elsewhere, before becoming a master himself. It was a great spur to the young on the threshold of their career. Most of the leading artists of the period evidently benefited greatly from this experience and none more so than Albrecht Dürer (q.v.) himself. His years as a journeyman, chiefly in the Upper Rhineland and in Basel, were spent under the powerful and widespread influence of Martin Schongauer (q.v.), a sure foundation that helped to bring about his later remarkable achievements as a draughtsman, engraver and designer of woodcuts. He was also stimulated by Italy, especially on his first brief visit there in 1494/5 which made a profound impression; however, it was the way in which he responded to his experience of nature that was so remarkable. On his Alpine journeys to and from Italy, he produced a series of landscape sketches in watercolour (see nos.39–43), which may be considered amongst the most inspired of all Dürer's works, and even now strike us with their extraordinary modernity. They include some of the first watercolours to have been done on the spot. The Nuremberg painters from Dürer's youth were predisposed to make the landscape background an important feature in their altarpieces, and perhaps this was what first prompted Dürer to draw views of his native city. His spontaneous records from his first Italian trip and shortly thereafter are a new development in European art which one might reasonably consider as Renaissance in character. These landscapes are explorations of nature, done for their own sake, and not, at least initially, with any specific end in view. The fact that A 'weierhaus' (no.42) was afterwards used as the basis for the background of one of his engravings does not lessen its independence as a work of art. Both in Dürer's case and with many of his successors, their artistic individuality is expressed most strongly in their drawings.

For obvious reasons one thinks of the Renaissance in terms of Italian art, but this influence was not the only factor which stirred artists north of the Alps. With Dürer, the leader of his generation, it was his 'attitude of mind' that was far more important. His awareness of his own genius and position as one who could – and did – rival the Italians, marks him out as a Renaissance man. His preoccupation with his own features in a series of self-portraits, both drawn and painted, as well as the abundance of surviving correspondence and diaries, show us how markedly Dürer differs from his predecessors. This overt self-consciousness, and its artistic consequences are quite as new and distinctive as the innovations of an Italian genius like Leonardo da Vinci (1492–1519). Dürer, in his unrelenting pursuit of the theoretical basis to his art, especially in his study of the proportions of the human figure, is as scientific as Leonardo da Vinci was in his more far reaching studies. But while Dürer himself became thoroughly Renaissance in outlook, his followers did not always absorb his inner perceptions and humanist interests.

Elsewhere in Germany in the early sixteenth century, chiefly around the River Danube, a group of artists flourished, including the young Lucas Cranach (q.v.), Albrecht (q.v.) and Erhard Altdorfer and Wolfgang Huber (q.v.). They have been called in modern times the *Danube School*. This group had a lively interest in landscape which always features prominently in their drawings, prints and paintings. At first sight, it may seem as though the forests were conceived by them merely as an imaginative backdrop, lending a mood of poetic fantasy to their subjects whether religious or secular. The idea of the dark, impenetrable woodland is to be found in Germanic and North European folklore and legend, a place of mystery, where the 'Good Knight' might expect to meet for instance, an unidentified Knight – a foe of evil and magic power. Albrecht Altdorfer (q.v.) captures this air of mystery in his drawings in a highly expressive way, and this interpretation is not exaggerated for even today such dense forests can be found near the Danube to the east of Regensburg. What is of particular note, however, is that such expression should be encountered in the opening years of the sixteenth century.

The forms, ornamental style and new themes of the Italian Renaissance were entering Germany from the south through a variety of means – the importation of books, prints, medals and so forth. One of the chief 'ports of entry' was the imperial city of Augsburg, which was the favourite residence of the Emperor Maximilian I and had strong commercial and banking links with Italy. It was here that the Mortuary Chapel of the Fugger Family was completed in the St Annakirche (*c.*1509–18) – the first religious architectural commission in Germany decorated in the Renaissance style. Dürer probably oversaw it himself, and certainly provided the designs for the large epitaph reliefs decorating the rear wall. But even here, its Renaissance character was not absolutely wholehearted as the vaulting of the chapel remained Gothic in style.

The leading artist at Augsburg at that time was Hans Holbein the Elder (q.v.), a painter who gradually accommodated Renaissance motifs into his designs, while still working according to the late Gothic tradition of large altarpieces for a widespread clientele. Portraiture is the one field in which he had few rivals. The freshness and spontaneity of his portrait drawings reflects the easy *rapport* that he established with his sitters, and his many drawings of Augsburg citizens capture their features and character in a matter-of-fact fashion. But the Augsburg artist of the beginning of the sixteenth century who most easily absorbed Renaissance motifs into his art was Hans Burgkmair (q.v.). A notable feature of his work was his representations of the exotic treasures and people of far-off lands, especially in his drawings and woodcuts of American Indians and their weapons (see no.158(a) & (b)). This was an interest that he shared with Dürer who also had an insatiable curiosity about the exotic of any kind: he travelled some distance in the hope of seeing a whale, only to find a walrus, which he duly drew (see no.74). Even Hans Holbein the Younger had once portrayed such primitive people, although he concentrated more on their reputation for wild behaviour and cannibalism, as seen in the border decorating his woodcut map of the world for Symon Grynaeus's *Novus Orbis Regionum ac Insularum Veteribus Incognitarum* of 1532. The benefits that Holbein reaped from his *Wanderjahre* (years of travel) were a broadening of his horizons and the encouragement and patronage of the Mayor of Basel, Jacob Meyer, which launched Holbein on his career. His ambition for the most prestigious, preferably royal, patronage, and the fears for his future aroused by the initial rumblings of the Reformation in Basel, spurred him on to go first to France and then England, where he finally settled, and providentially, left such a rich heritage. He portrayed the English court of Henry VIII with such perception that many of his sitters, important players in the pageant of English life and politics of the time, are revealed as proud, ambitious and greedy for power and riches.

Holbein's work must be seen as a whole arising from his early training in his father's studio in Augsburg. As all of his decorative schemes, apart from a few badly preserved fragments, have been destroyed, we must depend on his other works – namely devotional paintings and portraiture – to form an impression of his career. It is perhaps not incidental that the *Meyer Madonna*, possibly his greatest masterpiece, combines these two elements effectively, and seemingly with effortless ease. In this work he re-created the typical Medieval subject, the Virgin of Pity and this was produced, ironically, when the full vigour of the Reformation was about to burst upon the world – and wherever it held sway such forms of piety would be eradicated. Holbein's drawings amply reflect these activities and include preparatory sketches for parts of his now lost wall-paintings. An exceptional survival is his only cartoon, that for part of his Whitehall Mural (no.213). Besides these, there is an abundance of superb designs for glass-paintings, metalwork, jewellery, hand-weapons, and ornamentation for applied art objects of various kinds. It is, of course, in the field of portraiture in which Holbein had made his indelible mark not only as a painter but also as a draughtsman.

The last few years of Holbein's life, and the period immediately following his death in 1543 saw a considerable change in the artistic climate in Europe. This juncture in the century was also marked in Germany by the fact that so many artists and draughtsmen of wonderful talent and originality died, so that historians have naturally seen the age of Dürer and Holbein as a moment of prodigious activity followed by a period in which, for various reasons, the artistic achievement appears much less impressive. While one in this period of change should not over emphasise the effect of the Reformation, it is undoubtedly true that this new religious fervour did have a profound influence on people's attitude to life. The Church's unchallenged central position in people's lives was lost, even to some extent in countries and regions still faithful to the Catholic Church. Traditional demands for religious paintings stopped in the North, where the Protestants' 'religion of the Word' prevailed, only to be replaced by fewer commissions for paintings with much less varied iconographical subjects illustrative of the new doctrinal emphases. Often artists were obliged to become proficient in other fields; for instance, Heinrich Vogtherr the Elder (q.v.) was also the Imperial eye-specialist. This new attitude, decidedly bourgeois in tone, was firmly established in Germany by the middle of the century, especially in its most characteristic form – the full length portrait. In these, except from the usual means of identification, it is otherwise impossible to distinguish the banker from the prince, the city-mayor from the duke. In their portraits, all assure us of their claims to membership of the ruling class. In harmony with the times, the art became more pronouncedly patrician from the 1540s onwards.

Classifications like late Gothic and Renaissance have naturally continued to be useful pegs on which to hang our understanding of the fifteenth and sixteenth centuries in northern Europe. Provided they do not restrict our understanding and appreciation of the artists and their interaction with larger groups, whether studios, or the town where they worked, they have a useful function. Even though this great period of German art has already been studied with keen assiduity, especially by German scholars, it would be surprising if a fresh examination of these draughtsmen, with Dürer and Holbein at their head, was not fruitful, however seemingly familiar or unfamiliar their achievements might be to us.

John Rowlands

1 Austria and Bohemia, XV century

Anonymous artist

Bohemian c.1410–20

1 Sir John Mandeville's Travel Book

See colour plate section following p.80

Silverpoint and pen and black ink with watercolour, body-colour, and gold leaf, on light green prepared vellum. 16 folios, 22.5 × 18.1 cm

PROVENANCE: M. Pesch, whom it was said had acquired it from a friar, and had 'great reason to believe it had been purloined from the Vatican Library' (if this is true, then it could be from Queen Christina of Sweden's Library, rich in Bohemian manuscripts); Samuel Woodburn

British Library, Add Ms.24,189

LITERATURE: G. F. Warner, *The Buke of John Maundevill*, London, 1889; O. Pächt, *Burlington*, lxxxiii, 1938, pp.192 ff., repr.; J. Pešina, *Umění*, viii, 1960, p.119; J. Pešina, *Umění*, xiii, 1965, p.261; *Die Parler und der schöne Stil 1350–1400*, exhib. cat., Cologne, Kunsthalle, 1978–80, iii, pp.106f., repr. plate volume, nos.T.226 and T.227; J. Krása, *The Travels of Sir John Mandeville: a Manuscript in the British Library*, New York, 1983

In the later middle ages, travel accounts, especially those concerning the marvels of the East and in particular the Holy Land, had a considerable fascination for Christian Europe, and of all these by far the most popular, surpassing even that of Marco Polo's travels, was a text which first appeared in French in 1356/7. Claiming to be a guide for travellers bound for Jerusalem it was a typical mixture, much beloved of the medieval mind, of fact and fiction, and included in addition an account of the wonders of the East. During the last quarter of the fourteenth century, and for most of the following century, it was much copied and translated, and survives in about three hundred manuscripts. The identity of the author, who introduces himself as Sir John Mandeville from St Albans, continues to be something of a riddle; however, it is now thought that the writer who, despite flagrant dependence on earlier sources, does appear to have based some of his account on personal experience, was likely to have been either a physician of Liège, Jean de Bourgogne, or a chronicler also from Liège, Jean d'Outremeuse.

According to Otto van Diemeringen, author of a second version in German, who is portrayed here writing the *Travels* on folio 3 *recto* (the first illustration), Vavřinec of Březová, produced a Czech translation. It is with these two versions that the illustrations in this volume are most obviously linked. There is, however, no text in the volume and although the sheets have been cut, the size of the pictures speaks against there having been one. It was probably done for a bibliophile who was keen to have a *de-luxe* set of illustrations to accompany an unillustrated manuscript of Mandeville's *Travels* that he already possessed. The volume now consists of twenty-eight full-page miniatures, conceived as framed pictures painted in grey monochrome (the *camïeu* technique) on tinted vellum. Although originally thought to be Flemish, they were finally linked in 1938 by Pächt with Bohemia, when he described these illustrations as the work of a pupil or follower of an artist whose *œuvre* he defined and attempted to arrange chronologically, naming him the Master of the Dietrichstein Martyrology from Gerona. The works of this Master include the first illumination in the *Wenceslaus Bible* of 1402 in the Plantin Moretus Museum, Antwerp, and Pešina also attributed to him most of these illustrations to Mandeville's *Travels*. They provide superb examples of the so-called 'soft style' which evidently arose in Bohemia about 1400. This style, characterised by a sense of lyricism and courtly sophistication, spread westwards through Germany towards France. The most recent opinion about the possible identity of the hand responsible for the Mandeville illustrations is that of Josef Krása, who prefers to isolate him as a separate Master of the Mandeville Travels. He also found signs of his hand in two folios (92 *recto*, 92 *verso* and 93 *recto*) in the last part of the Gerona manuscript, in which the same tone of high seriousness apparent in the *Travels* is to be found.

The vision of this artist was broadened by the experience of the art of Paris and Northern Italy. The particular influence of the latter region is reflected in the exhibited illustrations: in that on the left, *Pope John XXII receiving a delegation from the Eastern Church* (7 *verso*) the characterisation of the figures owes much to the example of Northern Italian masters; while on the right, the manner in which two scenes are combined within the same framed space, *Three pilgrims in a ship approaching Tyre* and *Joppa and the pilgrims paying a bill outside the city gates* (8 *recto*) reminds us of North Italian manuscripts of the same period.

2

Master of the Vienna Adoration

Painter. This artist takes his name from the *Adoration of the Christ-Child*, a small panel-painting probably of *c*.1410/20 in Vienna (Museum Mittelalterlicher Österreichischer Kunst); a companion painting of the *Adoration of the Magi* by the same hand is in Budapest (Szépmüvészeti Múzeum). He was indebted to the works of Bohemian artists active in Vienna at the end of the fourteenth century, especially the Master of Wittingau (active *c*.1375–1400), and his followers. He was one of the earliest Viennese exponents of the 'soft style', and as such could have been the teacher of the next generation of Austrian artists, which includes among others, the Master of the Votive Painting of St Lambrecht (q.v.) and the Master of the Presentation in the Temple (active *c*.1420–40).

The early dating of the Master's activity has been questioned by G. Schmidt, who advances the date of the Vienna and Budapest panels to the end of the second decade. The incomplete series of Passion scenes by the same hand (formerly in the Durrieu collection, Paris) he considers to be painted at a later date, under the influence of an artist who ran a large Viennese workshop, to which, among others, the Master of the Votive Painting of St Lambrecht also belonged; however, the close and unmistakable links with the Master of Wittingau and his circle conclusively contradict these notions.

BIBLIOGRAPHY: Oettinger, *Tübingen*, pp.43ff.; Thieme-Becker, xxxvii, 1950, p.353; G. Schmidt, *Österreichische Zeitschrift für Kunst und Denkmalpflege*, Vienna, xx, 1966, pp.8, 13f.; Baum, *Österreichische Galerie*, p.28 (for further literature).

2 Christ carrying the Cross

Pen and black ink with grey wash, heightened with white body-colour, over a greyish-green ground, on vellum. 19.5 × 16.2cm

PROVENANCE: from a sixteenth-century album of Hungarian origin, which contained mainly prints

England, Private Collection

LITERATURE: Schilling, *Gesamm. Zeichn.*, p.17, no.2, repr.; Rowlands, *Private Collection*, p.8, no.1, repr.

There is a close affinity between the details and the general arrangement in this drawing and the paintings by the artist known as the Master of the Vienna Adoration. The features and the gestures of the holy women on the left of the drawing strongly resemble, for instance, those of the Virgin in the *Adoration of the Christ Child* (Vienna, Museum Mittel-alterlicher Österreichischer Kunst, inv.no.4909; Baum, *Österreichische Galerie*, p.29, no.10, col.pl.1). The shadowy chiseled face of the man beating Christ, has a decidedly Bohemian flavour, which accords well with the Master's supposed training. These characteristics, together with the restricted field of the composition, suggest that this drawing can be associated with the Master's incomplete series of panels with scenes from the Passion (formerly in

the Durrieu collection, Paris; Oettinger, *Tübingen*, pls.41b, 42, 43a). As a panel of *Christ carrying the Cross* is lacking from this it is not impossible that the drawing is a record of it. To judge from stylistic comparisons between the small group of paintings given to this Master, the attribution of the present drawing would seem highly probable.

Master of the Votive Painting of St Lambrecht

Active in Vienna c.1420–40

Painter. Little is known about this artist who was probably a pupil of the Master of the Vienna Adoration (q.v.) and was a leading representative of the so-called 'soft style' of the International Gothic in Austria. His name is taken from a painting of *c*.1430 which shows the Virgin of Mercy, and a battle between Ludwig of Hungary and the Turks, which was formerly in the Stift St Lambrecht and is now in the Joanneum, Graz. Benesch identified him with the Master of the Linz Crucifixion, named after a painting of the *Crucifixion* in the Landesmuseum Linz, although Oettinger and others consider this to be the work of an associate. Oettinger considered him to be the painter Hans von Tübingen (active 1433–62) but others, including Stange, who calls him 'Master Hans', have rejected this identification as the length of Tübingen's career appears to be inconsistent with the presumed period of activity of the present artist. Attempts to identify him with the sculptor and painter, Hans von Judenberg, who was active during the first half of the century in Vienna, are not convincing on stylistic grounds. Further examples of his paintings are to be found in Vienna (Museum Mittelalterlicher Öster-reichischer Kunst), Prague (National Gallery) and Wels (Stadtmuseum).

BIBLIOGRAPHY: O. Benesch, *Vienna Jahrbuch*, NF, ii, 1928, pp.63ff.; Oettinger, *Tübingen*; Thieme-Becker, xxxvii, 1950, p.348; Stange, xi, 1961, pp.11ff.; Baum, *Österreichische Galerie*, pp.30ff. (for further literature).

3 *Recto:* The Entombment
Verso: The Lamentation over the Dead Christ

Pen and black ink with grey wash. 14 × 20.8cm

PROVENANCE: Sloane bequest, 1753

5236–111

LITERATURE: K. T. Parker, *OMD*, i, no.2, 1926, p.24, pls.33, 34; Benesch, *Oesterr. Handz.*, pp.35f., nos.18, 19, repr.; L. Baldass, *Vienna Jahrbuch*, NF, ix, 1935, p.42; H. Mahn, *Schriften und Vörtrage der Württembergischen Gesellschaft der Wissenschaften* (Geisteswissen-schaftliche Abteilung), Heft 3, Stuttgart, 1937, pp.20–21, repr.; Oettinger, *Tübingen*, pp.8off., pls.75a and 75b; K. Oettinger,

3r

Zeitschr. f. Kunstwiss., vii, 1940, p.221, repr. (*recto*); O. Fischer, *Geschichte der deutschen Zeichnung und Graphik*, Munich, 1951, p.101, repr.; Stange, xi, p.18; Manchester, *German Art*, pp.12f., no.11; Vienna, *L'Art Européen vers 1400*, p.229, no.263; Baum, *Österreichische Galerie*, p.30

Parker, who first published the drawings on this sheet, associated them with a group of paintings, drawings and woodcuts brought together by Hugelshofer (Buchner, *Beiträge*, i, 1924, pp.24ff.) which he identified as the work of the Viennese school in the first half of the fifteenth century. Benesch subsequently described them as the only known drawings by the leading representative of the 'soft style' in Austria, the so-called Master of the Votive Painting of St Lambrecht. Parker's suggestion that the present drawings were possibly studies for a companion panel to the painting of the *Dead Christ at the foot of the Cross with the Virgin and St John* at Berlin-Dahlem (Gemäldegalerie, inv.no.1378) has much to recommend it. Although some scholars, including Oettinger and Stange, have attributed the Berlin panel to a contemporary associate of the Master of the Votive Painting of St Lambrecht, the Master of the Presentation in the Temple, an attribution to the former seems stylistically more convincing. In view of their high quality there would seem to be no objection to attributing these drawings to the St Lambrecht Master himself, rather than any associate, although Baldass and Oettinger have placed them amongst the works of the Master's circle, the latter proposing that they are by a follower whom he called the Master of the St Lambrecht Glass-Paintings after six panes now in the Joanneum, Graz (see Oettinger, *Tübingen*, pls.38a and 38b) from a window in St Peterskirche, at St Lambrecht, the building of which was begun in 1424 (see *Österreichische Kunsttopographie*, xxxi, Vienna, 1951, p.12).

3v

2 Bavaria, XV century

The Master of the Worcester 'Christ carrying the Cross'

Painter. Active during the first half of the fifteenth century, probably in Bavaria, and not Austria as some have considered. His name comes from a small panel painting, *Christ carrying the Cross*, of *c*.1420–30, formerly in the Worcester Collection, New York, and now in the Art Institute, Chicago. The various attempts which have been made to establish a stylistically cohesive group of drawings around this artist do not now appear convincing. Current scholarship does, however, support Oettinger's general idea that the master worked in Bavaria, although recent research indicates Regensburg rather than Munich as the centre of his activity. He appears to have exercised a strong influence on the succeeding generation of painters.

BIBLIOGRAPHY: K.Oettinger, *Zeitschr. f. Kunstwiss.* vii, 1940, pp.217ff.; Benesch, *Oesterr. Handz.* pp.41ff.; Thieme-Becker, xxxvii, 1950, pp.359f. (for further literature); Stange, x, pp.55ff.; *Regensburger Buchmalerei*, pp.94ff.

4 The Mocking of Christ

See colour plate section following p.80

Pen and black ink with grey, pink, brown and blue wash. The sheet has a curved top, which was probably cut at a later date, and is damaged at the bottom right-hand corner and along the lower edge. 18.1 × 27.2cm

PROVENANCE: H.Wellesley (anon. sale, Sotheby, 1862, 26 June, lot 134, bt *Evans 17s*); Sir J.C.Robinson; Malcolm

1895–9–15–962

LITERATURE: JCR, p.172, no.509; Parker, *German Schools*, p.26, no.3, repr.; O.Benesch, *Belvedere*, 9, ii, 1930, p.77; L.Baldass, *Vienna Jahrbuch*, NF, ix, 1935, pp.39, 45, pl.19; Benesch, *Oesterr. Handz.*, pp.18, 42, no.31, repr.; Oettinger, *Tübingen*, pp.112f.; K.Oettinger, *Zeitschr. f. Kunstwiss.*, vii, 1940, pp.219–22, pl.3; N.Csánky, *Budapest Jahrbuch*, x, 1940, p.71, pl.52; Stange, x, pp.55f.; Manchester, *German Art*, pp.13f., no.14; Falk, *Basel*, p.89, under no.199; Robert Suckale in *Regensburger Buchmalerei*, pp.93ff., repr.; G.Schmidt, *Kunstchronik*, xl, 1987, pp.510–11

Inscribed by the artist in black ink on the scroll, *profitisse quis te perkussit* (Vulgate, Matt. xxvi, 68); inscribed on the *verso* in brown ink, *No.783 June 28 1862* [sic] *from Dr H.Wellesley's Collection (portion sold at Sotheby's this date anonymously) J.C.Robinson*; and in pencil, *No.1205 John Malcolm* and *Old Dutch* (both cancelled)

J.C.Robinson, in the Malcolm catalogue, attributed this drawing to a member of the Augsburg School and dated it to *c*.1470, but, as Parker was the first to point out, it should be dated much earlier. Benesch attributed it to an anonymous artist together with, among other drawings, the *Study for a Golgotha* (Frankfurt, Städelsches Kunstinstitut, inv. no.6976), the *Three orientals on horseback* (Dresden, Kupferstichkabinett) and the *Rider blowing a horn* (Munich, Graphische Sammlung, inv. no.23839). He was known as the Master of the Worcester 'Christ carrying the Cross', so-called after his painting of *Christ carrying the Cross* of *c*.1420–30, formerly in the Worcester Collection, New York and now in Chicago (Art Institute, inv. no.1947.79; *Regensburger Buchmalerei*, p.94, repr. For other attributions of drawings to this master, see *Belvedere*, 1930, p.77). Although Benesch thought him to be an Austrian, and there are some reflections of the Viennese school of the time in his work, this artist is much more credibly located in Bavaria as Oettinger, Stange and others have suggested. Benesch's group of drawings does not seem particularly cohesive, but there are sufficient similarities between the artist's painting of *Christ carrying the Cross* and no.4 to suggest that the latter is probably a late work by the Master. The drawing's maturer, less child-like quality and well-organised composition would support this, and the work anticipates the firm sense of drama in the paintings of a probable pupil of the 'Worcester' Master, a Bavarian painter, the Master of the Tegernsee Altarpiece, named after his masterpiece of 1445/6, which was commissioned for the high altar of the Stiftskirche, Tegernsee in the Bavarian Alps.

The draughtsman responsible for the present drawing can also be associated, as proposed by Suckale, with the work of miniaturists; especially the two principal hands responsible for most of the fifteenth-century illustrations, not including some early illuminated work that can be related to the Salzburg school of the early part of the century, in the so-called Ottheinrich Bible (Munich, Bayerische Staatsbibliothek, inv. no.cgm 8010/1.2) which was written in a Bavarian dialect. It is not absolutely clear at present that the Master of the Worcester 'Christ carrying the Cross' worked specifically in Regensburg as a miniaturist, but as Suckale eloquently urges, it is certainly very likely that the Master of St Matthew and the Master of St Mark (named after the gospels in the Ottheinrich Bible which they illustrated), were from the circle of the 'Worcester' Master. Given the great similarities between the figures in the Chicago painting and those of the Master of St Mark there seems no reason why the latter's hand cannot be identified as the 'Worcester' Master's own; however, the sensitive outlines in the present drawing have been executed with a fine pen, and not with a brush, as Suckale appears to be suggesting in support of his argument. The 'Worcester' Master's wide influence on Bavarian illumination or perhaps more precisely that of Regensburg, if one accepts Suckale's persuasive view, makes him a key figure in the art of the region in the first half of the fifteenth century, even if a number of manuscripts associated by Suckale with the Master may be from other regions. This is a possibility noted by Schmidt, who refers to links with figures in the St Barbara altarpiece, formerly at Breslau (T. Dobrzeniecki, *Catalogue of the Medieval Painting*, National Gallery, Warsaw, 1977, pp.231–40, no.66).

More definite links, but of another kind, relating to the likely function of no.4 as part of a pattern book, are revealed through the later reappearance in an adapted but still recognisable form, of the 'Worcester' Master's *Mocking of Christ*. Christ and the surrounding group of five standing men, have been copied, either from no.4 or from the painting, now lost, of which the present drawing is presumably a record, by the artist responsible for the altarpiece, completed in 1477, in the cathedral of St Elizabeth at Kassa, formerly in northern Hungary (now Košice, Czechoslovakia). The *Mocking of Christ* appears with small variations, in a panel within the series of twenty-four scenes from the Passion, visible when the wings of this altarpiece are closed.

The kneeling figure in the left foreground of no.4 inspired a similar tormentor, shown in the reverse sense, in a drawing of the same subject by an artist from the workshop of Hans Holbein the Elder (q.v.) in Augsburg of *c*.1500, and not, as Parker supposed, of the same period as the present sheet (Basel, Kupferstichkabinett, inv.no.U.VIII 21; Falk, *Basel*, pl.55, no.199). This is a fairly loose connection, which suggests that the Basel drawing was probably copied from an intermediary drawing or painting; but it also serves to demonstrate the extent of the influence of the artist of the present sheet.

Anonymous artist

Mid fifteenth century

5 Firework Book

Manuscript codex containing 61 folios of text, 22 blank folios and 54 folios of drawings. Pen and black ink, with grey, blue, red, yellow and green wash. Each folio, 30.2 × 21.5cm

WM: oxhead surmounted by a stem with a flower (close to Piccard, xii, 486); and a tower (similar to Piccard, ii, 307)

5

PROVENANCE: Feldzeugmeister von Hauslab, Vienna; Feldzeugmeister Ritter von Hauslab-Liechtenstein; Prince of Lichtenstein; E. Weil; presented by the N.A.-C.F., 1950

Royal Armouries, HM the Tower of London, 1-34

LITERATURE: Auguste Demmin, *Guide des Amateurs d'Armes et d'Armures anciennes*, Paris, 1869, p.499, repr.; A. Essenwein, *Quellen zur Geschichte der Feuerwaffen*, Graz, 1969 (reprint of 1877 edition) i, p.111, ii, pl.B1f; Wilhelm Hassenstein, *Das Feuerwerkbuch von 1420*, Munich, 1941, p.87, no.c8; N.A.-C.F. *Report*, xii, 1950, p.37, no.1612, repr.

The earliest dated versions of the 'Firework Book' of Konrad Kauder are those in Munich (Staatsbibliothek, cod.germ.4902) of 1429 and in Heidelberg (Universitäts-bibliothek, cod.pal.germ.7877) of 1430. An even earlier version is in Weimar (Landesbibliothek, Q 342) prepared by Hanns Kenntz von Nürnberg 'jetziger Zeit Organist bei St Martin' in 1428.

The present version, which for a technical manual has remarkably lively illustrations, is, as Hassenstein points out, most clearly allied in its arrangement with cod.germ.734, Munich, Staatsbibliothek, produced in the 1460s. The two watermarks of the paper in the Tower of London manuscript are closest in type to two which are dated by Piccard 1447–50 and 1450 respectively. So bearing in mind its link with the version of the 1460s, just mentioned, it would seem likely that it was produced approximately either in the same decade or slightly earlier.

The sheets on display are folio 85 *verso* and folio 86 *recto*. In the former, the firemaster is supervising the weighing of the ingredients and the preparation of the fire pots, which are apparently fitted with fuses and carrying ropes. On the facing sheet, the firemaster directs an attack, using a cannon and fire-arrows shot from crossbows. The defenders remove fire-arrows from the roofs with hooks, and man the walls with small cannon and wall-guns, as well as cross-bows. The cannon had only recently become an efficient weapon of war with the invention of corned gunpowder, mentioned by Konrad Kauder in his version of the fire-work book of 1429 referred to above. Although rockets were known to be in use much earlier than the fifteenth century in Europe, and Roger Bacon had written about explosive powders as early as *c*.1260, the firemaster here is only using darts with lit fuses which ignite on reaching their target.

Mair von Landshut

Probably Freising c.1450–Landshut after 1504

Draughtsman, painter, engraver and woodcut designer. The association of Mair von Landshut with Nicolaus Alexander Mair (Nagler, *Monogr.* i, no.987; iv, no.1586), a painter who is documented in Landshut working for the Dukes of Bavaria in 1492, 1499 and 1514 is, according to Schubert, Stange and Lehrs, probably incorrect. Mair von Landshut is first mentioned in 1490, in the tax-register of Munich as a painter from Freising; in 1497 the Augsburg 'Stadtgerichtsbuch' refers to a Hans Mair, as a painter and citizen of Freising and as the brother-in-law of Michael Holbein, who was the father of Hans Holbein the Elder (q.v.; Lieb-Stange, p.3). Mair may have been an assistant of Jan Polack (died 1519) in Munich, since two panels of Polack's *St Peter Altarpiece* are partly attributed to him (*St Peter healing a madman*, in the Bayerisches Nationalmuseum, Munich and *St Peter in prison* in the Peterskirche, Munich). No documented paintings by Mair are known but there are about thirteen attributed to him through a comparison with his engravings, including: *Scenes from the Passion* dated 1495, in the sacristy of Freising cathedral; *Ecce Homo* (Trento, Museo Civico) dated *1502*; and the only known portrait, *Lady in black and gold* (Oxford, Ashmolean) of the early 1500s. His work reflects the influence of the Augsburg school of painters, especially Hans Holbein the Elder (q.v.).

His prints comprise twenty-two engravings and three woodcuts, many of which are signed MAIR, and ten of which are dated 1499. It is probable that he worked in Landshut since the coat of arms of this town is seen on one of his engravings (Lehrs, no.19) and revealed in the water-mark of an impression at Gotha (Landesmuseum) of another (Lehrs, no.4; Hollstein no.4); he also was evidently in contact with the Landshut publisher and block-cutter, Hans Wurm (active *c*.1501–4), who made a woodcut copy of his engraving, *Couple meeting in a gateway*, the unique impression of which is in the British Museum (Hollstein, no.20b). The technique with which Mair applied colour to his prints is interesting for its anticipation of chiaroscuro woodcuts; he used hand-tinted paper for impressions of fourteen prints, sometimes adding white heightening, to create the effect of a drawing.

Some thirteen known drawings are considered to be his work, three of which are signed (Vienna, Albertina, inv. no.4847; Munich, Staatliche Graphische Sammlung, inv. no.28379, and Venice, Accademia, inv.no.468); and some of which are dated, including his last known work of 1504 (Vienna, Albertina, inv.no.3052). Schubert considered that he may also have made designs for glass paintings.

BIBIOGRAPHY: Schubert, *Mair von Landshut*; Thieme-Becker, xxiv, 1930, pp.492f.; Lehrs, viii, 1932, pp.282ff.; Stange, x, 1960, pp.124–31; Hollstein, xxiii, 1979, pp.89ff. (for further literature); Andersson, *Detroit*, pp.302ff.

6

6 St John the Evangelist

Pen and black ink with grey wash. 19.3 × 13.4cm

WM: the upper part of a high crown (similar to Briquet, 4921)

PROVENANCE: C. Fairfax Murray; C. R. Rudolf (L. *Suppl*.2811b; sale, Sotheby, 1949, 2 Nov., lot 23, bt *Lacroix £220*); P & D Colnaghi; O. Manley; E. Schilling; presented by Mrs R. Schilling 1981-3-28-14

LITERATURE: J. Byam Shaw, *OMD*, ix, 1934, pp.35f., pl.36; L. *Suppl*. p.403, under no.2811b; Schilling, *Gesamm Zeichn*. p.59, no.22, repr.; Rowlands, *Private Collection*, p.43, no.39, repr.

Inscribed by the artist along the upper edge in black ink, *1498*; just underneath, there are traces of an illegible inscription made at a later date in pencil.

The sheet appears to belong to a series of drawings of Apostles and Evangelists by Mair. Four others are known from copies in the École des Beaux-Arts in Paris (Masson Collection, inv. nos.185–8) attributed, for no convincing reason, to Jörg Schweiger (active *c*.1507–28; for a documented drawing by Schweiger, see Falk, *Basel*, p.102, no.269, pl.68). Also executed in pen and ink with wash, they show seated saints in similar positions to that of St John, and were probably executed in Mair's studio. No.6

is of a higher quality than the Paris drawings, and, as Byam Shaw has observed, is stylistically close to a drawing attributed convincingly to Mair of *The Apostle Simon Zelotes* in the Pushkin Museum, Moscow (*OMD*, ii, no.7, 1927, pl.47), which may also be connected with the series although it is dated 1496, and is drawn in a more elaborate technique using pen and ink heightened with white on a green prepared paper.

The *St John the Evangelist* also shows striking similarities with Mair's painting of *St Oswald* (Bayerisches National-museum, Munich, inv. no.10/222; Stange, x, pl.210) which shows a seated saint in a position close to that of St John, but holding a sceptre in his left hand instead of a book. In particular, the block-like form of the stone seat in the painting is closely comparable with those seen in the series of drawings of Apostles, and with the architectural settings so often seen in his prints as well as his paintings.

Rueland Frueauf the Younger

Active in Passau 1497–1545

Painter. Son and probable pupil of the painter, Rueland Frueauf the Elder (1440/50–1507). He acquired citizenship in Passau shortly before 1497, and is recorded as a councillor there in 1533. The Augustiner Chorherrenstift, Kloster-neuberg possesses three painted cycles which have been attributed to him: four scenes from the Passion, four scenes from the life of St John the Baptist, and four scenes from the life of St Leopold with subjects relating to the foundation of the monastery. It is possible that he is to be associated with the Monogrammist RF, active in Nuremberg in the workshop of Michel Wolgemut (q.v.), who assisted the latter with the Peringsdörffer altarpiece (Nuremberg, Heiligkreuzkirche). The style of his paintings reveals the influence of Netherlandish art and, in its emphasis on landscape in which figures are shown on a relatively small scale, anticipates the interests of the artists of the Danube School.

Other paintings attributed to him include the *Crucifixion* dated *1496*, also at Klosterneuberg (see no.7); the *Perger Epitaph*, dated *1516*, at Kloster Vormbach near Passau, and works in Stift Neukloster (Wiener Neustadt).

BIBLIOGRAPHY: Thieme-Becker, xii, 1916, pp.534f.; *Altdorfer*, p.84.

7

7 *Recto:* Studies of eight scenes of martyrdom; St Christopher, and the Birth of Christ

Verso: Head of a horse

Pen and black ink. The lower left-hand corner of the sheet is missing. 20.5 × 28cm

PROVENANCE: G. Nebehay, Vienna; W. Schab, New York.

England, Private Collection

LITERATURE: Halm, *Deutsche Zeichn.*, p.24, no.23; F. Winzinger, *Österreichische Zeitschrift für Kunst und Denkmalpflege*, Vienna, XIX, 1965, p.151 repr.; Schilling, *Gesamm. Zeichn.* p.57, no.21, repr.; Rowlands, *Private Collection*, pp.42f., no.38, repr.

The artist who has filled this sheet with these compact scenes has a sense of rhythmic quality in his penwork and gives movement to his figures which are far more allied to Rueland Frueauf the Younger's work than to his father's, as Schilling and Peter Halm noted. Indeed, a comparison between this sheet and the similar way in which the figures around the foot of the cross are managed in the *Crucifixion* by Rueland Frueauf the Younger, dated *1496*, in the Augustiner Chorherrenstift, Klosterneuberg, near Vienna, speaks strongly in favour of a firm attribution to this artist.

3 Thuringia, XV century

Anonymous artist

c.1430

8 John the Baptist and St John the Evangelist

Pen and black ink with red wash, heightened with white body-colour. 12.7 × 9.3cm

PROVENANCE: Richard Philipps, Lord Milford (L.*Suppl.*2687); thence by descent to Sir John Philipps, Picton Castle, Pembrokeshire; F.C.Springell (L.*Suppl.*1049a)

England, Private Collection

LITERATURE: *Ten German drawings*, in Museum pamphlet, Boston, Museum of Fine Arts, 1958; Schilling, *Gesamm. Zeichn.*, p.19, no.3, repr.; Rowlands, *Private Collection*, p.10, no.3, repr.

Edmund Schilling identified the region and dated this drawing through a comparison with the panel paintings of *c.*1430 from Thuringia, now in Nuremberg (Germanisches Nationalmuseum, inv.nos.10 and 11; Lutze & Wiegand pp.179f.). They are wings with saints (the left-hand one includes the figures of John the Baptist and St John the Evangelist) from an altarpiece produced in a workshop in Erfurt, whose principal painting is the so-called 'Unicorn' altarpiece, formerly in Erfurt Cathedral, and subsequently in the Landesmuseum at Weimar (Stange, iii, pp.220–1, pl.281).

8

4 Cologne, XV century

Stefan Lochner

Probably Meersburg, Lake Constance, c.1410(?) – Cologne between 22 September and 24 December 1451

Painter. That his birthplace was Meersburg is suggested by a document of 16 August 1451, which mentions that his parents had recently died there. Förster concludes from paintings attributed to him that he probably went to the Netherlands early in his career. Recorded in Cologne in 1442 as 'Meister Steffen', when he was paid for decorations made in connection with the visit of Emperor Frederick III. Purchase and sale of his houses in Cologne are recorded between 1442 and 1448. Elected town councillor by the Painters' Guild in 1447 and in 1450. References to him

cease at the end of 1451, a year in which plague broke out in Cologne.

There are no pictures signed by Lochner but Dürer noted in his diary of 1520 that the *Adoration of the Magi* in the Town Hall chapel (now Cologne Cathedral) was painted by 'maister Steffan zu Cöln'. (No other painter of this name is recorded in the town during the period.) The great significance of this altarpiece is not only revealed by Dürer's admiration for it, but also by that of successive generations of artists. Other paintings attributed to Lochner on the basis of the *Adoration of the Magi* include the *Madonna in the Rose Garden* (Cologne, Wallraf-Richartz Museum); the *Presentation in the Temple*, dated 1445 (Lisbon, Gulbenkian Collection); the *Presentation in the Temple*, dated 1447 (Darmstadt, Hessisches Landesmuseum); two wings

9

10

from an altarpiece, the inner sides of which show Sts Matthew, Catherine and John the Evangelist (London, National Gallery) and Sts Mark, Barbara and Luke (Cologne, Wallraf-Richartz Museum); and an altarpiece of the *Last Judgement* (formerly Cologne, church of St Lawrence, now Cologne, Wallraf-Richartz Museum, Frankfurt, Städelsches Kunstinstitut and Munich, Alte Pinakothek). A few drawings and miniatures have been connected with Lochner's name and that of his workshop.

BIBLIOGRAPHY: J.J. Merlo, *Kölnische Künstler in alter und neuer Zeit*, Düsseldorf, 1895, pp.828ff.; F. Winkler, *Wallraf Jahrbuch*, iii–iv, 1926/7, pp.123ff.; Thieme-Becker, xxiii, 1929, pp.306ff. (for further literature); O.H. Förster, *Stefan Lochner*, Frankfurt-am-Main, 1938; Michael Levey, *National Gallery catalogue. The German School*, London, 1959, pp.59ff.; Munich, *Gemälde Köln*, pp.190ff.; *Late Gothic Art from Cologne*, exhib. cat., London, National Gallery, 1977, pp.42ff.

After Lochner

9 The Virgin adoring the infant Christ

Pen and black ink. 12.9 × 17.2 cm

PROVENANCE: F. Fagel; Sir J. C. Robinson; Malcolm (L.1489)

1895–9–15–1007

LITERATURE: JCR, p.184, no.549; BM *Guide* 1895, pp.52f., no.259; H. Schrade, *Wallraf Jahrbuch*, v, 1928, pp.61ff., fig.5; Stange, iii, 1938, p.108; Munich, *Gemälde Köln*, p.207

Inscribed on the *verso* in an (?) early sixteenth-century hand, in brown ink, *gergorij beck van norlingen.*

Robinson described the drawing as 'Early Flemish school *c.*1470'. The connection with Stefan Lochner was first made by Sidney Colvin in an annotation to the departmental copy of the Malcolm catalogue, where he observed that no.9 is related to the artist's painting of the *Adoration of the Christ Child* (Munich, Alte Pinakothek, inv. no.13169). The drawing is, as far as it goes, a virtually contemporary copy of the painting; the stable with the ox and the ass, and the angels in the background being omitted. The painting is on one side of the left wing of an altarpiece; the other side shows the *Crucifixion*. The right-hand wing, with the *Presentation of Christ in the Temple* (dated *1445*) and the *Stigmatisation of St Francis* is in the Gulbenkian Collection, Lisbon (inv. no.272).

Another early copy of the painting, which records the figure of the Virgin only, is to be found in a drawing in the École des Beaux-Arts, Paris (Masson Collection, no.128).

Follower of Lochner

10 The Virgin in the Temple with a kneeling donor

Pen and black ink. 23.1 × 14.2 cm

PROVENANCE: T. Banks (L.2423); Mrs L. Forster; A. Poynter (L.161 on *verso* of old mount); Sir E. J. Poynter (sale, Sotheby, 1918, 25 April, lot 254, bt *Colnaghi £17*); presented by O. Beit

1918–6–15–4

LITERATURE: Parker, *German Schools*, p.26, no.4, repr.; H. Schrade, *Wallraf Jahrbuch*, v, 1928. pp.57, 60, fig.3; Stange, iii, 1938, pp.106ff

Inscribed on the old mount, in a nineteenth-century hand, in brown ink, *Israel van Mentz.*; and in a modern hand, in black ink, *Flemish School/15th cent. No.3*

The style of this drawing strongly suggests a link with Stefan Lochner, the leading painter in Cologne during the middle of the fifteenth century. The position of the Virgin before a curtain held by angels, and that of the kneeling female donor, is reminiscent of Lochner's painting, the *Virgin with a violet*, which was probably made before 1443 (Cologne, Erzbischöfliches Diözesanmuseum; Cologne, *Spätgotik* no.1). No.10 may record a lost work by the master, or a member of his studio, since the partial noting of details is more suggestive of a copy than of a preparatory drawing.

The subject of the Virgin in the Temple, where she supposedly lived before her marriage to Joseph, comes from the apocryphal Gospels. Representations of it appear to derive from a votive image at one time in Milan Cathedral (see C. Dodgson, *Woodcuts of the Fifteenth Century in the Ashmolean Museum, Oxford*, Oxford, 1929, pp.23ff.). The Virgin is always shown in an attitude of devotion and is accompanied by angels, she wears her hair loose, and a belted robe. The dress is often embroidered with ears of corn, emblems of fertility, and she also usually wears a collar of rays around her neck; neither of these are present in no.10, yet in all other respects the Virgin conforms to traditional representations of the type. The number of versions of *die Ährenmadonna*, as the image is known, produced in the Rhineland during the fifteenth century bears witness to a flowering of the cult in this region (see A. Löhr, *Die Gottesmutter, Marienbild in Rheinland und Westfälen*, edited by L. Küppers, i, 1974, pp.171ff) to which the present sheet, together with the composition from the Lochner workshop it records, belong.

5 Swabia, XV century

Anonymous artist
c.1470

11 Design for the west tower of the Münster at Ulm

Pen and brown ink on two pieces of parchment, backed onto linen. 184 × 67.5 cm

PROVENANCE: M. Entris, Munich

London, Victoria and Albert Museum, 3547

LITERATURE: R. Pfleiderer, *Das Münster zu Ulm und seine Kunst-denkmale*, Stuttgart, 1905, pp.51 ff.; H. Koepf, *Die götischen Planrisse der Wiener Sammlungen*, Vienna, 1969, p.17, under no.35, repr.; Koepf, *Planrisse*, p.38, no.4, repr.; *Die Parler und der schöne Stil 1350–1400*, exhib. cat. Cologne, Kunsthalle, 1978–80, i, pp.325 ff., repr.

A considerable number of architectural drawings connected with the construction of Gothic cathedrals have survived; the present sheet is one of a group related to the Münster at Ulm. It is a design of *c.*1470 for the lower three storeys of the west tower, and is a fragment of a larger drawing which originally showed the whole tower, the appearance of which is recorded in an early sixteenth-century copy at Ulm (Ev. Gesamt-Kirchengemeinde; Koepf, *Planrisse*, pp.41 f. no.5, repr.) drawn in pen and ink on paper (110 × 23.7 cm). A further fragment, which shows the lower section of the pinnacle, and probably formed part of the present drawing since it is made in the same technique, and is also recorded in the copy, is in Ulm (Ev. Gesamt-Kirchengemeinde; Koepf, *Planrisse*, p.43, no.6, repr.). The copy, which corresponds closely with no.11 in its details, was published as an engraving by Elias Frick, in *Eigentliche Beschreibung von Anfang, Fortgang Vollendung und Beschaffenheit dess herrlichen Münster-Gebäudes zu Ulm*, Ulm, 1718, at which time the tower was only constructed as far as the gallery on the third storey, that is, just above the upper windows in the present sheet. The tower which was begun by Ulrich von Ensingen (*c.*1350–1419) is the work of various architects. This drawing probably represents the design of Moritz Ensinger (*c.*1430–82/3). The octagonal part of the tower, and the spire, were completed from 1885 to 1890, after the design of Matthäus Boblinger (active 1469–1505) with some variations.

Another drawing, which represents an earlier stage of the design, shows the upper tower and pinnacle from the gallery above the window of St Martin, which is seen in the centre of no.11, and is made in the same technique as the present sheet. It probably records the design of Ulrich von Ensingen or a member of his workshop (Ulm, Stadt-archiv, inv.no.1; Koepf, *Planrisse*, pp.29 ff., no.1, repr.).

Anonymous artist
c.1465

12 Design for a tabernacle

Pen and black and brown ink, with light yellow wash on seven pieces of paper. 258 × 31.8 cm

WM: bull's head with a crown (close to Briquet, 14591)

PROVENANCE: M. Entris, Munich

London, Victoria and Albert Museum, 3551

LITERATURE: R. Pfleiderer, *Das Münster zu Ulm und seine Kunst-denkmale*, Stuttgart, 1905, pp.51 ff.; Koepf, *Planrisse*, p.84, no.17, repr.; VAM, *Technique & Purpose*, p.43, no.118, repr. (VAM E.6101–1910 repr. in error in first edition)

The drawing was made in connection with the large stone tabernacle (26.25 m in height) in the Münster at Ulm, which was constructed between 1467 and 1471 (R. Pfleid-erer *op.cit.*, pls.14–16). The tabernacle in its completed state is considerably different to the present design, and has a rectangular shaped shrine for the sacrament, rather than the polygonal one indicated here; however, there is another design for it in Ulm (Stadtarchiv, inv.no.12 (new); Koepf, *Planrisse*, p.85, repr.) with which no.12 has sufficient similarities, particularly in the construction of the baldachin (see no.13) above the shrine for the sacrament, and also of the upper storeys, only half of which is represented in the present sheet, to suggest that no.12 was made as a pre-liminary study for the tabernacle. The Ulm drawing is made in a more elaborate technique on parchment, and is closer, particularly in the lower section, than the London drawing to the finished object.

An attribution of the design of the tabernacle was made at one time by Wilhelm Vöge to a 'Meister Wingarten' (from Weingarten, near Ravensburg) to whom payments were made in 1462 for work done possibly in connection with the tabernacle. It is quite probable, in any case, that the designs were made well before it was constructed. The tabernacle is embellished with sculpture, not seen in the preparatory drawings.

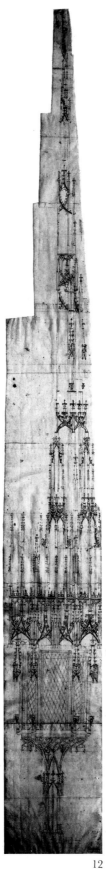

11

12

Anonymous artist

c.*1465*

13 Plan of groined vaulting for a tabernacle

Pen and brown ink, with numerous ruled incised lines and compass marks, parts gone over in black chalk. Trimmed along upper, lower and right-hand edges. 32.3 × 36.8cm

WM: bull's head with a crown (close to Briquet, 14591)

PROVENANCE: M.Entris, Munich

London, Victoria and Albert Museum, 3552

LITERATURE: R.Pfleiderer, *Das Münster zu Ulm und seine Kunstdenkmale*, Stuttgart, 1905, pp.51ff.; Koepf, *Planrisse*, p.87, no.18, repr.

Inscribed in the upper right-hand corner, by a later hand, in pencil, *Das [?]schnitt zu erst? Sacramenthaus.*

This drawing would appear to be a study for the vaulting on the baldachin above the shrine for the sacrament of the tabernacle in the Münster at Ulm (see no.12), or for one very similar to it. It is drawn on paper with the same watermark as that of no.12, which is of a type in use at Ravensburg, Ulm and elsewhere from 1465 (see R.Pfleiderer *op.cit.*, p.53). A similar plan for the vaulting of a baldachin is in Vienna (Akademie der bildenden Künste, inv.no.17002; H.Koepf, *Die gotischen Planrisse der Wiener Sammlungen*, Vienna, 1969, pl.378).

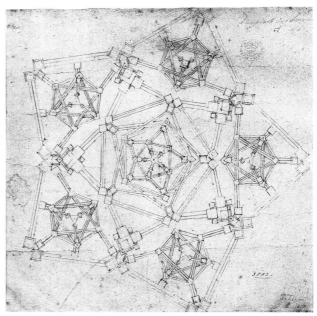

13

Bernhard Strigel

Memmingen November or December 1460 – Memmingen 1528 (between 1 April and 4 May)

Painter. Either the son of a painter, Hans Strigel the Younger, or possibly his brother, a sculptor, Ivo Strigel; their father Hans Strigel the Elder had a workshop established in Memmingen by at least 1430. Little is known of his early life and his first dated work is a drawing of 1490 (see no.14). He is thought to have assisted in the production of the altarpiece of the *Last Judgement*, made for the monastery of Disentis, Graubünden (now parish church, Graubünden) signed and dated by Ivo Strigel, *1489*. Some of the painted outer wings and the predella of the carved altarpiece in the Klosterkirche, Blaubeuren, dated *1493* and *1494* are attributed to him. During this period he was much influenced by the Ulm painter, Bartholomeus Zeitblom (*c.*1455/60– 1518/22) who also participated in the Blaubeuren altarpiece. In 1499 he received payment for work done in Chur, Switzerland. From 1512 he held various official posts in Memmingen on the town council, and in the shopkeepers' guild, to which painters there belonged. He was much patronised by the Emperor Maximilian I. In 1507 he made a portrait of the Emperor at Constance (formerly Strassburg, Musée des Beaux-Arts, destroyed

1947). In 1515 he was in Vienna for the Habsburg double wedding, where he painted *The Emperor Maximilian and his family* (Vienna, Kunsthistorisches Museum). Strigel's involvement with the Reformation is demonstrated by his defence of Christoph Schappeler, a Lutheran preacher working in Memmingen, against the Bishop of Augsburg at Dillingen in 1523, and at the Diet of Nuremberg in 1524. From 1523 to 1525 he acted as an envoy for the town over legal matters in various parts of southern Germany, and went to Innsbruck on numerous occasions to collect repayments of a loan made by Memmingen to the Emperor.

A large number of paintings by Strigel has survived. His *oeuvre* has been established round the portrait of *Johannes Cuspinian and his family* (Count Wilczek, Schloss Seebarn, Austria) which has an autograph inscription on the reverse, dated *1520* describing Strigel as court painter to the Emperor Maximilian; and the portrait of *Ulrich Wolfhard*, dated *1526* (Frau Neuerburg, Henef/Sieg) the only two known paintings to be signed. The Emperor's patronage must have stimulated further commissions, for Strigel was clearly a popular and successful portrait-painter. His best works include the portraits of *Hieronymus Haller*, 1503 (Munich, Alte Pinakothek); *Conrad Rehlinger and his children*, 1517 (Munich, Alte Pinakothek); *Eva von Schwarzenberg*, 1521 (private collection, Switzerland); and *Hans Rott and his wife*, 1527 (Washington, National Gallery of Art). Religious paintings which have been convincingly attributed to him, include an altarpiece of the *Adoration of the Magi* (Memmingen, Städtisches Museum), *The Legend of the True Cross*, which was probably commissioned by Maximilian (who is portrayed in the background) in 1507 and was formerly in S. Paolo fuori le mura, Rome, and of which only four panels survive (Schloss Kynžvart, Czechoslovakia); and

14r

14v

an altarpiece with the *Life of the Virgin* of 1507/8 for the Liebfrauenkapelle of the monastery at Salem (now Schloss Salem).

BIBLIOGRAPHY: Robert Visscher, *Prussian Jahrbuch* vi, 1885, pp.38–57; Thieme-Becker xxxii, 1938, pp.187ff.; Otto, *Strigel* (for further literature).

14 *Recto:* The Holy Family
Verso: Standing Virgin and Child, seen from the shoulders downwards

Pen and brown and black ink, heightened with white bodycolour, partly oxidised, on pink prepared paper, the *verso* in black ink with white bodycolour on pink prepared paper. The sheet has been cut down along the upper edge, apparently after the *verso* was drawn but before the drawing on the *recto* was made. 21.9 × 20.5cm

WM: a high crown surmounted by a cross (only partly visible, similar to Piccard, iv, 11)

PROVENANCE: S. Woodburn (sale, Christie, 1854, 21 June, lot 1132 as by 'Israel Van Meck', bt with 3 others *Tiffin £2*)

1854–6–28–22

LITERATURE: Waagen, *Treasures Suppl.* p.35; K.T.Parker, *Belvedere*, viii, 1925, pp.34ff., pls.8, 11; S.Freedberg, *Fogg Bulletin*, viii, 1938, p.21, fig.3; Otto, *Strigel*, pp.50, 107, no.88, pls.156, 164; Rettich, *Strigel*, pp.216ff.; E.Rettich, *Studien f. K. Bauch*, pp.101f., fig.1; Denison and Mules, *Pierpont Morgan Drawings*, p.37, under no.10

Inscribed by the artist in brown ink underneath the drawing, *Nehmt zu Dank 91* (letters in the first and third words are conjoined), and on the *verso, 90*

The sheet was first recognised as the work of Bernhard Strigel by Parker, who interpreted the *91* on the *recto* and the *90* on the *verso* to indicate respectively 1491 and 1490 — the earliest dates to be found on any of the known drawings attributed to Strigel. Rettich describes the sheet as belonging to the artist's circle, possibly his workshop, but the characteristics and vitality of the drawing on the *recto* are consistent with other drawings attributed to Strigel's early period, such as the *Two Lovers* in the Pierpont Morgan Library, New York (Acc. no.1,250) which also displays similar facial types. The two preparatory studies for Strigel's paintings on the high altar of the Klosterkirche at Blaubeuren, near Ulm (dated 1493 and 1494) are more elaborately executed than no.14, (Paris, Louvre, Cabinet des Dessins, inv.19182; Berlin-Dahlem, Kupferstichkabinett, inv.no.2407; Otto, *Strigel*, pls.158–9) but one encounters in them figures with the same, somewhat squat proportions as those in the *Holy Family*. A type of Virgin and Child comparable to the one in *Holy Family* is seen, in the reverse sense, in Strigel's devotional diptych for Hans Funk (Munich, Alte Pinakothek, inv.WAF 1067; Otto, *Strigel*, pl.10), which belongs stylistically to the 1490s. Strigel later copied the composition of the *Holy Family* in his painting, *The Child Servatius with Eliud and Memelia* (East Berlin, Staatliche Museen, formerly Deutsches Museum, inv.606D; Otto, *Strigel*, pl.96), which is a panel from an altarpiece representing the Holy Kindred (two further panels are in the National Gallery of Art, Washington) which has been dated to the period 1520–8.

The drawing of the *Virgin and Child* on the *verso* of no.14 lacks any strong individuality, but given the association with the *Holy Family* on the *recto* may reasonably be regarded as an early study by Strigel.

15 The Presentation in the Temple

Pen and black ink with grey wash and pink bodycolour for the flesh tones, heightened with white bodycolour, on blue prepared paper. 18.1 × 17.5cm

WM: crown surmounted by a heart

PROVENANCE: Bequeathed by Miss M.A.Whiteley

1956–7–14–1

LITERATURE: Augsburg, *Holbein*, p.157, no.179, pl.191; A.Shestack, *MD*, iv,no.1, 1966, pp.21ff., pl.15; E.Rettich, *Studien f. K. Bauch*, p.107, fig.6; G.Otto, *Memminger Geschichtsblätter*, Jahresheft 1967, 1969, p.26, pl.19

Inscribed by a later hand in brown ink in the lower left-hand corner, *Martin Shoen*, and on the *verso* by a different hand, in brown ink, $\frac{a}{e}$

The drawing was first published as a copy by Bernhard Strigel of the outer side of the right wing of the former high altarpiece, probably made *c*.1490–5, in the Catholic parish church in Bingen, near Sigmaringen (Augsburg, *Holbein*, p.133, no.129, pl.136). The inner side of the altarpiece was carried out by Bartholomeus Zeitblom (*c*.1455/60–1518/22) from Ulm, an important artist with a large workshop, but the outer side is by one of his assistants, probably the Master of the Pfullendorf Altar (B. Bushart, *Zeitschr. f. Kunstgesch.*, xxi, 1958, p.234), who gains his name from an altarpiece of *c*.1500 now dispersed and

15

partly destroyed (Frankfurt, Städelsches Kunstinstitut, Stuttgart, Staatsgalerie and Schloss Sigmaringen; see *Katalog der Staatsgalerie Stuttgart*, Stuttgart, 1957, pp.198f.). The copy is a free interpretation of the painting and contains only the main group of figures on the right. The draughtsman has created a greater sense of weight and volume than is perceived in the painting, by treating the drapery in a more elaborate fashion and by making the bodies more rounded in shape, changes one would expect from Strigel.

Following a suggestion of Winzinger's, Shestack attributed no.15 to Strigel on a stylistic basis, without knowing its connection with the Bingen altarpiece. He compared the use of pink flesh tones with a dark-coloured prepared paper to a drawing dated *1502* in Berlin-Dahlem (Kupferstichkabinett inv.no.4256; Otto, *Strigel*, pl.169) and to two drawings in Venice, which also display a similarly lavish use of white heightening to no.15 (Accademia, inv. nos.474, 475; Otto, *Strigel*, pls.167, 168).

16 St Vitus

See colour plate section following p.80

Pen and black ink with grey wash and red bodycolour for the flesh tones, heightened with white bodycolour on greenish-grey prepared paper. Areas of surface damage on the right side of the sheet have been made up in parts, notably in the saint's right hand, his left sleeve and around the belt of his tunic. 24 × 12.4cm

PROVENANCE: W.B.Tiffin

1855–7–14–67

LITERATURE: K.T.Parker, *Belvedere*, viii, 1925, p.38, pl.13; Otto, *Strigel*, pp.51, 108, no.95, pl.165; Rettich, *Strigel*, pp.215f; E.Rettich, *Studien f. K. Bauch*, pp.109f

The bodycolour is no longer oxidised, as stated by Parker and Rettich. Although the condition of the right-hand side of the sheet is not good, the penwork and handling of the wash on the drapery on the left, particularly that over the figure's right arm, is of a high quality, and makes Rettich's judgement of the drawing as the work of a studio assistant seem too fastidious.

As Parker and Otto have noted, no.16 is closely connected with the standing figure of St John the Baptist on one of four panels of an altarpiece, allegedly from the church of St Nikolaus in Isny (formerly in the Deutsches Museum, Berlin, inv.563A, destroyed 1945; Otto, *Strigel*, pl.101. Panels of the altarpiece which are known to have survived, are in the Gemäldegalerie, Berlin-Dahlem and the Kunsthalle, Karlsruhe). It is thought to be a late work by Strigel dating from the period 1520–8. St John the Baptist holds a different attribute and wears an animal skin instead of a tunic, but the position of the figure and the treatment of the drapery is very similar to that seen in the present sheet. A figure representing St Vitus, but unrelated in appearance to no.16, is seen on a different panel of the same altarpiece (Otto, *Strigel*, pl.98).

St Vitus, a Sicilian nobleman who lived in the fourth century AD, is patron saint of Bohemia, Saxony and Sicily, as well as of dancers and actors; the vessel refers to his martyrdom in a cauldron of boiling oil.

Anonymous artist

c.*1500*

17 St Margaret

Pen and black ink, heightened with white bodycolour on green prepared paper. 25.1 × 11.9cm

PROVENANCE: S. Rogers (sale, Christie, 1856, 6 May, lot 874); J. C. Robinson; Malcolm

1895–9–15–960

LITERATURE: JCR p.171, no.507

Inscribed on the *verso* in the lower left-hand corner, in a later hand in black ink, *Martin Schön*; and above, in a different hand, *101 J.C. Robinson 1856 bought from S. Roger's collection at the sale*

The old attribution to Schongauer is incorrect. The use of white heightening on a dark coloured paper is more typical of Swabian drawings than those of the Rhine region, and the handling of the white bodycolour in this sheet is fairly close to that of the pink heightening used by Hans Baldung (q.v.) in his early self-portrait of *c.*1502 in Basel (Kupferstichkabinett, inv.no.U.VI.36), most probably executed before his arrival in Nuremberg. The attention given to the volume of the figure in this depiction of St Margaret suggests that the draughtsman was copying a piece of sculpture. Its resemblance to the carved figures of Michel Erhart (*c.*1440–after 1522), and even more to those of his son, Gregor Erhart (*c.*1460–1540) is quite striking. Gregor Erhart's *Virgin and Child on the Crescent Moon* in the Ulrich and Afrakirche, Augsburg, executed *c.*1495–1500 (Augsburg, *Holbein*, p.185, no.257, pl.254) makes a fascinating comparison with the present drawing and strongly points to the region around Ulm where the Erharts came from, and to Augsburg in particular, where Gregor moved in 1494, as the likely place of origin of the sculpture.

17

6 Upper Rhineland, XV century

Anonymous artist
c.1440

18 A sibyl in an elaborate headdress

Pen and brown ink. 20.2 × 13.8cm

PROVENANCE: Daniell

1861-8-10-59

Acquired as a work by Schongauer, this finely executed drawing is, however, by another upper Rhenish hand and earlier in date. The features of the woman, who is evidently intended to be a sibyl, are rendered with much idiosyncrasy, and the pear-shaped head is curiously emphasised by an extravagant, bejewelled headdress. Similar facial types and head attire are seen in the paintings of Konrad Witz (1400/10–1444/6); such as his portrayal of Solomon, in *Solomon and the Queen of Sheba* (Berlin-Dahlem, Gemälde-galerie, inv.no.1701; Gantner, *Witz*, pls.26, 28) and Ahasuerus, in *Esther before Ahasuerus* (Basel, Kunstmuseum, inv.no.643; Gantner, *Witz*, pls.23, 25). This would suggest that the draughtsman of no.18 came from the immediate circle of Witz. A firm attribution to the master himself is difficult to make, since no other comparable drawings attributed to him are known to have survived. The few associated with Witz either have the appearance of copies (Erlangen, Universitätsbibliothek; Kuhrmann, *Erlangen*, pl.22; Berlin-Dahlem, Kupferstichkabinett, inv.no.1971; Bock, *Berlin*, i, p.88, ii, pl.118) or may be attributed to followers (Berlin-Dahlem, Kupferstichkabinett, inv.no.2169, Bock, *Berlin*, i, p.64, ii, pl.92, as Lochner; Erlangen, Universitätsbibliothek; Bock, *Erlangen*, nos.47, 48, 49, 52, repr.).

Anonymous artist
c.1465

19 Martyrdom of a pilgrim saint

Pen and black ink. 32.5 × 21.7cm

PROVENANCE: H. Eisemann

1930-4-14-37

The style is characteristic of artists working in the Upper Rhineland in the middle and second half of the fifteenth century. This vigorous use of the pen can be found in a series of ornamental studies, somewhat more precise in manner, from a pattern-book in use either in a goldsmith's shop or more probably a glass-painter's studio. Six sheets are at Karlsruhe (Kupferstichkabinett, inv.nos.VIII 1580, I–VI), four of which are probably by the same hand as a further three now at Basel (Kupferstichkabinett, inv.nos.U.1.4, U.1.8, U.1.9; Falk, *Basel*, nos.21–3, repr.). In discussing one of the latter (Falk, *Basel*, no.21) Parker described it as by a 'follower of the Monogrammist E.S. *c*.1470' (Parker, *Alsatian Drawings*, p.24, no.6 repr.), and this date is given some support by that proposed for the watermark of one of the sheets at Basel (an oxhead with a star; Falk, *Basel*, no.22), in a form noted by Falk as nearly identical with Piccard ix.333: Lahr, Mainz, Strassburg, 1469–71. The present drawing, although it lacks a watermark, can, however, be associated with the works of a particular artist active in the Upper Rhineland in the middle of the fifteenth century, Caspar Isenmann (*c*.1410–before 1490). Similar facial types occur in both this drawing and Isenmann's paintings. For instance, there is a striking comparison to be made between the head of the saint and that of Christ in Isenmann's painting of the *Arrest of Christ*, on the upper left-hand wing of the altarpiece, now dismembered, executed for the St Martinskirche, Colmar, which was commissioned in 1462 and completed in 1465 (Stange, vii, pp.12–14, pl.14). Types comparable with the executioner in the drawing can be found among the people by the city gate in the *Entry into Jerusalem* from the same altarpiece, especially the man on the right who lays a cloak on the ground.

Even though the quality of the drawing suggests that it is the work of a talented artist, these comparisons do no more than indicate that no.19 could be by someone active in Isenmann's circle. Parker has attributed to Isenmann himself a drawing now in Basel, a sheet of studies in silverpoint with two half-length figures and three heads (inv.no.U.VIII.15; Falk, *Basel*, no.18, repr.). Landolt's view, however, that these studies are copies is more plausible (Basel, *100 Master Drawings*, no.4, repr.) and it is conceivable that they were made from lost paintings by Isenmann, either by the artist himself or a leading assistant.

18

19

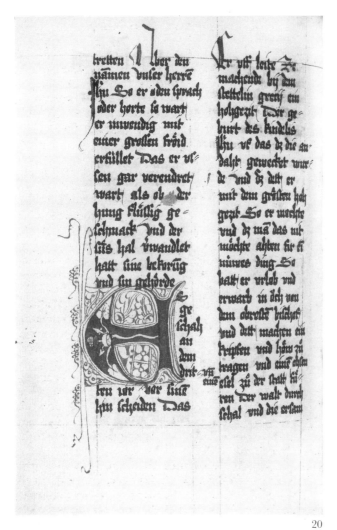

20

20

Sibilla von Bondorf

c.1450 – probably Strassburg soon after 1524

Probably a member of the noble family of the same name in the Black Forest, originally from Bondorf to the east of Freiburg-im-Breisgau. She joined the second order of St Francis, the 'poor Clares' very probably in Freiburg. Our knowledge of her life can be pieced together from scattered references in manuscripts and letters. Her first known work was a life of St Francis (see no.20) in which it is stated that the writing and illumination for it was finished in 1478 for the house of Clares in Lower Freiburg. In 1479/80 Sibilla was commissioned to add three pictures, the first of which she inscribed, *hec pictura e[st] a sorore Sibilla de Bondorf orate deu[m] pro ea*, to a manuscript middle-German translation of the rule of St Clare (British Library, Add.Ms.15,686) that belonged to the Convent of the poor Clares in Villingen im Schwarzwald, near Donaueschingen, where there was introduced at that time a stricter adherence to the rule. According to Konrad von Bondorf, a leading Franciscan and probably both a relative and the confessor

of Sibilla, in a letter of 1 March 1483 to a nun at Söflingen, Klara von Rietheim, he was with Sibilla when the women (presumably the Clares) moved from Freiburg to Strassburg. A Sibilla is listed as being in the house of the poor Clares at Strassburg from 1485 to 1524, when it was secularised: there are indications that this was Sibilla von Bondorf, since she is mentioned as *scriba*; later she became Prioress.

Other manuscripts that can be attributed to her in the late fifteenth century are the *Legends of St Clare* (Karlsruhe, Badische Landesbibliothek), which according to a later inscription belonged to the poor Clares in Freiburg-im-Breisgau, and can be dated before 1492; an illuminated prayer book (Donaueschingen, Fürstliche Fürstenburgische Bibliothek); and an illustration of *St John on Patmos* from the inside of a book-cover (Munich, Graphische Sammlung).

BIBLIOGRAPHY: C.v.Heusinger, *Zeitschr. Oberrheins*, cvii, 1959, pp.136ff.; D.Brett-Evans, *Zeitschrift für deutsche Philologie*, Berlin, lxxxvi, Sonderheft, 1967, pp.91ff.; N.Fabbretti and E.Silber, *I Fioretti di San Francesco*, Turin, 1981.

20 Life and miracles of St Francis

Pen and black ink with bodycolour and watercolour, illuminated with gold leaf. Sheet: 20.6 × 13.8cm

PROVENANCE: A. Asher

British Library, Add. Ms. 15,710

LITERATURE: *Add. Manuscripts*, p.13; D. Brett-Evans, *Zeitschrift für deutsche Philologie*, Berlin, lxxxvi, Sonderheft, 1967, pp.91ff.; N. Fabbretti and E. Silber, *I Fioretti di San Francesco*, Turin, 1981 (with reproductions throughout from Add. Ms. 15,710)

The manuscript is open at folios 135 *verso* and 136 *recto*, on the latter of which Sibilla has executed a miniature of St Francis holding the Christ Child at a mystical Nativity. This subject is closely related to a custom that grew up in the western church of the crib in which a model of the child was placed on Christmas Eve, to remain there until the Octave of Epiphany (13 January). Figures of the Virgin and St Joseph, various animals and shepherds were usually added, and the Magi, at Epiphany. It is thought that St Francis made the first such crib at Greccio in 1223.

Sibilla von Bondorf is but one of many women religious who played a highly distinctive role within the cultural life of the Upper Rhineland in the fifteenth century. She was certainly the most interesting of the sisters who expressed themselves in a charming way by illustrating manuscripts of devotion, essential to the enclosed life, with drawings of child-like simplicity. During the second half of the century the monastic life of these women had undergone considerable reform and a more specific provision for artistic activities was introduced. The sisters took full advantage of their opportunities, exercising their skills in writing, painting, weaving and embroidery. Everything they produced has an unmistakable character which, however, lacks any very marked individuality. It was all produced in a manner which reflected the overriding influence that weaving and embroidery played in the sisters' lives. The way in which Sibilla drew, for instance, would be unthinkable without her intimate knowledge of embroidery and tapestry design. The tapestries and embroideries of the Upper Rhineland region of the second half of the century with their bright but restricted colour range, naive arrangements of the figures, and chubby faces, possess a highly developed sense of background decoration. This is the formative influence behind all their artistic endeavours, which includes apart from the drawings already mentioned above a small drawing, now cut from a devotional book in the British Museum, *The infant Christ in the midst of flowers* (inv.no.1895-1-22-15; Dodgson, i, p.61, under no.A30). Although this is close to Sister Sibilla's work it is probably not by her. A further, even more naive example, also in the British Museum, is *The Christ Child holding the Host in a Corpus Christi procession* (inv.no.1972-u-677) which is of more interest as a reflection of local piety than as a work of art.

Master of the Drapery Studies

Upper Rhine (Strassburg?) active c.1470–c.1497

Draughtsman, designer of glass-paintings and painter, also known as the Master of the Coburg Roundels. About 150 drawings, many of drapery studies, have been attributed to this interesting and prolific artist. Approximately one-third of them are housed in the Veste Coburg. Thorlacius-Ussing was the first to identify the hand when he published a small number of drawings in Paris, Berlin, Copenhagen, Frankfurt and elsewhere, as being the sheets of a single sketchbook by a South German artist executed c.1490, possibly while on a journey. Buchner called the artist the Master of the Coburg Roundels after two drawings of roundels in the Veste Coburg (*The Adoration of the Magi.* inv.no.z.187–KI and *The Virgin and Child attended by Angels*, inv.no.z.232–KI) previously attributed to the Master of the Housebook and probably made for glass-paintings. He also associated with the artist eleven further drawings, and two paintings of the *Death of the Virgin* (Wallraf-Richartz Museum, Cologne, and National Museum, Cracow). Winkler expanded the list to about 100 drawings and named the artist, the Master of the Drapery Studies, due to the preponderance of this type of work. Many of his other drawings record paintings, sculpture and engravings of Netherlandish or German origin. Some of these compositions are lost (see no.21), but others have been identified as the work of artists such as Rogier van der Weyden (see no.23), Dirk Bouts (after 1420–75), and Martin Schongauer (q.v.).

Other paintings attributed to the artist include the *Ascension of Mary Magdalene* (Kunsthalle, Karlsruhe) and a related panel of the *Last Communion of Mary Magdalene* (M.H. de Young Memorial Museum, San Francisco); ten panels from an altarpiece with scenes of the Passion preserved in the church of Alt-St Peter, Strassburg, but probably originally in the Magdalenenkirche, Strassburg (Fischel, p.31); and an altarpiece showing scenes from the life of St Margaret, commissioned by a Strassburg family in c.1490 (Dard collection, Musée des Beaux Arts, Dijon, and private collection, Langenbruck, Basel). Further connections with Strassburg are indicated by the Master of the Drapery Studies' evident association with the Strassburg glass-painter, Peter Hemmel (c.1422–after 1501), some of whose work he recorded in his drawings, and for whom he may have produced designs; and by the false Schongauer and Dürer monograms on many of the Master's drawings which were inscribed by the Strassburg chronicler and collector Sebald Büheler (1529–95; see Andersson, pp.51f.) on drawings in his collection (see no.23).

The artist was clearly an inveterate copyist and it is very striking that there are no surviving copies by him of Dürer's earliest signed prints. This would seem to indicate that he had either abandoned copying or was already dead by 1497, the year in which Dürer produced his first dated engraving. Not all the drawings at present assigned to the Master are by him. Most of the Passion series at Coburg, first published by Kaemmerer, is by a different

21r

hand, possibly an associate. This series was made after the
Master of the Karlsruhe Passion, who has been identified
as Hans Hirtz (active in Strassburg, 1421–63), an artist
who clearly influenced the Master of the Drapery Studies
but did not necessarily train him as has been supposed.
Other drawings which should be reconsidered are mentioned
by Andersson (p.390), although her description of some as
'workshop productions' seems inappropriate since it is not
clear that the Master ever maintained a workshop.

BIBLIOGRAPHY: V. Thorlacius-Ussing, *Kunstmuseets Aarsskrift*,
xi–xii, 1924–5, pp.244ff.; xiii–xv, 1926–8, pp.137ff.; E. Buchner,
Munich Jahrbuch, NF iv, 1927, pp.284ff.; L. Kaemmerer, *Munich
Jahrbuch*, NF iv, 1927, pp.347ff.; F. Winkler, *Wallraf Jahrbuch*, NF
i, 1930, pp.123ff.; L. Fischel, *Oberrheinische Kunst*, vi (1934),
pp.27–40; Thieme-Becker, xxxvii, 1950, p.182; Andersson, *Detroit*,
pp.52, 108–44, 388–93 (for further literature).

21 *Recto:* Allegory of Salvation and Damnation

Verso: Allegory of the Way of Life and the Way of Death

Pen and brown ink. Trimmed down the left-hand side. 20.8 × 28.5cm

WM: fleur-de-lis within a crowned shield (similar to Piccard, ii, 1175)

PROVENANCE: Rodd

1847–3–6–12

21v

LITERATURE: F. Winkler, *Wallraf Jahrbuch*, NF i, 1930, pp.134, 152, pl.132 (*verso*)

There are inscriptions on both sides of the sheet, made by the artist in brown ink, which identify some of the figures and objects and indicate colours: on the *recto*: *gratia dei/astroth/allemanta[?]/superbia/avaritia/asmodius* or *asmodaeus/berith/luxuria/belphegor/ira/gula/Gel[b]/venite ad me o[mne]s[?] estis mat[er][?] huius mundi/[e]t ego po[r]tabo vos i[n] domum p[at]ris mei/per tribatione multi dirigu[n]tur ad gratia dei/tribulatio/belsebub/[i]nvidia/accidia*; and on the *verso*: *licht[?] den[?]/wiser/bopst[?]/obedientia/via vita/venite benedicti p[atr]is mei* (*Matt.* XXV, 34);/*rot/wasser/fron/avaritia/supe[r]bia/luxoria/i[n]obedientia/via mortis*. Inscriptions by a later hand have been added on the *recto*, to the left of the ship, *lucifer*, and along the lower edge, *Lucifer Belial Satanas leviathanon*.

The image of the Christian Church as a ship, seen in the centre of the *recto*, is well-known from early Christian writings. Its prevalence in the thought and literature of fifteenth-century Europe is reflected in a series of sermons in which the life of a Christian was likened to a voyage by sea, preached by Johannes Geiler von Kaysersberg in Strassburg (the probable home town of the Master of the Drapery Studies), in 1501, which is shortly after the period in which the artist is thought to have been active. A woodcut illustrating Geyler's allegory of the Ship of Salvation appears on a separately printed sheet inserted into *Das Schiff des Heils* by Johann Maier von Eck, published in Strassburg in 1512 (G. Llompart, *Gesamm. Aufsätze*, xxv, 1970, pp.311ff., pl.6; incorrectly dated 1507), but its composition bears no strong resemblance to the present sheet.

Pictorial representations of the Ship of the Church during the fifteenth century are not uncommon, but they are not usually shown in conjunction with representations of the Vices, as seen here. They often display a figure of Christ on the Cross as a mast, which is present in this composition, but instead of showing an actual building of a church, the ship is more usually filled with figures who represent the faithful on their voyage to salvation (see *Lexikon der christ. Ikonog.*, iv, pp.61–7); however, an anonymous woodcut of a German Romanesque church in a ship entitled *Ecclesia in navi cum suis remis inclinata fluctuante* appears in Johannes Lichtenberger's *Pronosticatio in Latino*, published in Strassburg, in 1488. (Facsimile edited by W. Harry Rylands, Manchester, 1890, signature B. i, with colour reproduction at end). All the same the simplicity of this work indicates that the composition of no.21 must derive from a different source.

It seems most likely, as Winkler pointed out, that the drawings are copied from a Netherlandish work, probably of the 1480s or 90s, which is otherwise unknown. The figures of devils are reminiscent of the style of Hieronymus Bosch (*c.*1450–1516); the motif of a figure seated under a canopy on the left-hand side of the *recto* is similar to that seen in the work of early Netherlandish artists such as the Master of Flémalle; and the type of Gothic architecture depicted is clearly inspired by Netherlandish, and ultimately French, rather than German buildings. The technique of the drawings and their inscriptions, some of which are in German are, however, typical of the Master of the Drapery

Studies. Similar inscriptions are seen on his drawing of the Last Judgement in Paris (Bibliothèque Nationale, inv. no.L.244; Lugt, *Bibl. Nat.*, pls.ii and iii) which also appears to be done after a Netherlandish work.

The composition of a sixteenth-century Spanish painting, the *Ship of the Church* in the Monasterio de las Descalzas Reales, Madrid, also bears some influence of Bosch and displays some similar ideas to the *recto* of no.21 (G. Llompart, *Gesamm. Aufsätze*, xxv, 1970, pp.324f., pl.7). In particular, the 'port' of salvation on the left plays an equivalent rôle in the painting to that of the seated figure who receives the blessed on the left of the sheet in the drawing.

22 *Recto:* An archer spanning a crossbow with a cranequin; study of a crossbow

Verso: Two archers spanning crossbows; a belthook and a double hook for a windlass

Pen and brown ink. The sheet has been cut down on all sides. 27.6 × 18.4cm

PROVENANCE: Durrell

1848–10–13–128

LITERATURE: BM *Guide*, 1928, p.33, no.302; Winzinger, *Schongauer*, pp.66ff., nos.35 (*recto*) and 36 (*verso*), repr.; J. Rosenberg, *MD*, iii, no.4, 1965, p.401

There are studies from life executed on both sides of the sheet, and while the figures on the *verso* are rapidly made in an abbreviated form, they are clearly by the same hand as the drawing of the crossbowman on the *recto* which has a more finished appearance. The drawings demonstrate different types of spanning devices for a crossbow in current use at the end of the fifteenth century. The weapon on the lower half of the *recto* is the most detailed study, and has a distorted perspective which was presumably made in order to show as much of the mechanism as possible. It is a crossbow with a cranequin, an early example of reduction gearing commonly used on sporting and hunting crossbows from the fifteenth to the seventeenth centuries. Comparable types of composite crossbow and cranequin of the late fifteenth century, German in origin, are in the Armouries at the Tower of London (inv.nos.XI.104 and XI.105). Other examples of German crossbows of this date are in the Wallace Collection (inv.nos.A.1032, A.1033, A.1034; Mann, *Arms and Armour*, pp.477ff., pls.158, 160). The figures on the upper part of the *recto* and on the left of the *verso* are shown winding the handle which operates the cranequin in order to span the bow.

A further spanning device, the belthook (a similar example of which is in the Livrustkammaren, Stockholm), is drawn along the upper edge of the *verso*, and shown in use by the kneeling figure on the right. It was worn attached to its owner's belt, who operated it by engaging the hook over the bowstring, as seen in the drawing, and straightening his body with his foot braced in a stirrup attached to the end of the tiller. The double hook seen underneath the belthook is probably for a windlass, an alternative spanning method which employed a series of pulleys. A comparable iron double hook from a crossbow windlass of English origin, dated to the late fifteenth or early sixteenth century, is in the Museum of London (inv.no.A.22501). Further drawings of a windlass may originally have been alongside, but have been lost through the trimming of the sheet.

The amount of specific detail apparent in these drawings makes it very unlikely that they were made, as Parker suggested (BM *Guide*), for a composition of the martyrdom of St Sebastian. They may perhaps have belonged to a series made to demonstrate the mechanics of a crossbow. Winzinger's attribution of no.22 to Schongauer (q.v.) is not convincing and, as Rosenberg correctly pointed out, the proportions of the figures on the *verso* are quite uncharacteristic of this artist. The style and technique of the drawings do, however, indicate an artist of the Upper Rhineland rather than a Nuremberg master as Parker originally suggested; indeed, they are so close to the work of the Master of the Drapery Studies, who was much influenced by Schongauer, that in the light of stylistic comparisons an attribution to him is the most credible answer. Comparable treatment of the drapery and the face and hands of the crossbowman on the *recto*, is seen in drapery studies by this master in Copenhagen (Statens Museum for Kunst, inv. no.6715, Gernsheim no.78912; repr. *Kunstmuseets Aarsskrift* xi–xii, 1924–5, p.245 *recto*, and xiii–xv, 1926–8, p.137 *verso*) and elsewhere. Particularly close comparisons may be made with a drawing of the *Resurrection* in Hamburg (Staatliche Kunsthalle, inv.no.22720 *verso*, Gernsheim no.20520), one of a series of twelve drawings of the *Symbolum Apostolicum* (see Andersson, *Detroit*, pp.112ff. for other examples of the series). The footwear of the sleeping guardsman on the left of this drawing is treated in a very similar fashion to that of the crossbowman on the *recto* of no.22.

23 *Recto:* Annunciation

Verso: Annunciation in an interior

Pen and black ink. 20.4 × 28.4cm

PROVENANCE: Anon. collector (sale, *Property of a Collector, many years deceased*, Sotheby, 1872, 20 Dec., lot 176 attributed to Schongauer, bt with one other, *Colnaghi 17s* for BM)

1873–1–11–53

Inscribed on the *verso*, in brown ink by Sebald Büheler, a false, crudely drawn Schongauer monogram (see biography)

The execution of the *Annunciation* on the *recto* is unusually vigorous for this artist, but there is no reason for not assigning it to him, like the more obviously characteristic drawing on the *verso*, both of which are records of paintings. The drawing on the *verso* of no.23 derives its composition from an Annunciation by Rogier van der Weyden (1397/1400–64), which is recorded in a panel painting, probably by a member of Rogier's school, now in Antwerp (Koninklijk

22r

22v

23v

23r

Museum voor Schone Kunsten, inv.no.39; Martin Davies, *Rogier van der Weyden*, London, 1972, pl.114), and also in a copy by a Swabian master, which was formerly part of the high altarpiece, dated *1489*, of the Klosterkirche of the convent at Lichental, near Baden-Baden, and is now in Karlsruhe (Kunsthalle, inv.no.806a; Karlsruhe, *Alte Meister*, pp.276f.). It is possible however, that the *verso* of no.23 records another, unknown version of the Rogierian composition as, although it contains many of the details, it is not a direct copy of either of the paintings mentioned above.

24 The Coronation of the Virgin

Pen and brown ink, with the addition of black chalk to indicate some leading, as guidance for the glass-painter. Diameter: 31.8cm

PROVENANCE: Campbell Dodgson bequest fund purchase, 1949

Oxford, Ashmolean Museum, P.330A

LITERATURE: *Annual Report*, *Ashmolean Museum*, Oxford 1949, p.52; Andersson, *Detroit*, p.142, under no.43.

Inscribed by the artist, *Siden dõch. mit blome[n]*

This roundel, together with those of the *Adoration of the Magi* and the *Virgin and Child* in the Veste Coburg (Kupferstichkabinett, inv.nos.z.187 and z.232; Andersson, *Detroit*, pp.109 and 143, repr.) whose compositions are on the same scale, evidently once formed part of a series of scenes from the Life of the Virgin, and as such may be considered one of the Master's few creations, the rest of his surviving drawings consisting almost entirely of records of the works of other artists. Among these records scholars have identified drawings that are copies of glass paintings produced in the workshops at Strassburg in the later decades of the fifteenth century. For instance, H.H.Naumann noted that the *Flagellation* and *Carrying of the Cross* on a sheet in Berlin (*Archives alsaciennes d'histoire de l'art*, Strassburg 1935, figs.45 and 46) were copied from two glass-paintings dated *1461* in the parish church at Walburg, Alsace, while Bergstrasser pointed to a similar link between a group of drawings by the Master of the Drapery Studies in Madrid and the cycle of glass paintings in the same church. Because the glass-paintings at Walburg have been attributed to Peter Hemmel of Andlau (*c*.1422–after 1501), the leading Alsatian glass painter of the period, much recent discussion

46

24

of the Master has been concerned with this visible relationship with Hemmel's workshop. The present drawing, and its companions in Coburg, if compared with glass-paintings produced in Strassburg, support the idea that the Master himself would have been employed there, even though, so far, it does not appear possible to associate the Master with a specific glass-painter's work. As glass-painters then apparently decorated cycles of windows as a team, this is perhaps not surprising; however, one can point to various windows that have more than a general kinship with the Coburg Roundels and the present drawing. Instances of this are the *Enthroned Virgin with Child and Angels* and the *Annunciation*, both in nave windows in the parish and pilgrimage church at Lautenbach, south of Baden-Baden in the

Black Forest, and datable *c.*1482 (see Becksmann, *Baden & Pfalz* pt.i, pp.176ff., figs.241, 249–50). A further glass-painting, from a nave window at Lautenbach and in the same style, the *Virgin and Child in glory on a crescent moon*, was formerly in the Kunstgewerbemuseum, Berlin (Becksmann, *op.cit.*, repr. text pl.XVIIId). The style and colouring of the glass-painting indicate the workshop responsible for these nave windows which formed part of the first phase of decoration at Lautenbach was in Strassburg and the master responsible called by some authorities the 'Lautenbacher Meister' was an associate of Peter Hemmel. The present drawing may be associated with the particular phase, and probably also the date, represented in these nave windows at Lautenbach.

Martin Schongauer

Probably Colmar c.1450 – Breisach 2 February 1491

Painter and engraver. One of five sons of a goldsmith, Caspar Schongauer (active 1440–81), who was a native of Augsburg and citizen of Colmar from 1445. Martin Schongauer is first documented in the matriculation register of Leipzig University, winter term 1465, as a Bavarian (Erler, *Leipzig*, p.254) when he was presumably in his early teens. He is described as a 'young apprentice' in van Heinecken's record of a drawing (no longer extant) inscribed by Albrecht Dürer (q.v.) who clearly admired the artist, *Diess hat der Hübsch Martin gerissen in 1470. jar da er ein junger gesell was. Das hab ich Albrecht Dürer erfarn, vnd jm zu ern daher geschrieben im 1517. jar.* (Rupprich, i, pp.208f., no.58). He was much influenced by Rogier van der Weyden (1397/1400–64) after whose *Last Judgement* altarpiece at Beaune he made a drawing of *Christ in Judgement*, inscribed by Dürer, *1469* (Paris, Musée du Louvre, Cabinet des Dessins). He also may have travelled to Burgundy and the Netherlands during this period. Payments for an altarpiece for the Dominican church at Colmar (studio work, Musée d'Unterlinden, Colmar) in 1471 indicate that Schongauer had established a workshop in Colmar by this date (Rott, p.51). He was recorded as a citizen of Breisach on 15 June 1489, where he executed wall-paintings of the *Last Judgement* for the Münster (*in situ*, heavily damaged). Other attributable paintings include the wings of an altarpiece for Jean d'Orliac, preceptor of the monastery at Isenheim, and an altarpiece for a member of the Stauffenburg family (both now Musée d'Unterlinden, Colmar) as well as several small panels of the *Madonna and Child* and *Adoration*, such as those in Berlin-Dahlem (Gemäldegalerie), Munich (Alte Pinakothek) and Frankfurt (Städelsches Kunstinstitut).

Schongauer was regarded with high esteem by his contemporaries, and he had numerous followers. The so-called portrait of Schongauer in Munich (Alte Pinakothek), variously ascribed to his pupil, Hans Burgkmair (q.v.), Thoman Burgkmair (q.v.) and the Master of the St Ulrich Legend (active mid-fifteenth century) and probably either a copy or an over-painted earlier work, is inscribed on the back by Hans Burgkmair, *Mayster Martin Schongauer Maler genent Hipsch/Martin von wegen seiner Kunst . . . 1488*. His work is best appreciated through his engravings, impressions of which have survived in fairly large numbers. They are the first significant group of prints to be produced by a painter, rather than a goldsmith, and were highly influential. Numerous copies have survived, made in a variety of media (many listed by Lehrs).

BIBLIOGRAPHY: Rosenberg, *Schongauer*; Lehrs, v–vi, 1925, 1927; H.Rott, *Zeitschr. Oberrheins*, NF xliii, i, 1929, pp.39ff.; Thieme-Becker, xxx, 1936, pp.249ff.; Baum, *Schongauer*; Flechsig, *Schongauer*; Winzinger, *Schongauer*; Bernhard, *Schongauer* (for further literature).

25 Christ as Teacher

Pen and black ink. 20.7 × 12.4cm

PROVENANCE: C.M.Metz (sale, T.Philipe, 1801, 5 May, lot 77); W.Y.Ottley (sale, T.Philipe, 1814, 17 June, lot 1254); Sir T.Lawrence (L.2445); S.Woodburn (sale, Christie, 1854, 21 June, lot 1132, bt with 3 others, *Tiffin £2*)

1854-6-28-23

LITERATURE: S.Colvin, *Prussian Jahrbuch*, vi, 1885, p.74, repr.; BM *Guide*, 1928, p.18, no.170; Panofsky, ii, p.73, no.629; Flechsig, *Schongauer*, pp.324ff., pl.21; Rupprich, i, p.209, no.59; Winzinger, *Schongauer*, pp.30ff., no.2, repr. (for further literature); Rosenberg, *MD*, iii, no.4, 1965, p.400; Rowlands, *Dürer* p.59, no.359, pl.xv; Strauss, vi, p.2898, no.xw.13, repr.

Inscribed by Dürer (first noted as his hand by Ephrussi, p.iv) in light brown ink, along the upper edge of the drawing, *Das hat hubsch martin gemacht jm 1469 jor.*

According to Rupprich, the inscription could have been added at the earliest about 1520. Despite its apparently

25

straightforward meaning, it has been variously interpreted. In all catalogues prior to its acquisition by the British Museum, the drawing was attributed to Martin Schongauer. Colvin, who first discussed it at length in 1885, took the inscription to mean that Dürer regarded the drawing as having been executed by Schongauer in 1469. Many scholars rejected this interpretation, and took the view that the inscription means that the drawing is a copy by Dürer after a work by Schongauer dated *1469*. In recent years, however, following Flechsig's trenchant attacks on this more complicated interpretation, there has been a return to Colvin's literal understanding of the meaning. Flechsig decried the notion, rightly in our view, that *gemacht* (made) could be understood to mean *erfunden* (invented). Such a possibility, especially when considered in the light of Dürer's inscription on a lost drawing noted by von Heinecken (see biography), seems very far fetched. While for Panofsky the inscription precluded the possibility of Dürer's authorship, he assigned the drawing with undue subtlety to a follower of Schongauer, who, he claimed, reinterpreted his master's style in a similar way to the young Dürer. Winzinger considered the inscription to date from about 1498–1501, and read the *hubsch* in it as *hubsh*. He had originally accepted the drawing as by Dürer (*Zeitschr. f. Kunstwiss*, 1953, pp.36ff. pl.15) and explained subsequently in his catalogue that this was because he had found difficulty in reconciling the figure of Christ with Schongauer's other representations of Him. A factor which caused Winzinger to change his attribution to Schongauer was Winkler's identification of the figure as an Old Testament prophet. But a series of thirteen prints of *Christ and the Apostles*, attributed to the Monogrammist IC (active end of fifteenth century) and probably based on designs by Schongauer, contains a figure of Christ of a very similar type to no.25 (Lehrs, vi, no.23).

Apart from the question of authorship based on stylistic analysis, the attribution of this drawing, and that of *Christ in Judgement*, in the Louvre, Paris (inv.no.18,785; Demonts, *Louvre*, ii, pl.ciii) with the inscription written by the same hand as in the present drawing, is clearly largely dependent on the way one interprets the inscription on *Christ as Teacher* (no.25). If the inscription on the latter is understood literally, then we may reasonably conclude that Dürer had understood that not only no.25, but also the present drawing and that in the Louvre were by Martin Schongauer. Although Dürer in his *Wanderjahre* travelled to Colmar to meet Schongauer, only to arrive too late as the artist had died on 2 February 1491, it is quite likely that through the deceased's brother, Ludwig, he would have had access to the studio; if so, this group, to which Dürer's inscriptions must add some authority as far as the attribution is concerned, is an early case of one artist collecting the work of another out of admiration. In 1515 Dürer, it will be recalled, was to exchange drawings with Raphael (P.Joannides, *The Drawings of Raphael*, Oxford, 1983, p.106, pl.37).

In my view, Colvin's opinion that these drawings are by Schongauer is correct; they are not copies by Dürer after Schongauer, as the majority of scholars, including Winkler and at first Winzinger, were to maintain later. Apart from the evident difference between the ink used for the inscriptions and that for the drawings, which has been confirmed by ultra-violet examination, it remains extremely doubtful whether Dürer, whose hand had become so distinctive by his *Wanderjahre*, would have been able or willing to disguise it so as to produce such a perfect imitation of Schongauer's hand.

It is unlikely that the drawing of the flower in the upper left-hand corner should be associated with the main subject of the young woman fanning a fire, which may be a reference to fanning the flames of desire.

26 A young woman fanning a fire with a bird's wing

See colour plate section following p.80

Pen and brown ink with touches of pink and red wash. 18.3 × 14.2cm

WM: three mounds, lacking the upper half (cf. Briquet, 11795–11803)

PROVENANCE: F.Fagel (sale, T.Philipe, 1799, 23 May, lot 423, bt with one other, *Baron £2–16s*); ?S.Rogers; presented by Mrs W.Sharpe

1884-9-13-14

LITERATURE: S.Colvin, *Prussian Jahrbuch*, vi, 1885, pp.69–74, repr.; BM *Guide*, 1895, p.53, no.260; BM *Guide*, 1928, p.33, no.300; Panofsky, ii, p.125, no.1277; Winkler, *Leben*, pp.15–16; Winzinger, *Schongauer*, pp.32ff., no.3, repr. (for further literature); Rowlands, *Dürer*, p.59, no.360; Strauss, vi, XW no.14, repr.

Inscribed by Dürer, in brown ink, on the lower edge, *1469* with Schongauer's monogram

27 Head of a high priest

Pen and brown ink over traces of black chalk. The drawing has been cut down on all sides; all corners have been made up, and a hole in the paper on the right edge has been repaired. 17.9 × 14.2cm

PROVENANCE: Sir T.Lawrence (L.2445); S.Woodburn (sale, Christie, 1860, 7 June, lot 840, bt *Evans £1–15s*); Phillips-Fenwick; presented anonymously

1946-7-13-130

LITERATURE: Popham, *Fenwick*, p.233; Winzinger, *Schongauer*, pp.37f., no.6, repr.; Rosenberg, *MD*, iii, no.4, 1965, p.399

Inscribed by the artist on the plate on the hat in brown ink, *ANFOH SEION*, a pseudo-Greek inscription written in Gothic script instead of the customary Holy Name of the Lord. The second word is doubtless intended to stand for Zion, but the first word does not correspond with any Greek word. The adornments of the headdress are freely based on William Durandus's description in *Rationale Divinorum Officiorum*, Book III, itself an elaboration of

27

Virgin praying (Florence, Uffizi, inv.no.1080E; Winzinger, *Schongauer*, pl.31) and reveals similar broad pen-work more rhythmically executed; but its damaged condition rules out any firm conclusion about its status.

Followers of Schongauer

28 Two rows of half-length figures

Pen and brown and black ink. 27.7 × 20.4cm

PROVENANCE: Sloane bequest, 1753

5236–165

LITERATURE: F.Winzinger, *Zeitschr. f. Kunstwiss.*, vii, 1953, p.34, pl.14a; Winzinger, *Schongauer*, pp.94f., no.70, repr.

Inscribed by a later hand, in brown ink, on the lower edge, *92*

In the 1845 Departmental Inventory of the Sloane Collection this is listed as the work of the engraver from Bocholt, Israhel van Meckenem (died 1503). The entry, however, was amended in pencil subsequently at some unspecified date, and the attribution changed to Martin Schongauer. Two draughtsmen appear to be responsible for the work on this sheet. The lower row of figures executed in brown ink is most probably by the same hand as the *Massacre of the Innocents* in the Uffizi (inv.no.2260), which may be identified, as Byam Shaw has proposed (*OMD*, 1932, pl.18) with the early work of the Monogrammist B.M. (active *c*.1480–1500). The upper row was added later by another hand in black ink and is the work of a more facile draughtsman who has also attempted, not very successfully, to strengthen parts of the lower row, and to rework sketchily the outline of the hands.

Anonymous artist

c.1480–1500

29 Young couple holding hands, grouped to form the letter A of an ornamental alphabet

Pen and brown ink over some traces of black chalk. 19.5 × 11.3cm

WM: part of an oxhead

PROVENANCE: Marquis C.de Valori (L.2500; sale, Paris, Roblin, 1907, 26 Nov., lot 159, attributed to Israhel van Meckenem); Colnaghi & Obach

1912–4–16–1

Very faintly inscribed in pencil on the lower edge, A:*1501 Israel v. mechlen* (clearly visible in the reproduction in the catalogue of the de Valori sale)

Exodus, xxviii,39. The two small half-moons however, appear to be Schongauer's own invention. According to Durandus, the plate was half-moon shaped. In the upper right-hand corner is the artist's monogram with the date *1470* executed in grey-brown ink by a different hand. The *verso* is inscribed in the lower left-hand corner, in pencil, by a later hand, *Maarten van Cleef.*

Popham published no.27 as the work of a follower of Schongauer. Rosenberg concurred with this, and described it as 'too rigid for Schongauer' in his review of Winzinger's catalogue (where it is described as one of the most important works of the artist's early period). In the arrangement of its drapery and the form of the knot, the drawing is indeed akin to the stylised manner of Schongauer's early engravings, before he achieves the more fluent organisation of such details in his mature work. It is interesting to compare the head of Christ in the print, *Christ as Man of Sorrows with the Virgin and St John* (Lehrs no.34) with that of the high priest in the present sheet. Relatively little is known about the extent and variety of Schongauer's early drawings, but even so one should be wary of taking too narrow a view. The impression of 'rigidity', about which Rosenberg complains, may possibly be created by the broad strokes from the type of pen that the artist used. While one cannot agree with Winzinger that the upper inscription on the *recto* was made by the artist it is conceivable that the date it records is correct as it may be a repetition of an earlier inscription. Another similarly disputed drawing, which has also been considered an early work, shows the

This drawing is of an isolated surviving Gothic letter from a 'figure alphabet'. Judging from its style it can be dated within the last two decades of the fifteenth century, and is probably from the Upper Rhineland. Although the influence of Martin Schongauer (q.v.) which it reflects was widely pervasive, the neat hatching which defines the folds of the drapery, and the sophisticated economy of the line suggest that the draughtsman, while lacking a strong individuality, was adept at producing an air of courtly refinement.

The production of letters made up of a mêlée of human figures and animals, positioned to form the curve of each letter, like a team of acrobats with infinitely flexible bodies defying, indeed ignoring gravity, emerged in Gothic decoration in the early thirteenth century, the date of the earliest 'Musterbuch' containing such an alphabet (Vienna, Nationalbibliothek Cod. vind.507) and waned rapidly with the rise of the roman letter in the early sixteenth century. Such animated letters formed, together with carved figures on choir-stalls, sedilia, and elsewhere inside and outside church buildings, a lively part of artistic expression in the high and late Gothic periods both north and south of the Alps. The immediate forebears of the letter in the present drawing may be found in those of the engraved series by the Master E.S. (active early 1440s–67), datable *c*.1466–7 (A. Shestack, *Master E.S. Five Hundredth Anniversary Exhibition*, exhib. cat., Philadelphia Museum of Art, 5 Sept.– 3 Oct. 1967, nos.72–5, repr.). The designs of these are finer and livelier than the present drawing which is very bland by comparison. Such animated initials also occur in various incunables; especially fine are those in the publications of Johann Zaimer of Ulm (active 1473–1500). Also one should mention, although produced in the Netherlands and not in Germany, the *Grotesque Alphabet* of 1464, perhaps the most entertaining late Gothic alphabet of its kind produced north of the Alps before 1500. Two surviving examples, one incomplete, and the other complete, the latter formerly belonging to Dysons Perrins, the notable collector of illuminated manuscripts, are now in the British Museum (A. M. Hind, *An introduction to a History of Woodcut*, London, 1935, i, pp.147–52). The series at Basel, although once considered originals, are early copies.

29

7 Nuremberg, XV century

Anonymous artist

Nuremberg, c.1420/25

30 The prayer book of Canon Georg, Graf von Löwenstein

Pen and black ink with red, pink, yellow, blue and grey wash and silver, over traces of black chalk.
Double spread: 27.7 × 39cm page: 27.7 × 19.5cm

WM: head of a negro (cf. Briquet, 15603–15611)

PROVENANCE: A. Asher

British Library, Add.Ms.15,695

LITERATURE: *Add. Manuscripts*, p.9, under the title of the first item in the prayer book, 'Das Deutsch Pater Noster, mit der glosz'.

The owner of the prayer book for whom it was specifically written and illustrated (as the repeated heraldic decoration of the von Löwenstein crest, helm and arms, clearly shows), was an influential and cultured ecclesiastic of the diocese of Bamberg, Georg von Löwenstein, son of Albrecht von Löwenstein and Udehild von Werdenberg, born *c.*1380. He was a canon at Bamberg Cathedral after 15 February 1399, and studied in Vienna in 1402 and at Heidelberg in 1405. Besides various livings in Bamberg, throughout his career he held benefices elsewhere, principally cathedral canonries, at Würzburg, Speyer, Worms and Mainz. He died at Bamberg on 10 August 1464 (see J. Kist, *Die Matrikel der Geistlichkeit des Bistums Bamberg, 1400–1556*, Lieferung 4, 1958, p.265, col.1, no.4065).

This private prayer book was intended for daily use and was written in the vernacular by a routine, not highly competent hand. It is decorated with subjects appropriate to the various devotional exercises. In accord with the then prevailing practice, Christ is represented as the *Man of Sorrows*, on folio 1 *recto*, at the beginning the text, kneeling in supplication before God the Father enthroned, and on the final sheet, folio 7 *verso*, exhibited here, as the *Man of Sorrows displaying the wounds of his Passion to the kneeling canon*. Surrounding them, are the arms of the canon's parents, Löwenstein and Werdenberg, and his grandmother's, Gräfin von Wertheim (on the father's side), and Gräfin von Kirchberg (on the mother's side). These arms are also to be found on the best-known work of art connected with Georg von Löwenstein, the diptych with his portrait, and *Christ as the Man of Sorrows*, now divided respectively between the Germanisches Nationalmuseum, Nuremberg (inv. no.GM128) and the Kunstmuseum, Basel (inv.no.1651). This was executed soon before the sitter's death in 1464

by Hans Pleydenwurff (*c.*1420–72), a painter from Bamberg who had acquired citizenship at Nuremberg in 1457. The positively youthful appearance of the canon in the prayer book, especially when considered with the style of the penwork of the drawing, indicates that it belongs to a much earlier decade in Georg von Löwenstein's life.

The prayer book gives no clue in its text as to its date, but the writing may well have been done locally; the spelling shows distinctive signs of the local Bavarian. The illumination gives much more guidance about its date, and the training of its draughtsman. The artist's work, while reflecting to some extent Bohemian art, especially in the series of the Apostles (folio 4 *recto* and *verso*) strongly suggests, through the influence of the painters of Nuremberg, that he was apprenticed there. One artist in Nuremberg whose paintings must have been well known to the draughtsman of the von Löwenstein prayer book, is the Master of the Bamberg Altar, who takes his name from an altarpiece of the *Passion*, dated *1429*, which was presented by Burckhardt Löffelholz to the Franciscan Church in Bamberg (now in the Bayerisches Nationalmuseum, Munich). The closest comparison can be made with this master's painted image of the *Virgin with Christ as the Man of Sorrows*, probably somewhat earlier in date than his Passion altarpiece, *c.*1420/25 (Germanisches Nationalmuseum, Nuremberg, GM1531; Nuremberg, *Gothic & Renaissance*, p.151, repr.). The type of Christ in this painting has marked similarities with the *Christ as the Man of Sorrows* on folio 7 *verso*, although the painter's image projects the effects of the Passion on Christ's body more tellingly. Von Löwenstein's figure of Christ concentrates on showing him in exultant triumph over death. Given the canon's youthful appearance, and the period of the Master of Bamberg's activity, it is very likely that the prayer book was decorated with its drawings in the 1420s, most probably in the earlier half of the decade.

Anonymous artist

c.1480

31 Design for part of a monstrance: two angels supporting the Host

Pen and brown ink, with pink wash on the faces of the angels and on the hands of the angel on the right, and yellow wash on their hair, over traces of black chalk underdrawing. 16.4 × 14.5cm

PROVENANCE: Probably J. Thane (traces of a collector's mark resembling L.1544 on the *recto*; sale, George Jones, 1819, 25

Das du mir erwerbest
an dem lieben kind stetik-
keit am kristenlichen
glauben wann rew gantz
und lauter beicht und
behut mich vor sunden
und vor werntlicher
schanden und bleibe mir
das ich deines lieben
kindes tod und marter
teglich vor mein augen
trag und das ich mein
gelubde also volbringe
das es got und dir muter
der barmhertzikeit sei
lobsam und verleihe
mir stetikeit an guten
wercken und gib mir ein
seliges zeit wenn ich so
diser werlt muß scheiden
und allen den die mir
guts in hertzen wunschte
mit worten od mit wer-
cken den erzaige ein
seliges ende den toten
das ewig leben den le-
wendigen ein selige zeit
auf erden das verleihe
mir und in got der vater
und der sun und d' heilig
geist amen amen

31

March, part of lot 134, as by 'I. van Mecklin'); Sir T. Lawrence (L.2445); S. Woodburn (sale, Christie, 1860, 7 June, lot 838 as by Schongauer, bt *Vaughan £4-15s*); Henry Vaughan bequest, 1900

1900–8–24–125

LITERATURE: BM *Guide*, 1901, p.16, no.A 69

Inscribed along the upper edge, in a later hand, in brown ink, *738*

The drawing entered the collection as '?School of Schongauer' and was described as 'approaching the manner of Schongauer' in the 1901 catalogue. The possible connection with this artist has not received support since, and the style and subject matter of no.31 would appear to suggest

a goldsmith's workshop active *c*.1480, possibly in Nuremberg, as a more plausible origin. A drawing of a similar type, which shows a kneeling angel whose arms are extended as if to support an object, is in Berlin-Dahlem (Kupferstichkabinett, inv.no.2136; Bock, *Berlin*, i, p.89, ii, pl.119) where it is classified as 'manner of Michel Wolgemut'.

Kohlhaussen, however, records no monstrance of Nuremberg origins of a date as early as we take this drawing to be, decorated with angels supporting the receptacle for the Host. The earliest that he lists with such a detail is one by Master Hans Payer and Master Frantz of 1490/91 which belongs to the church at Neunkirchen am Brand (Kohlhaussen, p.219, no.314, fig.343).

Anonymous artist

c.1485–95

32 The Mocking of Christ

Pen and black ink, with green and brown wash. 14.1 × 12cm

PROVENANCE: acquired on the Paris art market, *c.*1938

England, Private Collection

LITERATURE: *Exposition de dessins du XVe au XXe siècle*, Max Bine, Paris, 1927, no.10; Schilling, *Gesamm. Zeichn.* p.41, no.13, repr.; Rowlands, *Private Collection*, p.10, no.4, repr.

Inscribed by a later hand in greyish ink on the right-hand end of the step of the throne with the false date, *1467*

This undoubtedly is a characteristic drawing of the studio of Michel Wolgemut (q.v.), of which there are a relatively large number surviving, often differing quite widely in quality. The best, like the drawing in Berlin-Dahlem, a *Group of five standing men* (Kupferstichkabinett, inv.no. KDZ1027), has been attributed tentatively to Wolgemut, although Anzelewski considered that it may indeed be by the master himself. This he did on the basis of the separation that had been attempted by scholars recently of Wolgemut's work from that of his step-son, Wilhelm Pleydenwurff, with whom, as the contract, dated 29 December 1491, makes clear, Wolgemut collaborated in the provision of the illustrations of the 'Nuremberg Chronicle' (see Bellm, *Skizzenbuch, passim*). In the case of the present drawing Schilling, after comparing it with the woodcuts in the

32

'Nuremberg Chronicle', considered the possibility of it being by Wilhelm Pleydenwurff. These commendable endeavours to solve the vexed question of attributions within Wolgemut's circle, are hindered in my view, by the woodcuts being so varied in quality of design and execution, that it would appear rather more than two designers worked on the provision of illustrations for the book. The evident number of cutters employed has disguised the designers' individuality so successfully that firm conclusions about the possible division of labour cannot be defined with any certainty. Unfortunately, as far as Wilhelm Pleydenwurff's contribution to the 'Nuremberg Chronicle' is concerned, he must remain a shadowy figure.

Michel Wolgemut

Nuremberg 1434–Nuremberg 30 November 1519

Painter, designer of woodcuts. Trained with his father, Valentin Wolgemut (d.1469 or 1470). To judge from the Netherlandish influence in his work, he may have travelled as a journeyman to the Low Countries. At an early stage of his career he is thought to have assisted Hans Pleydenwurff (*c.*1420–72) in Nuremberg, since parts of this painter's *Hofer Altarpiece*, dated *1465* (Munich, Alte Pinakothek) have been attributed to him. Worked in Munich with the painter Gabriel Mälesskircher (*c.*1410/15–95) during the early part of 1471; later that year he was active in Nuremberg in his father's workshop which had been maintained by his mother since the former's death. In 1473 he married Hans Pleydenwurff's widow, thereby inheriting this artist's workshop.

Wolgemut taught Albrecht Dürer (q.v.) from 1486 to 1489. That Dürer held his master in high esteem is implied in a letter he wrote in 1506 from Venice to his friend Willibald Pirckheimer in Nuremberg, in which he recommends Wolgemut as a teacher for his younger brother Hans Dürer (q.v.); Dürer also painted a portrait of Wolgemut in 1519 (Nuremberg, Germanisches Nationalmuseum). Wolgemut's step-son, Wilhelm Pleydenwurff (*c.*1458–94), worked with him, and by 1491 had become his partner. The Wolgemut workshop was the most active in Nuremberg during this period; documented altarpieces amongst the several produced are: the *Life of the Virgin* for the Marienkirche, Zwickau, completed in 1479; the *Altarpiece of the Virgin* for the Stiftskirche, Feuchtwangen, 1484; the *Peringsdörfer Altarpiece, c.*1486 (Nuremberg, according to Neudörfer (1547) originally in the Augustinerkirche, from 1564 in the Heiligkreuzkirche); and the high altarpiece of the parish church of St John, Schwabach, executed from 1506 to 1508. In large commissions such as these, it seems clear that Wolgemut often worked in close collaboration with independent painters and sculptors, in addition to his own assistants, and so it proves difficult to establish precisely what part the master himself played in their execution. A number of portraits are attributed to Wolgemut, such as those of Hans Tucher, dated 1481 (Nuremberg, Germanisches Nationalmuseum) and Ursula Tucher (Kassel, Gemäldegalerie).

Together with Wilhelm Pleydenwurff, Wolgemut was responsible for the production of 645 woodblocks, from which about 1800 illustrations were made, for Hartmann Schedel's *Weltchronik*, the well-known best-seller published in 1493 by Anton Koberger in Nuremberg (see no.33). Other woodcuts convincingly attributed to Wolgemut and Pleydenwurff on the basis of the *Weltchronik* are those for *Der Schrein oder Schatzbehalter der wahren Reichtümer des Heils u. der ewigen Seligkeit* published by Koberger in 1491. A sketchbook in Berlin-Dahlem (Kupferstichkabinett, 78 b 3a), which contains 105 drawings of religious subject matter, generally based on standard popular formulae and presumably made for contemplative use, has been associated with the Wolgemut workshop because a few of the drawings are connected in a derivative manner with woodcuts in the Schatzbehalter. Bellm has attributed the drawings to four different hands (*Skizzenbuch*, pp.33ff) but his identification of the best hand with Wolgemut remains unconvincing.

BIBLIOGRAPHY: Neudörfer, *Nachrichten*, pp.128–30; Thieme-Becker, xxxvi, 1947, pp.175ff; xxxvii, 1950, p.306 (for further literature); Gerd Betz, *Der Nürnberger Maler Michel Wolgemut und seine Werkstatt* (typescript dissertation), Freiburg, 1955; Stange, ix, 1958, pp.51–60; Bellm, *Skizzenbuch*; Austin, *Nuremberg*, pp.92ff.

33 *Recto:* Design for the frontispiece of Hartmann Schedel's *Weltchronik* (The 'Nuremberg Chronicle')
See colour plate section following p.80

Verso: Manuscript text for folio XII recto

Pen and brown ink; with watercolour and gold leaf added later by a different hand on the shields. 38.6 × 24.6cm

PROVENANCE: W. Russell

1885-5-9-43

LITERATURE: Dodgson, i, p.246; Schilling, *Nürnberger Handz.*, p.26, no.6, repr.; Hind, *Introduction*, ii, pp.375f.; Bellm, *Skizzenbuch*, pp.44–6 (for earlier literature); E.Winkler, *Zeitschr. f. Kunstwiss.*, xv, 1961, p.153, fig.3; Manchester, *German Art*, pp.16f., no.23; Rowlands, *Dürer*, pp.61f., no.370; pl.xiv; Rücker, *Weltchronik*, pp.60f., fig.63; Kuhrmann, *Erlangen*, p.48, under no.37; Wilson, *Nuremberg Chronicle*, pp.76–9, repr.; Nuremberg, *Gothic & Renaissance*, pp.233f.

Inscribed, probably by a scribe rather than the artist himself, in red ink, on a scroll above God the Father, *Dixit deus fiat et facta sunt Omnia*; and below in the artist's hand in brown ink, *1490*. This is between the two shields, the fields of which were illustrated later (*left*, a man holding a purse and a cudgel; *right*, a pelican feeding her young).

The drawing is a detailed study for the woodcut which serves as the frontispiece to the 'Nuremberg Chronicle', an ambitiously conceived and highly successful publication

produced by Anton Koberger in 1493, in both Latin and German editions. The print, executed in the same direction as the drawing, reveals some small variations including a change in the inscription. The drawing is dated 1490, and was therefore made before the contract, dated 29 December 1491, between the authors of the illustrations, Michel Wolgemut and Wilhelm Pleydenwurff, and the commissioners of the book, Sebald Schreyer and Sebastian Kamermeister, was drawn up. This design, together with references in the contract to blocks already started, clearly demonstrates that the project was well under way before this contract was made, and indeed other records indicate that an earlier contract was drawn up in 1487 or 1488 (see Wilson, *Nuremberg Chronicle*, p.46).

Contrary to the traditional attribution to Wolgemut, Wilson gives the drawing to Dürer (q.v.), who worked in Wolgemut's workshop from 1486 to 1489. However, his attribution is untenable if other accepted drawings by Dürer of this period are taken into consideration. The fineness of the drawing, together with the important position the design was to occupy in the book, makes it reasonable to assume that Wolgemut, as the senior of the two artists, was responsible for it. Little is known of the activity of his stepson, Wilhelm Pleydenwurff, other than for the last five years of his life, 1490–4. Other drawings attributed to Wolgemut which show a similar style and technique to no.33 are in Erlangen (Universitätsbibliothek; Kuhrmann, *Erlangen*, pp.47f., no.37, repr.), and Berlin-Dahlem (Kupferstichkabinett, inv.no.KDZ 1027; Berlin, *Dürer und seine Zeit*, p.43, no.10, repr.).

Further drawings connected with the Nuremberg Chronicle are the pen and ink sketches which identify the illustrations in the two pre-publication manuscript layouts (Nuremberg, Stadtbibliothek, Cent. II, 98 and 99; Wilson, *Nuremberg Chronicle*, pp.55ff.); and five sheets with sketches of preliminary layouts which were used as end-papers for a two-volume bible (from which they have been recently removed), printed by Koberger in 1483 and presumably bound at a later date (Nuremberg, Stadtbibliothek, Solg. 68 and 69; Peter Zahn 'Neue Funde zur Enstehung der Schedelschen Weltchronik 1493', *Renaissance Vorträge*, Nuremberg, ii/iii, 1973, pp.2ff., repr.; A. Wilson, *MD*, xiii, no.2, 1975, pp.115ff., pls.1–5). The contract of 1491 states that Wolgemut and Pleydenwurff were charged with the preparation of the manuscript layouts, but these sketches appear to be made by different hands, none of which have been conclusively identified (Bellm, *Skizzenbuch*, p.58f. and n.53). Since they were produced merely as a guide to the printer, it is not surprising to find that none of them reveal the detailed treatment, or the quality of no.33.

The hand of the Latin text on the *verso* of the present sheet has been identified as that of Georg Alt (*c.*1450–1510), the city council scribe of Nuremberg who transcribed part of the Latin text for the layouts, and was responsible for its translation into German.

8 Albrecht Dürer

Nuremberg 21 May 1471 – Nuremberg 6 April 1528

Painter, engraver, etcher and designer of woodcuts. Third child of the goldsmith Albrecht, who took his surname from Ajtas, his birthplace in Hungary (Ajto means Tür, a door). His godfather was Anton Koberger, the leading German printer of his day. He received early training from his father, then from 30 November 1486 he was apprenticed to the painter Michel Wolgemut (q.v.) for three years, after which he travelled in the Upper Rhineland, and possibly to Holland. In 1492 he was in Colmar where he had hoped to meet Martin Schongauer (q.v.), but the latter had died on 2 February 1491. By August 1492 he was in Basel where he made an important contribution to book-illustration. He returned to Nuremberg after Whitsun in 1494 where he married Agnes Frey on 7 July. In the autumn he left for Italy and visited Venice and perhaps Padua and Mantua, returning to Nuremberg in the spring of 1495. He was influenced by leading Italian artists, especially Andrea Mantegna (c.1431–1506), Antonio del Pollaiuolo (c.1432–98) and Lorenzo di Credi (1456/59–1537) and he drew some watercolour landscapes (see nos.39, 41–3) as spontaneous records of nature on his journeys over the Alps and shortly after his return to Nuremberg.

He worked on various commissions for Friedrich the Wise Duke of Saxony c.1496, and his first dated engraving, *Four naked women*, was executed the following year. The first edition of the *Apocalypse*, illustrated with innovatory full-page woodcuts, was published in 1498. Examples of his revolutionary style of self-portraiture are dated 1498 (Madrid, Prado) and 1500 (Munich, Alte Pinakothek). His interest in the theory of proportions, which was stimulated by Jacopo de' Barbari (c.1440/50–c.1515) dates from c.1500, and is reflected in, amongst other works, his engraving *Adam and Eve* of 1504. His writings on the subject were published in *Underweysung der Messung* (1525), and *Vier bücher von menschlicher Proportion* (1528).

From 1505 to 1507 he again visited Italy, where he painted the *Feast of the Rose Garlands*, dated 1506, for the German merchants in Venice (Prague, National Gallery, now much damaged); by February 1507 he was back in Nuremberg. Between 1507 and 1512 he worked on a number of important paintings, including the *Adam and Eve*, dated 1507 (Madrid, Prado); the *Martyrdom of the Ten Thousand*, dated 1508 (Vienna, Kunsthistorisches Museum); and the *Adoration of the Trinity*, dated 1511 (Vienna, Kunsthistorisches Museum). He also published several series of prints during this period, such as the *Engraved Passion*, executed between 1507 and 1513; and the woodcut series of the *Life of the Virgin*, the *Great Passion* and the *Little Passion*, all of which were published in 1511.

From 1510 to 1519 Dürer executed commissions for the Emperor Maximilian I, who in 1515 granted him an annuity; these include woodcuts for the *Triumphal Arch* (1515–17) and the *Triumphal Procession* (1516–18), and two painted portraits of the Emperor dated *1519* (Nuremberg, Germanisches Nationalmuseum and Vienna, Kunsthistorisches Museum) which were made from a drawing dated *1518* which Dürer had drawn from life in Augsburg (now in Vienna, Albertina). In 1519 he visited Switzerland, and in 1520 travelled to the Netherlands where his Imperial salary was ratified by Maximilian's successor, Charles V. In his later years he came under the influence of Luther's writings. It is probable however that the biblical texts inscribed on the painting of the *Four Apostles*, dated *1526* (Munich, Alte Pinakothek) which Dürer had presented to his native city, were directed as much against the extreme Protestant sects then active in and around Nuremberg, as against the Catholic church.

Dürer's immense and innovatory output of graphic work included a small number of experimental drypoints and etchings.

BIBLIOGRAPHY: H.W.Singer, *Versuch einer Dürer-Bibliographie*, Strassburg, 1903; Thieme-Becker, x, 1914, pp.63ff.; Rupprich; Mende, *Dürer-Bibliographie* (for further literature); Strauss; Austin, *Nuremberg*, pp.96ff.; Nuremberg, *Gothic & Renaissance*, p.493.

Youth and Apprenticeship, 1484–90

34 *Recto:* A lady holding a hawk
Verso: A young man

Black chalk on paper, unevenly tinted in red, with a few spots of dark red oil paint which at the foot has been partly scraped away; the *verso* in black chalk with pen and brown ink. 27.1 × 18.4cm

WM: bull's head with a cross (close to Briquet, 14533)

PROVENANCE: Sloane bequest, 1753

5218–90

LITERATURE: Waagen, *Treasures*, i, p.230, no.90; Hausmann, *Naumann's Archiv*, p.35; Hausmann, p.107, no.12; Ephrussi, pp.3f.; Thausing, i, p.57; Lippmann, iii, no.208, repr.; Weisbach, *Junge Dürer*, pp.15f.; W.v.Seidlitz, *Prussian Jahrbuch*, xxviii, 1907, p.3; Conway, p.7, no.2; Pauli, p.5, no.6; BM *Guide*, 1928, p.18, no.169; Flechsig, *Dürer*, ii, p.316; Winkler, *Dürer*, i, p.8, no.2, repr.; Rupprich, i, p.205, no.4; Rowlands, *Dürer*, p.2, no.1; J.Rowlands, *Zeitschr. f. Kunstwiss.*, xxv, 1971, p.45, repr; Strauss, i, pp.6ff., nos.1484/2 and 3, repr. (for further literature)

Das ist och als hat
mic albrecht dürer
gemacht Ee er zum
maler kam in des
wolgemuts hus
off dem obern boden
in dem hindern huß
m beiwesen Cunrat
lomaiers seligen

35r

Inscribed on the *recto* by a contemporary of the artist, in brown ink to the left of the figure, *Das ist och alt. hat/mir albrecht dürer/ gemacht E. er zum/maler kam in des/Wolgemůts hus/vff dem obern boden/in dem hindern hus/in biwesen Cůnrat/Lomaÿrs säligen* 'This is also old. Albrecht Dürer did it for me, before he came to be a painter in Wolgemut's house, on the upper floor at the back of the house owned by the late Conrad Lomayer'. In the centre, below the lady's right foot, is a partially erased false Dürer monogram.

According to the inscription, this drawing was executed before 30 November 1486, when Dürer entered Wolgemut's studio. Its circumstantial nature suggests that we may rely on it. According to Flechsig the inscriber would appear to have come from Swabia, through his use of *hus*, *vff* and *biwesen*. Thausing had earlier noted a resemblance between this inscription and the writing of the calligrapher, Johann Neudörfer of Nuremberg, but he cannot have written it as he was only born in 1497.

This instance of Dürer's draughtsmanship when he was fifteen years old shows him attempting to give to the figure a certain plasticity. But one cannot as yet notice any clearly identifiable outside influence, such as Schongauer's series of engravings of the Wise and Foolish Virgins (Bartsch, vi, pp.153ff., nos.77–86), as Lippmann proposed. Its character merely reflects the general influence of his Nuremberg environment.

A slight unfinished sketch on a small scale probably for

a companion male figure evidently done at the same date is on the *verso*.

35 *Recto:* Knights fighting
Verso: Head of a knight

Pen and black ink. The absence of the 'T' from the collector's mark of Lawrence means that the drawing has been cut down on the left. 19.8 × 31.1 cm

PROVENANCE: General Count A.F.Andréossi; Sir T.Lawrence (L.2445); S.Woodburn; Dr C.D.Ginsburg (sale, Sotheby, 1915, 20 July, lot 14, bt with 5 others, *Leggatt £29*); presented by the Dürer Society

1915–8–23–1

LITERATURE: Conway, p.7, under no.11; Pauli, p.24, no.646; C.Dodgson, *Burlington*, xxviii, 1915, pp.7ff., repr.; BM *Guide*, 1928, p.18, no.172; Schilling, *Nürnberger Handz.*, p.27, no.11, repr.; Flechsig, *Dürer*, ii, pp.381–2; Winkler, *Dürer*, i, pp.18f., nos.17, 20, repr.; Rowlands, *Dürer*, p.2, no.2; Strauss, i, pp.34f., nos.1489/5 and 6 (for further literature)

Inscribed by the artist in light brown ink in the centre of the lower edge, *1489*, and probably also by Dürer, in black ink, with the artist's monogram and a swastika-like cross

Dodgson considered that the date, cross and signature,

which similarly occur on two other related drawings of the same year (Winkler, *Dürer*, i, pls.16 and 18) were inscribed by Dürer in this fashion for decorative effect. He believed that the young artist was adopting momentarily in his career the use of the cross in imitation of Schongauer's signature. Winkler explicitly and Flechsig implicitly considered the monogram and the cross as the additions of a later hand. Dodgson's arguments seem far more persuasive.

Together with the *Party of people on horseback* (Winkler, *Dürer*, i, pl.16) formerly at Bremen, and the *Three men-at-arms* at Berlin-Dahlem (Kupferstichkabinett, inv.no.KDZ.2; Winkler, *Dürer*, i, pl.18), which are similarly signed and dated, this constitutes an important indication of Dürer's ability as a draughtsman while he was still training in Wolgemut's studio. While one notes a general debt to his master in the type of background landscape in which the figures are placed, Dürer is already showing himself capable of defining the volumes of his figures convincingly with the pen, even though some of the attitudes in which they are represented are awkward and gauche. This is particularly the case with the horses in the present drawing. The possibility of a specific influence on Dürer here from the prints of the Master of the Housebook is debatable. Connections have been made by some critics with other works of the period, including contemporary book illustrations published in Nuremberg, but these are too general to be of particular significance. They merely reflect the artistic environment in which Dürer developed his early style. The head of a knight on the *verso*, was taken by Dodgson to be an improved version of the head of the fallen warrior; however, Flechsig's suggestion that it is of a soldier taking aim with a crossbow is surely correct.

Years of Travel (Wanderjahre), 1490–4

36 The Presentation of Christ in the Temple

Pen and black ink, strengthened with brown ink (with the point of the brush?) and with black and grey wash. 29.8 × 19.5 cm

PROVENANCE: Sloane bequest, 1753

5218–94

LITERATURE: Hausmann, *Naumann's Archiv*, p.38, no.94; Hausmann, p.109, no.80; W.v.Seidlitz, *Repertorium*, vi, 1883, p.204; W.v.Seidlitz, *Prussian Jahrbuch*, xxviii, 1907, p.7; J.Meder, *Vienna Jahrbuch*, xxx, 1912, p.189; E.Römer, *Prussian Jahrbuch*, xlvii, 1926, p.125, repr.; BM *Guide*, 1928, p.18, no.171; Tietze, i, p.86, no.w.2, repr.; Flechsig, *Dürer*, ii, pp.386f; Winkler, *Dürer*, i, pp.22ff., no.21, repr.; Winzinger, *Schongauer*, p.96, no.72(b); Rupprich, iii, p.443, no.5b; Rowlands, *Dürer*, p.3, no.5; Strauss, i, p.42, no.1491/1, repr. (for further literature)

Inscribed on the *recto*, by an early hand, in brown ink in the lower right-hand corner, *Albrech[t] Dürer hatt das stück/gemach jn*

36

sinn ledig[en] i[n]wand [er] jor[en]; and on the *verso* in a later hand, probably *c*.1600, certainly before 1637, the date on the binding of the Sloane volume, 5218, *Mensch gedenck dass Du Musst/scherben* [i.e. sterben] *unnd andtere dass dein/erben/Maria h[ilf]* (kindly elucidated by Drs C.Andersson and U.Barth)

According to the inscription this was done by Dürer during his *Wanderjahre*. If this statement is to be trusted, and in my opinion it seems reasonable to accept it, then, apart from its intrinsic quality, it is a document of prime interest for our knowledge of Dürer at this stage of his development and for his link with Martin Schongauer (q.v.). Like the drawings by Schongauer inscribed and owned by Dürer (see no.25), this drawing is further proof of Dürer's admiration for Schongauer's work, and strongly suggests that Dürer visited Schongauer's studio after the artist's death (2 February 1491) when it was taken over by Ludwig, Martin's supposedly younger brother, until he died in 1494.

This drawing is an unfinished free adaptation of a composition used in the studio of the Schongauer family at Colmar. A number of drawings survive, probably either from Schongauer's studio or his immediate circle, including

37r

37v

63

one preserved in the British Museum (inv.no.5218–93), which are all related to a panel of this subject, which formed part of an altarpiece by Martin Schongauer, painted *c*.1475 for the high altar of the Dominican church in Colmar (now in the Musée d'Unterlinden, Colmar; Baum, *Schongauer*, p.76, pl.160). An allied composition with a similar arrangement of the figures clearly derived from Schongauer's composition was used in a *Circumcision*, now in Colmar (Musée d'Unterlinden, inv.no.P14; Augsburg, *Holbein*, pl.124). This formed part of a dispersed altarpiece with scenes from the life of the Virgin, credibly attributed to Ludwig Schongauer (*c*.1440–94) of which other panels are in Darmstadt (Hessisches Landesmuseum, inv.nos.GK15A and B, the *Visitation* and the *Adoration of the Magi*; Augsburg, *Holbein*, pls.125–6), the Philadelphia Museum of Art (the *Birth of Christ*), and formerly in the collection of E. Sarre, Berlin (the *Annunciation*). Schongauer's composition for the Presentation persisted in use into the sixteenth century, as we find for instance in one of the large series of glass-paintings for the Carmelite Church in Nuremberg, after designs by Dürer and his followers (see no.91b).

No.36 was largely ignored by scholars in the last century except for von Seidlitz, who first proposed the attribution to Dürer. Flechsig and the Tietzes rejected this because they failed to appreciate the quality of the draughtsmanship, but the Tietzes' classification of 'workshop' is hardly feasible at this stage of Dürer's career. In this drawing for the first time Dürer has made substantial use of wash. It is certainly earlier than the first dated wash drawing, the *Female nude study* of 1495 in Paris (Louvre, inv.no.19.058; Winkler, *Dürer*, i, pl.85), which shows that Dürer had gained considerable confidence in his brushwork in the interval between the execution of the two drawings. In view of this, contrary to Winkler's opinion, the beginning rather than the end of Dürer's *Wanderjahre* would be the more likely time for its execution.

37 *Recto:* The seated Virgin and Child, and two drapery studies

Verso: The Virgin and Child seated at the foot of a tree, a study of a hand, and a drapery study

Pen and brown ink. 20.5 × 19.7 cm

WM: cross (repr. in Strauss)

PROVENANCE: Sir P. Lely (L.2092); W. Gibson; H. Howard, and thence to his brother, the Bishop of Elphin (sale, Sotheby, 1874, 27 Nov., lot 39, bt *Lauser £31*); G. Mayer; H. Oppenheimer; E. Korner; accepted by H.M. Treasury in lieu of tax and allocated to the British Museum

1983–4–16–2

LITERATURE: *Dürer Society*, iii, 1900, pp.4f., nos.III and IV, repr.; Flechsig, *Dürer*, ii, pp.113f.; Winkler, *Dürer*, i, pp.23f., nos.22 and 23, repr.; Rowlands, *Dürer*, p.4, no.11; Strauss, i, pp.48ff., nos.1491/4 and 5, repr. (for further literature)

Inscribed by a later hand, in brown ink, in the centre of the upper edge, *1519*, with above, a false Dürer monogram; and by W. Gibson in brown ink, in the upper right-hand corner, *8 [?£] 3 [?s]*; and on the *verso*, in brown ink on the tree trunk, a false Dürer monogram, and by a different hand, in brown ink, in the upper left-hand corner, BS NO 6.

The studies on this sheet belong to the artist's *Wanderjahre* (years of travel) chiefly spent in the Upper Rhineland. One of his aims was to fulfil his desire to meet Martin Schongauer (q.v.) the leading artistic figure of the time in Germany. Although Dürer only arrived in Breisach (where Schongauer had been working on wall-paintings in the Cathedral) after the artist's death on 2 February 1491, it would seem that Dürer had access to Schongauer's studio, as he may have then acquired some of the deceased's drawings (see nos.25–6). Given the young Dürer's admiration for Schongauer's work, it is hardly surprising to find his influence so strongly reflected in this sheet, especially in the oval-shaped face of the Virgin, with her large eyelids and downcast gaze. These studies of the Virgin and Child, together with the stylistically connected study (clearly of the same date) of the *Holy Family* in the Universitätsbibliothek, Erlangen (Winkler, *Dürer*, i, pl.25) have naturally been associated with the engraving of the *Holy Family with a butterfly* (Dodgson, *Dürer Engr.*, p.6, no.4, repr.). Other drawings also from the same period, but less obviously connected with the engraving, are those in Berlin-Dahlem (Kupferstichkabinett inv.no.KDZ 4174; Winkler, *Dürer*, i, pl.30) and formerly in the Gathorne-Hardy collection (Winkler, *Dürer*, i, pl.24).

Apart from his early isolated self-portrait in silverpoint of 1484 in Vienna (Albertina, inv.no.4839.D.30; Winkler, *Dürer*, i, pl.1), he first began to make intensive studies of his own features and parts of his body, especially his hands, during his *Wanderjahre* and afterwards in Italy. The most famous of these drawings is the *Self-portrait* on the *verso* of the sheet mentioned earlier at Erlangen (Winkler, *Dürer*, i, pl.26). Another sheet with an impressive self-portrait, which has a less piercing stare than the head at Erlangen, is now in the Metropolitan Museum, New York (Lehmann Collection; Winkler, *Dürer*, i, pl.27), and includes a study of the artist's raised left hand which anticipates in its fine penwork the *Study of hands* at Vienna (Albertina, inv. no.26.327 D35; Winkler, *Dürer*, i, pl.47). The study of a hand – probably the artist's own, despite Flechsig's objection – resting on a surface, on the *verso* of the present sheet is closer in its accomplished, if rather nervy penwork, to the rendering of the artist's hand in the *Self-portrait* at Erlangen.

The First Visit to Italy and the founding of the workshop in Nuremberg, 1495–1500

38 Three Orientals

Pen and black and brown ink with watercolour. 30.6 × 19.7cm

PROVENANCE: General Count A.F.Andréossi; Sir T.Lawrence (L.2445); S.Woodburn; Sir J.C.Robinson; Malcolm

1895·9·15·974

LITERATURE: JCR, p.175, no.521; Ephrussi, pp.200f., n.5; J.Janitsch, *Prussian Jahrbuch*, iv, 1883, pp.59ff.; BM *Guide*, 1895, p.55, no.272; Conway, p.23, no.381; Pauli, p.22, no.574; G.Pauli, *Bibliothek Warburg-Vorträge, 1921–2*, 1923, pp.54–5; BM *Guide*, 1928, p.23, no.218; Winkler, *Dürer*, i, p.58, no.78, repr.; F.Saxl, *Proceedings of the British Academy*, London, xxiii, 1937, p.410, repr.; B.Degenhart, *Prussian Jahrbuch*, lxi, 1940, pp.42f., repr.; Rowlands, *Dürer*, p.6, no.14; Strauss, i, p.284, no.1495/12, repr. (for further literature)

Inscribed by an early hand, in brown ink on the upper edge, *1514*, followed by the artist's monogram

This drawing and three others also of 'Turks', in the Albertina (inv.no.3196 D171; Winkler, *Dürer*, i, pl.79) and the Biblioteca Ambrosiana, Milan (inv.nos.F264 inf.32 and F.264 inf.35; Winkler, *Dürer*, i, pls.80 and 81) may be assigned on stylistic grounds to Dürer's first visit to Venice (1494–5) even though they are all inscribed by hands other than Dürer's, with dates subsequent to his second visit to Italy. Janitsch first noticed that the three figures in the present drawing appear to have been copied with some modifications from those in the background of a painting by Gentile Bellini (1429–1507), the *Corpus Christi Procession*, signed and dated *1496* (Venice, Accademia), by which year Dürer had left Venice. The three figures in the latter differ from those in Dürer's drawing, in that the man in the centre has a beard and the one on the right is a European, and not a negro slave, as Dürer depicted him. Dürer has also changed the position of the slave's left foot after an initial outline drawing of it in the same position as in Bellini's painting. The most likely explanation is either that Bellini was working on his commission over an extended period and Dürer might have seen it unfinished, or Dürer could have seen preparatory drawings. An interesting and possibly significant fact is that in late fifteenth- and early sixteenth-century Venetian paintings in which 'Turks' appear, they are mostly dressed as Egyptian Mamluks. As for the possibility that Dürer's Turks might have been drawn from a 'Turkish' costume-book rather than a drawing by Bellini, Dr Michael Rogers of the Department of Oriental Antiquities in the British Museum has informed me that the date at which 'Turkish' costume-books first arrived in the West is not known. But the evidence so far makes it unlikely that Dürer in this case could have used such a costume-book. It seems likely, however, that some sort of 'Turkish' source material was

38

available to West European artists from the second quarter of the sixteenth century onwards. For instance, woodcuts of Oriental warriors were designed by Erhard Schön (q.v.) Niklas Stoer (d.1562/3), Jan Swart van Groningen (c.1500–after 1553) among others, presumably based on Ottoman models. Saxl, however, ignored the existence of these prints when he linked with Gentile Bellini a group of drawings of Orientals in a manuscript, containing works ranging in date from the 1540s to about 1580, in the Biblioteca Querini-Stampalia, Venice (inv.no.CL.VIII.1). One of these, a Turk (fol.54 *recto*), he compares to the left-hand figures in the present drawing which, however, does nothing to further his idea of a specific link with Bellini.

39 View of the castle at Trent

See colour plate section following p.80

Pen and black ink with watercolour and light touches of white bodycolour. 19.6 × 25cm

PROVENANCE: General Count A.F.Andréossi; Sir T.Lawrence (L.2445); S.Woodburn; C.Goodrich (according to note in Departmental copy of JCR, 'bought from Miss C.Goodrich, 12 April, 1867 – £11'); Malcolm

1895-9-15-975

LITERATURE: BFAC, 1869, p.16, no.129; JCR, pp.175ff., no.522*; Ephrussi, pp.11, 109–10; Thausing, i, p.120; L.Klebs, *Repertorium*, xxx, 1907, p.400; Conway, p.9, no.51; Pauli, p.11, no.236; J.Meder, *Vienna Jahrbuch*, xxx, 1912, p.202; BM *Guide*, 1928, p.19, no.182; Tietze, i, p.16, no.67, repr.; A. Rusconi, *Graph.Künste*, NF, i, 1936, p.135, n.1; Winkler, *Dürer*, i, p.71, no.95, repr.; Winkler, *Leben*, p.45; Rowlands, *Dürer*, p.6, no.15; Koschatzky, no.9, repr.; Strauss, i, p.324, no.1495/32, repr. (for further literature)

Inscribed by the artist, in black ink along the upper edge, *trint*

The Prince bishop of Trent's 'Castel del buon consiglio' at a strategic position in the town, had been reconstructed in 1468, and has been comparatively little altered until the present day. Only the left half of the wall, from the central round tower to the outside of the castle, is missing following the order of Bishop Bernhard van Cles (1514–39) and the cone-shaped roof of the upper tower was taken down in 1809.

Thausing, who rightly rejected the first and incorrect identification of this watercolour as the 'Castle of Nuremberg' proposed in the BFAC catalogue, thought that it represented part of the town-wall of Trent and not the castle, which it was soon recognised to be. Most scholarship has thereafter been directed towards attempting to determine whether it was executed on the outward, or return journey of Dürer's first visit to Italy. Ephrussi, who thought that it had been done on his second Italian visit, has had no support. On the grounds of what Klebs considered an uncertain understanding of perspective, she concluded that it was done on the outward journey, as the Tietzes were to do later, but she complicated her case by allotting *Trent seen from the north* (formerly Bremen, Kunsthalle, inv.no.10; Winkler, *Dürer*, i, pl.96) to the return journey; however, if one accepts Winkler's view that they were executed on the same occasion – the return journey – (a view changed in 1957 without explanation), then Rusconi's observation of there being no snow visible on the mountains in *Trent seen from the north* would indicate, if one accepts his argument, that Dürer could not have done his drawings in Trent before the late spring. Furthermore, no.39 reveals a small but vital clue which should sway one conclusively in favour of the spring of 1495, namely the leafless vine in front of the castle, which would not have been so if the drawing had been done on the outward journey in the autumn of 1494. Amongst the landscape watercolours done on Dürer's first journey through the Alps, perhaps the closest in technical command and feeling are two views near Trent, the *Cambra valley near Segonzano* (Oxford, Ashmolean Museum, P.284; Winkler, *Dürer*, i, pl.99) and the *Castle at Segonzano* (Berlin-Dahlem, Kupferstichkabinett, inv.no.KDZ 24,622; Winkler, *Dürer*, i, pl.101).

40 A larch tree (*Larix decidua*)

See colour plate section following p.80

Brush drawing with green and brown bodycolour and watercolour 29.3 × 14.4cm

WM: imperial orb

PROVENANCE: Sir T.Lawrence (L.2445); ? W.Coningham; Colnaghi & Co.

1846-9-18-9

LITERATURE: Hausmann, *Naumann's Archiv*, pp.40f., under nos.161–4; Hausmann, p.111, under nos.138–41; Haendcke, p.31; L.Klebs, *Repertorium*, xxx, 1907, p.401; Conway, p.9, no.44; Pauli, p.12, no.246; BM *Guide*, 1928, p.19, no.181; Tietze, i, p.49, no.159, repr.; Flechsig, *Dürer*, ii, p.138; Winkler, *Dürer*, i, p.89, no.121, repr.; Rowlands, *Dürer*, p.6, no.16; Koschatzky, no.27, repr.; Strauss, i, p.396, no.1496/2, repr. (for further literature)

As with the landscape watercolours, this study, perhaps Dürer's finest portrayal of a tree, has been variously dated by scholars. Dating them both *c*.1506, Haendcke considered it to be a companion to the *Linden tree on a bastion* (Rotterdam, Museum Boymans-van Beuningen, inv.no.1958/T28; Winkler, *Dürer*, i, pl.63), which is now generally thought to be one of the earliest of Dürer's watercolours, executed in Nuremberg before he set out for his first visit to Italy. Klebs went to the other extreme, dating it before 1494. Subsequently it has been either placed, as Winkler proposed, with the Alpine watercolours done on the return from Italy in 1495 or shortly afterwards; or associated with the Nuremberg landscapes, either no.43 as proposed by Flechsig, or the *Mills on a river* (Paris, Bibliothèque Nationale, inv. no.B13 rés.; Winkler, *Dürer*, i, pl.113) according to the Tietzes. I still adhere to my cautious opinion that it presumably could have been done on his return from his first visit to Italy or soon afterwards; however, there is nothing to preclude a slightly later date.

41r

41 *Recto:* Study of rocks
Verso: Slight sketch of rocks

Brush drawing in watercolour and bodycolour over traces of black chalk; the *verso* in black chalk. 22.5 × 28.7 cm

WM: scales in a circle (close to Briquet, 2533)

PROVENANCE: Sloane bequest, 1753

5218–166

LITERATURE: Waagen, *Treasures*, i, p.231, no.166; Hausmann, *Naumann's Archiv*, p.41, no.166; Hausmann, p.111, no.142; Ephrussi, p.110; Thausing, i, p.127; Haendcke, p.29; L. Klebs, *Repertorium*, xxx, 1907, p.415; W. v. Seidlitz, *Prussian Jahrbuch*, xv, 1907, p.8; Conway, p.22, no.353; BM *Guide*, 1928, no.212; Tietze, i, p.125, no.A.124, repr. *recto*; Winkler, *Dürer*, i, pp.82f., no.110, repr. *recto*; Rowlands, *Dürer*, p.7, no.20; Koschatzky, no.19, repr.; J. Rowlands, *Zeitschr. f. Kunstwiss*, xxv, 1971, pp.46ff., repr. *verso*; Strauss, i, p.236, no.1494/19, repr. *recto* (for further literature)

Inscribed by an unknown but probably early hand, in brown ink, *1506*, with a false Dürer monogram

Thausing and Haendcke, regarded both the monogram and date as genuine, which Dodgson was inclined to do also; Seidlitz was among the first to question these opinions, a view followed in later scholarship. Klebs and the Tietzes went further and denied the attribution of the drawing to Dürer, the latter of whom described it as lifeless and wanting in any colour-sense, criticisms which are extraordinary in their insensitivity. Leading scholars have since accepted it as one of a group of studies, made in various mediums, evidently done in a quarry near Nuremberg, possibly in the Schmansenbuch on the outskirts of the city. Strauss, by contrast, relying on 'the evidence' of the watermark, which if it could be precisely classified would only provide us with a *terminus post quem*, considers that it should be dated to the beginning of Dürer's first Italian journey in 1494; this could certainly be a pointer in the right direction. In my view, the closest of Dürer's other watercolours to this study is the *Alpine road* in the Escorial near Madrid (Winkler, *Dürer*, i, pl.100) which, despite its poor condition, reveals similarities of handling, seen in details such as the rock faces. Since the discovery of the Escorial landscape by Beenken in 1928 and its publication by Winkler in the following year, most scholars have adhered to the latter's dating *c*.1495, with a minority suggesting the previous year. It seems most probable that the present drawing should be dated either in 1495 *en route* to Nuremberg, or very shortly after the artist's return there.

The sketch on the *verso*, as already suggested elsewhere, probably represents the beginnings of another study of rocks.

42 A 'weierhaus'

See colour plate section following p.80

Brush drawing with watercolour and bodycolour. 21.3 × 22.5 cm

PROVENANCE: Sloane bequest, 1753

5218–165

LITERATURE: Waagen, *Treasures*, i, p.231, no.165; Hausmann, *Naumann's Archiv*, p.34; Hausmann, p.106, no.4; Ephrussi, p.32; Thausing, i, pp.124f.; *Dürer Society*, ii, 1899, pp.8f., no.vii, repr.; Conway, p.12, no.148; Pauli, p.8, no.129; BM *Guide*, 1928, p.20, no.184; Winkler, *Dürer*, i, p.87, no.115, repr.; F. Zink, *Zeitschr. f. Kunstgesch.*, xii, 1949, pp.41ff., repr.; Rowlands, *Dürer*, p.6, no.17, repr.; Koschatzky, no.25, repr.; Strauss, i, p.404, no.1496/6, repr. (for further literature)

Inscribed by the artist on the lower edge, in black ink, *weierhaus*, with the artist's monogram added, in brown ink, to the right by a later hand

Thausing made the general observation that such small buildings served in time of war as outposts for the defence of the city of Nuremberg. They were normally used as fishermen's houses. This particular one has been identified by Zink, from Paul Pfinzinger's *Atlas* of 1595, in which there is a map of the waterways around Nuremberg, as the *Weyerhäusslein* at St Johannis, which at that time was just outside the city walls but today is a suburb of Nuremberg. In Dürer's day the building belonged to the Angerer family.

Both technically and in date this famous watercolour is close to the *Study of water, sky and pine trees*, also in the British Museum (no.43). The weierhaus appears in the reverse sense, in the background of Dürer's engraving of the *Madonna and Child with a monkey* (Dodgson, *Dürer Engr.*, p.29, no.22, repr.).

43 *Recto:* Study of water, sky and pine trees

See colour plate section following p.80

Verso: Sky study

Brush drawing in watercolour and bodycolour, the *verso* in watercolour and black chalk. 26.2 × 36.5 cm

PROVENANCE: Sloane bequest, 1753

5218–167

LITERATURE: Waagen, *Treasures*, i, pp.231f., no.167 (this is evidently it, although there are no vessels); Hausmann, *Naumann's Archiv*, p.41, no.167; Hausmann, p.111, no.143; Ephrussi, p.145, n.3; Lippmann, xxiii, p.3, no.219, repr.; Conway, p.12, no.147; Pauli, p.12, no.247; BM *Guide*, 1928, p.19, no.183; Flechsig, *Dürer*, ii, pp.137f.; Winkler, *Dürer*, i, pp.86f., no.114, repr. *recto*.; Manchester, *German Art*, pp.48f., no.119; Rowlands, *Dürer*, pp.6f., no.19; Koschatzky, no.26, repr.; J. Rowlands, *Zeitschr. f. Kunstwiss.*, xxv, 1971, p.50, repr. *verso*; Strauss, i, pp.400ff., nos.1496/4 and 5, repr. (for further literature)

The artist's monogram is inscribed in the sky in brown ink by a later hand

It is now generally agreed this landscape drawing, one of the most sensitive of Dürer's portrayals of nature, belongs to a group of landscapes of the countryside around Nuremberg, executed fairly soon after the artist's return from his first visit to Italy, most probably in either 1496 or 1497. The others are *A 'weierhaus'* (no.42) and *Mills on a river* in the Bibliothèque Nationale, Paris (inv.no.B.13 rés.; Winkler, *Dürer*, i, pl.113). The latter, perhaps the most magnificent of Dürer's completed landscapes, has much in common with the present drawing, which has been left unfinished. The colouring is very similar in each, although much less bodycolour is used in no.43, giving it a much more modern appearance than perhaps any other of his watercolours. As with the Paris sheet, the present drawing was done at evening with the sun setting. Even though the majority of scholars in the past, including Lippmann and Winkler, thought it was done at sunrise, the evidence of the unfinished, tentative *Sky study* on the *verso*, uncovered in 1971, supports Flechsig's view that the *recto* was done at sunset. As I suggested at the time of the discovery, it is probable that the slight sketch on the *verso* was executed on the same occasion. In it Dürer was entirely preoccupied with the sky, apart from two vertical lines in black chalk, doubtless intended to indicate the position of the trunk on the outside of the three trees in the clump to the right of the pool. The most obvious explanation for his abandonment of this study on the *verso*, is that the light-level became too low to continue working. The representation of the sky bears this out: dark clouds band the upper edge, and below, a fading glimmer of light breaks through between strips of purple and grey, with below them yellow strips and a small area of blue.

Over the intervening years observation of nature has confirmed my initial opinion that both the *recto* and *verso* were drawn at sunset.

44

44 The Prodigal Son

Pen and black ink. Cut down along upper and lower edges. 21.6 × 22cm

PROVENANCE: Sloane bequest, 1753

5218–173

LITERATURE: Waagen, *Treasures*, i, p.232, no.173; Hausmann, *Naumann's Archiv.* p.41, no.173; Hausmann, p.112, no.149; Thausing, i, p.217; W.v.Seidlitz, *Prussian Jahrbuch*, xxviii, 1907, p.9; Conway, p.11, no.110; Pauli, p.9, no.149; BM *Guide*, 1928, p.40, no.343; Winkler, *Dürer*, i, pp.95f., no.145, repr.; C.Dodgson, *Burlington*, lxxiv, 1939, p.233; Zink, p.95, under no.72; Rowlands, *Dürer*, p.10, no.43, repr.; Strauss, i, p.414, no.1496/11, repr. (for further literature)

This is a preparatory drawing, for the engraving of the *Prodigal Son* (Dodgson, *Dürer Engr.*, p.13, no.10, repr.) of *c.*1496, and is the only one for a print to have survived from the years before 1500. A copy drawn after the drawing, now in Nuremberg (Germanisches Nationalmuseum, inv. no.HZ8) shows the appearance of the present drawing before the sheet was cut down. The buildings in the background are depicted in the engraving standing closer together, while the pig with its foot in the trough is omitted, and the pig on the right-hand side of the drawing is moved forward in the engraving to a position behind the prodigal son, thus forming a circle of feeding pigs. Five piglets are added in the print to occupy the foreground.

A study for the figure of the prodigal son, now in Boston (the Museum of Fine Arts; Winkler, *Dürer*, i, pl.146) was executed on a somewhat larger scale, with the figure's head in an upright position. Although the increase in size might predispose one to consider it a copy, the execution is so characteristic of Dürer's draughtsmanship at this stage of his development that one must disagree with the Tietzes' and Panofsky's classification of it as a workshop copy (Tietze, i, p.213, no.w.6, repr.; Panofsky, ii, p.74, no.648).

45 Maurus rescuing Placidus from drowning with the assistance of St Benedict

Pen and brown ink with watercolour. 23.2 × 16.6cm

WM: oxhead (close to Piccard, xi, 347)

PROVENANCE: S.Woodburn (sale, Christie, 1854, 21 June, lot 1149, bt *Tiffin £2.12.6.* for B.M.)

1854–6–28–34

LITERATURE: Waagen, Treasures, iv, pp.38–9; Hausmann, *Naumann's Archiv*, p.35; Hausmann, p.107, no.11; S.z.Schweinsberg, *Berl. Mus.*, xlviii, 1927, pp.34ff.; BM *Guide*, 1928, p.21, no.195; Flechsig, *Dürer*, ii, pp.429ff.; Winkler, *Dürer*, i, p.141, no.200, repr.; Rowlands, *Dürer*, p.12, no.63; Strauss, vi, p.2948, no.xw.200, repr. (for further literature)

This belongs to a series of scenes from the life of St Benedict, which are designs for glass-paintings and have been thought to be by the so-called 'Benedict Master' (F.Winkler, Thieme-Becker, xxxvii, pp.40–1). On the basis of heraldic evidence on some of the drawings, it is generally assumed that they were made for the windows of the Chapel dedicated to the Virgin Mary of the Tetzel family, built in the middle of the fourteenth century in St Egidien, Nuremberg, the burial-place of this notable patrician family. Only one window still remains in the chapel that can be connected with the series of St Benedict. This is of the *Last Judgement with Christ and the Virgin as Intercessors*; the other associated surviving glass-paintings are now elsewhere. The work was probably commissioned about 1500; according to Winkler, it was on the occasion of the marriage of Friedrich Tetzel II to Ursula Fürer in 1499; this, however, U. Frenzel has discovered, had taken place earlier, on 6 February 1496 (Nuremberg, *Dürer*, 1971, p.387).

Nine related drawings in pen and ink are extant (Winkler, *Dürer*, i, pls.198–206). Together with no.45 two are in the British Museum (1927–3–23–1 and 1910–7–9–1). The rest are to be found in Vienna (Albertina, inv.no.3029), Paris (Louvre, inv.no.18.642) Nuremberg (Germanisches Nationalmuseum, inv.no.HZ 5480), Munich (Graphische Sammlung, inv.no.5633), Berlin-Dahlem (Kupferstich-

kabinett, inv.no.47) and Bucharest (formerly in the collection of Professor Cantacuzino). Three of these, including no.45, were executed with the addition of watercolour, and these, according to Winkler, were produced by Dürer first, before his interest in the project waned. It could be, of course, that he had been forced to turn to other work.

Two more designs are known from drawn copies, in Darmstadt (Hessisches Landesmuseum; Winkler, *Dürer*, i, pl.207) and in Schloss Hollenfels, Luxemburg (Winkler, *Dürer*, i, pl.208). A further design, *St Romanus giving the habit to St Benedict*, is known only from the glass-painting in the Schlossmuseum, Gotha (S.z.Schweinsberg, *Berl.Mus.*, xlviii, 1927, p.34, repr.). Two glass-paintings of subjects known already from drawings (Winkler, *Dürer*, i, pls.206 and 207), are in the Germanisches Nationalmuseum, Nuremberg, and the Isabella Stewart Gardner Museum, Boston, Mass.

The authorship of these designs has prompted much controversy among scholars. Thausing thought of the group as from Dürer's workshop, a view which Panofsky, Zink and Frenzel have later supported. Weisbach considered that they were by an older master than Dürer, and thus the idea of the 'Benedict Master' was born. Röttinger at first thought that this master was Hans Wechtlin, but later changed the attribution to a 'Master of St Bridget', curiously identified as Peter Vischer the Elder, so-called from the illustrations to the *Revelationes Sanctae Brigittae*, published by Anton Koberger (Nuremberg, 1500), with which the St Benedict series designs do have a certain affinity.

Some scholars saw someone from Dürer's circle of followers as their author. The Tietzes favoured Hans von Kulmbach (q.v.) while Flechsig proposed Schäufelein (q.v.). But neither of these is possible from a stylistic point of view, since the early drawings of both draughtsmen are quite different in character. There is, however, a steadfast body of opinion that continues to support Dürer's authorship of the series. Although initially advocating Wolf Traut (q.v.) as their author (Dodgson, i, p.502) Dodgson became finally convinced that they were by Dürer, a view which he underlined by acquiring two designs from the series for the British Museum, one of which he presented himself. Winkler and subsequently others, including Kuhrmann, Röttgen, Strobl and myself, have argued that the purpose for which drawings were intended must have a bearing on our view of their status. The fact that designs for glass-paintings required a simplification of composition and outline so that they could easily be transferred to glass, is a credible explanation for their work-a-day quality.

The question of attribution, when there is no external evidence, is particularly difficult to decide in the case of glass-painting designs on a larger scale than those from the St Benedict series. In these the lines are executed with a broad brush, further obscuring the artist's individuality. A good example of this is *St Augustine with six canons* (Rotterdam, Museum Boymans-van Beuningen, inv.no.DI 183(MB1953/T19); Winkler, *Dürer*, i, pl.210), a drawing attributed to

45

Dürer which has been associated with the St Benedict series, although it seems more likely in view of its subject that the design was intended for the Augustinian Convent at Nuremberg. The St Benedict series is a relatively more straightforward problem. Stylistically it can be compared with a pen and watercolour landscape, probably also of *c*.1500, the *Bridge at the Haller Gate (der Trockensteg)*, *Nuremberg* (Winkler, *Dürer*, i, pl.223) in the Albertina (inv.no.3065) whose authenticity has also been undeservedly questioned. Although it has been variously seen as the work of the 'St Benedict Master', and by Panofsky as a fair copy by Dürer of an earlier livelier version, there is no reason to regard it as anything else than an example of Dürer's use of a new medium for his watercolour landscapes. Here, by combining penwork with watercolour wash, he is employing a medium which he also used with notable success at that time for some of his costume studies (e.g. Winkler, *Dürer*, i, pls.224 and 225, dated 1500, both also in the Albertina).

Finally, the very conventional character of the composition in the St Benedict series cannot be considered an impediment to Dürer's authorship. For when he had more freedom he could produce in the same style such an imaginative drawing as the *Mass of angels* at Rennes (Musée des Beaux-Arts; Winkler, *Dürer*, i, pl.181). The artist would have been bound to carry out the instructions of whoever commissioned the work. Scenes from the lives of the Saints in the late Gothic period were depicted according to a set pattern, and this commission was not, in any case, an important one for the artist. But it would have provided a useful sum of money and possibly the prospect of further work.

46 A woman of Nuremberg dressed for church

Brush drawing in watercolour. 31.6 × 17.1cm

PROVENANCE: E. Knight; S. Woodburn (sale, Christie, 1854, 21 June, lot 1142, bt *Weber £4.8s*); W. Russell; Whitehead; Malcolm (bt from *Whitehead, 13 January 1869 – £25*, according to annotated copy of JCR)

1895-9-15-943

LITERATURE: Metz, *Imitations*, 1798, repr.; Waagen, *Treasures*, iv, p.188; JCR. pp.174ff., no.520*; Thausing, i, p.143, n; BM *Guide*, 1895, p.55, no.271; Conway, p.14, under 190; BM *Guide*, 1928, p.21, no.198; Tietze, i, p.56, under no.187; Schilling, *Nürnberger Handz*., p.28, no.16, repr.; Winkler, *Dürer*, i, p.162, no.232, repr.; Rupprich, i, p.205, no.15; Rowlands, *Dürer*, p.13, no.68; Strauss, ii, p.510, no.1500/4, repr. (for further literature)

Inscribed by the artist in black ink on the upper edge, *1500*, followed by the artist's monogram, and *Ein Nörmergerin/as man zw kirchen gatt*

This belongs to the small group of costume studies of Nuremberg women produced in or about 1500 (Winkler, *Dürer*, i, pls.224–8). Most nineteenth-century scholars, and many in this century, especially those who did not see

the drawing in the original (with the notable exception of Dodgson), assumed it to be a copy after the much better known drawing of the same subject in Vienna (Albertina, inv.no.3069; Winkler, *Dürer*, i, pl.224). In the Viennese version, which is more finished than the present drawing, the outline is clearly defined by the pen, but the individuality of the features is lost, which prompted the Tietzes to take an unfavourable view of the Vienna drawing. Its delicate washes suggest that the present drawing is a first study. The features of the woman, in so far as they are distinguishable, are similar to those of Dürer's wife Agnes, so it is very possible that she served as the model.

A similar relationship exists between the two versions of the *Nuremberg woman in her house-dress*, one in Milan (Biblioteca Ambrosiana, inv.no.F.264.2; Winkler, *Dürer*, i, pl.228), the other also in the Albertina (inv.no.3071; Winkler, *Dürer*, i, pl.226). Kuhrmann has noted that the Milan drawing (Munich, *Dürer*, p.21, no.20), to judge from the spontaneous application of the cool washes, appears to be a study freshly executed after the life, just like the present drawing. Dürer has used the pen in the Milan version with restraint, but in the second version in Vienna, he achieved the finished effect, of which the Tietzes did not approve.

The figure of the *Woman dressed for church* was employed by Dürer in his design for the woodcut of the *Betrothal of the Virgin* (Bartsch vii, p.131, no.82), and appears, in reverse, on the right of the print. A colour aquatint, published in 1798, was made by Conrad Metz (1749–1827) in the reverse sense after the drawing, when it was in the possession of Edward Knight. A sixteenth-century copy of no.46, made in pen and brown ink with grey wash, is also in the British Museum (Sloane 5218–174).

47 A Gothic table fountain

See colour plate section following p.80

Pen and brown ink with watercolour and traces of red chalk. The sheet is made up of three pieces of paper, the joins of which have been backed with two horizontal strips, *c*.1cm wide; numerous tears have been repaired. Trimmed along the lower edge. 56 × 35.8cm

WM: oxhead? (only partly visible)

PROVENANCE: Sloane bequest, 1753

5218-83

LITERATURE: Waagen, *Treasures*, i, p.230, no.83; Hausmann, *Naumann's Archiv*, p.38, no.83; Hausmann, p.109, no.77; V. Scherer *Die Ornamentik bei Albrecht Dürer*, Strassburg, 1902, p.90; W.v. Seidlitz, *Prussian Jahrbuch*, xxviii, 1907, p.19; Tietze, i, p.125, no.A.122, repr.; BM *Guide*, 1928, p.20, no.193; Winkler, *Dürer*, i, pp.163f., no.233, repr.; J.H.Whitfield, *OMD*, xiii, no.51, 1938, pp.31f., repr.; Manchester, *German Art*, pp.46f., no.114; Kohlhaussen, pp.258–60, repr.; Rowlands, *Dürer*, p.13, no.69; Strauss, i, p.456, no.1499/1 repr. (for further literature); Nuremberg, *Gothic & Renaissance*, p.283, under no.113

46

Inscribed on the *verso*, by a contemporary hand, in brown ink, *das aufzuglein das von silber ist und/sich anvecht von dem peck hat dy hoch/der Visirung lanck oder hoch* 'The mechanism which is silver and rises from the basin is equal in height to the length or height as in the design'; and below a ruled red chalk line, approx. 13.8cm, *das ist dy hoch der silbren poslein/eins teils hoher und lenger und/ein teils kurtzer* 'This is the height of the silver figurines, partly higher and longer, partly shorter'; and below a similar line, approx. 23.8cm, *das ist dy hoch der wasser/von den kindlein* 'This is the height of the water from the figurines of the children'; and below a similar line, approx. 36.5cm, *das ist dy hoch d/er wa/sser/der nackenden pos/sen/* 'This is the height of the water from the nude figurines'; and below a similar line, approx. 47cm, *das ist dy hoch der wasser der ewssen bossen/vom ausgang als der rotelstrich ausweist* 'This is the height of the water from the water figurines on the rim, as the red mark shows'

The above inscriptions on the *verso* (now visible, but formerly known to scholars only from a transcription), give information about the mechanism by which the fountain functions, and the height of the water or wine from the various apertures; this would have been supplied by the maker, who is likely to have been Hans Frey, Dürer's father-in-law. According to Neudörfer, Frey specialised in the production of such pieces of extravagant tableware. They played an important rôle in the ostentatious display of the late medieval banquet. From documentary evidence the use of such ornamental pieces at the courts of kings and grand nobility goes back at least to the thirteenth century, and probably derives from Byzantium and ultimately Sassanian Persia. One of the few from Medieval Western Europe to survive is the fragment, lacking its basin and foot, said to have been found in a garden in Constantinople, of a late fourteenth-century table fountain, now in the Cleveland Museum of Art (R.W. Lightbown, *Secular Goldsmiths' Work in Medieval France: a History*, London 1978, p.45, pls.xlviii–li).

Apparently the first mention of a drawing similar to no.47 was to one in the Imhoff collection (Heller, p.84, no.95); however, as this was drawn on vellum it is evidently one of the two surviving copies, and according to Anzelewski and Mielke (*Dürer: Kritischer Katalog*, Berlin, 1984, p.127, no.123) is now in Berlin-Dahlem (KDZ.766). They consider that the copyist was Hans von Kulmbach (q.v.).

A number of scholars, principally the Tietzes, have rejected Dürer's authorship of this design, the largest and most magnificent drawing of its kind to have survived. The draughtsmanship is, however, much finer than that of the copies, and the penwork and the deft use of wash, including the marbling effect on the stem of the fountain, are thoroughly characteristic of Dürer. It can be dated on stylistic grounds *c.*1500. The choice of colours and the application of the wash is closely similar to the pen and wash landscape, the *Trockensteg in Nuremberg* of *c.*1499 in Vienna (Albertina, inv.no.3065; Koschatzky, pl.24). The sculpture, if executed, must have been the most impressive of Frey's fountains, none of which have survived. Kohlhaussen has, however, proposed that three designs for table fountains at Erlangen should perhaps be associated with Frey's workshop (Kohlhaussen, pp.255ff., figs.395, 397, 398), none of which is executed by Dürer. A further design by Dürer for a smaller table fountain, as fanciful in conception as the present drawing, and with a twisted stem in imitation of intertwined branches (which was a typical late Gothic ornamental device in Central Europe), is in the Ashmolean Museum, Oxford (inv.no.P.285; Winkler, *Dürer*, iv, pl.946). It is a very similar creation to the partial designs for two other table fountains on a sheet in the British Museum (inv.no.5218–79; Winkler, *Dürer*, i, pl.235). A sheet for another design with studies for a variety of stems is in the Soane Museum, London (Kohlhaussen, fig.404).

48 Design for a Gothic cup

Pen and brown ink. 25.6 × 16.6cm

PROVENANCE: Sloane bequest, 1753

5218–78

LITERATURE: Hausmann, *Naumann's Archiv*, p.38, no.78; Hausmann, p.109, no.73; Conway, p.33, no.593; Pauli, p.43, no.1197;

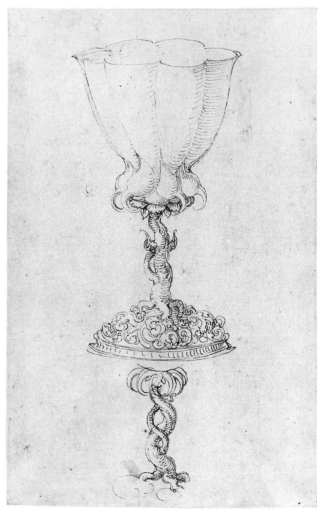

48

Wölfflin, *Handz.*, p.35, no.48, repr.; BM *Guide*, 1928, p.20, no.190; Tietze, i, p.65, no.216, repr.; Flechsig, *Dürer*, ii, pp.326–7; Winkler, *Dürer*, i, p.164, no.234, repr.; Panofsky, ii, p.147, no.1565; Kohlhaussen, p.357, repr.; Rowlands, *Dürer*, pp.13f., no.70; Strauss, i, p.468, no.1499/7, repr. (for further literature)

An alternative design for the stem of the cup is drawn below the base. The Tietzes, on stylistic grounds, rejected Wölfflin's dating of the middle of the second decade, regarding the drawing as roughly contemporaneous with the *Seven cups* (Bruck, fol.193 *recto*) at Dresden which they date *c.*1502–3. Flechsig notes a similarity between the design of the foot and shaft with those of the seven candlesticks which occur in *St John before the seven candlesticks* in Dürer's *Apocalypse* (Bartsch, vii, p.127, no.62) and he also thought that it was contemporaneous with the *Seven cups* at Dresden; however, he assumed that the sheet at Dresden must be dated after 1507, the earliest date noted in the book. But there is no necessity to be inhibited by this suggestion, as it is conceivable that the sheet could have been bound into the book at a later date. With regard to the difficulty of the present drawing, Flechsig notes the similarity of the design to that of the cup in the engraving *Nemesis* (Bartsch, vii, pp.91f., no.77) and the cup held by one of the kings in the painting, the *Adoration of the Magi* of 1504 in Florence (Uffizi, inv.no.1434; Anzelewsky, *Dürer*, pl.89), which prompts him to date it between 1503 and 1505. Winkler connects this drawing with a group of ornamental designs by Dürer, particularly of the *Gothic table fountain* (no.47), which he dates *c.*1500 on stylistic grounds. From the chronological sequence of the British Museum 1928 exhibition catalogue, it would appear that Dodgson placed the drawing somewhat between 1496 and 1500, although he does make the observation that it is probably of a later date than its position in the catalogue infers. It is also dated by Panofsky *c.*1500, but without further comment, and this date, judging from the penwork, seems to me to be the most likely answer.

Mature Works, 1500–5

49 Head of a suffering man

Charcoal. The drawing has suffered from exposure in a frame, at some stage before it was put in the Sloane volume no.5218 which is dated 1637. 31 × 22.1 cm

WM: oxhead (close to Briquet, 15379; and Piccard, xvi, 194)

PROVENANCE: Sloane bequest, 1753

5218–30

LITERATURE: Hausmann, *Naumann's Archiv*, p.36, no.30; Hausmann, p.107, no.30; Thausing, i, p.321; Conway, p.18, no.250; Pauli, p.12, no.262; BM *Guide*, 1928, p.22, no.207; Tietze, i, p.67, no.226, repr.; Flechsig, *Dürer*, ii, p.324; Winkler, *Dürer*, ii, p.8, no.271, repr.; Rowlands, *Dürer*, p.17, no.92; Anzelewsky,

Dürer, pp.174, 180; Strauss, ii, p.686, no.1503/17, repr. (for further literature)

Inscribed by the artist in charcoal in the upper right-hand corner, *1503*, with below, the artist's monogram

As noted in no.50, this appears to be a companion to that drawing. Both belong to an impressive group of charcoal portraits produced in 1503 (Winkler, *Dürer*, ii, pls.269–75). Flechsig's proposal, recently taken up by Anzelewsky, that it is a study after the life for the head of Christ in the painting commissioned most probably *c.*1500, by Albrecht Glimm, the *Lamentation over the Dead Christ* (Munich, Bayerische Staatsgemäldesammlungen, inv.no.704; Anzelewsky, *Dürer*, pl.69) is very unconvincing. The Tietzes also connect this drawing with a detail in another work by Dürer, namely the brutal visage of the threatening scourger on the title-page of the *Large Passion* (Bartsch, vii, p.117, no.4), which, apart from having the same type of beard, has nothing in common with the suffering man depicted here. Anzelewsky, however, does make another interesting suggestion when he links the painting of *The Head of St John the Baptist on a charger* (Nuremberg, Germanisches Nationalmuseum, inv.no.287; Anzelewsky, *Dürer*, p.180, repr.) with the present drawing and its likely companion, no.50. The various versions surviving of this subject, some of which are inscribed with the date *1503* and Dürer's monogram, are very probably copies after a lost original by Dürer. If such a painting was indeed executed by Dürer in 1503, as the existence of these copies would seem to suggest, this may be a further indication of the artist's state of mind during an unspecified illness in that year, to which he refers in his inscription on no.50.

50 Head of the dead Christ

Charcoal. Like no.49, the drawing has suffered from exposure in a frame. 31 × 22.1 cm

PROVENANCE: Sloane bequest, 1753

5218–29

LITERATURE: Hausmann, *Naumann's Archiv*, p.36, no.29; Hausmann, p.107, no.29; Ephrussi, p.86; Thausing, i, p.320; Conway, p.18, no.249; Pauli, p.12, no.261; BM *Guide*, 1928, p.22, no.209; Winkler, *Dürer*, ii, pp.8f., no.272, repr.; Rowlands, *Dürer*, p.18, no.93; Anzelewsky, *Dürer*, p.180; Strauss, ii, p.684, no.1503/16 repr. (for further literature)

Inscribed by the artist, below the drawing, in charcoal, *1503*, with the artist's monogram, and along the lower edge, faintly: *Die 2* [or, but much less likely, *Disz*] *angsicht hab ich uch erl?*| [*aus erfurcht?*, according to Strauss] *gemacht in meiner Kranckeit*

The two *angsicht* (countenances) mentioned in the more credible reading of the above inscription are presumably the present drawing, and the *Head of a suffering man* (no.49) which is of a comparable size. As both are portrayals of suffering, one of a man, the other of Christ, they would be a likely subject for Dürer to turn to during his illness. Certainly they appear to have been conceived as a pair.

49

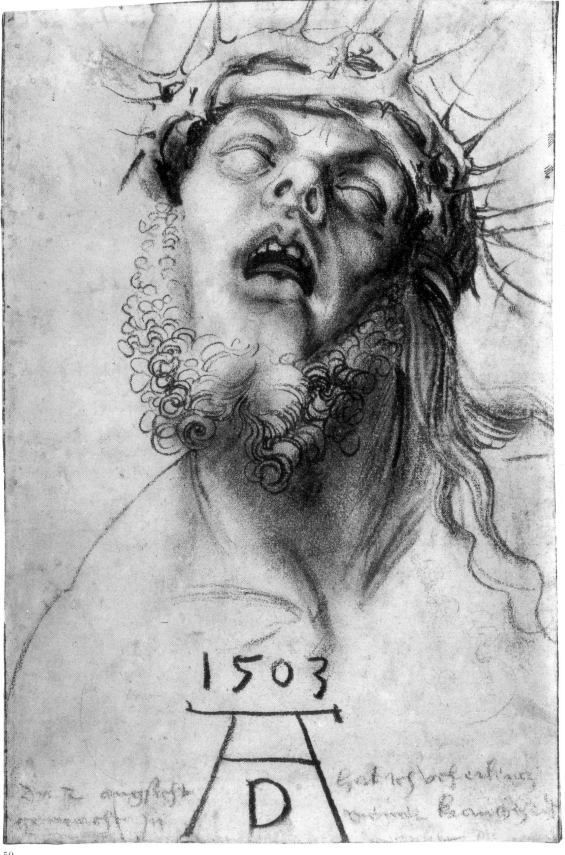

50

It is possible that there was a version, probably a copy of the present drawing, in the possession of Charles I. Abraham van der Doort listed one in his catalogue of Charles I's collections (*Walpole Society*, xxxvii, 1960, p.178, no.44) which from the description in very curious Dutch-English could be a copy of the present drawing, *itm krijst had Wit toren kran lucking opwurds don Wit a korius pensil giffen bij te jong hariot/don auffte albrt dur and giffen tu de king vor a niwjar bij te jong hariot/*'item Christ's head with thorn crown looking upwards done with a curious pencil given by the young Heriot [i.e. George Heriot (1563–1623/4), goldsmith, jeweller, and money-lender to James I] done after Albrecht Dürer and given to the king for a new year present by the young Heriot'. It is also listed (*Walpole Society, loc.cit.*, p.145, no.8) as 'Item upon blew paper drawen in black and white a head of Christ Crowned wth thornes – thought to bee a Coppy after Alberdure very Curiously done set in a black frame with a – shiver. Given to yor Maty by yor Mats Jeweller Mr Heriott'.

51 Apollo and Diana

Pen and brown ink, with additional work in black chalk on Apollo's hair, groin, thighs and his left arm; incised lines with the stylus divide the proportions of the god's head and body. 28.3 × 20.5 cm

PROVENANCE: Sloane bequest, 1753

5218–183

LITERATURE: Hausmann, *Naumann's Archiv*, p.42, no.183; Hausmann, p.112, no.157; Ephrussi, pp.74ff.; Thausing, i, pp.277f.; Conway, p.19, no.296; Pauli, p.9, no.154; E.Panofsky, *Prussian Jahrbuch*, xli, 1920, p.362ff., repr.; BM *Guide*, 1928, p.21, no.205; Flechsig, *Dürer*, ii, pp.153ff.; Winkler, *Dürer*, i, pp.180ff., no.261, repr.; M.Winner, *Berlin Jahrbuch*, x, 1968, p.188; E.Pogány-Balás, *Acta Hist. Art.*, xvii, 1971, pp.76ff., repr.; Rowlands, *Dürer*, p.18, no.95, repr.; Strauss, ii, p.580, no.1501/7, repr. (for further literature); Nuremberg, *Gothic & Renaissance*, pp.285f., under no.115

Inscribed by the artist, in brown ink, in the sun, *APOLO* in reverse, and along the upper left-hand edge, *ein 3 teil von 5 . . .* although the rest is unreadable, this is clearly a reference to Dürer's own system of proportions of the human body

The figure of Apollo in this drawing is one of the first of Dürer's studies of the proportions of the male body. The divisions of his scheme are marked by the incised lines mentioned above. This interest, which quickly developed into a passion, was awakened as the artist himself tells us through his acquaintance with the Venetian artist, Jacopo de'Barbari (*c*.1440/50–*c*.1515), who came to Nuremberg in 1500 to enter the service of Maximilian I. Evidently this is when Dürer met him, as his first proportional studies date from this time. As, however, Jacopo would not pass on the details of his own system, Dürer with some help from a reading of Vitruvius soon devised his own. The present drawing, which together with two other drawings of the male figure, the *Aesculapius* in Berlin-Dahlem (Kupfer-

stichkabinett, inv.no.KDZ.5017; Winkler, *Dürer*, i, pl.263) and the 'Poynter' *Apollo* in the Metropolitan Museum, New York (inv.no.63.212; Winkler, *Dürer*, i, pl.262) were produced at the same time, have been called the 'Apollo' group. They are drawn according to the same canon of proportions and constructional scheme, which is inevitable in the case of the 'Poynter' *Apollo*, as it is largely a tracing of the figure of Apollo in the present drawing. Dürer commonly made tracings in connection with his drawn studies of human proportions. They would have been made by placing the sheet in front of a source of light, or possibly as Schilling suggests (*Berl. Mus.*, NF, iv, 1954, p.22) on a specially constructed glass-topped table. These studies soon bore notable fruit in the production in 1504 of the engraving, *Adam and Eve*, (Dodgson, *Dürer Engr.*, pp.51ff., no.39, repr.). The figure of Adam, both in the preparatory work and the final engraving, is constructed according to the same proportions as the initial 'Apollo' drawings; indeed, the pose of the Adam is closely dependent on the figure of Apollo in no.51, which may well have been produced not long before the engraving.

In its general arrangement, no.51, an unfinished study for an engraving which was never executed, strongly recalls Jacopo de'Barbari's engraving of *Apollo and Diana* (Bartsch, vii, p.523, no.16). The question of the derivation of the pose of the god has been a matter of some contention. Those, like Flechsig, who are against the view that it derives from the *Apollo Belvedere*, the classical sculpture discovered at the end of the fifteenth century (Haskell & Penny, pp.148ff., repr.) do so on very slender grounds since they suggest that the sculpture was not generally accessible before *c*.1510, when it was placed in the Belvedere, and Marcantonio Raimondi (*c*.1470–*c*.1530) made an engraving based on it (Bartsch, xiv, pp.249ff., no.331). For Dürer could surely have known the sculpture from drawings of it, such as that in the *Codex Escurialensis* (fol.64) by an Italian hand of *c*.1495/1500 as well as the engraving, by Nicoletto da Modena (active *c*.1490–after 1511) (Bartsch, xiii, p.282, no.50) of *c*.1500. As Winner has noted, the way Dürer has drawn the god's hair can only be explained as a reflection of the *Apollo Belvedere*, and it is seen again in the head of Adam in his engraving of 1504. To a lesser extent, the influence of Andrea Mantegna (*c*.1431–1506) is revealed: the position of Apollo's legs is similar to that of the man with the cornucopia in Mantegna's engraving, *Bacchanale with the wine vat* (Bartsch, xiii, p.240, no.19), which would have been well known to Dürer.

The classical statue in its damaged state lacked hands, which gave Dürer a certain freedom in his interpretation. Apollo's snake was at first interpreted as the symbol of health, leading him in the Berlin drawings, mentioned earlier, to be identified with either Aesculapius, or 'Apollo medicus'. In the present drawing the god, through the presence of the solar disc and sceptre, was initially conceived of as the sun-god, Sol; however, there is nothing visible on the sheet to support Panofsky's idea that originally the *O* and *L* in the present inscription were preceded by

51

an S to form *SOL*. It is quite likely, however, as Panofsky has suggested that Dürer began the drawing with a solitary figure of the god Sol, under the influence of Jacopo's engraving, *Apollo and Diana*, with which the drawing has a clear relationship, and then transferred the subject to Apollo and Diana. At first Diana was drawn in in outline facing forward, but was later changed to a position with her back to the viewer, as she is seen in Jacopo's engraving. Dürer's engraving of *Apollo and Diana* of *c*.1504–5 (Dodgson, *Dürer Engr.*, p.46, no.34, repr., where it is dated too early, *c*.1502–3) is a different, maturer creation, influenced by the experience of composing and executing his *Adam and Eve*.

52 *Recto:* An elk

See colour plate section following p.80

Verso: A European bison

Recto: pen and brush and black ink with watercolour over traces of an underdrawing in pen and black ink; the *verso* in pen and black ink. 21.3 × 26cm

WM: high crown (Piccard, xii, 16-s)

PROVENANCE: Sloane bequest, 1753

5261–101

LITERATURE: H.David, *Prussian Jahrbuch*, xxxiii, 1912, pp.23ff., repr.; BM *Guide*, 1928, p.19, no.173; Flechsig, *Dürer*, ii, p.114; Winkler, *Dürer*, i, p.168, nos.242 and 243, repr.; Rowlands, *Dürer*, pp.8f., no.98; Strauss, ii, pp.568ff., nos.1501/1 and 2, repr. (for further literature); Koreny, *Tier-und Pflanzenstudien*, p.22, repr.

Inscribed by the artist at the cente of the lower edge in pen and black ink, *Heilennt*. Beneath this has been added later by another hand, in brown ink, the artist's monogram and *1519*

There has been a lack of agreement about the technique used on the *recto*. Dodgson proposed that it is in pen and ink, whereas Winkler with some hesitation regarded it as a pure brush drawing. In fact, it appears to be a pen and ink drawing elaborated with the brush: the areas of black ink along the back of the animal could only have been done with the brush, whereas certain strokes on and around the hind legs are clearly pen-work. There can be no question that the underdrawing has been executed with a fine pen.

First published by H.David who, whilst noting its obvious connection with the elk in the engraving of *Adam and Eve* (Bartsch, vii, p.30, no.1) of 1504, proposed that the drawing is not itself a study after nature, but might be after a stuffed specimen. On stylistic grounds he put its date back to 1500, and did not rule out the possibility of it having been done at the end of the 1490s. Winkler at first assigned no.52 to Dürer's first stay in Venice, and considered it along with the *Parrot* (Milan, Biblioteca Ambrosiana, inv. no.F.264.12; Winkler, *Dürer*, i, pl.244) and *Lion* (Warsaw, University Library; Winkler, *Dürer*, i, pl.246) to date from the mid-1490s. He subsequently modified this opinion

somewhat to take account of Flechsig's view that the way in which Dürer has written *Heilennt* was close in manner to, and thus presumably contemporaneous, with his writing on drawings of about 1500. Winkler also noted an historical circumstance that added weight to this later dating: King Maximilian, later Emperor, visited Nuremberg in 1501 from 13 to 21 April when, according to the chronicler, Heinrich Deichsler (1430–1506/7), he was presented with five bison as a parting gift (Deichsler, p.643, under 21 April, '*Item man schenkt dem kunig 5 aurerochsen, heten ein fremde gestalt*'). The drawing on the *verso* was presumably made in connection with this occasion. The bison appears later in a more finished form, in Dürer's pen and ink marginalia to the *Prayer Book* of Maximilian I of 1515 (Munich, Staatsbibliothek; Strauss, iii, p.1515, repr.).

Although the traces of the underdrawing on the *recto* are very slight, sufficient amounts can be seen to establish that the manner of its execution is the same as that adopted on the *verso*. This would support the view that the *recto* was executed at some stage from 1501–3 in the period when Dürer would have begun work on his engraving, *Adam and Eve* (see under no.53).

53 *Recto:* Studies for the hand and arm of Adam, rocks and bushes

Verso: Slight outline drawing of an arm

Pen and brown and black ink, the *verso* in black ink. 21.6 × 27.5cm

PROVENANCE: Sloane bequest, 1753

5218–181

LITERATURE: Waagen, *Treasures*, i, p.233, no.181; Hausmann, *Naumann's Archiv*, p.41, no.181; Hausmann, p.112, no.155; Ephrussi, p.70; Conway, p.19, no.300; Pauli, p.13, no.281; BM *Guide*, 1928, p.43, no.372; Winkler, *Dürer*, ii, pp.58f., no.336, repr. *recto*, appendix pl.xxi, *verso*; Rowlands, *Dürer*, p.19, no.101; Strauss, ii, p.754, nos.1504/13 and 14, repr. (for further literature); Nuremberg, *Gothic & Renaissance*, p.293, under no.120

Inscribed in brown ink, on the upper edge, *3*, with the artist's monogram

This is the only surviving sheet of studies of details for the engraving of *Adam and Eve* (Dodgson, *Dürer Engr.*, pp.51ff., no.39, repr.). The two studies for Adam's left arm with his hand holding an apple, one of which has part of the branch still attached, were drawn prior to the latest surviving sketch for the two figures of Adam and Eve drawn on two joined sheets of paper, and dated *1504*, in the Pierpont Morgan Library, New York (inv.no.1,257d; Winkler, *Dürer*, ii, pl.333).

The three studies of the hand without the apple were drawn after Dürer had decided that Adam should not hold the fruit offered by Eve. The study of the hand in the centre shows it with the fingers and thumb as they are in the engraving, although reversed.

The study of Adam's right arm was, however, done just to establish the position of the right arm and hand before

PLATE I

Martin Schongauer: *A young woman fanning a fire with a bird's wing* (no.26)

PLATE II

Anonymous: *Sir John Mandeville's Travel Book*, folio 7, verso (no.1)

PLATE III

Anonymous: *Sir John Mandeville's Travel Book*, folio 8, recto (no.1)

PLATE IV

(*Above*) Master of
the Worcester
'Christ carrying
the Cross':
*The Mocking of
Christ* (no.4)

Bernhard Strigel:
St Vitus
(no.16)

PLATE V

Michel Wolmegut:
*Design for a
frontispiece*
(no.33 recto)

PLATE VI

Albrecht Dürer: *View of the castle at Trent* (no.39)

(*Facing page*) Albrecht Dürer: *A larch tree* (no.40)

PLATE VII

PLATE VIII

Albrecht Dürer: *A 'weierhaus'* (no.42)

PLATE IX

Albrecht Dürer: *Study of water, sky and pine trees* (no.43 recto)

PLATE X

Albrecht Dürer:
A Gothic table fountain
(no.47)

PLATE XI

Albrecht Dürer:
A bird (no.62)

Albrecht Dürer:
An elk (no.52 recto)

PLATE XII

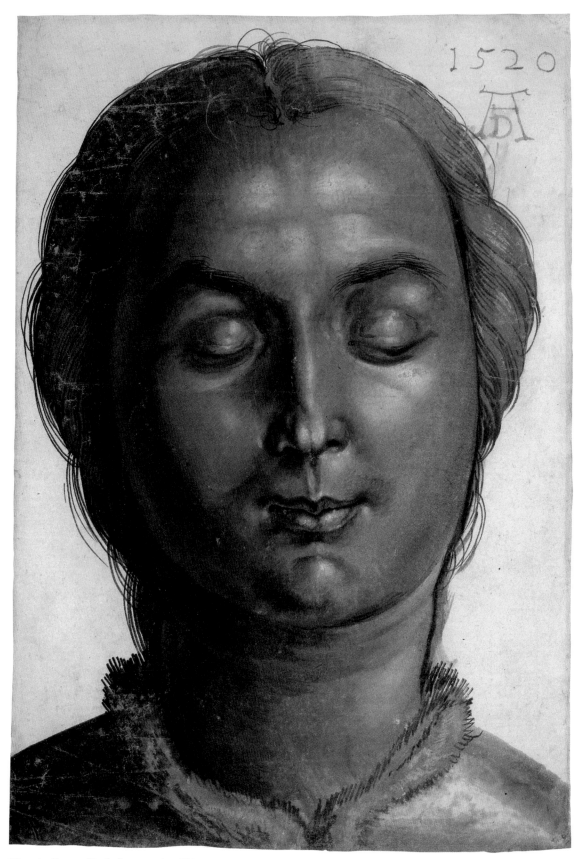

Albrecht Dürer: *Head of a woman* (no.71)

PLATE XIII

Albrecht Dürer: *Portrait of a man, supposedly Paul Hofhaimer* (no.70)

PLATE XIV

Georg Pencz: *Head and shoulders of a young man* (no.104)   Hans Baldung: *Head of an old woman* (no.90)

PLATE XV

Hans von Kulmbach:
Design for an altarpiece
(no.100)

Wolf Traut:
The ordeal of St Kunigunda
(no.109)

PLATE XVI

Georg Beck: *Dedicatory frontispiece* (no.148)

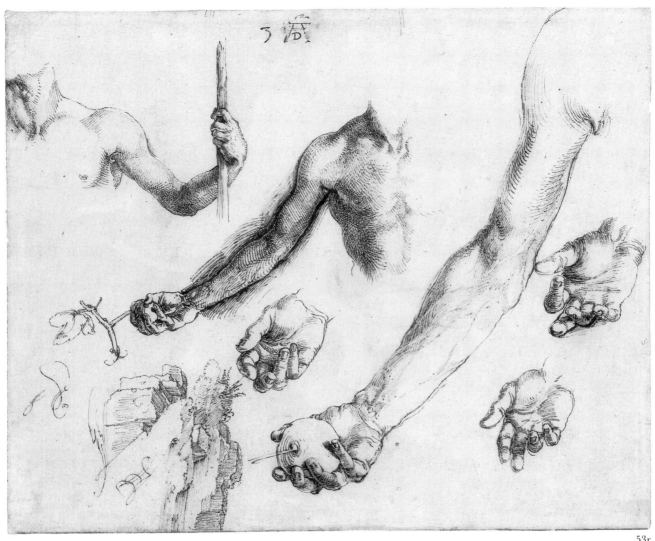

53r

he had decided how he would draw the branch. Whereas all these studies on the sheet are drawn in reverse to the engraving, the study of rocks and bushes in the background of the engraving, which is not followed at all closely, is drawn in the same direction as in the print.

54 *Recto:* Death riding

Verso: An owl

Charcoal. Trimmed on the left-hand side. 21.1 × 26.5 cm

WM: imperial orb (close to Briquet, 3058)

PROVENANCE: Sir J. C. Robinson (according to his note on the *verso*, acquired at Amsterdam in 1857); Malcolm

1895-9-15-971

LITERATURE: JCR, p.174, no.518; Ephrussi, p.103; Thausing, i, pp.207f.; C. Dodgson, *OMD*, iii, no.9, 1928, pp.11ff., repr. *verso*; BM *Guide*, 1928, p.22, no.211; Tietze, i, p.127, no.A.133, repr.

recto; Winkler, *Dürer*, ii, p.87, no.377, repr. and appendix pl.xv; Manchester, *German Art*, p.50, no.122, repr. *recto*; L. Grote, *Zeitschr. f. Kunstwiss*, xix, 1965, p.156, pp.163ff., repr. *verso*; Rowlands, *Dürer*, p.20, no.115; Strauss, ii, p.884, nos.1505/24 and 24a, repr. (for further literature)

Inscribed by the artist in charcoal in the upper left-hand corner, *ME/[M]ENTO/MEI/1505*, with his monogram above the horse's right hind hoof in the centre

It is usually assumed, with its foreboding of death, that this drawing was prompted by the plague that had broken out in Nuremberg in 1505. Death, here crowned, riding on a horse, is an image which derives ultimately from the moment in the Apocalypse (Revelations, vi, 8) when the fourth seal is opened and there appears 'a pale horse: and his name that sat on him was Death . . .'. Only the Tietzes reject this outstanding drawing; they likewise regarded the monogram as spurious.

The incomplete sketch of an owl on the *verso*, first noted by Dodgson, has been connected with an undated broad-

81

54r

sheet with an anonymous poem, illustrated with a woodcut by Dürer of *An owl attacked by four birds*, the unique impression of which is preserved in the Veste Coburg (Kurth, pl.300). It was published in Nuremburg by the *Briefmaler* Hans Glaser (active 1540–61). The woodcut has been dated by Meder about 1515 which could be rather late; however, there is no more than a general similarity between the owl in the sketch and that in the woodcut. There is also an owl perched with outspread wings over the arch in the woodcut, *The Marriage of the Virgin* (Kurth, pl.180) which belongs to that part of the *Life of the Virgin*, finished before Dürer left for Venice in 1505. It is by no means certain, however, that the sketch on the *verso*, merely because of the date on the *recto*, should be considered a preliminary idea for this owl. Grote has associated the *verso* sketch with the owl in the gold background of the painting of the *Man of Sorrows* at Karlsruhe (Staatliche Kunsthalle, inv.no.2183; Anzelewsky, *Dürer*, pl.8), but this seems improbable.

The Second Visit to Italy, 1505–7

55 Portrait of a peasant woman

Pen and brown ink and brown wash. 41.6 × 28.1 cm

PROVENANCE: Marquis de Lagoy (L.1710); ?S.Woodburn; H.Danby Seymour (L.176); A.Seymour; MrsA.Seymour; Miss J.M.Seymour (sale, Sotheby 1927, 26 April, lot 21, bt *F.Sabin* £2,500); H.E.ten Cate; purchased with the aid of contributions from the N.A.-C.F. and an anonymous donor, 1930

1930–3–24–1

LITERATURE: C.Ephrussi, *Gazette*, xvi, 1877, pp.432ff., repr.; Ephrussi, pp.111f.; Conway, p.22, no.354; Pauli, p.14, no.316; Nuremberg, *Dürer*, 1928, p.110, no.243; Tietze, ii, p.21, no.287, repr.; C.Dodgson, *Burlington*, lvi, 1930, pp.237f, repr.; C.Dodgson, *BMQ*, v, 1930, pp.9f., repr.; Winkler, *Dürer*, ii, p.86, no.375, repr.; Rupprich, i, p.206, no.28; Manchester, *German Art*, p.48,

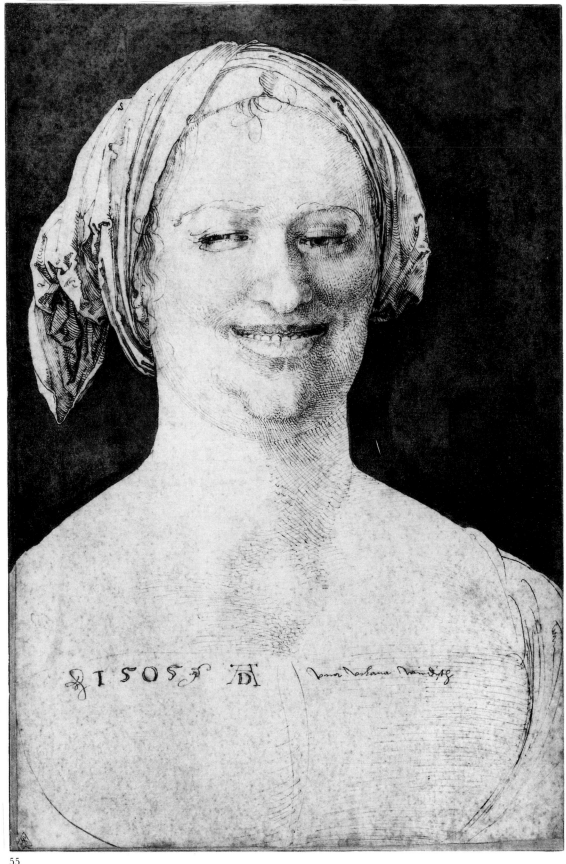

55

no.118; H.T.Musper, *Pantheon*, XXIX, 1971, pp.474ff., repr.; Rowlands, *Dürer*, p.21, no.117; BM *Portrait Drawings*, p.10, no.18; W.Stechow, *The Art Bulletin*, lvi, New York, 1974, p.265; Strauss, ii, p.890, no.1505/27, repr. (for further literature); F.Winzinger, *Zeitschr.f. Kunstwiss.*, xxix, 1975, pp.28ff., repr.

Inscribed by the artist in brown ink, across the bodice, *1505*, within calligraphic flourishes, his monogram and *Vna vilana Windisch*

This peasant woman (*una vilana*, a coarse woman) was, as the inscription indicates, from the Windisch Mark, the old name for a region of Southern Austria, the area around Gurk in Carinthia. This portrait drawing, in which the artist has marvellously caught the low cunning in the expression of the sitter, could have been done either *en route* to Venice or in that city, where such peasants could have found work. In an earlier pen drawing, the *Laughing woman* of 1503 (Winkler, *Dürer*, ii, pl.277) formerly in Bremen (Kunsthalle) Dürer had successfully depicted a similar facial expression with telling effect.

Generally the present drawing is regarded by scholars as one of the finest of Dürer's pen portraits, although the Tietzes comment adversely on what they saw as the drawing's want of a sense of depth. Undoubtedly its surface has suffered at some time before it entered the collection from the old-fashioned use of the knife to remove marks caused by foxing. The brown wash background is characteristic of Dürer and it is not, as the Tietzes suggest, a later addition.

The version of this drawing executed on vellum, now in a continental private collection (pen and brown ink and wash, 32.5 × 26.2 cm), recently published by Musper, cannot be considered an original by Dürer, let alone the original of which he assumes the present drawing to be an inferior copy. Despite the support from a graphologist, who has pronounced on the relative merits of the inscription on the two drawings at length (M.Peter, *Zeitschrift für Menschenkunde*, Vienna & Stuttgart, xl, 1976, pp.211ff., repr.) the relative quality of the two drawings emphatically favours the present one. Through the courtesy of the owner of the version on vellum, it has been possible for me to examine it closely. From this my conclusion is that whoever executed this second drawing lacked the necessary skill to organise the shading with the spontaneity one finds in the British Museum drawing. In general the lines lack rhythm in their execution and, in particular, the shading around the right eye is faulty. Significantly, the draughtsman of the second version had made the left eye too open so that the telling expression seen in no.55, is quite absent. Furthermore, one cannot see any sign of Dürer's assurance with the pen either in the hatching about the chin, or in the peppered effect of dots, for instance, to the left of the nose and chin. All this indicates that the drawing on vellum is an attempt by someone of moderate talent to produce a copy reasonably close in its details to the present drawing, a view also taken by Winzinger. Winzinger's proposal that the drawing on vellum could be from Dürer's workshop seems unlikely.

56 Head of a woman

Silverpoint, heightened with white bodycolour, on pink prepared ground. 21.8 × 18.1 cm

PROVENANCE: E. Piot; Sir J.C.Robinson; Malcolm

1895-9-15-978

LITERATURE: JCR, p.176, no.525; Conway, p.23, no.370; Pauli, p.37, no.1065; BM *Guide*, 1928, p.28, no.269; Flechsig, *Dürer*, ii, pp.291f.; Winkler, *Dürer*, ii, pp.15f., no.286, repr.; Tietze, iii, p.121, no.A.344, repr.; Panofsky, ii, p.117, no.1169; Rowlands, *Dürer*, p.22, no.124; Strauss, i, p.434, no.1497/3, repr. (for further literature)

Like no.57, this silverpoint drawing, about which widely differing views have been expressed, is difficult to date, and some have even denied that it is by Dürer at all. Both Flechsig and Winkler waver between 1497 and 1503, although the former is more in favour of the earlier date. As Colvin has proposed (see BM *Guide*), it seems probable it was executed *c*.1506. The intense interest shown here in the finished rendering of the face which, by the brushwork, gives the effect of a polished surface, is just like that which is so evident in the preparatory brush drawings for the *Rosenkranz Madonna* (Prague, Nationalgalerie, inv.no.O.P.2148; Anzelewsky, *Dürer*, pl.95), especially in the *Head of an angel*, signed and dated *1506*, in the Albertina (inv.no.3099; Winkler, *Dürer*, ii, pl.385). No doubt because Dürer has used the silverpoint here he has been more generous with the brush in defining the features. This technical difference is not an adequate reason for denying Dürer's authorship, as both the Tietzes and Panofsky do.

The resemblance of the features to those of Dürer's wife, Agnes, is not close enough for one to be sure that the drawing is of her.

57 Head of a boy, inclined to the left

Silverpoint, heightened with white bodycolour on grey prepared ground. 27.2 × 21.4 cm

PROVENANCE: Sloane bequest, 1753

5218-41

LITERATURE: Waagen, *Treasures*, i, p.230, no.41; Hausmann, *Naumann's Archiv*, p.108, no.41; Conway, p.18, no.258; BM *Guide*, 1928, p.24, no.231; Flechsig, *Dürer*, ii, p.326; Winkler, *Dürer*, ii, p.14, no.284, repr.; Nuremberg, *Dürer*, 1971, p.58, no.88, repr.; Rowlands, *Dürer*, p.22, no.125; Anzelewsky, *Dürer*, p.181, under no.78; J.Rowlands, *MD*, x, 1972, p.383; Strauss, i, p.438, no.1497/5, repr. (for further literature)

Most scholars have had difficulty in deciding the possible date of this unfinished drawing, and have quite reasonably been cautious and attempted only to give a general indication of one. Flechsig considered that it most probably belonged to either the last decade of the fifteenth or the beginning of the sixteenth century. Winkler proposed dating it *c*.1503-5, but the style suggests to me that it was done during or just after the second visit to Italy. The refinement of execution would be consistent with this later

56

date, even though there is no other silverpoint drawing that one can date with certainty in the same period. The *Head of a woman* (no.56) is an isolated instance which may possibly be datable *c.*1506.

There is a certain similarity between the boy in this drawing and the study, *Head of the twelve-year-old Christ* in the Albertina (inv.no.3106; Winkler, *Dürer*, ii, pl.404), for the painting, *Christ among the Doctors*, dated *1506*, and proudly inscribed by Dürer, *opus quinque dierum* (the work of five days), now in the Thyssen-Bornemisza Collection, Lugano (inv.no.90; Anzelewsky, *Dürer*, pl.117). This connection was kindly pointed out to me by Anzelewsky (letter of June 1973), who thought it such a close similarity that he wondered whether the present drawing might not be a 'starting point' for the drawing in Vienna. Anzelewsky had earlier linked no.57 with the small painting on canvas, *Head of a Boy, inclined to the right*, one of a pair of heads of boys now in the Bibliothèque Nationale, Paris (inv.no.6(B13 rés.); Anzelewsky, *Dürer*, pl.87. He indicated a date of *c.*1503–5, in which he was evidently following Winkler's view, although he also commented favourably on the Tietzes' comparison of the paintings in Paris with a head in the background of the painting in Lugano, evidently the one behind and to the left of that of Christ.

The Mature Painter and Imperial Service, 1507–18

58 Portrait of Conrad Merkel

Charcoal. 29.4 × 21.6cm

PROVENANCE: Sloane bequest, 1753

5218–27

LITERATURE: Hausmann, *Naumann's Archiv*, p.36, no.27; Hausmann, p.107, no.27; *Dürer Society*, v, 1902, p.9, no.x, repr.; A.Weixlgärtner, *Mitt. Kunst.*, 1903, p.78, repr.; Conway, p.18, no.251; BM *Guide*, 1928, p.23, no.222; Winkler, *Dürer*, ii, pp.110f., no.429, repr.; Panofsky, ii, p.108, no.1043, repr.; Rupprich, i, p.206, no.34; Manchester, *German Art*, p.49, no.120; V.Oberhammer, *Pantheon*, xxiv, 1966, p.154, repr.; Rowlands, *Dürer*, p.24, no.130; BM *Portrait Drawings*, pp.10f., no.21, repr.; Strauss, ii, p.1064, no.1508/25, repr. (for further literature)

Inscribed in charcoal by the artist across the top of the drawing *hÿe Conrat Verkell altag 1508* with his monogram in a later hand

Dodgson proposed that the inscribed date may originally have been 1503, and that it was later changed to 1508. There seems to be no pressing stylistic evidence to support this. He did, however, consider the interesting possibility that the sitter might be the painter, Conrad Merkel (or Merklin; d.1518) of Ulm, only to reject the idea because it was impossible to read the first letter of his surname as 'M'. However, it is known from a note of Dürer's attached to a poem of his, dated 1510 (Rupprich, i, pp.132–3), that Conrad Merkel was a good friend of his. The verses he

sent were in answer to a light-hearted letter from Merkel, who pretended that he had an obsession which the learned men of Ulm could not cure. He said that, as Dürer was a clever man, he had no doubt that he could eradicate his fantasy. The witticism concerned a play on words, which Dürer takes up in his reply. Panofsky has ingeniously proposed that this type of humour is to be found in the drawing's inscription, which he translates as, *Here* (i.e. *with me) it's always Conrad Hog*. By changing Merkel to Verkell (i.e. *Ferkel*: piglet) Dürer has made a pun on the surname which matches perfectly the grotesque facial appearance he has drawn in the portrait.

A misleading reference in Thieme-Becker (xxiv, p.417), led Rupprich to state that in the Berlin Print Room there is a portrait drawing by the Master BB, erroneously identified as Conrad Merkel. The drawing in fact, is a doubleportrait, dated *1512*, of Jacob Mercklin von Ulm and of Jörig Koch von Basel (inv.no.KDZ335; Bock, *Berlin*, ii, pl.98). This Jacob may well be a relative of Conrad's and a painter, for Conrad and a Jacob Merkel are listed in the *Bruderschaftbuch* of Kloster Wengen as 'pictor noster'.

59 Study for the tomb of a knight and his lady

Pen and brown ink. 25.9 × 17.9cm

PROVENANCE: General John Guise bequest, 1765

Oxford, Christ Church, 1109

LITERATURE: Bell, p.42, pl.xxxi; Winkler, *Dürer*, ii, pp.148f., no.489, repr.; Tietze, ii, pp.154f., no.w.75, repr.; Nuremberg, *Dürer*, 1971, p.381, no.704, repr.; Strauss, iii, p.1232, no.1510/16, repr. (for further literature); Byam Shaw, i, p.344, no.1422, ii, pl.389

As Byam Shaw and others have pointed out, this finely executed drawing cannot be later in date than 1510, as the female figure reappears as the servant behind Salome in the woodcut dated that year, of the *Beheading of St John the Baptist* (Bartsch, vii, pp.142ff., no.125). It is now generally accepted that the drawing is not only the best of three versions, but also the original executed by Dürer. The Tietzes' reservations about it, which caused them to grade it as a studio work, is not in keeping with its excellence. The other drawings are two early copies, each with false Dürer monograms and the date *1517* (Berlin-Dahlem, Kupferstichkabinett, inv.no.KDZ 27; Lippmann, i, pl.48; Florence, Uffizi; Winkler, *Dürer*, ii, appendix pl.xxv).

This drawing was used for two different epitaphs which were cast in bronze in the Vischer foundry in Nuremberg (see nos.110–11): for Count Hermann VIII von Henneberg (d.1535) and his wife, Elisabeth von Brandenburg (d.1507) in the town church at Römhild (Meller, *Vischer*, p.134, fig.70) and for Count Eitel Friedrich II von Hohenzollern (d.1512) and his wife, Magdalena von Brandenburg (d.1496) in the Collegiate church at Hechingen, near Tübingen (Byam Shaw, i, fig.110). Of the two, the epitaph

58

59

60

at Römhild has fewer differences from Dürer's sketch than that at Hechingen; the former has been attributed to the so-called Arthur Master, who was responsible for the figures of the Kings Arthur and Theoderich, on Emperor Maximilian's tomb in the Hofkirche at Innsbruck.

60 Christ on the Cross and a portrait head, with a slight drapery study

Pen and brown ink, with the drapery study in black chalk. 28 × 20.5 cm

WM: trident with a small circle

PROVENANCE: Sloane bequest, 1753

5218–116

LITERATURE: Hausmann, *Naumann's Archiv*, p.39, no.116; Hausmann, p.110, no.98; Conway, p.29, no.491; Pauli, p.23, no.592; BM *Guide*, 1928, p.24, no.232; Winkler, *Dürer*, iii, p.48, no.588, repr.; Rowlands, *Dürer*, p.26, no.154; Strauss, iii, p.1280, no.1511/14, repr. (for further literature)

Inscribed by the artist in brown ink above the man's head, *her Jorg vo[n] eblingn*, and to the right of Christ, *1511*, with below the artist's monogram

The Christ on the Cross is a preliminary sketch for the figure in the engraving, also dated *1511*, *Christ on the Cross* (small plate) in the engraved Passion (Dodgson, *Dürer Engr.*, p.71, no.53, repr.). Nothing is known of the sitter, Herr Jorg von Eblingen.

61 *Recto:* Christ among the Doctors in the Temple

Verso: St Jerome kneeling in Penitence

Pen and brown ink. 9.8 × 9.3 cm

WM: flower on a stem, part of an unidentifiable mark

PROVENANCE: Sloane bequest, 1753

5218–61

LITERATURE: Hausmann, *Naumann's Archiv*, p.37, no.61; Hausmann, p.108, no.57; Ephrussi, p.96, n.3; Conway, p.27, no.450, *verso*; BM *Guide*, 1928, p.26, no.251; Flechsig, *Dürer*, ii, p.439; Tietze, i, p.128, no.A.139, repr.; Winkler, *Dürer*, i, pp.132f., no.195 repr., appendix, pl.XVIII; Panofsky, ii, p.66, no.551; Rowlands, *Dürer*, p.26, no.155; Strauss, ii, p.1092, nos.1509/11 and 12, repr. (for further literature)

61r

61v

Inscribed by a later hand in brown ink on the lower edge with Dürer's monogram, and to its left, perhaps by another hand, *EH*

On the *recto* is a sketch possibly for a woodcut considered for the *Little Passion* series (Kurth, pls.222–58), but not executed. The subject of *Christ among the Doctors* had already occurred among the prints for the *Life of the Virgin* of *c*.1504–5 (Kurth, pl.189). Winkler connected the drawing with this woodcut, placing it in the years *c*.1500–2. Flechsig, unconvinced by Winkler, went on to reject Dürer's authorship, as did also the Tietzes and Panofsky.

They, however, failed to notice that the present drawing is of about the same size as the woodcuts of the *Little Passion*, and that in the general arrangement of its figures is strongly reminiscent of another woodcut in the series, *Christ before Pilate* (Kurth, pl.237). The large dominant figure of a doctor in the left foreground of our drawing has strong affinities with that in the right foreground of the woodcut. In the preparatory drawing for that print this figure would have also been on the left. Possibly these similarities may have been partly responsible for Dürer's abandonment of the subject of *Christ among the Doctors* in the *Little Passion*, in which it would have come after the *Nativity*. Alternatively, after the supposed abandonment of *Christ among the Doctors*, Dürer may have decided to adapt the design for use as *Christ before Pilate*. If one accepts this connection, there is no objection on stylistic grounds to dating the sketch *c*.1509, when it would have been executed with this series in mind.

The rudimentary drawing on the *verso* is probably just a slight note made by Dürer himself.

62 A bird

See colour plate section following p.80

Pen and brown ink with blue, green, yellow, pink, grey and brown wash. 45 × 32.7cm

PROVENANCE: Sloane bequest, 1753

5218–84

LITERATURE: Hausmann, *Naumann's Archiv*, p.38, no.84; Hausmann, p.109, no.78; BM *Guide*, 1928, p.24, no.227; Winkler, *Dürer*, iii, p.102, no.702, repr.; Rowlands, *Dürer*, p.30, no.182; Strauss, iii, p.1372, no.1513/25 repr. (for further literature)

Inscribed by the artist, in brown ink, on a scroll above the bird's head, *GI GI GIG* (presumably its cry), and at the foot of the drawing, *1513*.

Like the companion drawing, *An emblem with a lion*, inscribed with the motto, *FORTES FORTUNA IUVAT* and also dated *1513*, in Berlin-Dahlem (Kupferstichkabinett, inv.no.KDZ. 1269; Winkler, *Dürer*, iii, pl.703) no.62 was probably intended as a design for a device to be used by a jouster at a tournament. Winkler's suggestion that they were for glass-paintings is less convincing in view of their subjects, as well as the type of design which, if for a glass-painting, would be unusual on such a scale. In this period, it was fashionable for jousting contestants to compete under the guise of emblems rather than coats-of-arms. Thus they emphasised the elements of courtly make-believe at jousts, which had increased the more unrelated the sport had become to methods of warfare.

The finished and tinted state of these two designs indicates that they were probably intended to be shown to clients

63a

63b

1928, p.24, no.228; Flechsig, *Dürer*, ii, p.325; Tietze, iii, p.121, no.A.345, repr.; Winkler, *Dürer*, iii, p.66, no.627, repr.; Panofsky, ii, p.91, no.884; Rowlands, *Dürer*, p.31, no.197; Strauss, vi, p.3060, no.xw.627, repr. (for further literature)

for approval. Dürer would then have either painted the emblems himself, or given the designs to a mutually agreed painter, perhaps a specialist, to complete the work for him.

63(a) Two women and a man making music

Pen and brown ink. 18.6 × 9.8cm

PROVENANCE: Sloane bequest, 1753

5218–131

LITERATURE: Waagen, *Treasures*, i, p.230, no.131; Hausmann, *Naumann's Archiv*, p.39, no.131; Hausmann, p.110, no.107; Ephrussi, pp.44, 47; W.v.Seidlitz, *Repertorium*, vi, 1883, p.205; M.J.Friedländer, *Prussian Jahrbuch*, xvi, 1895, p.242; BM *Guide*,

This and no.63(b), are designs for the decoration of the two narrow ends of a casket, which could have been either of metal or wood. Although Winkler thought that the designs were done for a goldsmith, Kohlhaussen does not include them in his study of Dürer's drawings for gold and silver-ware.

The Tietzes and Panofsky, who denied Dürer's authorship on slender and unconvincing stylistic grounds, favoured instead either Hans von Kulmbach (q.v.) or Hans Baldung (q.v.). Other scholars have accepted them as by Dürer and, given the type of commission, such a rapid schematic execution is to be expected. It is difficult, however, to date them with any precision. Flechsig saw links with the linear style of drawing Dürer adopted to decorate the margins of the *Prayer Book of Emperor Maximilian*, dated *1515* (Munich, Staatsbibliothek; Strauss, iii, p.1478, ff., repr.), but he also thought a date of *c.*1520–1 might be possible. Winkler favoured the latter solution on the strength of a comparison with the three roundels on the design for a large wall decoration, dated *1521*, in the Pierpont Morgan Library, New York (inv.no.1,257; Winkler, *Dürer*, iv, pl.921). I am now inclined to agree with Winkler.

(b) Allegory of youth, age and death

Pen and brown ink. 18.7 × 9.9cm

WM: Star (? part of an Imperial orb)

PROVENANCE: Sloane bequest, 1753

5218–132

LITERATURE: Waagen, *Treasures*, i, p.230, no.132; Hausmann, *Naumann's Archiv*, p.39, no.132; Hausmann, p.110, no.108; Ephrussi, p.44; W.v.Seidlitz, *Repertorium*, vi, 1883, p.205; M.J.Friedländer, *Prussian Jahrbuch*, xvi, 1895, p.242; Conway, p.27, no.463(2); Pauli, p.28, no.772; BM *Guide*, 1928, p.24, no.229; Winkler, *Dürer*, iii, p.66, no.628, repr.; Rowlands, *Dürer*, p.31, no.198; Strauss, vi, p.3062, no. xw.628, repr. (for further literature)

See no.63(a).

64(a) Two ornamental designs for the foot of a monstrance

Pen and brown ink. 14.6 × 17.4cm

WM: part of a trident with a small circle

PROVENANCE: Sloane bequest, 1753

5218–142

LITERATURE: Waagen, *Treasures*, i, p.231, no.142; Hausmann, *Naumann's Archiv*, p.40, no.142; Hausmann, p.111, in error nos.117 to 121 (it should read no.118); Ephrussi, p.206; Thausing, ii, p.52; Conway, p.33, no.594; Pauli, p.29, no.814; Röttinger, *Doppelgänger*, p.7; BM *Guide*, 1928, p.26, no.246; Winkler, *Dürer*, iii, p.113, no.722, repr.; Rupprich, i, p.209, no.61; Fritz, *Gestochene Bilder*, pp.184ff., repr.; Kohlhaussen, pp.211–12, 229–30; Rowlands, *Dürer*, p.32, no.199; Strauss, iii, p.1686, no.1517/25, repr. (for further literature)

Inscribed by the artist in brown ink by the alternative head for the lady in the margin *Do mach welchsh/kopfle du wilt* 'make whichever head you like', and the artist's monogram has been added in brown ink by a later hand in the upper right-hand corner

As J.M.Fritz has pointed out, a comparison between the designs on this sheet and those on no.64(b), and late gothic masterpieces of Dürer's time, makes it clear from their shape that they were not intended for the decoration of spoons but for the engraving on the feet of monstrances.

They cannot have been for chalices, an idea advanced by Röttinger, because unlike monstrances all the sections of the foot on chalices are not oblong but of equal size.

The style of this and no.64(b) is consistent with the customary dating of *c.*1515 and the next few years, after Dürer's younger brother, Endres Dürer (1484–1555) had become a master goldsmith and with whom these and similar designs are usually, and probably rightly, associated.

(b) Three ornamental designs for the foot of a monstrance

Pen and brown ink. 14.3 × 17.6cm

PROVENANCE: Sloane bequest, 1753

5218–141

LITERATURE: Waagen, *Treasures*, i, p.231, no.141; Hausmann, *Naumann's Archiv*, p.40, no.141; Hausmann, p.111, no.117; Ephrussi, p.206; Thausing, ii, pp.51f.; Conway, p.33, no.594; Pauli, p.29, no.815; Röttinger, *Doppelgänger*, p.7; BM *Guide*, 1928, p.26, no.247; Winkler, *Dürer*, iii, pp.113f., no.723, repr.; Fritz, *Gestochene Bilder*, pp.184ff., repr.; Kohlhaussen, pp.211f.; Rowlands, *Dürer*, p.32, no.200; Strauss, iii, p.1686, no.1517/26, repr. (for further literature)

The artist's monogram has been added in brown ink by a later hand in the upper left-hand corner.

See no.64(a).

65 Rhinoceros

Pen and brown ink. 27.4 × 42cm

WM: trident with a small circle

PROVENANCE: Sloane bequest, 1753

5218–161

LITERATURE: Heller, p.48; Hausmann, *Naumann's Archiv*, p.33, no.1; Hausmann, p.106, no.1; Thausing, ii, pp.124f.; Conway, p.35, no.643; Pauli, p.26, no.725; BM *Guide*, 1928, p.24, no.230; Winkler, *Dürer*, iii, pp.64f., no.625, repr.; Rupprich, i, p.208, no.57; Rowlands, *Dürer*, p.33, no.211; T.H.Clarke, *Connoisseur*, clxxxiv, 1973, pp.3ff., repr.; Strauss, iii, p.1584, no.1515/57, repr. (for further literature); BM *Animals in Art*, pp.127f.; Clarke, *Rhinoceros*, pp.20, 181, no.1, repr.

Inscribed by the artist in brown ink along the upper edge, *RHINOCERON 1515* and along the lower edge, *Ite[m] in 153 jor adi i maÿ hat man unserm küng van portigall gen lisabona procht ein sold lebendig tir aws India das nent man Rhynocerate das hab ich dir von Wunders wegen müssen abkunterfet schicken hat ein farb wÿ ein/ krot vnd van dicken schaln überleg fast fest vnd ist in d[e]r gros als ein helffant aber njdrer vnd ist des helfantz tott feint es hat for[n] awff der nasen ein starck scharff hore[n] und so dz tir an helfant Kumt mit jm zw fechten so hat es for albeg sein/hore[n] an den steinen scharbff gewestzt vnd lauff dem helfant mit dem Kopff zwischen dy fordere[n] pein dan reist es den helfant awff wo er am düsten hawt hat vnd erwürgt jn also der helfant fürcht jn ser übell den Rhÿnocerate dan er erwürgt jn albeg wo er den*

64a

64b

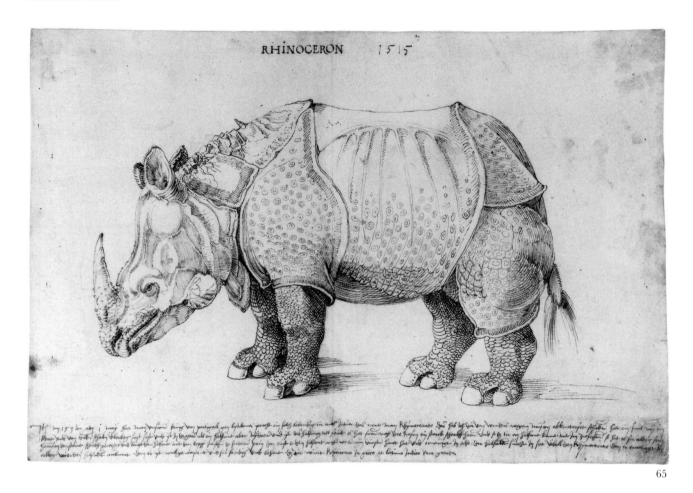

65

helfant aukumt dan er ist woll gewapent vnd ser freidig und behent D[a]z tir würt Rhinocero in greco et latino Indico vero gomda 'In the year 15[1]3 [this should read 1515] on 1 May was brought to our king of Portugal in Lisbon such a living animal from India called a Rhinocerate. Because it is such a marvel I considered that I must send this representation. It has the colour of a toad and is covered all over with thick scales, and in size is as large as an elephant, but lower, and is the deadly enemy of the elephant. It has on the front of the nose a strong sharp horn: and when this animal comes near the elephant to fight it always first whets its horn on the stones and runs at the elephant with its head between its forelegs. Then it rips the elephant where its skin is thinnest, and then gores it. The elephant is greatly afraid of the Rhinocerate; for he always gores it whenever he meets an elephant. For he is well armed, very lively and alert. The animal is called rhinocero in Greek and Latin but in Indian, gomda'

Dürer has evidently transcribed this account from what was probably a newsletter, sent to the artist with the drawing on which no.65 was based, either by a member of the German mercantile community in Lisbon, or, according to Clarke – who based his opinion on that of Donald F. Lach – by the Moravian printer active in Lisbon, Valentim Fernandes. The circumstances surrounding the arrival of the animal in Europe and its fate may be briefly stated (for a detailed account, see Clarke, op.cit, pp.16–23). This rhinoceros had been presented by the ruler of Gujarat,

Sultan Muzafar II to the governor of Portuguese India, Alfonso d'Albuquerque, who despatched it to King Manuel I in Lisbon, where it arrived on 20 May 1515. There it was stabled near the Casa du Mina e India. Later in the year, in order to further ingratiate himself with the Pope, Leo X (he had already sent him a famous elephant, Hanno, the previous year) the king sent the animal to Rome *via* Marseilles, where it was inspected by Francis I of France, and his Queen; however, it did not to reach the Pope alive, if at all. One account says the beast was drowned and lost at sea, while another states that its carcase was stuffed and delivered to Leo X.

It has been rightly said that Dürer's image, perpetuated by the woodcut that he produced based on the present drawing, which then passed through several editions into the following century, has had such a powerful effect on successive generations of artists, that even when in the eighteenth century people became aware of Dürer's inaccuracies they were reluctant to abandon his imaginative view of the animal for a fully accurate observation of it. Considering that Dürer never saw a rhinoceros face to face the drawing is an extraordinary feat.

66a

66b

66(a) Christ bearing the Cross

Pen and black ink on vellum. 13.8 × 10.4cm

PROVENANCE: Sloane bequest, 1753

5218–149

LITERATURE: Waagen, *Treasures*, i, p.231, no.149; Hausmann, *Naumann's Archiv*, p.40, no.149; Hausmann, p.111, no.128; Thausing, ii, p.154; Conway, p.35, under no.638; Pauli, p.28, no.764; BM *Guide*, 1928, p.26, no.257; Winkler, *Dürer*, iv, p.96, no.925, repr.; Rowlands, *Dürer*, pp.33f., no.216; Strauss, iv, p.2286, no.1525/7, repr. (for further literature)

Inscribed by the artist in red ink at the foot, *QVI NON TOLLIT CRVCEM/SVAM ET SEQVITVR ME/NON EST ME DIGNVS* (Matthew, x, 38); and above in the upper left-hand corner on a tablet with a gilded frame, by another hand *In libertatem voca/ti estis tantum/ne libertatem detis/in occasionem carni* (Galatians, v.13)

See no.66(b).

(b) A Christian bearing his cross

Pen and black ink on vellum. 13.7 × 10.4cm

PROVENANCE: Sloane bequest, 1753

5218–150

LITERATURE: Waagen, *Treasures*, i, p.231, no.150; Hausmann, *Naumann's Archiv*, p.40, no.150; Hausmann, p.111, no.129; Thausing, ii, p.154; Conway, p.35, under no.638; Pauli, p.28, no.765; BM *Guide*, 1928, p.27, no.258; Winkler, *Dürer*, iv, p.96, no.926, repr.; Rowlands, *Dürer*, p.34, no.217; Strauss, iv, p.2288, no.1525/8, repr. (for further literature)

Inscribed by the artist in red ink on a decorative scroll at the foot, *NAM SI AMBVLAVERO INMEDIO/VMBRE MORTIS NON TIME/BOMALA QVONIA[M] TV MECV[M] ES* (Psalm xxiii), and above, in the upper right-hand corner on a tablet with a gilded frame, probably by another hand, *Domine du quod/iubes et iu/be quod/vis* (cf. Thomas à Kempis, *De imitatione Christi* for similar expressions of devout humility, e.g. Liber Secundus, cap. xvi, 'Da quid vis, et quantum vis et qn vis' (*Opera*, Paris, 1523); certainly the present quotation is in the tradition of 'Devotio moderna' piety)

This and no.66(a) were obviously conceived as companions. It may be, as their styles, heraldic additions, and subjects suggest, that they were done for the man kneeling before a *prie-dieu* pictured in the drawing in the Schlossmuseum, Weimar (Winkler, *Dürer*, iv, pl.924), which is also on vellum and of a similar design and format. The identity of

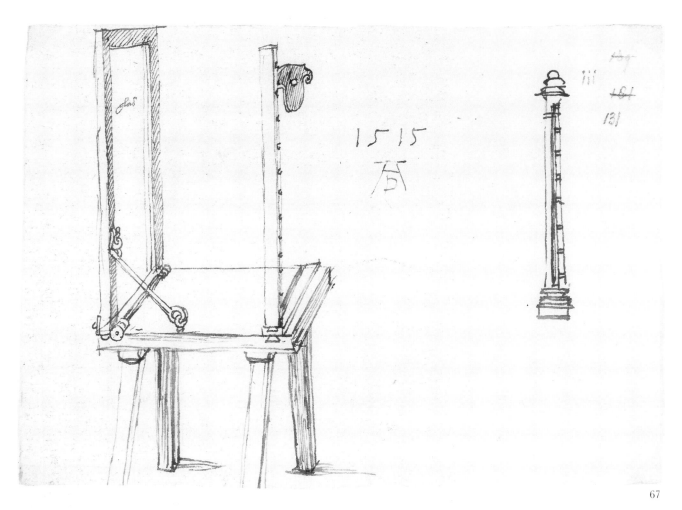

67

the holder of the coat-of-arms on this latter drawing has not been finally determined, but the same coat-of-arms, similarly tinctured, has been added to the present drawing by a hand other than Dürer's. It appears to be that of Lazarus Spengler (1479–1534), the town clerk of Nuremberg; although, as Dodgson has pointed out, the tinctures have been reversed.

67 Perspective apparatus

Pen and brown ink. 12.2 × 17.5 cm

PROVENANCE: Sloane bequest, 1753

British Library, Department of Manuscripts, Add. Ms. 5229, fol. 131 *recto*

LITERATURE: Rowlands, *Dürer*, p.45, no.290; Strauss, vi, p.2846, NO.A.S: 1515/1, repr. (for further literature)

Inscribed by the artist, in brown ink, in the centre of the sheet, *1515* with below, the artist's monogram; and within the frame, *glas* (glass)

This is a drawing of the apparatus that features in the woodcut of an *Artist drawing a seated man* (Dodgson, i, p.343, no.150) an illustration in the fourth book of Dürer's *Underweysung der Messung*, a treatise on the art of measurement that first appeared in 1525. Dürer writes of such an apparatus that is good for all those who wish to make a portrait, but who cannot trust their skill. An earlier design for the same apparatus, signed and dated *1514*, is in the album containing sketches by Dürer, chiefly preparatory drawings for his publication on the proportions of the human body in the Sächsische Landesbibliothek, Dresden (Ms.R-147) the so-called 'Dresden Sketchbook' (Bruck, pl.135).

68 Portrait of a man

Charcoal. The drawing has been cut down on all sides. 41.6 × 22.7 cm

WM: crossed arrows

PROVENANCE: Sloane bequest, 1753

5218–44

LITERATURE: Waagen, *Treasures*, i, p.230, no.44; Hausmann, *Naumann's Archiv*, p.35; Hausmann, p.106, no.8; Conway, p.37, no.668; Pauli, p.30, no.846; BM *Guide*, 1928, p.26, no.249; Winkler, *Dürer*, iii, p.31, no.564, repr.; Rowlands, *Dürer*, p.35,

68

no.230; BM *Portrait Drawings*, p.10, no.20; Strauss, iii, p.1636, no.1516/10, repr. (for further literature)

Inscribed by the artist in charcoal at the foot of the drawing *1516*, with below the artist's monogram which lacks the lower part. All this is inscribed below a horizontal line, a feature which the present drawing shares with the portrait supposedly of Conrad Peutinger of 1517 (Paris, Louvre, Cabinet Rothschild; Winkler, *Dürer*, iii, pl.566)

According to the late Ernst Otto, Graf zu Solms-Laubach, the sitter in this drawing is the founder of his line, Graf Otto zu Solms. This identification is based on a comparison with the medals of him by Hans Schwarz (active 1512–32) of 1518 and 1520 (see G.Habich, *Die Deutsche Schmaumünzen des XVI Jahrhunderts*; i, pt.i, Munich, 1929, no.141, pl.xxi.3. and no.194, pl.xxvi.4). Unfortunately the face of the sitter in each successive medal is obscured by a growing beard, which makes it difficult to be certain of this identification; however, what we can see of the features in Schwarz's medal does appear to have a similarity with those of the sitter in the present drawing.

69 *Recto:* The Virgin crowned by two angels

Verso: Head and shoulders of a man looking down

Pen and brown ink. 14.8 × 10cm

PROVENANCE: Malcolm (noted by Robinson in annotated copy of JCR, 'Bought from Colnaghi and Co; March 2, 1872; £25 -')

1895–9–15–981

LITERATURE: JCR, p.176, no.528*; Ephrussi, pp.192ff.; Conway, p.38, under no.709; BM *Guide*, 1928, p.45, no.427; Winkler, *Dürer*, iii, p.19, no.541, repr. *recto*, appendix, pl.iv *verso*; Rowlands, *Dürer*, p.37, no.240, repr. *recto*; Strauss, iii, p.1730, nos.1518/15 and 16, repr. (for further literature)

Inscribed by a later hand in brown ink, on the stone in the foreground, *1518*, with the artist's monogram

This is a carefully executed preparatory drawing for the engraving of the same subject (Dodgson, *Dürer Engr.*, p.114, no.87, repr.) dated *1518*, the first of a group of such designs for four engravings of the Virgin, produced in the years 1518–20. The others are the *Virgin suckling the Child* in the Albertina, Vienna (inv.no.3131 D.137; Winkler, *Dürer*, iii, pl.542) for the engraving, dated *1519* (Dodgson, *Dürer Engr.*, p.118, no.89, repr.); the *Virgin with the Child in swaddling clothes*, formerly in the Koenigs collection, Rotterdam (Winkler, *Dürer*, iii, pl.543) signed and dated *1520* (the latter in mirror image) for the engraving of the same year (Dodgson, *Dürer Engr.*, p.123, no.93, repr.); and the *Virgin crowned by an angel* (Winkler, *Dürer*, iii, pl.544) in Melbourne for the engraving of this subject (Dodgson, *Dürer Engr.*, p.124, no.94, repr.). The ex-Koenigs drawing is not as close to its corresponding engraving as the Albertina and the present design are to theirs; however, there was also in the Koenigs collection a drawing evidently

69r

by Dürer (Winkler, *Dürer*, iii, appendix pl.iv) of the outlines only, executed precisely as they are in the finished engraving (Dodgson, *Dürer Engr.*, 93) although in reverse. A pen study for the inclined head of the Virgin as it was adopted in the engraving in preference to the erect pose of the initial design (Winkler, *Dürer*, iii, pl.543) is in the Kunsthalle, Hamburg (Winkler, *Dürer*, iii, appendix pl.iv).

As Winkler has proposed, the slight sketch on the *verso* of the present drawing is also by Dürer.

70 Portrait of a man, supposedly Paul Hofhaimer

See colour plate section following p.80

Charcoal and brown chalk. 37 × 27.6cm

PROVENANCE: Sloane bequest, 1753

5218–52

LITERATURE: Waagen, *Treasures*, i, p.230, no.52; Hausmann, *Naumann's Archiv*, p.37, no.52; Hausmann, p.108, no.51; Ephrussi, p.258; B.Haendcke, *Zeitschr. f. christ. Kunst*, xi, 1898, p.158; F.Dörnhöffer, *Kunstgesch. Anz.*, 1904, no.2, p.58, n.1; C.Dodgson,

Burlington, vii, 1905, p.152, repr.; Conway, p.39, no.711; C.Dodgson, *Vasari Society*, vii, 1910–11, no.25; Pauli, p.39, no.1114; BM *Guide*, 1928, p.26, no.254; Winkler, *Dürer*, iii, pp.37f., no.573, repr.; Anzelewsky, *Dürer*, p.51; Rowlands, *Dürer*, p.38, no.245, repr.; BM *Portrait Drawings*, p.10, no.15; Strauss, iii, p.1738, no.1518/20, repr. (for further literature); Anzelewsky, pp.191, 198, repr.

Haendcke thought the sitter was Oswald Krell from a comparison with Dürer's portrait at Munich (Bayerische Staatsgemäldesammlungen, inv.no.WAF.230; Anzelewsky, *Dürer*, pl.58) but this did not gain acceptance. Dörnhöffer was the first to identify the sitter as Paul Hofhaimer (1459–1537), organist to the Emperor, on the basis of a comparison with the representation of a court organist, evidently Hofhaimer, who is depicted by Burgkmair (q.v.) in the *Triumphal Procession* of Maximilian I (Dodgson, ii, p.98, no.123), and by Hans Weiditz (q.v.) in his woodcut, *Maximilian I hearing mass* (Bartsch, vii, p.184, no.31). The identification of the organist as Hofhaimer in the former is confirmed by the description of the woodcut in the programme of the Triumph that Marx Treitzsaurwein, the Imperial Secretary, wrote under Maximilian's direction (Vienna, National-bibliothek, Cod. 2835; for an English translation, see S.Appelbaum, *The Triumph of Maximilian I*, New York, 1964, p.5, col.1). The musician in the second woodcut is recognisable as Hofhaimer by a comparison with Burgkmair's portrayal of him. At all events, the style of the present drawing does suggest that it could have been done in 1518 when Dürer was at Augsburg for the Reichstag, and when he would certainly have had the opportunity of meeting Hofhaimer.

Hofhaimer was highly favoured by Maximilian, who to secure the famous musician's attachment knighted and ennobled him in 1517 with the title 'obrister Organist' (first Organist). His playing technique was very influential through its dissemination by his many pupils. As Paracelsus said of him, 'was der Hofhaimer auf der Orgel, ist der Dürer auf der Malerei'. An up-to-date assessment of the significance of his work by Manfred Schuler is to be found in the *New Grove Dictionary of Music and Musicians*, edited by S.Sadie, viii, London, 1980, pp.631–3.

Anzelewsky suggested that the sitter might be Lazarus Spengler (1479–1534), the friend of Dürer and Pirck-heimer, who on more than one occasion represented Nuremberg at meetings of the Reichstag. The supporting evidence Anzelewsky has produced, however, is merely an inferior seventeenth-century print which too imprecisely records a lost portrait of Spengler (see Heller, p.248). Although there is no surviving contemporary likeness definitely known to be of Spengler, there is a small portrait drawing by Dürer in Weimar (Schlossmuseum; Winkler, *Dürer*, iv, pl.924) which may represent him (see no.66(b)), but the facial features of this figure are too sketchily drawn to bear comparison with the detailed portrayal of the individual seen in the present drawing.

The Journey to the Netherlands, 1520–1

71 Head of a woman

See colour plate section following p.80

Brush drawing in black and grey bodycolour, heightened with white bodycolour. 32.4 × 22.8cm

PROVENANCE: Sloane bequest, 1753

5218–43

LITERATURE: Hausmann, *Naumann's Archiv*, p.37, no.43; Hausmann, p.108, no.43; Conway, p.40, no.739; Pauli, p.36, no.1030; Veth & Muller, i, p.32, no.xviii, repr.; BM *Guide*, 1928, p.27, no.264; Winkler, *Dürer*, iii, p.39, no.576, repr.; Rowlands, *Dürer*, p.39, no.257; Strauss, iv, p.1912, no.1520/5, repr. (for further literature)

Inscribed by the artist with the brush in grey bodycolour in the upper right-hand corner, *1520* with below, the artist's monogram

Evidently, the same model had been used for a similar study dated *1519*, *Head of a woman* (Winkler, *Dürer*, iii, pl.575) formerly at Bremen, which, however, lacks the abundant use of bodycolour. There has been strong disagreement about whether the present drawing has been done from life or is the result of theoretical construction. In the British Museum Guide of 1928, Dodgson, following Justi, favoured the latter idea, while Winkler strongly rejected it. By this date the artist had become so engrossed in the detailed study of the proper proportion of the human body, that this inevitably affected all his output. The aim of these theoretical studies was after all to achieve through practical means an 'elixir' of just proportions. It would be preferable to see this as a formal drawing with its sitter, although sapped of character, represented with such refinement as to make it difficult to decide whether it was at least initially a work done after nature, as it seems was the case with the related study, formerly at Bremen. It might possibly have been done on Dürer's journey to or stay in the Netherlands, and one can point to a similarity between the features of the sitter in no.71 and those of the young woman on the silverpoint sheet in Bremen (Kunsthalle; Winkler, *Dürer*, iv, pl.782) who has been indentified by Veth and Muller, without any degree of certainty, with Zoetje, the daughter of Tommaso Bombelli, the Genoese silk merchant in Antwerp. The Bombelli are much referred to by Dürer in his diary, and were evidently most friendly to the artist during his stay.

72

72 The Münster at Aachen

Silverpoint on pinkish prepared paper. 12.6 × 17.4 cm

PROVENANCE: J.D.Böhm (sale, Vienna, A.Posonyi, 1865, 4 December and following days, lot 1135); A.Grahl (L.1199; sale, Sotheby, 1885, 27 April, lot 82, bt *Thibaudeau £290*); Malcolm

1895-9-15-982

LITERATURE: Ephrussi, pp.284f.; Conway, p.42, no.768; Pauli, p.34, no.1006; Veth & Muller, i, p.24, no.III, repr.; BM *Guide*, 1928, p.27, no.267; Schilling, *Sketchbook*, p.20, repr.; Winkler, *Dürer*, iv, p.15, no.763, repr.; Rotterdam, *Erasmus*, i, no.278; Rowlands, *Dürer*, p.40, no.263; Goris & Marlier, pp.70, 182, no.2, repr.; Strauss, iv, p.1946, no.1520/22, repr. (for further literature)

Inscribed by the artist, in silverpoint, in the upper right-hand corner, *zu ach das münstr*; and on the *verso* by a later hand, in pencil, in the lower left-hand corner, *Böhm*

Although described as anonymous Italian *c.*1500 in Posonyi's sale catalogue, it was always thereafter recognised as a sheet from Dürer's silverpoint sketchbook, used on his trip to the Netherlands in 1520 and the following year, which is referred to by the artist in the diary he kept then as *mein büchlein*. From the diary we know that he was at Aachen between 10 and 23 October 1520, and he specifically mentions visiting the Münster. Charles V was crowned there on the last day of Dürer's stay in the city. Dürer evidently took this view from the town hall, which he also drew on another sheet of the silverpoint sketchbook, now in the Musée Condé, Chantilly (Winkler, *Dürer*, iv, pl.764).

73 *Recto:* A dog resting

Verso: Studies of two women

Silverpoint on prepared paper. Trimmed on all sides. 12.8 × 18 cm

PROVENANCE: Baron D.Vivant Denon (L.779); W.Beckford; Smith

1848-11-25-3

LITERATURE: Pérignon, *Description*, p.161, no.622; Waagen, *Treasures*, i, p.235; Hausmann, *Naumann's Archiv*, pp.34-5; Hausmann, p.106, no.5; Thausing, ii, p.184; Ephrussi, pp.283f.; Conway, p.42, nos.765 and 766; BM *Guide* 1928, p.27, no.266;

73r

73v

Schilling, *Sketchbook*, p.21, repr.; Winkler, *Dürer*, iv, pp.16f., nos.767 and 766, repr.; F.Grossman, *Warburg Journal*, xiii, 1950, pp.234f., repr.; Rowlands, *Dürer*, p.40, no.264; Goris & Marlier, p.182, nos.5 and 6, repr.; Strauss, iv, pp.1948ff., nos.1520/23 and 24, repr. (for further literature)

Inscribed by the artist in silverpoint in the upper right-hand corner, *zw ach gemacht* (done at Aachen), with below the monogram

As the inscription indicates, this most sensitive sketch of a dog was made during Dürer's stay at Aachen, in October 1520. He made in the following year at Antwerp another drawing, of the same type of dog, in the silverpoint sketchbook (Berlin-Dahlem, KDz 34, *verso*; Winkler, *Dürer*, iv, pl.777). Both drawings were in the collection of Baron Vivant Denon at the beginning of the nineteenth century.

Of the two female figures on the *verso*, that of a young woman (left) is taken from a brass statuette, one of those which formerly decorated the sides of the tomb of the Duchess Isabella of Bourbon (d.1465), the first wife of Charles the Bold, Duke of Burgundy. Her tomb was constructed either in 1476, or 1478, in the Abbey Church of St Michel, Antwerp. It was formerly thought that Dürer had copied the figure from the tomb of Joan of Brabant, then in the Carmelite Church in Brussels. Although the church and tomb in Antwerp were destroyed in the eighteenth century, we know of the latter's appearance from the effigy of Isabella preserved in Antwerp Cathedral, from drawings made before the tomb's destruction, and from the ten statuettes in the Rijksmuseum, Amsterdam, thought to have come from this tomb (see Müller, pp.61f., pls.106, 107A–C). These figures were copied from those on the tombs of Louis de Mâle in Lille, and of Joan of Brabant in Brussels, which had been commissioned by the Duke of Burgundy, Philip the Good, in the middle to late 1440s. They were, however, produced in reverse positions from those on the earlier tombs, the people represented were changed and details of their dress and poses were somewhat modified.

The right-hand figure on the *verso* appears again in a pen and ink sketch, most probably on a sheet from such a sketchbook used by Dürer on his journey to the Netherlands (Winkler, *Dürer*, iv, pl.751). This is in the Biblioteca Ambrosiana, Milan (inv.no.F264 inf.5) and is inscribed by the artist, *ein türgin* (a Turkish woman) or, as Erica Tietze interpreted, *ein bürgin* (a woman from the Austrian province of Burgenland). Albrecht Altdorfer (q.v.) drew a woman with the same kind of headdress in the margin of the Emperor Maximilian's *Prayer Book* as part of the decoration, which was chiefly done by Dürer in 1515 (Besançon, Bibliothèque Nationale; Winzinger, *Altdorfer*, pl.88). No basis is known for Dürer's identification of the woman as a Turk, and research by Ursula Mende (*Kunstgeschichtliche Aufsätze von seinen Schülern und Freunden . . . des K.H.Ladendorf*, Cologne, 1969, pp.24–40) has established that such a costume was worn during this period by women in Bohemia, Silesia, and some parts of Austria. This indicates that Conrat's interpretation of Dürer's inscription is probably

the correct one. The headdress is also seen in Dürer's engraving, *The Crucifixion in outline* (Dodgson, *Dürer Engr.*, pl.107). As earlier in his career, Dürer was much interested in recording costumes, in addition to dressing well himself. While in Antwerp, a centre of international trade, he also made drawings of Irish men and Lithuanian women.

74 Head of a walrus

Pen and brown ink with watercolour. 21.1 × 31.2cm

PROVENANCE: Sloane bequest, 1753

5261–167

LITERATURE: Conway, p.42, no.776; Pauli, p.39, no.1104; Veth & Muller, i, p.37, no.xxxvii, repr.; BM *Guide*, 1928, p.28, no.275; Flechsig, *Dürer*, ii, pp.234, 250; Winkler, *Dürer*, iv, p.42, no.823, repr.; Rupprich, i, p.209, no.69; Rowlands, *Dürer*, pp.40f., no.266; Goris & Marlier, p.186, no.73, repr.; Strauss, iv, p.2048, no.1521/27, repr. (for further literature); BM *Animals in Art*, p.128, no.174, repr.

Inscribed by the artist in brown ink in the upper left-hand corner, *1521/Das dosig thÿr van dem jch do das hawbt/contrefett hab ist gefangen worden/jn die niderlendischen see vnd/was XII ellen lang/brawendisch mit fŭr fussen*, followed by his monogram; and by a later hand, in pencil, in the lower left-hand corner, (?) *Fricheohus I.*

This inscription, added subsequently by the artist, may be translated as '1521 that stupid animal of which I have portrayed the head was caught in the Netherlands sea and was twelve brabant ells long with four feet'

Although the inscription is dated *1521* this study after nature was evidently done on his visit to Zeeland in December 1520, where he had gone partly in the hope of seeing a stranded whale of 'more than a hundred fathoms long' (Goris & Marlier p.76). Dürer, like so many of his contemporaries, was thoroughly fascinated by the strange and exotic in nature. In the event, by the time Dürer had reached Ziericzee where he hoped to see the whale, its carcase had floated off with the tide. So Dürer had to content himself with this walrus, not, however, mentioned by him in his diary, which was subsequently used in 1522 as the model for St Margaret's dragon, in one of his sketches now at Bayonne (Musée Bonnat, inv.no.1275/1504; Winkler, *Dürer*, iv, pl.855) for a *Sacra Conversazione* which was never painted.

75 Portrait of Christian II of Denmark

Charcoal. 39.9 × 28.7cm

WM: jug with a flower (close to Briquet, 12627)

PROVENANCE: Sloane bequest, 1753

5218–48

LITERATURE: Heller, pp.16f.; Hausmann, *Naumann's Archiv*, p.37, no.48; Hausmann, p.108, no.47; H.W.Singer, *Monatshefte*, iv,

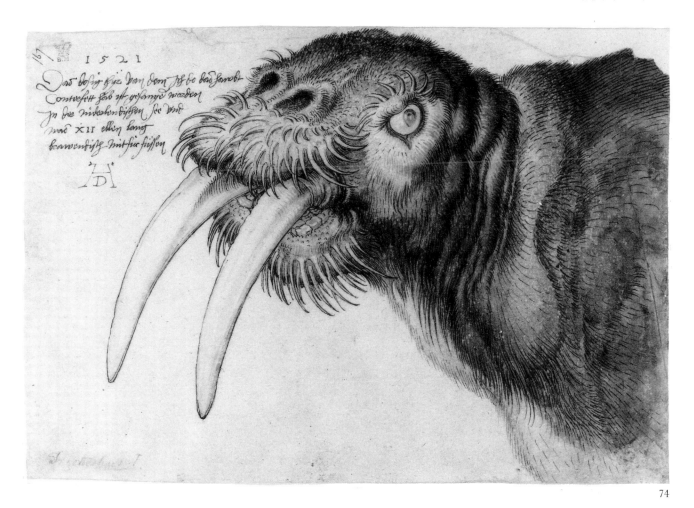

74

1911, p.415; BM *Guide*, 1928, p.28, no.279; Winkler, *Dürer*, iv, pp.37f., no.815, repr.; G.Glück, *Kunstmuseets Aarsskrift*, xxvii, 1940, pp.22ff.; Rowlands, *Dürer*, p.41, no.267; Anzelewsky, *Dürer*, pp.53, 264f.; Goris & Marlier, pp.99, 185, no.63, repr.; Nuremberg, *Dürer*, 1971, pp.292f., no.542; Strauss, iv, p.2058, no.1521/33, repr. (for further literature); E.Kai Sass, *Hafnia*, iv, 1976, pp.164ff., repr.; *Dürer aux Pays-Bas*, pp.77f., no.88, repr.; *Woodner Coll.*, 1987, p.148, n.3. Inscribed by the artist *1521*, with his monogram

At the end of Dürer's sixth and final stay in Antwerp, the artist records in his diary that on 2 July (1521) he was summoned by Christian II, King of Denmark, to do his portrait and he states, *Das thet ich mit dem kohln* (i.e. charcoal; Rupprich, i, p.176, col.2). He also did a portrait of Anton van Metz, the King's representative with the German Princes. Dürer also presented to the King 'choice things', i.e. prints, from his trunk to the value of five gulden. Having obviously made a good impression, he was commanded to accompany Christian II to Brussels, where he witnessed the King's formal reception by the Emperor Charles V, his brother-in-law, and Margaret of Austria, Regent of the Netherlands. There on 7 July Dürer executed the King's portrait in oils for which he received thirty gulden. This latter work has apparently not survived – certainly it cannot be recognised amongst the portraits that remain.

But the charcoal drawing of the King has been identified with the present one, an idea first proposed by Singer in 1911. There have subsequently been some dissenting voices, led by Gustav Glück; however, Kai Sass has disposed of these objections very convincingly. The first concerned the King being represented without the Order of the Golden Fleece, which according to the rules he was obliged to wear. In fact, Christian II had just been travelling *incognito* across many miles of enemy territory, and furthermore, the drawing would have been primarily done to establish the features of the sitter, which agree more than tolerably well with the succession of surviving portraits of the King by various artists in different media from 1515 onwards. These include works by Michel Sittow (*c.*1469–1525) Lucas Cranach the Elder (q.v.) and the circle of Quentin Massys (*c.*1466–1530). According to the second objection, Dürer fails to give in this drawing any sense of a regal presence, and the sitter's headgear would not have been worn by a king. This can easily be laid to rest as Christian II appears in several portraits wearing such a cap. In any case, in the days immediately following the execution of this drawing, a considerable sum was spent in purchasing suitably sumptuous attire for the King's reception by the Emperor, made necessary through his

75

sudden departure from the Danish Court and his secret journey. This is confirmed by an independent witness, referred to by Kai Sass, the Venetian Ambassador, Gasparo Contarini, who states in his description of the event, sent to the *Signoria* in Venice, that Christian II was wearing a cap of black silk. Finally, I think one can say that of all the surviving portraits of the King, this is the one in which the scheming, cunning nature of the sitter has been captured most successfully. Other artists tended to represent Christian II in too extrovert a manner. Only Dürer has portrayed someone whom one could readily imagine had perpetrated that extraordinary act of treachery in the previous year, the 'Stockholm Massacre', when the Swedish nobility were invited to a banquet and all slaughtered at the table.

76 Portrait of a man

Charcoal. Repairs below sitter's right temple and below his right shoulder; made up in the upper right-hand corner and along the lower edge. Trimmed on all sides. 36.9 × 25.4 cm

WM: Gothic P surmounted by a stem, on which there would have been a flower which is now obliterated (very close in form to Briquet, 8536, but this has no stem with a flower; the upper part of the letter is close to Briquet, 8622, 8633-4, 8638, all with flowers on stems. The feet of the letter in these cases are different)

PROVENANCE: V. Röver (as the so-called self-portrait of Lucas van Leyden, according to information kindly supplied by J.G. van Gelder); ? J. Goll van Frankenstein (sale, Amsterdam, Vries, Brondgeest, Engelberts and Roos, 1833, 1 July and following days, Kunstboek AA., no.12); Earl of Warwick (L.2600; sale, Christie, 1896, 20 May, lot 115, bt *Salting £430*); George Salting bequest, 1910

1910-2-12-103

LITERATURE: BFAC, 1869, p.22, no.184; Pauli, p.39, no.1108; BM *Guide*, 1928, p.28, no.271; Flechsig, *Dürer*, ii, pp.237; Winkler, *Dürer*, iv, p.35, no.809, repr.; Rowlands, *Dürer*, p.41, no.269; Goris & Marlier, p.185, no.60, repr.; BM *Portrait Drawings*, p.10, no.17; Strauss, iv, p.2052, no.1521/30, repr. (for further literature)

Inscribed by a later hand, in brown ink, in the lower left-hand corner, *15/25* with a false Lucas van Leyden monogram, and *Effigie[s] Luca Leidensis*. This partly obliterates Dürer's monogram and *1521* in charcoal, neither of which are likely to have been inscribed by the artist

For a long time the sitter was thought to be the well-known Dutch artist, Lucas van Leyden (? 1494-1533) whom Dürer met in Antwerp in 1521. This clearly cannot be the case, since one has only to compare it, for instance, with Dürer's portrait drawing of him now in Lille (Musée des Beaux-Arts, inv. no. PI.918, Winkler, *Dürer* iv, pl.816) to see the difference in the features of the two sitters. The mistaken identity goes back at least to a seventeenth-century etching, made after a design based on the present drawing and much reduced in scale, which Bartsch classified as a print by Lucas van Leyden (Bartsch, vii, p.433, no.173). This print has a false monogram and the date *1525*, and is

inscribed, *Effigies lucae Leidensis. Propria manu incidere.* The error is repeated in the engraved portrait of Lucas van Leyden by Philipp Kilian (1628-93) after Joachim von Sandrart (Sandrart, *Teutsche Academie*, p.93, repr.) which was probably based on the etching rather than the present drawing. Winkler's dating of this drawing to 1521 and proposal that it was done in the Netherlands seem quite credible. Flechsig's doubts about this seem to me unnecessary, as the execution is closely associated to that of portrait drawings certainly drawn there at this date. The drawing has evidently been cut down all round, as Dürer's portrait drawings of the period are usually done within a large margin on which he usually put the date, which explains its absence here.

77 St Christopher

Pen and black ink, heightened with white bodycolour, on dark grey prepared paper. 18.6 × 14 cm

PROVENANCE: Sloane bequest, 1753

5218-178

LITERATURE: Waagen, *Treasures*, i, pp.232-3, no.178; BM *Guide*, 1928, p.27, no.265; C. Dodgson, *OMD*, iii, no.9, 1928, p.11, repr.; Flechsig, *Dürer*, ii, p.466; Tietze, iii, pp.128f., no.A377, repr.; Winkler, *Dürer*, iv, pp.30f., no.801, repr.; Panofsky, ii,

77

p.85, no.802; Rowlands, *Dürer*, p.41, no.271; Goris & Marlier, p.184, no.48, repr.; Strauss, iv, p.2026, no.1521/15, repr. (for further literature)

This was first noted by Waagen as a drawing of Dürer's 'later period' because of the 'free motif' of the Infant Christ and the 'full forms' of the saint. Subsequently, on the strength of Parker's suggestion and supported by Winkler, Dodgson, in the British Museum exhibition catalogue of 1928, rescued it from a mistaken attribution to Baldung to which, however, Flechsig later adhered.

It seems very likely, both from the style and the use of a characteristically Flemish ground, that no.77 was done during Dürer's stay in the Netherlands, and presumably was conceived in connection with his two engravings of St Christopher, both dated *1521* (Dodgson, *Dürer Engr.*, pp.125f., nos.95 and 96, repr.). A related sheet, with nine pen and ink studies of St Christopher, also dated *1521*, in Berlin-Dahlem (Kupferstichkabinett, inv.no.KDZ4477; Winkler, *Dürer*, iv, pl.800) was thought by Panofsky to have been produced in connection with four drawings of St Christopher, heightened with white on grey paper, which Dürer recorded as making for Joachim Patinir (d.c.1524), 'der gut landschafft mahler' in May 1521 (Rupprich, i, p.172, col.1). This may be possible, but they could also have been drawn in preparation for the engravings. It is also conceivable, however, that the present drawing might be one of the St Christophers given to Patinir. Certainly the rejection of the attribution of this drawing to Dürer by the Tietzes, which later found support from Panofsky, has nothing to recommend it, given the high quality of the draughtsmanship.

78 Head of a man

Leadpoint, heightened with white bodycolour, on dark grey prepared paper. 28.4 × 21.1 cm

PROVENANCE: Sloane bequest, 1753

5218–42

LITERATURE: Hausmann, *Naumann's Archiv*, p.36, no.42; Hausmann, p.108, no.42; Ephrussi, p.337; Conway, p.44, no.811; Pauli, p.37, no.1064; BM *Guide*, p.28, no.268; Winkler, *Dürer*, iv, p.52, no.848, repr.; Rowlands, *Dürer*, p.43, no.276; Strauss, iv, p.2172, no.1521/95, repr. (for further literature)

Inscribed by the artist in leadpoint, in the upper right-hand corner, *152[?1]* with below, his monogram

This study is evidently for the head of St Joseph, who was included in a sketch now in Bayonne (Musée Bonnat, inv.no.1277/1505; Winkler, *Dürer*, iv, pl.839), probably the second of four extant, for the composition of a painting, which was never executed, of the Virgin and Child enthroned, surrounded by saints with attendant musician angels. The specific attitude of the head adopted in the present drawing is not evident in what appears to be an earlier sketch for the composition in the Louvre (inv.no. RF.1079, Winkler, *Dürer*, iv, pl.838), although the figure of

St Joseph is present and his name is inscribed by Dürer above his head. But St Joseph with his head inclined as here can be clearly seen in the drawing at Bayonne. St Joseph is subsequently excluded from the other two sketches, one of which is dated *1522* (Bayonne, Musée Bonnat, inv.nos.1275/1504 and 1277/1506; Winkler, *Dürer*, iv, pls.855, 856) which were rapidly done for upright and less crowded compositions. What are probably the earliest stages of Dürer's ideas for the composition are represented by two pen drawings, both dated *1521*, at Chantilly (Musée Condé; Winkler, *Dürer*, iv, pl.837) and in the Louvre (inv.no.19604; Winkler, *Dürer*, iv, appendix, pl.6), the second of which is clearly a copy after a lost original. Surprisingly both of them are worked out in considerable detail. In the first, in the left foreground, is the figure of an elderly bearded man leaning against a column, absorbed in reading a book, who could be either St Jerome or, more probably, St Joseph. This figure, however, is missing in the copy, but St Joseph occurs again bearded in the putative first sketch in the Louvre.

Similar studies of saints to the present one for the same composition are those of *St Apollonia* in Berlin-Dahlem (Kupferstichkabinett, inv.no.KDZ 1527; Winkler, *Dürer*, iv, pl.846), *St Barbara* in the Louvre (inv.no.18.590; Winkler, *Dürer*, iv, pl.845), and the *Female saint crowned with roses* (probably St Dorothy) in the Biblioteca Ambrosiana, Milan (inv.no.F264, inf.27; Winkler, *Dürer*, iv, pl.847), all signed and dated *1521*.

79(a) Two designs for the reverse of a projected medallion portrait of Dürer

Pen and brown ink. 15.3 × 9.4 cm

PROVENANCE: Sloane bequest, 1753

5218–67

LITERATURE: Hausmann, *Naumann's Archiv*, p.38, no.67; Hausmann, p.109, no.62; *Dürer Society*, xii, 1911, p.20, repr.; BM *Guide*, 1928, p.26, no.255; Winkler, *Dürer*, iii, pp.112f., no.720, repr.; Kohlhaussen, p.435, no.451; Rowlands, *Dürer*, pp.39f., no.260; Strauss, iii, p.1788, no.1519/17, repr. (for further literature)

Inscribed by the artist in brown ink in the upper design, *IMAGO/ ALBERTI·DVRER./ALEMANI: QVAM. SVIS/MET. IPSE. EFFINXIT M/ ANIBVS·ANNO·AETATIS/SVAE·XLVIII SALVTIS/VERO M.D./XIX*; and in the lower design, *IMAGO·/ALBERTI·DVRER·/ALEMANI·QVAM·SV/ ISMET.IPSE EFFINXIT*

These two alternative designs were undoubtedly done by Dürer for the reverse of a medal of himself, most probably the one he asked Hans Schwarz (c.1492–after 1532) to do. According to a note in Dürer's diary (Rupprich, i, p.157, col.2), he sent from Antwerp in September 1520 two gold guilders through the merchant bankers, the Fuggers, to Schwarz in Augsburg for his portrait ('für mein angesicht'); however, only the medallist's boxwood model for the obverse is known to have survived, and is now in the Herzog Anton Ulrich-Museum, Brunswick (see G. Habich, *Prussian Jahrbuch*, xxvii, 1906, pp.34f., 58, repr.). It is quite possible

78

79a

that Schwarz did not complete the commission. Another version of the text of the inscription is to be found among the autograph material in the Department of Manuscripts, British Library, (Sloane Ms.5229, fol.51 *recto*).

The Last Works, 1522–8

(b) *Recto:* The arms of Dürer
Verso: Musical tablature

Charcoal. 16.8 × 13.5 cm

PROVENANCE: Sloane bequest, 1753

5218–68

LITERATURE: Hausmann, *Naumann's Archiv*, p.38, no.68; Hausmann, p.109, no.63; Conway, p.47, no.868; Pauli, p.41, no.1158; BM *Guide*, 1928, p.26, no.256; Winkler, *Dürer*, iv, pp.101f.,

no.941, repr.; Rowlands, *Dürer*, p.40, no.261; Strauss, iv, p.2206, no.1523/1, repr. (for further literature) and vi, p.3187, appendix 6:4 *verso*, repr.; J.M.Massing and C.Meyer, *Zeitschr.f.Kunstgesch.*, xlv, 1982, p.254, *verso*, repr.

This is a rapid preparatory sketch in reverse for the woodcut, *The Arms of Albrecht Dürer*, signed and dated *1523* (Kurth, pl.327). Dürer's arms, consisting of an open door over three hillocks, was adopted from the arms of his father, which he painted on the back of his *Portrait of Albrecht Dürer the Elder* in the Uffizi, Florence (inv.no.1086; Anzelewsky, *Dürer*, pl.2). The family name was often spelt 'Thürer' (hence Tür, door) and Dürer's forbears came from a village in Hungary called Ajto, which is Hungarian for door. Even so, it is not impossible that the Dürer family was German in origin.

The supposed cypher written on the *verso* is, in fact, an academic musical exercise, a succession of eleven four-part chords without any indication of the rhythm which Massing and Meyer very plausibly consider to have been written by Dürer in organ tablature, a system of notation that signifies to the player what action he should perform. Certainly, the exercise, the work of an amateur, appeared to be like other examples elsewhere among Dürer's writings (Massing and Meyer, op.cit. pp.252–3) written in the artist's hand. The only difficulty seems to be that the kind of tablature apparently used by Dürer (the *New Grove Dictionary of Music and Musicians*, edited by S. Sadie, xviii, London, 1980, p.508, under Tablature 2. Keyboard iii) is of a type that only had currency from about 1570 onwards;

79b

however, the fact that Dürer has surely been writing exercises could explain this discrepancy, as the new system was a simple adaptation of the older one which was in use in Germany from about 1430 until about 1570.

80 Portrait of Henry Parker, Lord Morley

Leadpoint with traces of white bodycolour on green prepared paper. The sheet is creased and much rubbed. 37.8 × 30.5cm

PROVENANCE: General Count A.F.Andréossi; A.Firmin-Didot (sale, Paris, Danlos & Delisle, 1877, 16 April, lot 18); W.Mitchell (sale, Frankfurt, Prestel, 1890, 7 May, lot 29, bt *Deprez & Gutekunst 6650 RM* for the BM)

1890-5-12-155

LITERATURE: Ephrussi, pp.326ff.; Conway, p.46, no.855; Pauli, p.41, no.1151; BM *Guide*, 1928, p.28, no.280; Winkler, *Dürer*, iv, pp.83f., no.912, repr.; R.A., *British Portraits*, p.167, no.537; Rupprich, i, p.209, no.75; Rowlands, *Dürer*, pp.43f., no.282; Anzelewsky, *Dürer*, pp.86, 268, under no.171z, repr.; M.Levey, *Anz. Germ. Nat.*, 1971–2, pp.157, 163, n.8; J.Rowlands, *Zeitschr. f. Kunstgesch.*, xxxvi, 1973, pp.211f.; BM *Portrait Drawings*, p.10, no.16; Strauss, iv, p.2238, no.1523/17, repr. (for further literature)

Inscribed by the artist with leadpoint at the foot of the drawing, *heinrich morley aws engellant 1523* with below, the artist's monogram

This was drawn at Nuremberg, where Henry Parker (1476–1556) newly created on 15 April 1523 Lord Morley, had come on a Garter embassy to confer the Order on the Archduke Ferdinand. On 19 November Lord Morley wrote from Nuremberg to Cardinal Wolsey 'we [have waited] the space of one month and three days th[e coming] to Nuremberg of Domfurnando. Are assured that within six days of the date of th[is letter] he will be here, and will be met by most of the gre[at] princes of Almayn, to hold a great diet', (*Letters and Papers, Foreign and Domestic, of the reign of Henry VIII*, edited by J.S.Brewer, London, vol.iii, pt.2, 1867, p.1473, no.3546).

Evidently during the time of waiting Morley sat for this drawing, and also almost certainly had a painted portrait done by Dürer. For in the 1590 inventory of Lord Lumley's collection we find listed: 'Of the old Lo: Henry Morley, A°1523 done in watercolor by Albert Duer' (L.Cust, *Walpole Society*, vi, 1917–18, p.23). Its description suggests that this is not, as Cust implies, the present drawing, the provenance of which indicates that it would not have been in England at this date, but rather a painting executed in tempera on canvas, which is a medium very susceptible to damage from careless handling or neglect. A rare survival of such a portrait by Dürer, is that of Jakob Fugger now in Augsburg (Bayerische Staatsgemäldesammlung inv.no.717; Anzelewsky, *Dürer*, pl.168) which is not in good condition. Although the portrait in the Lumley collection passed into that of the Earl of Arundel (M.L.Cox, *Burlington*, xix, 1911, p.286, col.2), its subsequent fate is unknown and it evidently has not survived. Anzelewsky did raise hopes when he noted a portrait whose description appeared to fit the lost work, seen by Waagen at Belvoir Castle in the

collection of the Duke of Rutland (Waagen, *Treasures*, iii, p.398). But unfortunately this portrait can be identified as one by a Bavarian master, perhaps from the circle of Hans Wertinger (q.v.) which was lent by the then Duke of Rutland to an exhibition at the Guildhall, London, in 1892 (see *Reproductions of some works in the loan exhibition of pictures in the Guildhall*, 1892, pl. facing p.6) and it is still at Belvoir Castle.

Henry Parker was not the only Englishman whose portrait Dürer made. The artist mentions in his Netherlands diary that he made a portrait of an English nobleman in Antwerp in 1521 (Rupprich, i, p.172, col.2) for which he was given one gulden. But this has not been identified among the surviving portrait drawings, Shortly afterwards the same man commissioned Dürer to paint his coat-of-arms (Rupprich, i, p.173, col.1), which to judge from a surviving drawing was to form part of a hanging candelabra. This sketch is at Frankfurt (Städelsches Kunstinstitut, inv.no.695; Winkler, *Dürer*, iv, pl.829) and its significance was first noted by Schilling (*Städel-Jahrbuch*, i, 1921, pp.126f.). Levey has established that the person concerned was a member of the Abarowe family of the manor of North Charford, Hampshire (*The Victoria History of the Counties of England: Hampshire and the Isle of Wight*, iv, 1911, p.561). The arms drawn by Dürer agree with those of the Abarowe family (sable two crossed swords, argent their hilts and pommels downwards between fleur de lis or).

81 Portrait of Helius Eobanus Hessus

Silverpoint on prepared paper. 16.9 × 11.7cm

PROVENANCE: Sloane bequest, 1753

5218-21

LITERATURE: Ephrussi, pp.333ff.; Thausing, ii, p.260; Dodgson, i, p.345, under no.1; Conway, p.48, under no.913; Pauli, no.1184; BM *Guide*, 1928, p.30, no.293; Winkler, *Dürer*, iv, p.79, no.905, repr.; Rotterdam, *Erasmus*, i, no.293; Rowlands, *Dürer*, p.45, no.294; Strauss, iv, p.2308, no.1526/2, repr. (for further literature)

Inscribed by the artist in silverpoint on the right-hand edge, *1526*, and below, the artist's monogram; and by a later hand in ink in the upper left-hand corner, *Eobanus Hessus*

The identity of the sitter is confirmed by a woodcut portrait after this drawing included in an Elegy by Hessus addressed to Johann Friedrich, Duke of Saxony, published in Nuremberg by Friedrich Peypus in 1526. Dodgson notes a complete copy of the first edition in the Berlin Print Room. Helius Eobanus (1488–1540), the classical scholar and poet whose family name was probably Koch, had come to Nuremberg in 1526 to teach at the new Gymnasium in the Aegidienkloster founded by Melanchthon, and remained there until 1533. Eobanus became briefly a close friend of Dürer until the artist's death. He lamented his passing in an *Epicedion in Funere Alberti Dueri . . .*, Nuremberg, 1528, as well as giving vent to more intimate expression

81

82

in a short poem, the 'Dream about Dürer', published with it. For a detailed monograph on Eobanus see Carl Krause, *Helius Eobanus Hessus: sein Leben und seine Werke . . .*, 2 vols., Gotha, 1879.

82 Design for a turnip-shaped cup

Pen and black ink with yellow wash. 19.2 × 13.6cm

PROVENANCE: Sloane bequest, 1753

5218–81

LITERATURE: Hausmann, *Naumann's Archiv*, p.38, no.81; Hausmann, p.109, no.75; Ephrussi, p.205; *Dürer Society*, xii, 1911, p.25, repr.; BM *Guide*, 1928, p.29, no.285; Flechsig, *Dürer*, ii, p.472; Tietze, iii, pp.129f., no.A.380, repr.; Winkler, *Dürer*, iv, pp.100f., no.939, repr.; Kohlhaussen, pp.352, 530, repr.; Rowlands, *Dürer*, p.46, no.298; Strauss, iv, p.2332, no.1526/14, repr. (for further literature)

Inscribed by the artist in black ink in the centre of the upper edge, *1526*, with the artist's monogram added subsequently in brown ink

Although this design belongs to the naturalistic and illusionist manner adopted by the late Gothic goldsmith designers,

it could also be, as Flechsig has suggested, that Dürer is indulging his humour at the expense of the peasants after the troubles of the previous years, not unlike his projects of mock monuments to them published in 1525 in the third book of his *Underweysung der Messung* (cf. no.67).

The penwork is fully characteristic of Dürer's latest style. The Tietzes have been alone in rejecting it, although Dodgson initially had some doubts.

83 Portrait of Ulrich Starck

Black chalk. 40.7 × 29.7cm

WM: Crowned shield containing crowned letter 'L', between two fleur-de-lis with 'b' attached below (close to Briquet, 8329)

PROVENANCE: Sloane bequest, 1753

5218–51

LITERATURE: Waagen, *Treasures*, i, p.230, no.51; Hausmann, *Naumann's Archiv*, p.37, no.51; Hausmann, p.108, no.50; Ephrussi, p.328, n.1; A. Hagelstange, *Mitt. Kunst*, 1905, pp.25f., repr.; C. Dodgson, *Burlington*, vii, 1905, p.157, repr.; Conway, p.49, no.924; Pauli, p.43, no.1199; BM *Guide*, 1928, p.29, no.286; Tietze, iii, pp.64f., no.977, repr.; Winkler, *Dürer*, iv, p.89, no.919,

83

repr.; Rowlands, *Dürer*, p.47, no.308; BM *Portrait Drawings*, p.10, no.19; Strauss, iv, p.2352, no.1527/1, repr. (for further literature)

Inscribed by the artist, above right, in black chalk, *1527*, with the artist's monogram below

It is possible, as the Tietzes have suggested, that Dürer may have intended this drawing to serve as a preparatory study for a large woodcut similar to that of *Ulrich Varnbühler* of 1522 (Dogson, i, p.340, no.146). But it is certain that this was the basis for the portrayal of Ulrich Starck on the Nuremberg medal of 1527, through which the identity of the sitter in this drawing was first established by Hagelstange. There is no necessity for thinking that Dürer would himself have provided the reduced design from which the medallist worked. Ludwig Krug (*c*.1488/90–1532) has been proposed as a likely candidate. The present drawing, which is the only certain surviving work of any note from the year before the artist's death, despite the accomplished sculptural modelling of the face, indicates how lifeless and tired the sick and ageing artist's hand had become.

84 Emblematical design

Pen and black ink. 15.1 × 13.8cm

WM: Cardinal's hat, possibly with a letter or letters (cf. Briquet, 3401–3516).

PROVENANCE: Sloane bequest, 1753

5218–65

LITERATURE: Hausmann, *Naumann's Archiv*, p.37, no.65; Hausmann, p.109, no.61; Ephrussi, pp.215f.; Conway, p.49, no.919; Pauli, p.43, no.1203; BM *Guide*, 1928, p.30, no.290; Tietze, iii,

pp.126f., no.A.371, repr.; Winkler, *Dürer*, iv, p.101, no.940, repr.; Winkler, *Leben*, p.345; Kohlhaussen, p.414, repr.; Rowlands, *Dürer*, p.46, no.299; Strauss, iv, p.2386, no.1528/1, repr. (for further literature)

The various figures in the composition have been identified by Dürer's inscriptions, in black ink: on the left, *Affrictio* (for *Afflictio* 'misfortune'), who beats a heart held in tongs by *immodia* (? for *invidia* 'envy'); in the centre, *Consolatio* ('consolation') points heavenwards; and at the base of the altar is inscribed *tristitia* ('sorrow'). A later hand has inscribed the artist's monogram in the upper left-hand corner.

The Monogrammist IB (active *c*.1525–30) produced an engraving based on this drawing in 1529, the year after Dürer's death, with certain small changes to the allegory. In the engraving, the heart is held by *invidia* and struck by *tribulatio*. The design was made for Dürer's close friend, Willibald Pirckheimer, whose emblem appears on the anvil, and evidently refers to some difficulty in Pirckheimer's life. Strauss has plausibly proposed that this could be a reference to the matrimonial problems of Pirckheimer's daughter Felicitas, in 1528. If correct, this would have been one of Dürer's latest drawings, and undoubtedly the last work that he did for his friend.

Most scholars have accepted the attribution of the drawing to Dürer, the notable exception being the Tietzes who attributed it, as well as the subsequent engraving, to Georg Pencz (q.v.) who at that time was generally assumed, following Friedländer's argument, to be identifiable with the Monogrammist IB at the beginning of his career. Many, including Pauli and Hind have not accepted this, and it is very likely, as a result of a recent examination of the problem, that Friedländer's case must be finally abandoned (Landau, *Pencz*, pp.10ff.).

84

9 Nuremberg, XVI century

Anonymous artist

c.1520

85 Design for a goblet with a lid surmounted by a bird

Pen and black ink. Curved top 42.9 × 15.5cm

WM: high crown with a star, the lower part cut off (Piccard, v.2)

PROVENANCE: Sloane bequest, 1753

5218–77

LITERATURE: Hausmann, *Naumann's Archiv*, p.38, no.77; Hausmann, p.109, no.72; Ephrussi, p.205; BM *Guide*, p.32, no.296; Lippmann, vii, p.20, no.841, repr.; Panofsky, ii, p.147, no.1571 (for further literature); Kohlhaussen, pp.351f., 357, pl.513; Rowlands, *Dürer*, p.54, no.336; Strauss, i, p.489, no.13, repr.

Most of the drawing is executed in outline which suggests that it has been traced; only the surmounting bird and a small portion of the ornamental top of the cover have been worked up in more detail. This sheet evidently comes from a goldsmith's workshop and was done as a record for future possible use. The estimated date for the production of the paper, 1515/19, according to Piccard, indicates that the record was made on the brink, even in conservative circles, of the change to Renaissance forms and ornamentation.

The style of the cup has of itself suggested an earlier date and other associations. In the 1928 Dürer exhibition it was placed by Dodgson and Parker with works whose attribution to Dürer is not entirely rejected. Although they saw the completed part as drawn in 'the hard manner of a fifteenth-century engraver', by which they were doubtless thinking of engravers such as Wenzel von Olmütz (active *c.*1480–*c.*1500) and Israhel van Meckenem (d.1503), they nevertheless proposed that it might be an early unfinished drawing by Dürer. At first, Winkler in Lippmann's series had accepted the attribution to Dürer, earlier implied by Ephrussi, only later to exclude it from the main body of his own catalogue. Kohlhaussen, like Flechsig and the Tietzes, rejected the attribution to Dürer, but he was convinced that the design of this cup in the form of two bundles of turnips with their roots intermeshed could only owe its creation to Dürer, and that this tracing records a design by him. It is possible to point to other metalwork designs by Dürer, as well as such work represented in his paintings as, for instance, in the *Adoration of the Magi*, dated *1504* (the Uffizi, Florence, inv.no.1434) with similar fanciful elements, in various vegetable, fruit and plant shapes. Designs of this sort were not, however, the sole invention of Dürer, although he did, of course, produce outstanding examples, but were of a type of ornamental metalwork favoured by his predecessors' patrons, and taken up in turn by Dürer and his contemporaries. For instance, there is a design recorded in a tracing at Basel (Kupferstichkabinett, inv.no.U.XIII.81; Falk, *Basel*, pl.116, no.535) of a monstrance in a fanciful vegetable form, which belongs to the large collection of metalwork designs there, and which has been claimed by Major as a copy after Urs Graf, and is certainly of Basel origin. This also belongs to a trend in design that held sway in the late Gothic period in Central Europe.

Anonymous artist

before 1530

86 Design for a perpendicular window

Pen and brown ink with watercolour, on two joined sheets cut subsequently into a late Gothic curve. 42 × 30.4cm

WM: shield with fleur-de-lys and a Gothic b below (Briquet, 1827)

PROVENANCE: W.Esdaile (L.2617); D.Laing; Royal Scottish Academy; transferred to the National Gallery, 1910

Edinburgh, National Gallery of Scotland, D.959a

LITERATURE: C.Dodgson, *Vasari Society*, vii, 1911–12, no.25, repr.; K.Harrison, *The Windows of King's College Chapel, Cambridge*, Cambridge, 1952, pp.63f.; H. Wayment, *MD*, xxiii–xxiv, no.4, 1986, pp.506ff., repro.

The inscriptions in black ink, although not by the artist, are probably contemporary. The phonetic rendering of the English suggests that they were probably written by a Fleming or a German. They form a corrected list of the subjects, which partly differ from those drawn by the draughtsman, for each group of lights in the window: from left to right in the upper row of lights, *mandaet* [i.e. mandate, that is, the washing of the feet on Maundy Thursday]; *the mōute of oly|vet*; *ther criste|was take*; *cruisfix*; *takyn[ge] frō the|crosse*; *Resurexion* [crossed through]; *there criste is|berryt*; *the hell[e] brekyn[ge]*; and in the lower row, from left to right, *ecce homo*; *the sentens|of pylaet*; *the crossbearer*[?]; *helle brekynge* [crossed through]; *Crusfix*; *Resurexion*; *apuryn[ge] to o[u]r lady*; *Resurrexion* [crossed through]; *apurn[ge] to the Marys*. The outer flanking lights of both rows each contain a full-length figure of a saint, inscribed by the same hand, from the upper left, *Scs petrus*; *scs paulus*; *scs thomas*; *scs wilhms* [i.e. Wilhelm] (the last two saints most probably being St Thomas of Canterbury and St William of York); also inscribed at the top of the sheet, *5*

Dodgson who first drew attention to the drawing, proposed that it was by an artist trained in Nuremberg whose draughtsmanship reflects the influence of Hans von Kulmbach (q.v) a view which carries conviction, and to which Winkler gave his verbal support. This design, a 'vidimus' produced for the patron's approval (see also nos.100, 142, 173(a) & (b)) was clearly made for a commission in England since the window is designed in the Perpendicular style, which is only to be found in late Gothic English ecclesiastical buildings. It is unusual in being thirteen lights wide, that is most probably about thirty feet across. The east and west windows of King's College Chapel, Cambridge, have each only nine lights, but those in St George's Chapel, Windsor Castle, and Eton College Chapel have fifteen. With the key position given to the Crucifixion, the present drawing would normally be for an east window. According to Harrison, the 5 at the head of the sheet may imply that the design was part of a series for windows of a chapel or church with some nine or ten windows in the scheme.

Given the inclusion of St Thomas of Canterbury, it can be assumed that the work was ordered before 1535, when the saint's appearance was banned; and according to Arthur Lane in a letter to the National Gallery of Scotland, after the construction of the east window of King's College Chapel, which was made c.1526–30. Harrison proposed that the scheme could be for the decoration of Cardinal Wolsey's chapel at York Place; however, Peter Newton, in a letter to the National Gallery in 1978, while supporting the idea that the commission was for Cardinal Wolsey, is less sure than it could be for York Place about which little is known. He suggested that the commission was intended for Christ Church, Oxford before Wolsey's fall in 1529. A connection with the art of Nuremberg could also be a reflection of the Cardinal's taste, since this was frequently transmitted through the works of Flemish artists whom he is known to have patronised (see J.J.G.Alexander & E.Temple, *Illuminated Manuscripts in Oxford College Libraries*, Oxford, 1985, p.83, nos.827–8). The surviving glass-paintings that Wolsey had ordered for Christ Church, which was taken over by Balliol College after the Cardinal's fall, bears witness to this, since the glass in the chapel includes designs based on Dürer's engravings of the Passion.

With the rediscovery of an album containing a group of twenty-four drawings, similar to no.86, in the Musées Royaux des Beaux-Arts, Brussels, missing for many years, the present drawing has been provided with a wider context. They are likewise, 'vidimuses' for English windows and are very probably, as proposed by Hilary Wayment, designs for the windows of Cardinal Wolsey's Hampton Court Chapel, which were evidently fully glazed before Wolsey's fall from power in 1530. As Wayment points out, there is a close stylistic relationship between no.86 and the newly found drawings in Brussels; indeed several of the subjects are based, in their compositions, on no.86, which supports Harrison's idea that the present drawing records a window at York Place. The drawings at Brussels do not

85

contradict Dodgson's association of no.86 with Nuremberg, but the style of its execution and of the associated drawings in Brussels does not lead one to think that they could be either by Erhard Schön (q.v.) or from his workshop, as proposed by Wayment. None of Schön's signed drawings is sufficiently similar in style to make this credible.

Franconian, Bamberg

1508/9

87 Heiligthumer in Bamberg der Domkirche (Reliquary Book of Bamberg Cathedral)

Pen and greyish-black ink with watercolour, over traces of black chalk. Some sheets made up. Double spread: approx. 48.1 × 62 cm; page: 48.1 × 31 cm

PROVENANCE: A. Asher

British Library, Add. Ms. 15,689

LITERATURE: *Add. Manuscripts*, p.8; R. Kroos, *Zeitschr. f. Kunst-*

87

gesch, xxxix, 1976, pp.105ff.; R. Baumgärtel-Fleischmann, *Bericht des historisches Vereins Bamberg*, Bamberg, cxii, 1976, pp.161ff.; R. Baumgärtel-Fleischmann, *Anz. Germ. Nat.*, 1978. p.26.

This manuscript formed the basis for the printed *Heilthumbsbuch*, published by Johann Pfeyl in Bamberg, 1509, and it has been assumed that it was executed just prior to the appearance of this publication. According to Baumgärtel-Fleischmann, the drawings are by the Bamberg painter, Hans Wolf (d.1542). If this attribution is correct, these drawings, which are chiefly records of the contents of the Cathedral treasury, including reliquaries, crosses, and church vessels of all kinds, would constitute one of his earliest commissions. The final folio (36 *recto*) on display is unlike the rest, although certainly by the same hand, and represents the *Procession at Easter with the shrine of St Heinrich* (the Emperor, and founder of the Cathedral which was begun in 1003/40) with on the left, the east end of the Cathedral, and in the background, the *Kaiserpfalz*, the old Imperial palace (see no.109). The procession is shown proceeding around the east choir, and re-entering the Cathedral by the left portal, the *Adampforte*, as laid down in the ordinal, and as it appears in both the Pfeyl edition of 1509, already mentioned, and in the title-page woodcut of the *Bamberg Heiltumsbuch* of 1493 (Munich, Bayerisches Staatsbibliothek, cod. lat. 428. fol.253 *verso*; R. Kroos, *op.cit.* p.113, fig.2). The shrine itself is now lost, and either the first shrine, which was made between 1147 and 1170, or a possible later replacement, is represented in the drawing on folio 36 *recto*.

Hans Baldung, called Grien

Schwäbisch-Gmünd (Osten, Baldung, p.303) 1484/5–Strassburg, September 1545

Painter, engraver, designer of woodcuts and glass-paintings. Born into a professional family from Schwäbisch-Gmünd. At least two of his relatives, an attorney and a doctor, settled in Strassburg in the 1490s. Nothing is recorded of his apprenticeship, although it is possible that he received early training in either Strassburg or Swabia (Yale, *Baldung*, p.5) and, to judge from the style of his earliest work, highly probable that he worked as a journeyman with Albrecht Dürer (q.v.) in Nuremberg from 1503 to *c*.1507. The origin of Baldung's nickname, *Grien*, which was conceivably first dubbed when he was in Dürer's workshop and to which the G in his monogram used from 1507 refers, may either point to his immaturity, or to a predilection for the colour green; or may come from *Grienhans*, meaning devil (Osten, *Baldung*, p.301) with reference to the demonic fantasies which appear in some of his work.

The *St Sebastian* altarpiece of 1507, his earliest dated painting (Nuremberg, Germanisches Nationalmuseum) was made with the probably somewhat earlier *Adoration of the Magi* (Berlin-Dahlem, Gemäldegalerie) for the Stadt-kirche, Halle. Baldung was recorded at Strassburg in 1508, where he became a citizen in the following year. During this period he obtained the patronage of the Markgraf Christoph I of Baden, for whom he made a large votive painting of the Markgraf and his family (Karlsruhe, Staat-liche Kunsthalle).

From 1512 to 1517 he was recorded working in Freiburg-im-Breisgau. There he created his masterpiece, the *Coronation of the Virgin*, signed and dated *1516*, for the high altar of the Münster (still *in situ*). The payment he received for this commission was very high for the period and can be seen as a measure of the esteem in which he was held (Yale, *Baldung*, p.12). Amongst other work during this very fruitful period, he made a number of unusual wood-cuts, including the *St Sebastian* of 1514 and the *Christ carried to Heaven by Angels* of *c*.1515–17, and he was em-ployed with Dürer, Lucas Cranach the Elder (q.v.) and others to illustrate the margins of the *Prayer Book of Emperor Maximilian* of 1515 (Besançon, Bibliothèque). The paintings of Mathis Grünewald (q.v.), whose altarpiece in nearby Isenheim was completed in *c*.1515, quite probably made a considerable impact on Baldung, and a heightened sense of pathos and dramatic intensity appears in much of his work from 1512 to 1516. By May 1517 he had returned to Strassburg, where from 1533 to 1545 he was an unpaid magistrate (*Schöffe*) of his guild. He produced a number of paintings with classical and mythological subjects, such as the *Hercules and Antaeus*, signed and dated *1531* (Kassel, Staatliche Gemäldegalerie), particularly after the Reformation arrived in Strassburg in *c*.1530.

A prolific painter and draughtsman, Baldung's art is highly original, characterised by an intensity of colour and an expressive use of line, although he developed a rather mannered style in his later works. He designed over 500 woodcuts, the majority for book illustrations, and a few engravings. He was one of the first to use the chiaroscuro technique of printing woodcuts. Over 250 of his drawings, which cover a wide range of subjects, have survived.

BIBLIOGRAPHY: Thieme-Becker, ii, 1908, pp.403ff.; Koch; Karlsruhe, *Baldung*; Basel, *Baldung*; Mende, *Baldung*; Yale, *Baldung*; Osten, *Baldung* (for further literature); Andersson, *Detroit*, pp.56ff.; Austin, *Nuremberg*, pp.136ff.; Nuremberg, *Gothic & Renaissance*, p.493.

88 St Martin and the Beggar

Pen and black ink. Diameter: 17.3 cm

PROVENANCE: A. Grahl (L.1199); H. Oppenheimer (sale Christie, 1936, 14 July, lot 355, bt *Smith 32gs*); anonymous collector (sale Sotheby, 1965, 25 March, lot 115, bt *Betts £200*); P. & D. Colnaghi

Edinburgh, National Gallery of Scotland, D4902

LITERATURE: Keith Andrews, *Old Master Drawings from the National Gallery of Scotland*, Colnaghi's, 1966, no.6, pl.5; *Pictures for Scotland*, p.139, fig.134; J. E. von Borries, *Burlington*, cxxvii, 1985, p.98, repr.

88

This appeared in the Oppenheimer sale catalogue as the work of Baldung, where it was also stated that it had formerly been attributed to Hans Leu (q.v.). Andrews has associated it with Baldung's woodcut of the same subject, usually dated 1505–7, which falls within the period Baldung worked in Dürer's workshop during the master's absence in Italy. But it is much more closely related in its wayward style and immature charm to what must be the earliest of his surviving paintings, the *Knight with a woman and Death* (Paris, Louvre, inv.no.RF2467; Osten, *Baldung*, pl.1), which when first published was dated *c*.1503–5 through comparison with other drawings and woodcuts produced then in Nuremberg by Baldung. Of all these, one can now say that the Edinburgh drawing has the most in common with it. As von Borries has pointed out, the most notable similarities are seen in the facial types, and distinctive profiles, the rendering of the landscape, and the ambiguity in the placing of the figures within the allotted space. The lack of control over the indication of shapes and volume, and a want of subtlety in handling the pen as compared for instance with his *Virgin on the crescent moon*, dated *1503* (no.89) persuade one that it is among the first of Baldung's surviving drawings.

89 The Virgin on the crescent moon

Pen and black ink. 22.3 × 17 cm

PROVENANCE: R. Udny (L.2248); Mrs M. J. Hay (sale, Sotheby, 1953, 18 Nov., lot 46, as 'German School')

England, Private Collection

LITERATURE: Halm, *Deutsche Zeichn.*, pp.26f., no.33, repr.; Karlsruhe, *Baldung*, p.64, no.99, repr.; Oettinger-Knappe, p.123,

89

no.14, repr.; Rowlands, *Dürer*, p.50, no.318; H.C.von Tavel, *Zeitschr. f. schweiz. Arch.*, xxxv, 1978, p.228, repr.; Bern, *Deutsch*, p.429, no.267, repr.; Schilling, *Gesamm. Zeichn.*, p.43, no.14, repr.; Osten, *Baldung*, pp.16, 19, 42, repr.; Rowlands, *Private Collection*, p.25, no.20, repr.

Inscribed by the artist in dark brown ink on the crescent moon, *1503*

This drawing demonstrates that, even when working in Nuremberg under the shadow of Dürer, Baldung had already begun to develop his own distinctive style as a draughtsman, especially when using the pen. It was recognised by Schilling as a work of the young Baldung at the Sotheby's auction in 1953. The highly characteristic use of the pen, with short curling strokes defining the folds of the drapery, establishes its place as a drawing from the Nuremberg period: two other closely allied drawings by Baldung, also dated *1503*, are the *Aristotle and Phyllis* in the Louvre, Paris (inv.no.34; Koch, pl.1) and the *Landsknecht and Death* in Modena (Galleria Estense; Koch, pl.2). The only known drawing by Baldung which can be dated earlier than the present sheet is the *St Martin and the Beggar* (see no.88).

90 Head of an old woman

See colour plate section following p.80

Charcoal heightened with white chalk, on red tinted paper. 26 × 18.8cm

PROVENANCE: Sloane bequest, 1753

5218–76

LITERATURE: Hausmann, *Naumann's Archiv*, p.36, no.36; Hausmann, p.107, no.36; Ephrussi, p.84; BM *Guide*, 1895, p.57, no.284; Bock, *Grünewald*, p.131; Schmid, *Grünewald*, ii, p.283, repr.; BM *Guide*, 1928, p.22, no.216; Winkler, *Dürer*, ii, pp.84f., no.373, repr.; Schoenberger, *Grünewald*, p.47; Oettinger-Knappe, p.318, pl.142; F.Winzinger, *Zeitschr. f. Kunstwiss.*, xxv, 1971, pp.51ff. repr.; Rowlands, *Dürer*, p.17, no.91; M.Y.a.Libman, *Kniga i Grafika*, pp.188ff., repr.; Strauss, vi, p.3024, no.xw.373, repr. (for further literature)

The attribution of this drawing has always remained a bone of contention. After its initial acceptance by Ephrussi as a Dürer, Colvin proposed that this and a drawing now generally given to Kulmbach (no.99) were both by Mathis Grünewald (q.v.). This possible solution was soon challenged by Schmid, who saw no.90 as nearer to Dürer and Kulmbach. In the light of the discovery of the chalk and charcoal drawings by Grünewald in the von Savigny collection, the majority of which are now in Berlin, Winkler saw clearly the unacceptability of the attribution to Grünewald. He also wisely rejected a suggested attribution to Wolf Huber (q.v.). Although he could find no technical parallel with any other drawings by Dürer, he nevertheless attributed no.90 to him, albeit with a certain reserve, with a date of *c.*1505.

In the 1928 *Guide*, Dodgson accepted Dürer's authorship without any reservation. Winzinger sought his solution of the problem by reference to the *Portrait of an old woman*, dated *1516* with a false Dürer monogram in Copenhagen, which Winkler described as a strongly Grünewaldesque ('stark Grünewaldische') chalk drawing. Following Schilling's perceptive attribution of this portrait to Hans Schäufelein (q.v.; *Kunstmuseets Aarsskrift*, 1951, p.56), Winzinger proposed, by a comparison of the two drawings, that the present one is also by Schäufelein executed shortly after the Copenhagen drawing. In the compiler's view, however, the British Museum drawing lacks the somewhat coarse incisiveness of the lines in the Copenhagen portrait. The two drawings do not appear to be by the same hand, and neither does there seem any necessity for viewing the present drawing as Winzinger does, as a 'paraphrase' of Dürer's *Portrait of his mother* (Winkler, *Dürer*, iii, pl.559).

In 1971 the compiler accepted Dodgson's solution as the most convincing, a view which he now feels compelled to abandon. This has been prompted by a comparison of no.90 with three circular glass-paintings, *Death and the revellers* and *Judith and Holofernes* at Dresden, and the *Rape of Europa* in an English private collection. The first and last of these were attributed to Dürer by Winkler, who dated them *c.*1500–3 (Winkler, *Dürer*, i, pls.215–16), while *Judith and Holofernes* he attributed to Kulmbach (Winkler,

K&S, pl.116). Schilling was the first to see that all three drawings belong together and are by the same hand, which he identified as that of Baldung (E. Schilling, *Zeitschr. f. Kunstgesch.*, xxiv, 1961, p.91; *Festschrift O. Pächt*, pp.196ff.). This view has received support from Winzinger, and if one accepts that they were done during Baldung's stay in Nuremberg, perhaps *c.*1505 during his *Wanderjahre*, then their strong dependence on Dürer is entirely explicable. The present drawing also would fall into the same category, and makes the attribution to the young Baldung entirely credible.

Another recent investigator of the problem of these drawings is the Russian scholar, M. Ya. Libman whose surprising conclusions have been summarised for me by Mr George Morris. Libman reaffirms the attribution of the present drawing to Dürer despite analogies that he noted between it and *Death and the revellers* which he maintains, like Winkler, is by Kulmbach. The same sort of link he observes with the *Judith and Holofernes* but he fails to see that they are all by the same hand. Libman's solution is that the two drawings at Dresden are both by Kulmbach. There is a drawn copy of the present drawing in the Museum of Fine Arts at Karkov in the Ukraine (inv.no.94) which, to judge from the photograph kindly made available to me by Dr Charita Mesenseva, is by a much later and not very competent hand.

See also nos.112–15 for further works by Baldung.

Dürer Workshop

91 (a) St Martin dividing his cloak with the beggar

Pen and brown ink over black chalk. Diameter 33.2cm

WM: tower with a crown (Piccard, ii, 496)

PROVENANCE: W. Y. Ottley (sale, T. Philipe, 1814, 6 June, lot 68, bt with one other, *Roscoe £1*) Sir T. Lawrence (L.2445); S. Woodburn (sale, Christie, 1860, 5 June, lot 440, bt *Tiffin £1.10s for BM*)

1860-6-16-54

LITERATURE: Térey, iii, no.197, repr.; BM *Guide*, 1928, p.37, no.323; M. Weinberger, *Mitt. Kunst*, no.2/3, 1932, pp.37ff., repr.; Koch, p.208; Rowlands, *Dürer*, p.50, no.321, repr.

Inscribed by a later hand, in brown ink, on the left, *281*.

Térey tentatively attributed this to Baldung, an opinion which was accepted without reservation by Parker, and subsequently by myself. This appears to me now however, quite mistaken, as the drawing should be more closely linked with Dürer himself. The design of the present drawing is a free adaptation from that of a woodcut for a *Salūs animae* of 1503 (C. Dodgson, *Holzschnitte zu zwei Nürnberger Andachtsbüchern . . .*, Berlin, 1909, p.18, no.81, pl.xii) produced in Dürer's studio. According to Weinberger, the present drawing should be connected with two other drawings, both

91a

attributed to Dürer himself by Winkler, the *Anna selbdritt* in Budapest (Szépmüvészeti Múzeum, inv.no.CE.17.14; Winkler, *Dürer*, i, pl.222) and the *St Augustine* in Berlin-Dahlem (Kupferstichkabinett, inv.no.KDZ 1283; Winkler, *Dürer*, i, pl.221). The design in Budapest was used for a glass-painting in the Gumbertus-kirche, Ansbach, near Nuremberg which is one of a series dated *1520*. Because of this, Weinberger described the artist of these drawings, which he thought, mistakenly in my view, were all by the same hand, as the 'Erster Zeichner der Ansbacher Fenster'. Despite this confusion Weinberger certainly was pointing more or less in the right direction, in that the present drawing which is not fine enough to be Dürer's own hand, should be associated with his studio. It is likely to have been produced towards the end of the artist's career, and was used after Dürer's death for a painted glass-roundel with the arms of Martin Geuder, and his wife, Juliana, *née* Pirckheimer. This was one of a series of five, two of which are dated *1533* and was commissioned for the Klarakloster at Nuremberg, but destroyed in the Second World War (see H. Schmitz, *Die Glasgemälde des Königlichen Kunstgewerbe-Museums in Berlin*, Berlin, 1913, i, p.162, pl.46, ii, pls.284–8).

There is a drawn copy of the drawing at Dresden.

Hans Leu the Younger

Probably Zurich, c.1490–battle of Gubel, 24 October 1531

Painter, designer of woodcuts and glass-paintings. Son of the Zürich painter, Hans Leu the Elder (*c.*1460–before 1507). During his *Wanderjahre* (years of travel) he was employed, first by Albrecht Dürer (q.v.), *c.*1510, and subsequently very probably by Hans Baldung (q.v.) in Freiburg-

91b

im-Breisgau. He was evidently back in Zürich by 1514 at the latest, and there established himself as the leading painter of the city. Thereafter his career can be charted through a succession of mostly signed and dated works, chiefly drawings, until the late 1520s.

BIBLIOGRAPHY: Thieme-Becker, xxiii, 1929, pp.142f.; Karlsruhe, *Baldung*, pp.125ff. (for further literature); *Meister um Dürer*, pp.139ff.

(b) The Virgin at the loom ministered to by angels

Pen and black ink. Curved top. 27.9 × 19.7cm

PROVENANCE: Giuseppe, Duca di Cassano Serra, Naples: Obach & Co

1909–1–9–16

LITERATURE: Obach & Co., *Old Master Drawings*, no.48, repr.; C. Dodgson, *Vasari Society*, v, 1909/10, p.27, repr.; W. Hugelshofer, *Anz.*, xxv, 1923, p.165, repr.; Röttinger, *Doppelgänger*, p.93, n.1.; BM *Guide*, 1928, p.37, no.322; Koch, p.189, under no.A4; Karlsruhe, *Baldung*, p.125; K.-A. Knappe, *Zeitschr. f. Kunstwiss.*, xv, 1961, p.62, n.15; *Meister um Dürer*, p.139, under no.235; Oettinger-Knappe, pp.61, 109, n.309; Rowlands, *Dürer*, p.55, no.344.

Inscribed by the artist, in black ink, on the foot of the loom, *1510* with below, his monogram.

This is the earliest known surviving drawing by Leu, which shows him, as one would expect, strongly influenced by Dürer in whose studio he was working at the time. That Leu was an assistant of Dürer is confirmed in a letter written by Dürer in 1523 to Propst (Provost) Felix Frey in Zürich, in which he sent his greetings to Leu, amongst other acquaintances in Zürich, and enclosed some prints and a drawing, the *Dance of the monkeys* now in Basel (Kupferstichkabinett, inv.no.1662.68; Strauss, iv, p.2247, repr.; Rupprich, i, pp.106f., no.51). The artist's monogram has been generally accepted as convincing evidence of the authorship of no.91(b). Oettinger and Knappe regarded it as a copy by Leu after a design by Hans Baldung (q.v.) for which one can see no compelling stylistic grounds. What is more, the copies after lost drawings by Baldung, which Koch tentatively attributed to Leu (Koch, pls.A3 and A4) have no perceptible connection with the present drawing. There is no reason to doubt that this design is Leu's own conception, given its evident naivety, and immaturity of expression. It is a preparatory design for one of a large cycle of small scale glass-paintings with scenes from the New Testament, which was produced from 1503 to 1513 to decorate the crossing in the church of the Carmelite Priory at Nuremberg. The majority of the designs for the windows are based on compositions by Dürer and a few are after designs by Hans Baldung (q.v.) and Hans von Kulmbach (q.v.). The glass-painting which corresponds to no.91(b) shows the arms of the Petz family, and a label containing the initials *hl*, and is now, together with a number of others, in the parish church at Grossgründlach, just outside Nuremberg (Oettinger-Knappe, col.pl.x). A large group from the series is now in St Bartholomew's Church at Wöhrd, a suburb of Nuremberg, while others are at Henfenfeld, and in museums outside Germany, including the Victoria and Albert Museum which possesses the *Last Supper* (inv.no. c.409–1919).

See also no.186.

Sebald Beham (old German: Peham)
Nuremberg 1500 – Frankfurt-am-Main 22 November 1550

Miniaturist, engraver, etcher, designer of woodcuts and glass-paintings. There is no documentary evidence for the name Hans which appears in the early literature. The H in Beham's monogram, ⊢SB or ⊢SP probably represents the second syllable of the artist's surname.

Beham's early works show a strong influence of Albrecht Dürer (q.v.). In January 1525, together with his brother Barthel Beham (1502–40) and Georg Pencz (q.v.), he was banished from Nuremberg for making atheistic and anarchistic statements in support of the Peasants' War, but was permitted to return in September of the same year. In 1528, after publishing a book on the proportions of the horse, *Dises büchlein zeyget an und lernet ein mass oder proporcion der Ross*, he was accused of plagiarising unpublished work by Dürer, and again fled from Nuremberg; he returned in 1529. Woodcuts by him were published in Ingolstadt in 1527, 1529 and 1530. In 1530 he was in Munich, where he witnessed the triumphal entry of the Emperor, Charles V, an event which he commemorated in one of his finest woodcuts, printed from five blocks, *The Military Display, 10 June 1530*. In 1530/31 he worked for Cardinal Albrecht of Brandenburg, for whom he illuminated, together with Nikolaus Glockendon (d.1534) two prayer books (Kassel, Bibliothek, and Aschaffenburg, Königliche Bibliothek) and painted a table-top, signed and dated *1534* (Paris, Musée du Louvre). From 1532, Beham seems to have lived mostly in Frankfurt, where his work was published by Egenolf. He became a citizen of Frankfurt in 1540, having renounced his Nuremberg citizenship in 1535.

Known as one of the so-called 'Little Masters', from the small scale of his engravings (see Heinrich Aldegrever (q.v.), and Georg Pencz (q.v.)), he was one of the most productive graphic artists of his generation, with an output of about 250 engravings and over 1000 woodcuts.

BIBLIOGRAPHY: Dodgson, i, 1903, pp.439ff.; Thieme-Becker, iii, pp.193ff. (for further literature); Hollstein, iii; *Meister um Dürer*, pp.73ff.; Zschelletzschky; Andersson, *Detroit*, pp.202ff.; Austin, *Nuremberg*, pp.176ff.

92 The multiplication of bread and fish

Pen and brown ink, with grey and pink wash. Diameter: 23.2 cm

PROVENANCE: Francis Douce bequest, 1834

Oxford, Ashmolean Museum, P.274

LITERATURE: Parker, *Ashmolean*, p.117, no.274, repr.; Lloyd, *Ashmolean Drawings*, p.19, under no.14

Inscribed by a later hand below in the centre of the lower margin, *Albert Durer*. This inscription, by the same hand, occurs at the same point on many other drawings from the same series and on others associated with Beham

This drawing belongs to a series of roundel designs for glass-paintings of scenes from the life of Christ of varying quality, some of which are dated *1522* by the artist (for instance, the *Denial of Christ by Peter* in the British Museum (inv.no.1920–4–20–3) and the *Massacre of the Innocents* in Berlin-Dahlem (Kupferstichkabinett, inv.no.KdZ 15098; Berlin, *Dürer und seine Zeit*, pl.78)). At least twenty-five drawings survive associated with this series, all originally of the same dimensions, of which one of the largest groups is in the National Museum, Stockholm (Bjurström, *German Drawings*, nos.11–16, repr.). The finest designs in the series like the present drawing, are the most worked up, to which washes, and frequently colour notes and indications of the leading are added. The presence or absence of some or all these additions is not, however, a sure guide, as Bjurström suggests, as to whether or not a glass-painting

was produced. For instance, the well-executed *Christ before Pilate* from the collection of Mrs Cleeve, Guildford is drawn in pen and brown ink alone, and has no notes of any kind (see Rowlands, *Private Collection*, p.19, no.12, repr.), and a glass-painting based on this design, or one closely related to it, is in the Cloisters, the Metropolitan Museum of Art, New York (inv.no.11.93.10).

93 St Lawrence

Pen and brown ink. Diameter: 31.3 cm

PROVENANCE: Sloane bequest, 1753

5218–55

LITERATURE: BM *Guide*, 1901, p.17, no.A78; C. Dodgson, *Dürer Society*, vi, 1903, pl.xiv; BM *Guide*, 1928, p.39, no.332; Rowlands, *Dürer*, pp.51f., no.327

Inscribed by the artist, in brown ink, to the left of the saint, *1521*, below which has been added in black chalk by a later hand, Dürer's monogram

This design for a glass-painting and a companion, of *St Sebald*, of the same size, now in the Lessing Rosenwald collection, National Gallery of Art, Washington, D.C., have a similar decorative surround of a branch with fruit, with the arms of Nuremberg, the *Jungfernadler* and the city arms. The drawing at Washington was formerly in the Weigel and von Lanna collections. St Lawrence and St Sebald are the two patron saints of Nuremberg, to whom the two principal churches of the city are dedicated.

Beham evidently had this drawing in mind when he later designed for Hector Pömer (1495–1541), a book-plate (Dodgson, i, p.484, no.159) with a figure of St Lawrence

93

dependent on the present drawing. Pömer, who came from a patrician family, was a priest from *1520* and provost of St Lawrence's church, Nuremberg.

In Berlin-Dahlem (Kupferstichkabinett, inv.no.KDZ 53) there is a design by Beham for a quatrefoil window dated *1520* with a full-length figure of St Lawrence, with the border characteristically decorated with a vine-branch. A companion to this of St Sebald has not so far been traced.

Peter Flötner

Thurgau? 1486/95 – Nuremberg, 23 October 1546

Sculptor, engraver, designer of woodcuts, furniture and decorative objects. It is thought from stylistic evidence, that he travelled in Italy in *1520* or *1521*, and perhaps also in *c.*1530. He possibly trained in Augsburg, and was active briefly in Ansbach before he arrived in Nuremberg in *1522* where he became a citizen on 8 October *1523*.

Flötner was one of the most innovative sculptors and printmakers of the German Renaissance and his work is notable for its variety. His earliest wood-carvings in Nuremberg were possibly the capitals and consoles for the town hall, made in *1520/21* (destroyed *1945*). Extant examples of his sculpture are rare; the only signed wooden sculpture by him to have survived is the *Adam* of *c.*1525, in Vienna (Kunsthistorisches Museum). He designed the interior decoration of a number of patrician houses in Nuremberg, including the sculpture and possibly the architecture, for the garden room of the Hirschvogelhaus, erected in *1534*, the ceiling of which was painted by Georg Pencz (q.v.). The house was destroyed in *1945*; the remains of the garden room are now in the Stadtmuseum Fembohaus,

Nuremberg. Flötner's designs for organs, altarpieces, fountains and other objects are to be found in Berlin-Dahlem (Kupferstichkabinett), Erlangen (Universitätsbibliothek), Basel (Kunstmuseum) and elsewhere. His most important surviving sculpture, the *Apollo Fountain*, dated *1532*, and cast in brass by Pankraz Labenwolf (*1492–1563*), for which Flötner's original drawing is known (see under no.94) was made for the Herrenschiesshaus, Nuremberg (now on loan from the city to the Germanisches Nationalmuseum, Nuremberg). He produced wooden models for the *Silver Altarpiece* of *1531–8* (Cracow Cathedral) made for Sigismund I of Poland, to which Georg Pencz (q.v.), Hans Dürer (q.v.) and others also contributed.

His carving on the *Coconut Goblet*, made before *1540*, is a good example of his decorative work (Nuremberg, Germanisches Nationalmuseum). He also made stone reliefs and models for metal plaquettes which were apparently much sought after; a large quantity of his plaquettes were found in the well-known Amerbach collection in Basel when it was inventoried in *1586* (now Basel, Historisches Museum). His prints include designs for ornament and single leaf woodcuts and broadsheets which often show satirical subjects. Many of his woodcuts are signed with the monogram, *PF* and a chisel and mallet, evidence that he regarded himself primarily as a carver.

His models and designs were reproduced by other craftsmen well into the sixteenth century. Despite numerous collaborative ventures, and the apparent popularity of his work, he was not successful during his lifetime, for he died in debt.

BIBLIOGRAPHY: Thieme-Becker, xii, 1916, pp.108ff.; Charles L.Kuhn, *Art Quarterly*, xvii, 2, 1954, pp.109ff.; Austin, *Nuremberg*, pp.224ff. (for further literature); Nuremberg, *Gothic & Renaissance*, p.494; John Rowlands, *Print Quarterly*, iv, 2, 1987, pp.158ff.

94 Apollo playing a *lira da braccio*

Pen and black ink with watercolour, over traces of black chalk. A tear and a few holes repaired at the foot of the drawing. 28.7 × 18.5cm

PROVENANCE: Sloane bequest, 1753

5218–171

LITERATURE: Waagen, *Treasures*, i, p.232, no.171; Hausmann, *Naumann's Archiv.*, p.41, no.171; Hausmann, p.112, no.147; Ephrussi, p.138; BM *Guide*, 1928, p.33, no.298; Winkler, *Dürer*, ii, appendix, pl.xx; Panofsky, ii, pp.92f., no.900; Rowlands, *Dürer*, p.49, no.317; Strauss, ii, p.1012, no.1507/9, repr.

Inscribed above the tree at the upper edge, probably by an early hand in black ink, *1507*, with a false Dürer monogram.

Ephrussi noted that the drawing must be connected with a print by the north Italian artist, Benedetto Montagna (active *c.*1500–41). The figure is in fact closely based, in reverse, on the seated figure of Orpheus in Montagna's engraving, *Orpheus playing to the animals* (Hind, *Early Italian Engraving*, vii, pl.745). In the drawing, Orpheus becomes

Apollo crowned with laurels, and sits on a large tree stump instead of the Mantegnesque rocks seen in the print, the background of which is omitted. The German draughtsman makes Apollo's dress and hair-style less severely classical than those of Orpheus, and also omits the sympathetic strings from the musical instrument.

Panofsky's idea that no.94 derives from an Italian original known through an illumination in a manuscript at Wolfenbüttel (Codex 277A Extr.) and attributed by Berenson to Giovanni dai Libri, must be rejected since the connection between the two compositions is too tenuous to be meaningful. Ephrussi regarded the drawing as by Dürer (q.v.) but despite Strauss's statement to the contrary, he did not see it as a preparatory study for a woodcut illustration of Apollo, published in two books by Erhard Oeglin in Augsburg in 1507: Petrus Tritonius, *Melopoiae sive Harmoniae*; and Guntherus Ligurinus, *De gestis Imp. Caesaris Friderici primi Augusti*. The figure of Apollo in the woodcut is in a similar position to the present Apollo, but does not correspond closely enough to suggest that it was made after the drawing. It is more probable that the composition of the woodcut derives from that of the Wolfenbüttel

manuscript mentioned by Panofsky. The print has been associated by some with Dürer, an attribution rightly rejected by Dodgson (Dodgson, i, p.266); it is more likely to be connected with Kulmbach (q.v.)as Winkler has suggested (Winkler, *Kulmbach*, p.37, pl.4). The fact that the date of 1507 on the sheet is the same as that of the two publications in which the woodcut appears, seems to indicate that a mistaken connection was made between the drawing and the print by the author of the inscription.

The technique and slightly mannered style of the drawing do, in fact, suggest that it was made later than 1507. It is drawn in the manner of certain artists from Nuremberg, where a self-conscious antiquarian tone was much in vogue among the patrician patrons during the sixteenth century. This style is chiefly associated with members of the Vischer family (see Peter Vischer the Younger). The present drawing is however, closest in execution to works by Peter Flötner whose drawings were similarly inspired; in particular to his preparatory study, dated *1531* (formerly in the collection of the Grand Duke of Saxe-Weimar), for the *Apollo fountain* (Nuremberg, *Gothic & Renaissance*, p.439, fig.139). This sheet is drawn in pen and ink with wash, and it displays many similar passages in the rendering of the different parts of the body. One is strongly inclined to regard both drawings as by the same hand, and it seems likely that no.94 also dates from the 1530s. This more than bears out my earlier idea that the present drawing is a pastiche produced by Flötner or an associate of his.

A copy of no.94, inscribed with the date *1517*, which Ephrussi states is in Munich, can no longer be found. Since the inventories of the Graphische Sammlung were burnt during the last war, it has not been possible to verify Ephrussi's assertion.

95 Design for a dagger with the Triumph of Bellona on the scabbard

Pen and black ink with black, yellow and grey wash over traces of black chalk. The sheet is made up of three pieces of paper, the lower corners cut diagonally. 34.7 × 7.6cm

PROVENANCE: F. Fagel (sale, T. Philipe, 1801, 27 May, lot 57, bt *Ottley £1.17s*); W. Y. Ottley (sale, T. Philipe, 1814, 11 June, lot 665); W. Beckford

1848–11–25–8

LITERATURE: Waagen, *Treasures*, i, p.236; Reid, pl.5; Woltmann, i, p.435, ii, p.135, no.196; His, pl.xxxii, no.1; LB, ii, p.342, no.39; Chamberlain, ii, p.278; White, p.570, no.185; Rowlands, *Dürer*, p.53, no.335, repr.

In the early literature, this drawing was considered to be by Hans Holbein the Younger (q.v.), although Edouard His stated that the sheath design seemed to be after Holbein, and was drawn by a different hand to that of the hilt. Binyon also considered that the drawing was done by two different hands, with the sheath by Holbein and the hilt probably by Peter Flötner, a solution accepted by

94

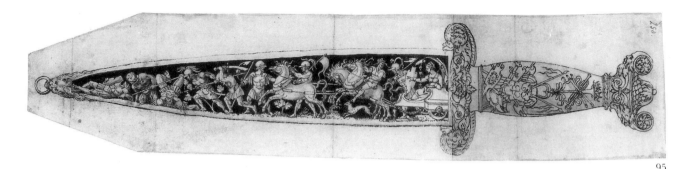

95

Chamberlain. The design is, however, a consistent whole and can be attributed to Flötner with confidence. The hilt is similar in design to his woodcuts of three ornamental hilts (Hollstein, viii, p.155, nos.75–7; repr.), one of which has a Roman breast cuirass and is particularly close in composition (no.77). The sheath, both in its details and the use made of a favourite device, the setting-off of the figures against a dark background, finds parallels in other drawings by Flötner, and the style of the drawing as a whole is comparable to a finely drawn and elaborately organised design for a dagger, dated *1539*, in Berlin-Dahlem (Kupferstichkabinett, inv.no.16779; Nuremberg, *Gothic & Renaissance*, p.448, pl.259).

A Swiss dagger, of possibly nineteenth-century origin, displays on its sheath the same composition of the *Triumph of Bellona* as seen in the present drawing. However, the difference in the design of the chape and the hilt of the dagger suggests that it was not made after this drawing, but after an intermediary design of a later date (Danish private collection; Schneider, *Schweizerdolch*, p.147, no.76, repr.).

Augustin Hirschvogel

Nuremberg 1503 – Vienna February 1553

Etcher, glass painter, cartographer, potter and mathematician. Son of the foremost glass painter of Nuremberg, Veit Hirschvogel the Elder (1461–1525) who worked after designs by artists such as Albrecht Dürer (q.v.) and Hans von Kulmbach (q.v.). He was active in his father's workshop until the latter's death, after which he established his own workshop producing glassware in the Venetian style. In August 1536 he was in Laibach (Ljubljana) where he worked, for some of the time as a maiolica painter, until *c.*1540. During this period he established his reputation as a cartographer, the profession for which he was best known during his own day. His maps include one of the Turkish borders made in 1539 for the Nuremberg council, and numerous commissions for the Emperor.

After a short stay in Nuremberg in 1543 he settled in Vienna in 1544. His pioneering use of triangulation in maps of Vienna, made after the Turkish siege of 1543 for the future defence of the city, and completed in 1547,

received wide acclaim. He appears to have taken up etching after 1543, producing some 300 prints, most of which are signed and dated. The majority were made for book illustrations, but he also produced ornament prints and, most notably, landscape etchings which reveal the influence of the Danube School artists, Albrecht Altdorfer (q.v.) and Wolf Huber (q.v.) and which constitute his most impressive artistic achievement.

BIBLIOGRAPHY: Thieme-Becker, xvii, 1924, pp.138ff.; A. Schmitt, *Berl. Mus.* iv, 1954, pp.8ff.; Yale, *Danube School*, pp.88ff.; J.S. Peters, *MD*, 1979, pp.359ff.; J.S. Peters, *Anz. Germ. Nat.*, 1980, pp.79ff.; Hollstein, xiiiA, 1984, pp.141ff. (for further literature).

96 *Recto:* A monastery (? Salem) in a wooded valley

Verso: A wooded gorge

Pen and black ink. Trimmed, 10.5 × 15.9cm

PROVENANCE: P.J.Mariette (L.2097); Obach & Co.

1909-1-9-15

LITERATURE: Obach & Co., *Old Master Drawings*, no.32, repr., *verso*; Parker, *German Schools*, p.35, no.65, repr., *recto*; P.Halm, *Die Landschaftzeichnungen des Wolf Huber*, dissertation, Munich, 1927, pp.224–7; Winzinger, *Huber*, i, pp.158f., nos.232 and 233, ii, pls.232 and 233

Inscribed by the artist on the *recto*, in black ink, on the upper edge, *1536*, and below, on the right, *83*; on the *verso* by later hands, in brown ink, in the lower right-hand corner, *Alberto durer*, and on the right-hand edge, *wolff horber*

Both *recto* and *verso* have been drawn by the same hand, even though the drawing on the *verso* is less freely done. It was thought, when acquired, that this was Huber's; however, Parker expressed his doubts, and Halm proposed Hirschvogel. There are some strong indications that this idea is correct. The way the foliage on the large tree in the foreground on the *recto* is depicted in clumps is so prevalent throughout Hirschvogel's landscapes as to amount to a signature (see particularly *Landscape with a river in a gorge* and *Landscape with a church*, Bartsch, ix, pp.187f., no.63, p.189, no.68). The *verso* is put together with the same sense of charming effect common to similar scenes among his etchings, of which the *Village with an arched stone bridge over a river*

96r

96v

(Bartsch, ix, p.185, no.56) is of a kindred type. This neater type of pen-work is met again in another landscape drawing, also attributed to Hirschvogel, *A watermill at the foot of a hill* in an English private collection (Rowlands, *Private Collection*, p.46, pl.42).

Bushart's suggestion (in course of publication) that the abbey represented here is Salem is most interesting as, if correct, not only would it be the oldest known view of this historic site, but it also would be particularly enlightening, since the abbey church and its surrounding buildings have changed so much through rebuilding over the intervening centuries. Fortunately the outward characteristics of the medieval Cistercian abbey church, with its three long lancet windows at the east end of the choir, and its high-pitched roofs to choir and transepts are still to be seen. There are sufficient similarities between this view and what remains today at Salem for Bushart's proposal to be given some credence.

Hans Süss von Kulmbach, known as Hans von Kulmbach

Probably Kulmbach, c.1480 – Nuremberg between 29 November and 3 December 1522

Painter, designer of woodcuts and glass-paintings. It is evident from the style of his early graphic output that he worked in some capacity although not necessarily as an apprentice (*Lehrjung*) as Neudörfer stated, with Jacopo de' Barbari (*c.*1450–1515/16) who was in Nuremberg from April 1500 until 1503 (see Winkler, *Kulmbach*, p.9). It is also highly probable that he joined the workshop of Albrecht Dürer (q.v.) as an assistant at some time during this period (see no.97) and also collaborated with him in later life (see no.99). On 15 March 1511 he became a citizen of Nuremberg. He was a successful portraitist, and executed altarpieces for churches in Nuremberg and Cracow, Poland, which he may have visited. Apart from Dürer, Kulmbach was one of the most prolific painters and draughtsmen of the first two decades of the sixteenth century in Nuremberg.

About twenty altarpieces, few of which have survived in their entirety, have been associated with Kulmbach. They include eight panels of an altarpiece with *Scenes from the Lives of Sts Peter and Paul* (Florence, Galleria degli Uffizi) of *c.*1507/8, probably made for a church in Cracow; an altarpiece with *Scenes from the Life of the Virgin*, signed and dated *1511*, and probably made for the monastery 'na Skalce' in Cracow, of which the main panel, an *Adoration of the Magi*, is in Berlin-Dahlem (Gemäldegalerie), and further panels are in Cracow (National Museum, and the monastery 'na Skalce'); the Tucher altarpiece, showing the *Virgin and Child with Saints*, signed and dated *1513*, in the church of St Sebald, Nuremberg (see no.99); the altarpiece of *St Catherine*, signed and dated *1514* and *1515*, made for the church of St Mary, Cracow, and still *in situ*; and an altarpiece of *St John the Evangelist* for the same church, of

which only the predella, dated *1516*, is known to have survived (Warsaw, National Museum).

One of Kulmbach's best known portraits is that of *Casimir von Brandenburg*, signed and dated *1511* (Munich, Alte Pinakothek) which displays the light clear colours characteristic of his paintings. Further portraits by him, many of which are dated and signed with his monogram, *HK*, are to be found in Berlin-Dahlem (Gemäldegalerie), Nuremberg (Germanisches Nationalmuseum), Munich (Alte Pinakothek) and elsewhere.

About half of the approximately 150 known surviving drawings, many of which are attributed to him on a stylistic basis, were made as studies for glass-paintings, including a number for windows still *in situ* in the church of St Sebald, Nuremberg (see no.97). For this work, Kulmbach must have maintained close connections with the workshop of the glass-painter Veit Hirschvogel (1461–1525; G. Frenzel, *Zeitschr. f. Kunstgesch.*, xxiii, 1960, pp.193ff.). Kulmbach's designs for glass-paintings form the most comprehensive collection of drawings of this type to have survived from the early sixteenth century.

BIBLIOGRAPHY: Neudörfer, *Nachrichten*, pp.134ff; Thieme-Becker, xxii, 1928, pp.92ff.; Stadler, *Kulmbach* (for further literature); F. Winkler, *Prussian Jahrbuch*, vol.62, 1941, pp.1ff.; Winkler, K&S; Winkler, *Kulmbach*; K.-A. Knappe, *Zeitschr. f. Kunstgesch.*, xxiii, 1960, pp.184ff.; *Meister um Dürer*, pp.97ff.; F. Winkler, *Kunstchronik*, xiv, 1961, pp.265ff.; Andersson, *Detroit*, pp.104ff.; Austin, *Nuremberg*, pp.130ff.; Schallaburg, *Polen*, p.213; Nuremberg, *Gothic & Renaissance*, p.495; Butts-Mende (in preparation).

97 St Peter

Brush and black ink with grey wash, and traces of black chalk which indicate the lead-lights. The sheet consists of five pieces of paper attached horizontally with slight overlapping on the top join; the other joins, and the lower left-hand corner, have been made up. 100.2 × 38.8cm

WM: high crown surmounted by a cross (in four of the pieces of paper) very close to Briquet, 4895; see also Meder *Dürer*, pl.iv, 20; and Strauss, vi, pp.3285ff

PROVENANCE: A. Casabianca

1882-3-11-60

LITERATURE: BM *Guide*, 1928, p.35, no.308; Winkler, K&S, pp.29f., 71f., no.63, repr. (for further literature); Winkler, *Kulmbach*, pp.23f., pl.12; K.-A. Knappe, *Zeitschr. f. Kunstgesch.*, xxiii, 1960, p.186; G. Frenzel, *Zeitschr. f. Kunstgesch.*, xxiii, 1960, p.201, pl.5 (detail); Knappe, *Bamberger Fenster*, pp.69ff., figs.60, 61, 67; Oettinger-Knappe, pp.104, 318; Rowlands, *Dürer*, p.54, no.338; Kuhrman, *Erlangen*, p.79, under no.66; B. Butts, *MD*, xxiii–xxiv, no.4, 1986, p.525, n.13

The largest known drawing by Kulmbach, no.97 is the only surviving cartoon for one of the sixteen sections of the window given by Veit Truchsess von Pommersfelden, Bishop of Bamberg, in the east choir of the church of St Sebald, Nuremberg. The window, whose measurements

(105.5 × 41.5cm) are very close to those of the cartoon, is one of the finest examples of glass-painting produced in Nuremberg during this period, and was executed in the workshop of Veit Hirschvogel (Knappe, *Bamberger Fenster*, pl.4, fig.7) to replace a window designed by Wolf Katzheimer between 1493 and 1495. The attribution of no.97 to Kulmbach was first suggested by Parker in the exhibition catalogue of 1928, and convincingly supported by Winkler who initially dated the sheet to *c.*1515, but later altered this correctly to an early point in Kulmbach's career (Winkler, *Kulmbach*). A record of payment by the Bishop of Bamburg to Veit Hirschvogel for the completed work is documented in the year 1502–3 (Knappe, *Bamberger Fenster*, pp.18f.) and since the then Bishop, Veit Truchsess von Pommersfelden, was consecrated on 16 July 1501, and visited Nuremberg on 15 August, the drawing could have been made during the latter part of 1501, or early in 1502.

The influence of Dürer is immediately apparent in the treatment of the figure, and in the use of brush and wash, also seen in Kulmbach's drawings of *c.*1501, in Coburg (Kunstsammlungen der Veste Coburg, inv.z.2320, z.2321; Andersson, *Detroit*, pp.104ff., nos.26 and 27, repr.). This would argue in favour of Kulmbach making the drawing during, or soon after, his period as an assistant in Dürer's workshop. The watermark is of a type commonly seen in paper used by Dürer in his drawings and prints, and it must have been easily available not only in his workshop, but also throughout Nuremberg. Kulmbach used paper with a similar watermark on at least one other occasion (see no.98). Knappe's initial attribution of the drawing to Dürer himself, supported by Butts, was made on account of its early date, but is not convincing on a stylistic basis. The drawing is identical in treatment to the cartoon of *St Michael and an angel* from a composition of the fall of the rebel angels in Boston (Museum of Fine Arts, inv.no. 97,623; Nuremberg, *Gothic & Renaissance*, p.243, no.160, repr.) and to the cartoon of *St Leonhard* in the Universitätsbibliothek, Erlangen (inv.no.B.151) both of which can be firmly attributed to Kulmbach. The cartoon of St Augustine, attributed to Dürer in the Boymans-van Beuningen Museum, Rotterdam (inv.no.MB 1953/T19; Winkler, *Dürer*, i, pl.20) with which Knappe evidently compares the present sheet, is not by the same hand; the handling of the brush, particularly in the hands and faces, reveals a different mind at work; however, Knappe later changed his opinion, since in Oettinger-Knappe the drawing of St Peter is noted as 'executed by Kulmbach?'

A study by Kulmbach for another section of the Bamberg window showing Sts Henry and Kunigunda is in Dresden (Kupferstichkabinett, Winkler, K&S, pl.74) and studies by him for further windows in St Sebald have also survived (Winkler, K&S, pls.75–80).

97

98

98 Two standing female allegorical figures

Pen and brown ink. 12.9 × 15.9cm

WM: part of a high crown (? Briquet 4902, Strauss, vi, pp.3285f.)

PROVENANCE: Sloane bequest, 1753

5218–113

LITERATURE: Hausmann, *Naumann's Archiv*, p.39, no.113; Hausmann, p.110, no.95; BM *Guide*, 1928, p.35, no.313; Stadler, *Kulmbach*, p.103, no.4, repr. (for further literature); Winkler, K&S, p.56; no.28, repr.; H. Landolt, *Jahresbericht der Öffentlichen Kunstsammlung Basel*, Basel, 1962, pp.33f., repr.; Winkler, K&S, p.56, no.28, repr.

On the *verso*, there are five lines of illegible inscription made in pencil or black chalk

The nude woman on the left holds a pair of scales in which a feather outweighs two clasped hands, a symbol of fidelity. The figure on the right is clothed in fashionable attire and holds what appears to be, for it is only suggested with a few light pen-strokes, a harness, rather than a palm of martyrdom as Winkler suggested. The figure on the left represents 'fair-weather' friendship, which fades with the onset of adversity. The idea of a feather possessing more weight than this worthless association is described in the book of emblems by Guillaume de la Perrière, *Le Théâtre des bons engins* of 1536, no.14 (first illustrated edition, Paris 1539; Henkel-Schöne, pp.1430f.). The figure on the right probably represents temperance, since the harness is commonly associated with allegories of this virtue (Henkel-Schöne, p.1361). The two figures are possibly studies for sections of a glass-painting, although why one should be nude and the other clothed is not altogether clear. A fashionably dressed woman holding scales which contain a feather and a pair of clasped hands is also seen in a Swiss glass-painting of *c*.1515 (Zürich, Schweizerisches Landesmuseum, inv.no.LM 6432). In this case, however, the direction of her superficial friendship, or fidelity, is made clear, since she is in the company of an elderly man who supports the heavier scale containing the feather with his hand, and gazes lovingly in her direction.

The drawing is typical of Kulmbach's delicate, somewhat faltering line. It is similar in treatment to the artist's drawing of a *Standard bearer*, which is dated *1510* (formerly Kiel, Kupferstichkabinett des Schleswig-Holsteinischen Kunstvereins; Winkler, k&s, pl.27) and was probably made at about the same time.

99 St Catherine and St Barbara

Charcoal. The sheet shows signs of staining, particularly across the lower edge. 28.2 × 19.7 cm

PROVENANCE: Sir T. Lawrence (L.2445); W. Coningham (L.476); Sir J. C. Robinson; Malcolm

1895–9–15–955

LITERATURE: JCR, p.177, no.529; BM *Guide*, 1895, p.57, no.285; Bock, *Grünewald*, pp.129f.; Conway, p.29, no.493; Schmid, *Grünewald*, ii, pp.283f., repr.; BM *Guide*, 1928, p.35, no.310; Stadler, *Kulmbach*, pp.118f., no.76, repr. (for further literature); Winkler, k&s, pp.84f., no.89, repr.; Rowlands, *Dürer*, pp.54f., no.340

Inscribed, probably by an early hand, in charcoal on the upper edge with Dürer's monogram; and to the right of St Catherine's wheel, by a different but also early hand, in charcoal(?), now much faded, with Dürer's monogram and the date *1514*; and by a later hand, in brown ink in the upper left-hand corner, *251*

The false Dürer monograms, which quite often appear on Kulmbach's drawings, may partly account for the attribution of this drawing to Dürer in the Malcolm catalogue. It was then attributed to Grünewald, before Parker published it in 1928 as a typical charcoal drawing by Kulmbach, of which other examples, one signed (Budapest, Museum of Fine Arts) are known (Winkler, k&s, pls.44–7). The drawing is a preliminary sketch for the saints on either side of the enthroned Virgin, in the central panel of Kulmbuch's painting of the *Virgin and Child with Saints*, signed and dated *1513*, which he was commissioned to make in memory of Provost Lorenz Tucher, in the church of St Sebald, Nuremberg. In the painting, the positions of both saints are turned more to the left, and St Barbara's tower is removed to the background. Related drawings by Dürer make it quite clear that he also played a formative part in the development of Kulmbach's composition. A detailed study for the whole altarpiece in Berlin-Dahlem (Kupferstichkabinett, inv.no.kdz.64; Winkler, *Dürer*, ii, pl.508) and a pen and ink study for the central Virgin and Child group in Vienna (Albertina, inv.no.3127, D.140; Winkler, *Dürer*, ii, pl.509) by Dürer are both signed and dated *1511*. The position of St Catherine in the present sheet is particularly close to that of St Catherine in the Vienna drawing. A further pen drawing of St Catherine in the National Gallery of Ireland, possibly also related to the Tucher altarpiece, has been attributed by some to Kulmbach (*Dublin Master Drawings*, p.54, repr.) but from a stylistic point of view is clearly by Dürer, as Winkler suggested (Winkler, *Dürer*, pl.510).

The colouring and composition of the Tucher altarpiece reveal a strong influence of contemporary Venetian paintings, particularly those of Giovanni Bellini (*c*.1430–1516).

This provides a further indication of the close collaboration between Dürer and Kulmbach, who could not have known works such as Bellini's San Zaccaria altarpiece, dated *1505*, in which a figure of St Catherine is seen in a similar position to her namesake in the Tucher painting. It seems most likely that Dürer would have conveyed knowledge of such paintings to his former pupil after his return from Venice to Nuremberg in 1507.

100 Design for an altarpiece

See colour plate section following p.80

Centre: the Coronation of the Virgin
Left wing: St Wolfgang and Mary Magdalene
Right wing: St George and St Giles
Predella: the Death of the Virgin

Pen and brown ink with yellow, pink, blue, grey and green wash over traces of black chalk. The wings and the predella are drawn on separate pieces of paper, the wings stuck onto the sheet on which the centre and outer frame are drawn. Overall dimensions: 34.4 × 35.7 cm

PROVENANCE: Sloane bequest, 1753

5218–124, 125, 126 and 127

LITERATURE: Hausmann, *Naumann's Archiv*, p.39, nos.124–7; Hausmann, p.110, nos.100–3; BM *Guide*, 1901, p.16, no.A72; BM *Guide*, 1928, p.35, no.311; Stadler, *Kulmbach*, p.121, no.81, repr. (for further literature); Winkler, k&s, p.80, no.82, repr.; Rowlands, *Dürer*, p.55, no.342; B. Butts, *MD*, xxiii–xxiv, no.4, 1986, pp.519ff. repr.

Inscribed by a later hand, in black ink, on the bed in the predella, the monogram of Georg Pencz (q.v.) and *1552*; and by a different hand, in brown ink along the lower edge, on the left wing, *89* and on the right wing, *90*

Listed by Hausmann as a drawing by Dürer, no.100 was first attributed to Kulmbach, possibly by Lawrence Binyon, in the 1901 exhibition catalogue, on account of its resemblance to a study dated *1514*, for the Markgraf's window in the church of St Sebald, Nuremberg (Dresden, Kupferstichkabinett; Woermann, *Dresden*, ii, nos.45–6, pl.7) also attributed to Kulmbach. Winkler noted the similarity in execution of the drawing to Kulmbach's studies for the Maximilian window dated *1514*, also in St Sebald (Winkler, k&s, pls.77–80) in which the use of coloured wash is handled in an identical fashion. No.100 is not connected with any known painting, but probably also dates from this period.

Detailed drawings for altarpieces with movable shutters as seen in the present sheet were usually made for the patron's approval of a particular design. Several such drawings exist by Lucas Cranach the Elder (see no.142) but no.100 is the only one of this type known by Kulmbach.

101

101 Orpheus and Eurydice

Pen and brown ink. 15.9 × 28.7 cm

PROVENANCE: Francis Douce bequest, 1834

Oxford, Ashmolean Museum, P.307

LITERATURE: Stadler, *Kulmbach*, pp.48, 131, no.129, repr. (for further literature); Parker, *Ashmolean*, pp.137f., no.307, repr.; Winkler, K&S, p.60, no.41, repr.; Winkler, *Kulmbach*, pp.13, 92; Lloyd, *Ashmolean Drawings*, pp.6f., no.6, repr.

Inscribed by the artist in brown ink, with his monogram and dated *1518*, above in the centre on the trunk of the tree

The penwork has that charming frailty of line characteristic of Kulmbach; however, as has been pointed out elsewhere, the influence of the prints of Jacopo de' Barbari (*c.*1440/50–1515) particularly the way he treated such subjects from classical mythology is very evident. This drawing is an isolated example of Kulmbach treating such a theme, although one finds an anticipatory detail in his earlier *St Christopher* at Christ Church, Oxford (inv.no.1106; Byam Shaw, ii, pl.841; Winkler, K&S, pl.35), which Winkler dated convincingly *c.*1510. In this he includes some sea monsters that likewise recall such fantastic beasts in the prints of Jacopo de' Barbari and, of course, Albrecht Dürer (q.v.).

Peter Vischer the Younger (q.v.) had earlier produced a drawing of the same subject on the *verso* of a sheet now in Nuremberg (Germanisches Nationalmuseum, inv.no. Hz.5551; Zink, pp.128f., no.102, repr.). Dated *1514*, it is the earliest known drawing attributed to Peter Vischer

the Younger, whose bronze plaquette of *Orpheus and Eurydice* of *c.*1515, apart from the similarities of the physique of Orpheus's body with no.101, has comparable vegetation (J. Pope-Hennessy, *Renaissance Bronzes from the Samuel H. Kress Collection*, London, 1965, no.435, repr.).

Hans Dürer

Nuremberg 1490–Cracow 1534

Painter, brother and pupil of Albrecht Dürer (q.v.). He also worked in his youth in the workshop of Michel Wolgemut (q.v.). Albrecht Dürer executed a portrait drawing of his younger brother in 1503, now in the Washington National Gallery of Art, Rosenwald collection (Winkler, *Dürer*, ii, pl.280). It has also been suggested that the study, *Head of a boy inclined to the left* (no.57), is an earlier portrait of him but its date does not support this identification. Hans is recorded for the last time in Nuremberg in 1510. Eventually he journeyed to Poland where he settled. Payments for work in Cracow begin in 1527. He was one of the artists employed in decorating the principal rooms in Wawel Castle at Cracow, and from 1529 he was appointed court-painter to King Sigismund I. In 1532 he painted the *Tabula Cebetis* in the Deputies' room in the castle, after which he commenced the decoration of two other rooms, with friezes of military parades and tournaments, which on his death were completed by an otherwise unknown artist, Antoni from Wroclaw (Breslau) in Silesia. His death is noted in 1534 in the account book of the royal salt-mines, although a payment due for work in the royal castle is recorded in the following year.

A number of attempts to reconstruct his *œuvre* have been made, but they have been hampered by the heterogeneous nature of surviving works of the period signed with the monogram *H.D.* The most plausible and interesting solutions are noted among the literature listed below.

BIBLIOGRAPHY: H. Beenken, *Zeitschr. f. bild. Kunst*, lxiv, 1930/31, pp.88ff.; H. Beenken, *Prussian Jahrbuch*, lvi, 1935, pp.59ff.; F. Winkler, *Prussian Jahrbuch*, lvii, 1936, pp.65ff.; K. Sinko-Popielowa, *Biuletyn Historii Sztuki i Kultury*, v, 1937, pp.141–63; *Meister um Dürer*, pp.92f.; Jan Bialostocki, *The Art of the Renaissance in Eastern Europe*, Oxford, 1976, pp.24, 60.

102 Virgin of Sorrows

Charcoal and brown chalk. 19 × 13.5 cm

PROVENANCE: E. Rodrigues (sale, Amsterdam, Muller, 1921, 12 July, lot 117, bt *Colnaghi 650 guilders*)

1921–10–12–4

LITERATURE: Röttinger, *Doppelgänger*, p.201; H. Beenken, *Zeitschr. f. bild. Kunst*, lxiv, 1930–31, p.94, repr.; E. Wiegand, *Berlin Jahrbuch*, lx, 1939, pp.142, 147

102

Inscribed by the artist with charcoal on the left-hand side, the artist's monogram, *HD*; on the *verso* inscribed in a florid hand *Matthys Van Aschenhaw* (Aschenbaw) or *Eschenhaw* (Eschenbaw) which probably refers to an early owner of the drawing

For a discussion of this drawing see no.103.

103 Christ on the Cross, and two studies of his hands

Charcoal heightened with white bodycolour, outlines pricked. 38 × 29.1 cm

PROVENANCE: J. C. von Klinkosch (sale, Wawra, Vienna, 1889, 15 April and following days, lot 363)

1895–12–14–62

LITERATURE; C. Dodgson, *Vasari Society*, iv, 1908–9, no.30, repr; Röttinger, *Doppelgänger*, pp.156ff.; H. Beenken, *Zeitschr. f. bild. Kunst*, lxiv, 1930/31, p.95, repr.; E. Wiegand, *Berlin Jahrbuch*, lx, 1939, p.142

Inscribed by the artist in charcoal on the lower edge with his monogram, *HD*.

This drawing and no.102, are clearly by the same hand. They are linked with a further charcoal drawing, also signed with the monogram in the same form, *An audience*, in Erlangen (Universitätsbibliothek, inv.no.B.212; Bock, *Erlangen*, ii, p.88, no.212, repr.). To these can now be added another drawing, clearly by the same hand, also executed in charcoal and with the same kind of monogram, the *Portrait of a man with a beard seen in profile facing left* (20 × 15cm) in the University Library, Warsaw (inv.no. 2b.d.581/1). The chief problem with this group of drawings is whether the Monogrammist HD who executed them can be identified with Albrecht Dürer's younger brother, Hans. Certainly they fit well into the development of painting and draughtsmanship in Franconia in the first quarter of the sixteenth century, and show, as we would expect, some indebtedness to Albrecht Dürer, especially the *Virgin of Sorrows* (no.102). The *Last Judgement* executed with pen and blue ink and watercolour in the Louvre, Paris (inv.no.19.044; Demonts, *Louvre*, i, pl.lxvi) was attributed by Schilling on the basis of a fragmentary inscription on its *verso*, *Hans Durer und . . .*, to Hans Dürer. Despite the difference in the medium from the group of drawings in charcoal, there is a good case to be made for accepting Schilling's proposal. The drawing is competently but not brilliantly done, and the composition itself shows knowledge of Dürer's designs for the same subject, two drawings now in the British Museum (Rowlands, *Dürer*, p.13, nos.65 and 66) both datable *c*.1500. The most natural solution is that this group and the drawing in the Louvre are by Hans Dürer. A strong pointer in support of this is that the watermark of the paper of *An audience* in Erlangen indicates that it is Polish (see J. Smiarska-Czaplicka, *Filigrany Papierni Położonych na obszarze Rzeczypospolitej Polskiej od Początku XVI do Połowy XVIII Wièku*, Wroclaw, Warsaw & Cracow, 1969, p.15, plate xxxviii, closest to no.737 (arms with a

103

dart surrounded by a dragon, that of the Lithuanian family Chneptavius, chief among whom was Vrysztof Szydloweicky (d.1532), Chancellor to King Sigismund I)). Unfortunately what is known of the provenance of the portrait drawing in the University Library, Warsaw (mentioned above), is too slight to be useful, as all we know is that it came from the collection of the Warsaw Society of Friends of the Sciences, given in 1923.

The only other drawings which may reasonably be attributed to Hans Dürer are the pen drawings executed on the vellum attached to the back of the panel of the painting *Portrait of a young man*, signed with the artist's monogram and dated *1511* (Rome, Galleria Spada). They are not only from Nuremberg, as has been suggested, but also the largest of them, *A fantastic bird with a scroll* can be linked with Albrecht Dürer's own drawings, in particular, those surviving on the remaining fragments of Willibald Pirckheimer's Latin translation of the *Hieroglyphica* of Horapollo, probably from the period 1514–17 (see Rowlands, *Dürer*, pp.34–5, nos.224, 225 for those in the British Museum).

The three pen drawings at Erlangen, two of which are signed with the monogram HD cannot, however, be considered to be by Hans Dürer (Bock, *Erlangen*, pp.64–5, nos.213–5). They are certainly the work of a minor talent, chiefly influenced by Lucas Cranach the Elder. It may be that the late inscription, *Herman Döring*, on Bock, *op.cit.*,

no.213 reflects an old tradition; however, such an artist is not known. Perhaps it is a mistake, and Hans Döring, an artist who worked for the Grafs zu Solms was intended (see E. Ehlers, *Hans Döring*, Karlsruhe, 1919).

Georg Pencz

c.1500 – Leipzig October 1550

Painter, engraver and designer of woodcuts. Nothing is known of his origins or education: first recorded in 1523 as a painter in the citizen's register of Nuremberg. He was influenced by Albrecht Dürer (q.v.) and is believed to have executed Dürer's designs for the decorations of the main hall in Nuremberg town hall in 1521 (destroyed) although this has never been confirmed (Landau, *Pencz*, pp.6ff.). Certain writers have considered Pencz to be the same artist as the Monogrammist JB (Jörg Bentz) who made engravings from 1523 to 1530, although this view is not entirely convincing for stylistic reasons (Landau, *Pencz*, pp.10ff.). Together with Bartel and Sebald Beham (q.v.) he was expelled from Nuremberg in January 1525 for anarchistic statements made in support of the Peasants' War, but was re-admitted in September of the same year. It is assumed from stylistic evidence that he visited northern Italy, probably towards the end of the 1520s, and possibly Rome from 1539 to 1540 (Landau, *Pencz*, p.44, n.87). He was appointed painter to Duke Albrecht I of Saxony at Königsberg, but died *en route* at Leipzig.

His paintings include the *Passion of Christ* on the exterior of the wings of the *Silver Altarpiece* of 1531–8, made for King Sigismund I of Poland (Cracow Cathedral), a project to which Peter Flötner (q.v.), Hans Dürer (q.v.) and others also contributed. The most impressive of his painted works are portraits, such as the *Portrait of a Young Man*, dated *1534* (Berlin-Dahlem, Gemäldegalerie); the *Portrait of a Youth*, dated *1544* (Florence, Uffizi); the *Portrait of Jörg Herz*, dated *1545* (Karlsruhe, Staatliche Kunsthalle) and the *Portrait of a Man* dated *1549* (Dublin, National Gallery of Ireland). Influenced by works seen in Mantua, he apparently introduced *trompe l'oeil* ceiling decoration into Nuremberg, where he was commissioned to paint a series of ceiling paintings for the houses of a number of patrician families (see nos.105, 106).

The majority of his known engravings, the most distinguished side of his surviving work, was made in the manner of the so-called 'Little Masters' (see Sebald Beham and Heinrich Aldegrever).

BIBLIOGRAPHY: *Meister um Dürer*, pp.151ff.; H.G. Gmelin, *Munich Jahrbuch*, iii, NF, xvii, 1966, pp.49ff.; Landau, *Pencz* (for further literature); Andersson, *Detroit*, pp.326ff.; Austin, *Nuremberg*, pp.203ff.; Nuremberg, *Gothic & Renaissance*, p.496.

104 Head and shoulders of a young man

See colour plate section following p.80

Pen and black ink, with red, black and white chalk, and water-colour on buff paper. 24.6 × 17.4cm

PROVENANCE: Sir A.Fountaine (sale, Christie, 1884, 10 July, lot 846, bt *Thibaudeau £19* for BM)

1884–7–26–26

LITERATURE: P.Wescher, *Pantheon*, xviii, 1936, pp.281ff., repr.; Rowlands, *Dürer*, p.57, no.351; BM *Portrait Drawings*, p.8, no.12

The artist has inscribed his monogram in black chalk in the centre of the upper edge

Quite apart from the presence of the monogram, the portrayal of the sitter is so characteristic of Pencz, that there can be little doubt about his authorship. Wescher considered the drawing to belong to Pencz's early period because of the Düreresque style of the penwork. In addition, the young man's features, particularly the somewhat arch expression and the highly mannered pose, link it closely with Pencz's earliest known painting, of *Judith*, signed and dated *1531* (Munich, Alte Pinakothek, inv.no.L.271; H.G.Gmelin, *Munich Jahrbuch*, iii, NF, xvii, 1966, p.73, no.1, pl.12). This painting represents Pencz's refined reflection of the work of contemporary Venetians, especially Palma Vecchio (1480?–1528), whom he obviously much admired. The use of wash with coloured chalks is consistent with Pencz's other known drawings, such as the signed portrait of the *Young man wearing a fur cap* in Florence (Uffizi, inv.no.1052). A similar portrait drawing, signed and dated *1536*, was formerly in the Koenigs collection on loan to the Boymans-van Beuningen Museum, Rotterdam, in 1936 (reproduced in a sale catalogue, Amsterdam, de Vries, 1922, 25 January, lot 422).

For want of further pointers it seems reasonable to date no.104 to about the same time as the *Judith* in Munich.

105

105 Design for an illusionist decoration

Pen and black ink, with grey and blue wash. 19.6 × 11.6cm

PROVENANCE: George Grote bequest, 1872

London, University College G.1624

LITERATURE: Hind, *Select List*, p.14, no.18; E.Kris, *Mitt. Kunst*, 1932, pp.65ff., repr.; H. and E.Tietze, *OMD*, xiv, 1939, p.18; *Meister um Dürer*, p.160, no.269; Zink, p.131, under no.103; Byam Shaw, i, p.346, under no.1429, fig.111; Landau, *Pencz*, p.34, n.65; Geissler, *Deutsche Zeichner 1540–1640*, i, p.38, no.A34, repr.

See no.106.

106 Design for an illusionist ceiling decoration

Pen and brown ink with brown and pinkish-brown wash. 23.8 × 15cm

PROVENANCE: General John Guise bequest, 1765

Oxford, Christ Church, 0964

LITERATURE: Bell, p.84 (as Tommaso Sandrino); H. and E.Tietze, *OMD*, xiv, 1939, pp.18f., pl.15; Manchester, *German Art*, p.54, no.137; *Meister um Dürer*, p.160, under no.269; Zink, p.131, under no.103; Byam Shaw, i, p.346, no.1429 (for further literature), ii, pl.848; Landau, *Pencz*, p.34, n.65

The connection between this and no.105 was first referred to by the Tietzes, while Kris had perceived that the description in Sandrart's *Teutsche Akademie* (1675) of a ceiling painting by Pencz of a room in a garden pavilion, at the end of a gallery in Herr Volkamer's house in Nuremberg, was connected with no.105. It was painted, so Sandrart indicates, as though the room were still in the process of being built with workmen bearing in planks and others raising a hoist, in order to complete the roof, through which was visible the open sky with clouds and birds. From this it is clear that, of the two designs, the University College drawing fits the description more closely; however, both are obviously for the same commission. A third drawing, by Pencz, *Two nude workmen seen from below in foreshortening* (Paris, Louvre, Cabinet des Dessins, inv. no.18,946; *Meister um Dürer*, p.160, no.270; E.Kris, *Mitt. Kunst*, 1932, p.66, pl.2) was obviously done in general preparation for his work on the design of ceiling-paintings.

While studying the perspective problems associated with such oblique views, Albrecht Dürer (q.v.) executed a drawing, *c*.1514, of two men hoisting a basket through an oval opening to the sky, which because of its subject has been associated with the Volkamer commission and thus attributed mistakenly to Pencz (Vienna, Albertina, inv. no.3139; Albertina, *Dürer*, no.87, repr.).

All Pencz's designs for ceiling paintings reflect the influence of such works that he saw in Italy, chiefly on his first visit in *c*.1528/9. It has been suggested such illusionist designs may have been inspired by the frescoes of Andrea Mantegna (*c*.1431–1506) at Mantua. Byam Shaw has proposed a later date for the Volkamer commission, although Landau specifically mentions the year 1534 when Peter Flötner (q.v.) was commissioned to work with Pencz on a garden painting for the Hirschvogel's town house, at the beginning of a new and fruitful stage in Pencz's career when he was called upon to decorate various garden rooms for patrician families in Nuremberg. A ceiling painting on canvas of that year of the *Fall of Phaethon* (preparatory drawing by Pencz in the Germanisches Nationalmuseum, Nuremberg, inv.no.HZ.5212; Zink, p.132, repr.) executed for the Hirschvogel family's garden pavilion, but now in a much repainted state in the Stadtmuseum Fembohaus, Nuremberg, was created when the impressions that the decorations of Giulio Romano (1492 or 1499–1546) of the Palazzo del Tè at Mantua made upon him were still vividly remembered, especially the *Marriage of Cupid and Psyche*.

Erhard Schön

Nuremberg, after 1491 – Nuremberg September/December 1542

Painter, designer of woodcuts. Very few details are known about the life of Schön, although he is thought to have designed over 1200 woodcuts. A follower and imitator of the style of Albrecht Dürer (q.v.) he was also influenced by Hans Springinklee (q.v.) with whom he designed woodcuts for the *Hortulus Animae* (1516; for other editions see Oldenbourg, *Hortulus Animae*) and the *Biblia* (1518) produced by Anton Koberger. He contributed a few illustrations for Emperor Maximilian's *Theuerdank* (1517) and *Triumphal Arch* (1515–17, and 1526). He was employed by virtually every printer and 'Briefmaler' (producer of broadsides and minor printed matter) in Nuremberg, in addition to printers in Bamberg, Vienna and Lyons; and, after Dürer's death, he became the most prolific designer of woodcuts in Nuremberg. Apart from his early devotional work, his woodcuts illustrate mythological and historical subjects, in addition to the satirical anti-clerical allegories used by the Protestant reformers, for which he is best known.

Only one signed painting, dated *1538*, by Schön is known (Nuremberg, Germanisches Nationalmuseum) and a handful are attributed to him. Dated drawings by him which have survived were made between 1530 and 1542; some of them are signed with his mark, an acute angle opening to the left (see no.107). A number of other drawings made in pen and ink, his preferred technique, have been attributed to him on a stylistic basis.

BIBLIOGRAPHY: Dodgson, i, pp.418ff.; Thieme-Becker, xxx, 1936, pp.218ff. (for further literature); Andersson, *Detroit*, pp.330ff.; Austin, *Nuremberg*, pp.162ff.

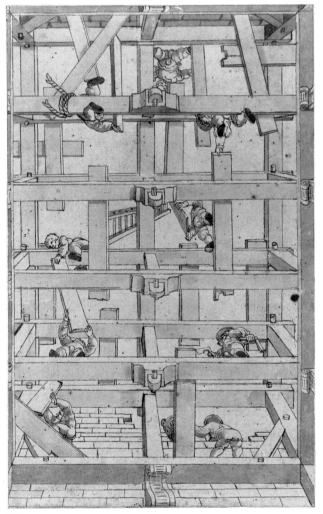

106

107

107 The death of Marcus Curtius

Brush drawing with black ink, heightened with white bodycolour, on a dark brown prepared ground. The sheet has been cut down on all sides. 15.3 × 10cm

PROVENANCE: Mrs Hamilton-Gell (Christie, 1910, 18 July, lot 30, bt with one other, *Obach 27s.6d*); Campbell Dodgson bequest, 1949

1949-4-11-123

LITERATURE: C. Dodgson, *Vasari Society*, x, 1914–15, no.21, repr.

Inscribed by the artist on the lower edge in white bodycolour, *1541*, with part of an acute angle, the artist's mark

Most of Schön's drawings, of which there is an abundance surviving, are executed on a similar scale to the present drawing in pen and ink. No.107, drawn in the year before the artist's death, has been executed unusually in an elaborate way with bodycolour. Two other similar drawings, both likewise from the end of Schön's career, and noted by Dodgson, are the *Judith with the head of Holofernes*, dated *1537*, on red prepared paper in the Louvre, Paris (inv.no. 18.918; Demonts, *Louvre*, ii, pl.cii, no.284) and a *Standard-*

bearer, dated *1540*, executed on a light green ground in the Edmond de Rothschild collection in the same museum.

Hans Springinklee

Active in Nuremberg 1512–c.1524

Painter, designer of woodcuts, block-cutter and miniaturist. Little is recorded of Springinklee's life. He is best known as a pupil and, at times slavish imitator, of Albrecht Dürer (q.v.) in whose house he lived in Nuremberg (Neudörfer, p.144). He designed over 200 woodcuts of varying merit, some of which were formerly attributed to his master, and others of which are signed with his monogram, *HSK*. He made a significant contribution, both as Dürer's assistant, and as an independent designer, to the *Triumphal Procession* (1516–18) and the *Triumphal Arch* (1515–17) of the Emperor Maximilian I. His earliest dated woodcut is the *Horoscope* of *1512*.

In 1520 the Nuremberg Council commissioned the 'young Springenclee' together with 'other good painters' to decorate a ceiling of the castle, on the occasion of the visit of Emperor Charles V (destroyed in 1945; Dettenthaler, p.177, no.9; Fehring-Ress, *Nuremberg*, p.156). The majority of Springinklee's work was for book illustrations produced *c*.1515–22, published by Koberger in Nuremberg and Lyons. His best-known woodcuts were for the *Hortulus Animae*, first published in an edition of 1516 (Lyons) to which Erhard Schön (q.v.) also contributed. None of his prints is dated later than 1522, although some were published after this date (Dodgson, p.369, n.1). In his catalogue of Springinklee's paintings, Dettenthaler attributed fifteen unsigned works to the artist, to which the authenticated ceiling painting in Nuremberg castle is added. These include the high altarpiece for the parish church of St Ursula in Ergersheim of *c*.1515, and the *Welser Altarpiece* of *c*.1521–2 (the former high altarpiece of the Frauenkirche, Nuremberg, of which two surviving panels are in the Germanisches Nationalmuseum, and the remaining sculpture *in situ*). Dettenthaler also attributed to the artist the design of the woodwork of both these altarpieces (pp.152, 161). A wing of an altarpiece with *St George and the Dragon*, in the parish church of St George at Wedelstein (on loan from the Germanisches Nationalmuseum) is considered to be a late work, of *c*.1523–4.

Only two signed drawings by Springinklee are known, *Christ as the Man of Sorrows* in the Kupferstichkabinett, Basel, and *The Rest on the Flight into Egypt*, dated *1514*, in the British Museum (no.108); a few other drawings have been attributed to him on the basis of these. Similarities to the style of the Danube school in his signed drawings, and in some of the paintings attributed to him, suggest that Springinklee was influenced by Albrecht Altdorfer (q.v.) with whom he worked on Maximilian's *Triumphal Arch*.

BIBLIOGRAPHY: Neudörfer, *Nachrichten*, pp.144ff.; Dodgson, i, pp.369ff.; K.T.Parker, *OMD*, i, 1926, p.12, viii, 1928, pp.62ff.; Thieme-Becker, xxxi, 1937, pp.412ff.; *Meister um Dürer*, pp.187ff.; F.Winkler, *Kunstchronik*, xiv, 1961, p.270; J.Dettenthaler, *Mitt. Nuremberg*, 63, 1976, pp.145ff. (for further literature); Austin, *Nuremberg*, pp.152ff.

108 Rest on the Flight into Egypt

Pen and black ink, heightened with white bodycolour, on greenish-brown prepared paper. Some staining across the upper part of the sheet; a small patch of the tree-trunk at the upper edge and the upper left-hand corner are touched in. 22.4 × 16.1 cm.

PROVENANCE: T.Dimsdale; ?S.Woodburn; W.Mayor (L.2799)

1876–12–9–618

LITERATURE: *Mayor Collection*, p.51, no.273; *Mayor Collection 1875*, p.100, no.479; C.Dodgson, *Dürer Society*, vii, 1904, p.11, no.xii, repr.; K.T.Parker, *OMD*, i, 1926, p.12; BM *Guide*, 1928, p.38, no.328; Manchester, *German Art*, p.53, no.133; Rowlands, *Dürer*, p.60, no.366.

Inscribed by the artist, in white bodycolour, on the left-hand edge above the tower, *1514*, and on the tree trunk, with his monogram

Mayor thought the drawing to be by Albrecht Altdorfer (q.v.) and it was registered as such on entering the Museum. The correct attribution to Springinklee was first made by

108

Dodgson, who pointed out the existence of the date and the monogram. Like the only other signed drawing by Springinklee, the *Christ as Man of Sorrows* in the Kupferstich-kabinett, Basel (inv.no.1959.110; *Meister um Dürer*, pl.67), no.108 reveals the influence of Altdorfer and the Danube School, particularly in the treatment of the landscape.

Wolf Traut

Nuremberg c.1485 – Nuremberg 1520

Painter, designer of woodcuts and glass paintings. Apprenticed to his father, Hans Traut (*c.*1460–1516) a native of Speyer, who became a citizen of Nuremberg in 1477. The earliest woodcuts to be firmly attributed to him were for Ulrich Pinder's *Der Beschlossen Gart des Rosenkranz Maria* of 1505, which he must have made while in the workshop of Albrecht Dürer (q.v.); and he was probably also an assistant of Hans von Kulmbach (q.v.). From 1512 to 1513, Dürer employed him to make woodcuts for his *Triumphal Arch*. His most important painting, the Artelshofener altarpiece, signed and dated *1514*, and originally in the Lorenzkirche, Nuremberg, is now in Munich (Bayerisches National museum). From 1513 to 1518 he executed altarpieces for the monastery at Heilsbronn (now Heilsbronn Münster, and Nuremberg, Germanisches Nationalmuseum). A few drawings have been attributed to Traut on a stylistic basis; they are to be found in Paris (Louvre), Erlangen (Universitätsbibliothek), Nuremberg (Germanisches Nationalmuseum) and elsewhere.

BIBLIOGRAPHY: Dodgson, i, pp.500ff.; Rauch; C.Dodgson, *OMD*, xvi, 1930, pp.72ff.; Thieme-Becker, xxxiii, 1939, pp.351ff. (for further literature); *Meister um Dürer*, pp.204ff.; Austin, *Nuremberg*, pp.158ff.; Nuremberg, *Gothic & Renaissance*, p.497.

109 The ordeal of St Kunigunda

See colour plate section following p.80

Pen and black ink with watercolour on the architecture. 35.5 × 31.3 cm

WM: bull's head with a serpent and cross (close to Briquet, 13,375-7)

PROVENANCE: A.Firmin-Didot (sale, Paris, Hotel Drouot, 1877, 12 May, lot 2); presented by Mrs Alfred Morrison

1924–12–13–1

LITERATURE: C.Dodgson, *OMD*, i, no.3, Dec. 1926, pp.32ff., pl.39; Thieme-Becker, xix, 1926, p.597; *Meister um Dürer*, p.212, under no.376; F.Anzelewsky, *Zeitschr. f. Kunstwiss.*, xix, 1965, pp.137ff., repr.; Berlin, *Dürer und seine Zeit*, pp.45f., under nos.12 and 13; Rowlands, *Dürer*, p.60, no.367

A preparatory drawing for the central subject of Traut's woodcut broadside, *The Legend of Sts Henry and Kunigunda*, dated *1509* (Dodgson, i, pp.511f.) of which there are two impressions in the Munich Library. The figures in the foreground are in reverse, whereas the two labourers in the middle distance and the buildings in the background, the old Imperial Palace at Bamberg (the Kaiserpfalz) are in the same direction.

Dodgson, who first published the drawing, attributed it to the Bamberg artist, Wolfgang Katzheimer (active 1465–1508?) through comparison with drawings of Bamberg, including one of the Palace, attributed to him, at Berlin-Dahlem (Kupferstichkabinett, inv.no.KDZ 15346; Berlin, *Dürer und seine Zeit*, pl.12). He dated the present drawing for topographical reasons before 1487, but in this he appears to have been mistaken. The drawing of the Kaiserpfalz at Berlin shows the tower of the palace before the changes apparently brought about the fire of 1 October 1487, whereas the present drawing, the broadside, and painting of *The Ordeal* (Bamberg, Staatsgalerie, inv.no.L.1031; Stange, *Tafelbilder*, iii, p.122, no.296) which has been attributed to Wolfgang Katzheimer the Younger (active 1493–1508), all show a new timber roof with four slender turrets – a change which is recorded in 1489. In addition, details of the costumes argue strongly against an early date and are consistent with the date of the broadside. Thus, despite any similarities that may be seen in the execution of the buildings in the Berlin drawings and the present one, the style of draughtsmanship of the rest of the drawing prompts one to support strongly Anzelewsky's suggestion that this drawing is by Wolf Traut.

St Kunigunda (d.1033) was the wife of the Emperor Henry II, seen here in the centre of the group on the right-hand side of the drawing. Accused of infidelity, she underwent trial by ordeal, and walked unharmed over red-hot ploughshares. An ecclesiastical reformer, who was also canonised, Henry II founded Bamberg Cathedral, where he and Kunigunda are buried (see no.87).

Hans Vischer

Nuremberg c.1489 – Leipzig 1550

Sculptor and draughtsman. Third son of Peter Vischer the Elder (*c.*1460–1529) and brother of Peter Vischer the Younger (q.v.). Hans worked in the family foundry in Nuremberg from *c.*1512, and was in charge of it after his father's death in 1529.

Röttinger identified Hans Vischer with the Monogrammist HV. He considered Vischer to have worked early in his career as a painter with Hans Springinklee (q.v.), and also attributed to him various designs for woodcuts and drawings connected with commissions for Maximilian I.

As a sculptor, Hans controlled the Vischer foundry during its period of greatest productivity. His sculptures are difficult to differentiate from those of his assistants, but amongst the best works, one must number the double funerary monument of the Electors Joachim and Johann Cicero in Berlin Cathedral, completed by 1530; and the large brass screen, originally commissioned in 1512 by the

Fugger family for a funerary chapel, and probably initially designed by Hans's brother, Hermann the Younger (*c.*1486–1517), which was adapted and completed by 1540 for the Great Hall of Nuremberg town hall (now Annecy, Château de Montrottier).

BIBLIOGRAPHY: Röttinger, *Doppelgänger*, pp.147ff.; Meller, *Vischer*, pp.204ff.; Thieme-Becker, xxxiv, 1940, pp.411ff. (for further literature); Nuremberg, *Gothic & Renaissance*, p.497.

110 Christ and the Canaanite woman

Black chalk. The paper at the bottom is much creased. 41.1 × 29cm

WM: high crown (similar to Piccard, vii, 13)

PROVENANCE: acquired between the compilation of the 1815 inventory, in which it is not listed, and that of 1837 in which it features

Ee.1–29

According to a nineteenth-century inscription on the old mount, the drawing was thought to be after Hans Vischer. It is, in fact, a very close record, without the details of the inscription and arms, of the bronze plaque, dated *1543*, originally on the gateway of the Castle at Neuberg an der Donau, and erected by the Pfalzgraf Ottheinrich in com-

110

memoration of the arrival of the Reformation in Neuberg in 1542 (now Munich, Bayerisches Nationalmuseum; see Weihrauch, p.20, no.25, repr.). The design of the plaque is based on the bronze memorial relief, dated *1521*, of Frau Margarete Tucher, in Regensburg Cathedral, which is inscribed with the sign of the workshop of Peter Vischer the Elder (*c.*1460–1529) and attributed by Meller to Paul Vischer who died in 1531 (Meller, *Vischer*, pl.141). The Neuberg plaque would have been produced by the Vischer foundry after Hans took control in 1529, and its composition is similar in most details to the *Tucher Epitaph*. Variations occur principally in the architecture beyond the domed gateway, where in the plaque a pediment of classically inspired proportions replaces the round archway of the earlier relief; and in the decoration of the spandrels of the arched frame, where putti entwined with wreaths replace the circular motifs of the Epitaph.

It is possible that no.110 was made by Hans Vischer himself, although not much is known of his, or any other work by the Vischer family in the medium of black chalk used on its own. It was, in any case, made for the purpose of possible future reference by a member of the foundry.

Peter Vischer the Younger

Nuremberg 1487 – Nuremberg 1528

Sculptor and draughtsman. Son of Peter Vischer the Elder (*c.*1460–1529), whose father, Hermann the Elder (active 1453–87) became a citizen of Nuremberg in 1453 where he established the Vischer brass foundry which, during the first third of the sixteenth century, was to become the most important in Germany. Peter the Younger probably travelled to northern Italy in 1507–8, and 1512–13. Together with his brothers, in particular Hermann the Younger (*c.*1486–1517) and Hans (q.v.), he was responsible for the introduction of Italian Renaissance stylistic elements into German sculpture, notably seem in his *Epitaph of Dr Anton Kress*, dated *1513* (Nuremberg, Lorenzkirche) and in the *Shrine of St Sebald* (Nuremberg, Sebalduskirche), begun by his father in 1508, and completed in 1519. The numerous brass putti on the *Shrine*, generally attributed to Peter the Younger, were produced by the so-called lost-wax method, a technique which originated in Italy. His sculptured work also includes brass plaquettes, medals and ink-stands.

The most important group of drawings by the Vischer family is in Paris (Louvre, Cabinet des Dessins). This consists of records of Italian architecture of both antique and Renaissance origin, and nude studies, made in a classicising manner which reveals the influence of both Dürer's drawings and of north Italian art. The subject of Peter the Younger's earliest dated drawing, *Scylla, 1514* (Nuremberg, Germanisches Nationalmuseum), reveals an interest in classical literature which was also referred to by Neudörfer, who stated that Vischer's illustrated works of

the classical poets were done with the advice of the humanist, Pankratz Schwenter. The latter's manuscript of the life of Hercules, *Histori Herculis*, dated *1515*, contained three of Vischer's drawings (Nuremberg, Stadtbibliothek, and Berlin-Dahlem, Kupfterstichkabinett). Vischer also made a series of drawings for Boccaccio's Decameron.

BIBLIOGRAPHY: Neudörfer, *Nachrichten*, pp.33ff.; Edmund Schilling, *Städel-Jahrbuch*, vi–viii, 1932, pp.149ff.; Demonts, *Louvre*, ii, pp.74ff.; Thieme-Becker, xxxiv, 1940, pp.410f. (for further literature); Stafski, *Vischer*; Berlin, *Dürer und seine Zeit*, pp.64ff.; Austin, *Nuremberg*, pp.219ff.; Nuremberg, *Gothic & Renaissance*, p.497

111 Bath-house scene

See colour plate section following p.200

Pen and brown ink with watercolour over black chalk on vellum. 22 × 15.8cm

PROVENANCE: Campbell Dodgson bequest, 1949

1949–4–11–126

LITERATURE: Manchester, *German Art*, p.53, no.132; Rowlands, Dürer, p.61, no.369

The overtly classical style of the bath-house in this drawing was doubtless the outcome of Vischer's close association with humanist circles in Nuremberg, in addition to his interest in Renaissance works which he would have seen in Italy. Similar elongated figures, drawn in the same technique, may be seen in his illustrations in Berlin-Dahlem, for Pankratz Schwenter's manuscript, *Histori Herculis*, dated *1515* (Kupferstichkabinett, inv.nos.KDZ 1082 and 1083; Berlin, *Dürer und seine Zeit*, pp.64f., nos.57, 58, repr.) and the present drawing may well have been made at the same period.

10 Upper Rhineland, XVI century

Hans Baldung, called Grien

For biography, see before no.88

112 Study of the heads of two men

Red chalk with some preliminary work in black chalk. 28.8 × 20.1 cm

WM: hand in sleeve (similar to Briquet, 11401 and 11410)

PROVENANCE: Earl of Warwick (sale, Sotheby, 1936, 17 June, lot 89, bt *Colnaghi*), Campbell Dogson bequest, 1949

1949–4–11–106

LITERATURE: Winkler, K&S, p.160, no.75, repr.; E.Schilling, *Zeitschr. f. Kunstwiss*, ix, 1955, pp.164–6; Rowlands, *Dürer*, p.50, no.322

This was published by Winkler, who had not seen the original, as by Schäufelein (q.v.). Dodgson, contrary to Winkler's statement, did, in fact, favour Baldung as its author, a view which Friedländer also supported (letter to Dodgson of 1 August 1936). Dodgson similarly noted that Schilling agreed with him; however, subsequently the latter expressed support for Winkler's opinion, seeing it as a late work by Schäufelein. The types of heads here are far more consonant with Baldung, both in their physical structure, a matter which Schäufelein tended to disregard, and in their characterisation, which with Schäufelein, from his maturity onwards, often amounted to little more than a convenient formula, as in his *Portrait of a bearded Man*, signed and dated *1520* in Berlin-Dahlem (inv.no.KDZ 1295). The power of the line and the mastery of details of the features such as the ears, emphatically point to Baldung, and the drawing was most probably made *c*.1512. The head of the bearded old man recalls that of the figure of St Thomas, who kneels on the right in the painting of the *Crucifixion with saints and a donor* (Basel, Kunstmuseum, inv.no.17), signed and dated *1512*, and probably executed on the artist's arrival in Freiburg-im-Breisgau for a church there. No.112 is a spirited drawing but lacks the masterly finesse of his later drawing of the *Head of Saturn*, dated *1516* (Vienna, Albertina, inv.no.17549; Washington, *Albertina*, pl.16). A copy in red chalk, inscribed *1545*/G ☙ B, from the collections of Sir Thomas Lawrence (probably S.Woodburn, sale, Christie, 1860, 5 June, lot 438, as by Baldung, 'Two heads of saints – *red chalk*' bt with one other, *Dale 9s*) and V.Koch, and acquired in 1938 by the Kunsthalle, Bremen, now presumably destroyed. It was much inferior in quality and was probably executed by an amateur who shied away from the more demanding parts of his copying.

113 Head of a fool

Charcoal. Much surface damage and numerous old repairs; the upper right-hand corner has been made up. 26.7 × 19.2 cm

WM: head of an eagle in a shield, i.e. the arms of Freiburg-im-Breisgau (Briquet, 2207)

PROVENANCE: Archduke Leopold Wilhelm (listed in his inventory of 1649 as 'Eines Narrensz Kopff mit ein Capuccio vnd offenem Maul. Mit schwartzer Kreide gezeichnet'; see *Vienna Jahrbuch*, i, 1883, p.clxiii); the Fürsten Liechtenstein; W.Feilchenfeldt, Zürich, from whom acquired by E.Schilling; presented by Mrs R.Schilling in memory of her husband, 1978

1978–3–4–2

LITERATURE: Schönbrunner-Meder, iii, no.253, repr.; C.Koch, *Festschrift Winkler*, pp.197ff., repr.; Yale, *Baldung*, p.217, no.54, repr.; Schilling, *Gesamm. Zeichn.*, p.49, no.17, repr.; Rowlands, *Private Collection*, p.25, no.21, repr.

Inscribed by the artist in black chalk, in the lower left-hand corner, B, the second letter of the artist's monogram, from which it is clear that the drawing has been cut on the left

Meder first suggested the attribution to Baldung, but together with some other drawings executed in chalk it was not included by Koch in his *catalogue raisonné*. Encouraged, however, by Schilling, who had meanwhile acquired the drawing himself, largely for its documentary interest, Koch acknowledged its significance in Baldung's *oeuvre*. He connected the fool depicted here with the figure crouching at the foot of the cross in Baldung's *Crucifixion* which was painted on the reverse of his high altarpiece, the *Coronation of the Virgin*, completed in 1516 and still *in situ* in the Münster, Freiburg-im-Breisgau.

114 Head of an old man with a heavy beard

See colour plate section following p.200

Pen and black ink, heightened with white and rose-pink bodycolour, on dark brown prepared paper. 26.2 × 19 cm

WM: ?traces of a shield with a crown and fleur-de-lis

PROVENANCE: Sloane bequest, 1753

5218–26

LITERATURE: Hausmann, *Naumann's Archiv*, p.35; Hausmann, p.106, no.7; Parker, *Alsatian Drawings*, pp.29f., no.36, repr.; BM *Guide*, 1928, p.38, no.325; Koch, pp.33, 129, no.105, repr.; O.Benesch, *Mitt. Kunst*, 1932, p.13 (reprinted in Benesch, *Collected Writings*, iii, p.384); Manchester, *German Art*, p.52, no.129; Yale, *Baldung*, p.229, no.59, repr.

Inscribed in black ink by the artist, *1518*, with a false Dürer monogram added below by a later hand

112

Previously kept with the drawings doubtfully attributed to Dürer, Parker first attributed it to Baldung but with reservations. As first noted by Benesch, Parker's hesitations now seem unnecessarily cautious because the brilliant execution of the drawing and the type of head both appear to be thoroughly characteristic of Baldung in 1518. The two drawings, both formerly in the Koenigs collection, Haarlem, with which Parker compares it, *Head of a bearded old man looking down*, signed and dated *1519* (Koch, pl.106, present location unknown) and the *Virgin and Child* (Koch, pl.112; New York, Woodner Collection) appear to be closely allied in style. Although, judging now only from good photographs, the head in the former is less impressive than the present drawing in its linear details, especially the fine lines in white bodycolour, both it and the *Virgin and Child* are clearly by the same accomplished hand.

115r

115 *Recto:* A rearing unicorn for a heraldic crest, and a drapery study

Verso: Sketch of the head of a unicorn and its front legs

Brush and black ink heightened with white bodycolour, on grey-blue tinted paper, the *verso* in black chalk. The sheet has been cut down on the upper and side edges. 19.7 × 26.6cm

WM: orb surmounted by a cross, within a shield (similar to Briquet, 3019–20 but smaller)

PROVENANCE: most probably Friedrich Carl von Savigny (1779–1861), from the first of two albums discovered in the 1910s and 1920s by his grandson, Geheimsrat von Savigny, Berlin, among the family possessions, at the instigation of Max J. Friedlander; ?Konsul Julius Licht; presented by Gustav Nebehay

1926–6–21–2

LITERATURE: Parker, *Alsatian Drawings*, p.32, no.50, repr.; Koch, p.150, no.142, repr.; Karlsruhe, *Baldung*, p.279, under no.77, p.285 under no.84; Yale, *Baldung*, p.277, no.88, repr.; Osten, *Baldung*, p.303

Inscribed by the artist in white bodycolour in the lower right-hand corner, *1544*

The heraldic crest of a rearing unicorn forms part of the arms of the Baldung family, of which the artist produced two woodcuts earlier in his career. The first of these (Hollstein, ii, p.149, no.264 repr.), probably dates from the early 1520s, and certainly before 1532 when it was used by the artist's elder brother, Dr Caspar Baldung, as an ex-libris. This we know from Caspar's inscription, dated *[15]32* on the partly coloured impression in the Kunstmuseum, Basel (Basel, *Baldung*, p.80, no.96). This eliminates Parker's suggestion that no.115 is a preparatory drawing for Hollstein 264. The second woodcut is a variant of the preceding, and now possibly only survives in the impression in the British Museum, inv.no.1919–6–16–49 (Karlsruhe, *Baldung*, p.286, no.85, repr.). The only other known impression, inscribed *Die Baldung*, and recorded in an old photograph

in the British Museum, was in a sixteenth-century armorial formerly in the library of the Zeughaus (Arsenal) in Berlin, but is now missing. The pose of the unicorn in the present drawing resembles that in this supposed *unicum*, although the drapery is different. Quite apart from the fact that the unicorn is drawn facing in the same direction as in the woodcut, there is no pressing reason for considering it as a preliminary study for it. The compilers of the Karlsruhe exhibition catalogue (op.cit., p.286) rightly point to the close stylistic link between the putto in the woodcut, and the drawings of putti in Bern (Koch, pls. 154–5) which have been dated to *c*.1530. The renderings of their rotund limbs by regular pen-strokes in these two designs for borders corresponds to the shading in the woodcut, which suggests that it also should be dated *c*.1530.

Koch suggested that no.115 was made in connection with Baldung's woodcut of *The bewitched groom* of *c*.1544 (Hollstein, ii, p.139, no.237 repr.) in which the artist's crest appears in a small shield on a wall at the back of the room. As is stated in the Yale catalogue, it seems unlikely that a drawing as elaborate as the present one would have been made in preparation for such a small detail. Perhaps Baldung originally intended his crest to play a larger part in the composition; but, while this supposition cannot be proved, it is safer to argue that the study was probably made for a separate, unknown composition.

145

116

Follower of Baldung

116 The rape of Proserpine

Pen and black ink, heightened with white bodycolour on brown prepared paper. Much surface damage, in particular along and near the lower edge, with several old repairs badly executed. Cut down on all sides. 20.4 × 29cm

PROVENANCE: J. Heywood Hawkins; Colnaghi

1861–8–10–11

LITERATURE: C. Dodgson, *OMD*, ii, no.7, 1927, p.45, repr.; J. Byam Shaw, *Burlington*, liii, 1928, p.152

Inscribed by the artist in white bodycolour above the god's head, *PLVTO*, and on the lower edge, *151 . . .*, or *154 . . .* (Although Byam Shaw has favoured the first reading, it is possible that the third number could be a '4')

This drawing entered the collection as by Aldegrever (q.v.), but Dodgson, convinced that it was by a Nuremberg artist, attributed it to Erhard Schön (q.v.). This attribution was, however, soon questioned by Byam Shaw, who rightly pointed out the draughtsman's familiarity with Baldung's work, and considered it to be by someone in that artist's circle. This is supported by the fact that the drawing abounds in details strongly reminiscent of features in particular drawings by Baldung. For instance, the horses' heads recall those in the *Four fighting horses*, dated *1531*, in Karlsruhe (Staatliche Kunsthalle; Koch, pl.131) and Proserpine's head that of the *Bowed woman walking on balls tied to her feet* (Koch, pl.61) in Vienna (Albertina, inv. no.3222). The hand that executed the present drawing may be the same as that which was responsible for the *Lamentation over the dead Christ* in Constance (Wessenberg-Museum; Koch, pl.A.11), a copy after Baldung.

Monogrammist GZ

Active 1516–22

Designer of woodcuts. His name is taken from the monogram on a group of single-sheet woodcuts and book-illustrations published between 1516 and 1522 in Basel, Mainz, Hagenau and Strassburg. His works shows the influence of artists of the Danube school, particularly Lucas Cranach the Elder (q.v.), and of Mathis Grünewald (q.v.) and Hans Baldung (q.v.). An identification with the Basel painter, Gabriel Zehender (active 1525–35) to whom a double portrait, dated *1525*, in a New York private collection has been attributed, has not proved conclusive.

BIBLIOGRAPHY: Thieme-Becker, xxxvii, 1950, p.399; Karlsruhe, *Baldung*, p.128 (for further literature).

117 The Virgin and St John standing before Christ on the Cross

Pen and black ink, heightened with creamy white bodycolour on brown prepared paper. 23.4 × 15.8cm

PROVENANCE: F.E.Whelan

1880–2–14–345

LITERATURE: F.Stiassny, *Kunstchronik*, NF, v, 1893–4, col.140; Térey, iii, p.xcvii, under no.9; K.T.Parker, *Anz.*, NF, xxvi, 1924, pp.43ff.; Parker, *Alsatian Drawings*, p.33, no.53 repr.; A.Stange, *Zeitschr. f. Kunstgesch.*, xx, 1957, pp.263f.; Karlsruhe, *Baldung*, p.128

Acquired as by Baldung, it was first attributed to the Monogrammist GZ by Parker, who dated it towards the end of the second decade of the sixteenth century, on the strength of the relationship with the woodcut by this artist, the *Crucifixion* of 1517, and the similarity between the St John in this drawing and the St Philip in his woodcut series of apostles (see H.Koegler, *Zeitschrift für Bücherfreunde*, Bielefeld & Leipzig, xii, 1908–9, p.442). There is a copy, made in the same medium as the present drawing, at Berlin-Dahlem (Kupferstichkabinett, inv.no.KdZ.291; Térey, i, p.xii, no.32, repr.) dated *1524*, which Térey described as a studio repetition after Baldung. The date on the Berlin drawing strongly suggests that Parker's dating of the present drawing could well be right. Stiassny was the first to notice that the Berlin drawing is a close copy after no.117; Térey nevertheless denied that the original was the British Museum drawing without, however, giving any reason, although he does reject the possibility of a connection with Baldung. A version of no.117, perhaps a copy, drawn on a blue ground with a different landscape, was with Colnaghi's in June 1948. Its present whereabouts is unknown.

117

Heinrich Vogtherr the Elder

Dillingen 1490–Vienna 1556

Printer, designer of woodcuts, block-cutter, etcher, draughtsman, painter, author of religious tracts, and eye-specialist. He may have trained under Hans Burgkmair (q.v.). After working from about 1522 in Wimpfen, he moved to Strassburg in 1525 when he became a citizen and member of the guild. From 1536 he began a printing business, chiefly publishing medical works, some evidently written by himself. In 1544/6 he was in Zürich employed by the leading printer, Christoph Froschauer (1521–64). After four years in Strassburg again, he became court-painter in Vienna and eye-specialist to the Emperor Charles V in 1550. Vogtherr is now chiefly remembered for his woodcuts which are more remarkable as works of technical skill than of artistic orginality.

BIBLIOGRAPHY: Thieme-Becker, xxxiv, 1940, pp.499ff.; Geissler, *Deutsche Zeichner 1540–1640*, i, p.46 (for further literature).

118

118 Battle between the Amalekites and the Israelites

Brush drawing in blue wash, heightened with white bodycolour, on grey-blue prepared paper. 15 × 29.9cm

PROVENANCE: B.Geiger (sale, Christie, 1920, 10 Dec., lot 455, bt *Colnaghi £8*)

1921–6–14–5

LITERATURE: Campbell Dodgson, *Belvedere*, i, 1922, pp.88–9, pl.xli; W.Wegner, *Zeitschr. f. Kunstgesch.*, xxii, 1959, p.35, n.14; J.Rowlands, *MD*, viii, no.2, 1970, p.171; Geissler, *Deutsche Zeichner 1540–1640*, i, pp.46f., no.A.42, repr.; *Die Renaissance im deutschen Südwesten*, exhib. cat. Heidelberger Schloss, 21 June–19 Oct. 1986, i, p.305, repr.

Signed by the artist in white bodycolour, on a shield to the left, with his monogram, *HVE* (the 'E' signifies *ältere* 'elder', adopted by Vogtherr in 1541 when his son became a master), and dated, *1542* on a flag above; and inscribed in black ink, on a scroll to the left, *AMALEK* and on flags to the right, *RVBEN, IOSVA, DAN*.

The battle illustrated here is described in Exodus, xvii. This drawing may be compared with Vogtherr's large woodcut, printed from eight blocks, *Judith and Holofernes* of 1543, in which a similar mêlée of opposing cavalry are in conflict. In both works the artist reveals his dependence on the work of the Augsburg school, which is a feature of his *œuvre* throughout his career. Although he is thought to have been trained by Hans Burgkmair (q.v.) the most prevalent influence appears to have been that of Jörg Breu the Elder (q.v.) and the Younger (q.v.). Both in the present sheet, and in a similar but unsigned battle-scene drawing, *Gideon putting the Midianites to confusion*, in the Courtauld Institute collection (inv.no.4701), we find the same rather quaintly domesticated version of the Augsburg tradition that Vogtherr adapted for his Strassburg patrons.

11 The Middle Rhineland, XVI century

Mathis Nithart Gothart, called Grünewald

Würzburg c.1480 (or c.1470/75) – Halle August 1528

Painter, architect, hydraulic engineer. He is not likely to have been a sculptor, as has been proposed. It has proved difficult to use scattered fragments of evidence, which are much debated, to reconstruct an outline of this artist. By a century and a half after his death, when Sandrart published the first account of the artist's career and work, he had sunk into such obscurity that not even his proper name was known. Sandrart refers to him in error as Grünewald (green wood) and this has been enshrined in our minds by the literature and through common usage. Probably the earliest reference, although mistaken, to the artist as Grünewald is to be found in the gold lettering of the Apocalypse on an album in the British Museum (1911–7–3–103/150) containing principally woodcuts by Matthias Gerung (*c*.1500–68/70) which reads: APOCAL: GRVNE/WALT 1637. Gerung usually signed his prints with the monogram *MG* which explains the confusing misattribution of the woodcuts to Grünewald. In contemporaneous documents concerning him, the artist is referred to usually as 'Meister Mathis maler'. The name 'Gothart' (full of God) appears for the first time in 1516, and 'Nithart' (full of evil) in 1527; however, it is not clear which of these was his family name, and which was a given name.

The earliest certain reference, dated 10 October 1505, relates to the painting and lettering by an assistant of Mathis, on an epitaph of Johann Reitzmann, vicar at Aschaffenburg, recently deceased. Grünewald entered the service – probably from 1509 – of Uriel von Gemmingen, Archbishop of Mainz, at whose castle in Aschaffenburg he supervised the building works. In 1511 he painted wings with saints in *grisaille* for an altarpiece for a merchant at Frankfurt, Jakob Heller, who also employed Albrecht Dürer (q.v.) for similar work. In 1512 Grünewald began to work on his masterpiece, the altarpiece for the Antonite Church at Isenheim, Alsace (now in the Musée d'Unterlinden, Colmar); he probably completed it in 1515. By August 1516 he was once more in the service of the court at Mainz, with Archbishop Albrecht von Brandenburg, in whose employ he remained until 1526. Probably being suspected of Lutheranism, he fled to the safety of the nearby city of Frankfurt. In 1527 he moved to Halle, where he was employed as a hydraulic engineer.

BIBLIOGRAPHY: Schmid, *Grünewald*; Thieme-Becker, xv, 1922, pp.134ff.; Sandrart, *Teutsche akademie*, pp.81ff.; Behling, *Grünewald*; Ruhmer, *Grünewald*; G.Testori and P.Bianconi. *L'opera completa di Grünewald*, Milan, 1972 (for further literature).

119 Half-length figure of a woman with clasped hands

Black chalk. 38 × 24cm

PROVENANCE: Francis Douce bequest, 1834

Oxford, Ashmolean Museum, P.297

LITERATURE: Schmid, *Grünewald*, i, pl.48, ii, p.268; Parker, *Ashmolean*, pp.131f., no.297, repr.; Behling, *Grünewald*, pp.36f., 99f., no.10 repr.; Ruhmer, *Grünewald*, pp.87f., no.xvi, repr.; G. Testori & P.Bianconi, *L'opera completa di Grünewald*, Milan, 1972, p.98, no.52 repr.; Lloyd, *Ashmolean Drawings*, pp.8ff., no.7, repr. (for further literature)

Inscribed in the centre of the left-hand edge, in black chalk, *[M]athis*, with above in ink *Matsis*, evidently in imitation of the inscription below it. The inscription in black chalk has been regarded by some scholars as a signature of the artist; however, just as many have rejected this. It is now often thought to be by the same hand as that of the inscription in ink on the right, which has been identified by Schmid as the hand of Philip Uffenbach (1566/70–1630/39) who, according to Sandrart, possessed an album by Grünewald, which Uffenbach would have inherited from his teacher, Hans Grimmer, who was in turn a pupil of Grünewald himself. The inscription on the right, in ink, is as follows, *Disses hatt Mathis von/Ossenburg des Churfürsten v[on]/ Mentz Moler gemacht/und wo du Mathis ge/schriben findest das ha[tt]/ Er mit Eigener handt/gemacht* 'This was made by Mathias of Aschaffenburg painter to the Prince Elector of Mainz, and where you find Mathias written, that he has done with his own hand'. This statement would appear to contradict those who consider that the 'signature' in black chalk on the left is by the same hand as the right-hand inscription

This empassioned study was doubtless executed for a figure in a composition of one of the Passion scenes, like the *Crucifixion*, now lost, known to us from the painted copy at Donaueschingen by Christoph Krafft, dated *1648*. A closely related, similarly forceful study, for another swooning woman is in the Museum am Römerholz, Wintherthur. Grünewald's characteristic use of chalk with strokes of varied intensity mirrors the dramatic effects that he sought in his painting. His skill as a draughtsman stands out, not like Dürer, through the refined precision of line, but from an apparently wayward, shaky use of nervy contours well suited to his highly-charged language. His drawings are not easy to date, even when the probability of an association with a known commission is envisaged, because the technique adopted is uniformly employed through his career. In the present case, however, it has been generally assumed that this and the study in Winterthur were executed just before he began work on the Isenheim altarpiece of *c*.1512–15.

12 Bavaria and Tyrol, XVI century

Austrian or S. German artist

Early sixteenth century

120 Book of Hours of the Blessed Virgin Mary, and other offices (Horae Beatae Mariae Virginis et Officia Varia)

Pen and black ink with bodycolour and gold-leaf on vellum.
19.3 × 13.5 cm (leaf)

PROVENANCE: P. C. Webb (ex-libris); Mrs Margetts, from whom purchased with funds donated by Charles, Lord Farnborough, Jan. 1847

British Library, Egerton MS 1146

LITERATURE: *Add. Manuscripts*, p.385; J. Backhouse, *Books of Hours*, London, 1985, p.12, pl.8 (folio 13 *verso*); Ray Desmond, *Wonders of Creation. Natural History drawings in the British Library*, London, 1986, p.27, pl.10 (folio 293)

As in other areas with flourishing schools of illumination, the German-speaking regions, following in the wake of Flemish examples, produced devotional manuscripts, chiefly books of Hours, whose margins were decorated with flowers of different kinds, small animals and insects. These are chiefly the familiar flowers of the country lane and garden, accurately drawn and coloured so that they are almost always readily recognisable. The margins of this small

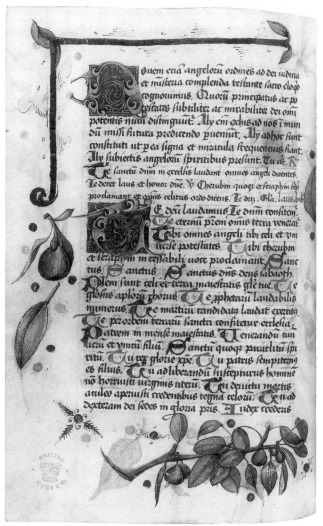

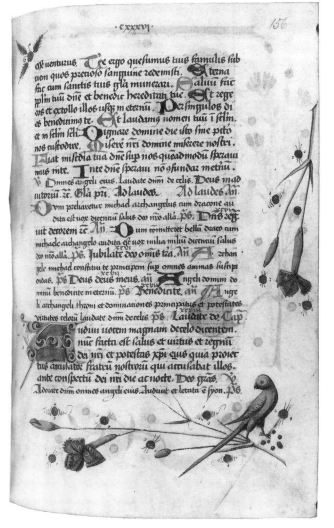

120

quarto manuscript are filled with very finely executed and accurate watercolour drawings of plants. The accompanying drawings of animals and birds are more obviously repetitions of earlier drawings and engravings, while those of the plants, although arranged for decorative effect, do on the whole reflect nature. The book is displayed to show a typical opening (folios 155 *verso*, 156 *recto*): on the left, at the foot, a cut branch from a fig tree with its fruit, and in the left-hand margin, a fig with its stalk and leaves and a detached leaf. On the right are two sprigs of carnations. A parakeet-like bird clearly modelled on a pattern book drawing or an engraving stands nearby.

Janet Backhouse dates the manuscript *c.*1500, and on the basis of the small hunting scenes that decorate the leaves of the calendar, places it in south Germany or Austria. Her proposal that it was produced for a member of the Emperor Maximilian's court is not impossible, given the Emperor's passion for the chase. But this was, of course, endemic in courtly circles then. The saints included in the calendar give credence to Miss Backhouse's general location of the manuscript.

121

Anonymous artist

Bavarian c.*1520*

121 *Recto:* The Birth of Christ

Verso: A barrel-roofed interior with women sorrowing over a dead body

Pen and black ink with grey wash, heighened with white bodycolour on reddish-brown prepared paper, the *verso* in pen and black ink on light-brown prepared paper. 16.9 × 13cm

England, Private Collection

LITERATURE: F. Winzinger, in *Festschrift Karl Oettinger*, Erlanger Forschungen, Reihe A, xx, 1953, pp.370–1; Winzinger, *Huber*, i, p.154, no.216, repr.; Schilling, *Gesamm. Zeichn*, p.189, no.39, repr.; Rowlands, *Private Collection*, p.45, no.40, repr.

Winzinger initially associated this drawing with an artist from Regensburg, Michael Ostendorfer (*c.*1490–1559) but later attributed it to an artist whom he named, after a small painting in the Thyssen Collection, Lugano, the Master of the Thyssen Adoration. This work was clearly done by a close follower of Wolf Huber (q.v.). Unfortunately, the stylistic basis by which Winzinger links the Lugano painting not only with the present drawing, but also with the *Interior of a church*, a drawing in Munich, dated *1518* (Staatliche Graphische Sammlung, inv.no.1024; Winzinger, *Huber*, ii, pl.217) is difficult to perceive. It seems prudent, therefore, to classify this drawing, whose technique and style is so characteristic of southern Bavaria, as a work of that region of about 1520.

Hans Maler zu Schwaz

Schwaz active c. *1500*–c.*1530*

Painter. Originally from Ulm, he settled in Schwaz, near Innsbruck. He is documented in 1510 as the painter of two portraits of Maria of Burgundy, which were commissioned by Emperor Maximilian I. He was much patronised by the Archduke Ferdinand, grandson of Maximilian and younger brother of Emperor Charles V, and by the Fugger family of Augsburg. A small *œuvre* of portraits has been established around the *Portrait of a man* dated *1523* and signed, *HM MZS* (Duke of Sutherland, Ellesmere Collection) and the *Portrait of Anton Fugger*, inscribed on the reverse *Hans Maler von Ulm Maler zvo Schwatz* with the date, *1524* (Vienna, Count Thun). His paintings reveal the influence of the Swabian artists, Bartholomeus Zeitblom (*c.*1455/60–1518/22) and Bernhard Strigel (q.v.).

BIBLIOGRAPHY: G. Glück, *Vienna Jahrbuch*, xxv, 1905, pp.245ff.; Thieme-Becker, xxiii, 1929, p.591 (for further literature).

122 Portrait of Ferdinand, Archduke of Austria (1503–64), later Emperor Ferdinand I

Pen and black ink, and bodycolour, with a background of olive green over bright blue ground which is visible in places. 38 × 26.8cm

PROVENANCE: General John Guise bequest, 1765

Oxford, Christ Church, 1108

LITERATURE: Bell, p.86, pl.cx; K.T.Parker and W.Hugelshofer, *Belvedere*, viii, 1925, p.52, repr.; K.T.Parker, *OMD*, vii, 1932, p.27; Otto, *Strigel*, p.103, no.66, repr.; Byam Shaw, i, p.345, no.1428 (for further literature), ii, pl.843

A comparison with other documented portraits of Ferdinand, who was the younger brother of the Emperor Charles V and was crowned Emperor in 1556, makes it certain that he is the sitter in this drawing. Parker abandoned his acceptance of Bell's attribution to Bernhard Strigel (q.v.) for the convincing proposal that it is by Hans Maler, who was employed by the Archduke on several occasions between 1521 and 1525 to produce pairs of portraits of himself and his wife. In the present portrait, the sitter appears to be the same age, that is about seventeen, as in Maler's earliest

123

painted portraits of the Archduke, in Vienna (Kunsthistorisches Museum, inv.no.831), Stuttgart (Altertümer Museum), formerly at Worlitz (Gotisches Haus) and formerly in a Bavarian private collection. The last three of these, which are repetitions of the Vienna portrait, all bear the inscription: *REX FERDINANDUS, Etatis 17, 1521*.

123 The Adoration of the Magi

Pen and brown ink. Cut down most obviously on the upper and vertical edges. 18.3 × 13.5cm

PROVENANCE: H.S.Reitlinger (sale, Sotheby, 1954, 14 April, lot 276, as 'German *c.*1515', bt *Schidlof* £9); E.Schilling; H.Schaeffer, New York; A.Laube, Zürich

1984-11-10-1

LITERATURE: H.S.Reitlinger, *Old Master Drawings, A Handbook for Amateurs and Collectors*, London, 1922, p.121, pl.12 (as 'German 1500–1520'); E.Schilling, *OMD*, viii, Sept. 1933, pp.28f., pl.30

This would appear to be an isolated example of a composition sketch by Hans Maler. The attribution hinges on the similarity that Schilling adroitly perceived between the facial types in the drawing, especially of the king standing

122

on the left, with those in two paintings from a series of martyrdoms of the apostles, of St Bartholomew and St Andrew in Nuremberg (Germanisches Nationalmuseum, inv.no.HG 550 and 551; Lutze & Wiegand, p.88, nos.263 and 264). These panels, formerly attributed to Michael Ostendorfer (*c.*1490–1559) and then Bernhard Strigel (q.v.), were subsequently very convincingly reattributed to Hans Maler through the remarkable likeness of the features of the executioner on the left in the *Martyrdom of St Bartholomew* to those of the sitter in the black chalk drawing of a *Portrait of an old man* in Karlsruhe (Kunsthalle, inv.no.VIII 1655), signed by the artist with his monogram (Karlsruhe, *Altdeutsche Zeichn.*, no.16, repr.).

The Master of Mühldorf

Mühldorf am Inn, active early sixteenth century

Painter, designer of woodcuts, draughtsman. His name is taken from the paintings on two wings and the predella of an altarpiece of the *Passion*, dated *1511*, which was probably made for the Salvatorkirche, Ecksberg, but since the mid-nineteenth century, it has been in the parish church of St Lorenz at Altmühldorf, near Mühldorf am Inn. A drawing of the *Annunciation*, dated *1514* (Sacramento, E.B.Crocker Art Gallery), considered to be by the same artist, bears the monogram W, which Hausberger has suggested is that of Wilhelm Pätzsold (Thuringia *c.*1470/80–Mühldorf 1521), a painter recorded as active in Mühldorf. The interpretation of the name by some authorities as Wilhelm Beinholt is, according to Hausberger, due to a mis-reading of the inscription on Pätzsold's tomb-stone in the church of St Nicholas, Mühldorf (Hausberger, p.130). From the few known works attributed to this master, it would appear that as a journeyman he travelled in Austria and Bavaria, and settled in Mühldorf in 1511.

Among his most notable paintings are the *Pfeffinger Family Tree*, dated *1516* (Munich, Bayerisches National-museum); the *Martyrdom of St Leodegar* (Nuremberg, Germanisches Nationalmuseum); and the *Sermon of St Paul* (Innsbruck, Tirolisches Landesmuseum Ferdinandeum). His work to some extent reflects the influence of the early works of Lucas Cranach the Elder (q.v.) and among the other artists of the Danube School, in particular Albrecht Altdorfer (q.v.).

BIBLIOGRAPHY: Thieme-Becker, xxxvii, 1950, p.237; Linz, *Don-auschule*, pp.143ff.; Yale, *Danube School*, pp.74f.; Hausberger (for further literature)

124 The Virgin of Altötting

See colour plate section following p.200

Pen and black ink, heightened with white bodycolour, on brown paper. Somewhat water-stained. The back of the drawing is, according to Dodgson, covered with red chalk, but this is difficult to verify through the backing. 22.3 × 17.8cm

PROVENANCE: T.Thorp; Campbell Dodgson bequest, 1949

1949-4-11-122

LITERATURE: C.Dodgson, *Munich Jahrbuch*, NF, xii, 1937/38, pp.45ff., repr.; *Altdorfer*, p.164, no.731; Winzinger, *Zeitschr. f. Kunstwiss.*, xxii, Heft 1/2, 1968, pp.18f., repr.; Hausberger, pp.96ff., repr. Inscribed by the artist, in black ink, *1518*

The *Annunciation* in the E.B.Crocker Art Gallery, Sacramento, dated *1514* with a monogram (*Old Master Drawings from the E.B.Crocker Collection: the German Masters, 15th to 19th centuries*, exhib. cat., Sacramento, California, 1939, German Masters, Group One, no.11, repr.) was the only drawing which was attributed to the Master of Mühldorf prior to Winzinger's reappraisal and expansion of the Master's œuvre. Indeed, the Sacramento drawing is the sole basis for Winzinger's attribution of a small group of prints and drawings to him. Of these additions, the present drawing is the one which has perhaps the most to recommend its attribution, on grounds of style, if we allow for the differing purposes for which the two drawings were evidently made. While it cannot be said that any decisive points of close comparison are available to us, the representation of the raised head of an archangel in the *Annunciation* and the heads of the boyish angels betray a mannerism common to both. The attribution of this drawing to the Master of Mühldorf is reinforced by the subject, which represents a local image. Although Dodgson attributed the drawing to the Innsbruck artist Sebastian Scheel (*c.*1479–1554), he correctly identified the subject as the earliest known representation of the statue of the Virgin in the Holy Chapel at Altötting, near Mühldorf 'Die Gnadenmutter von Altötting' (C.Dodgson, op.cit., pl.1). The Virgin is shown in the drawing with clothing and adornments which would have been draped round the statue in votive offering, and surrounded by angels which are not there today. The year 1518 was the high point of the image's veneration immediately before the Reformation, for it was then that the Emperor Maximilian I presented the chain, depicted in the drawing, as a votive offering, on the engagement of his nephew, Ferdinand, son of Philip the Fair, to Anna of Hungary and Bohemia. It is possible to make out, hanging from the chain in the drawing, the arms relating to this prospective union: the two upper arms are of Austria and of the Sforza of Milan, symbolising the marriage of Maximilian I and Bianca Sforza, and below, the arms of Ferdinand.

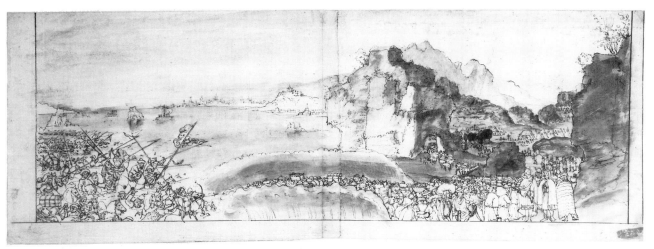

125r

Ludwig Refinger

Ingolstadt? c.1506 – Munich 1548/49

Painter and designer of glass-paintings. Active in Munich from 1528, when he was in the workshop of Wolfgang Muelich (active 1520–before 1542), and where he was an assistant of Barthel Beham (1502–40) whose workshop he took over in 1540, and whose widow he married.

His work for the Bavarian Dukes of Munich and Landshut included contributions to the series of painted scenes from classical history commissioned by Duke Wilhelm IV for a garden room and to which, among others, Jörg Breu (q.v.), Hans Burgkmair (q.v.) and Albrecht Altdorfer (q.v.) also contributed. Only three of Refinger's paintings for the series are known to have survived: *The death of Marcus Curtius*, dated *1540* (Munich, Alte Pinakothek); *Horatius Cocles halting the advance of Lars Porsena* and *The duel of Manlius Torquatus with a Gaul* (both Stockholm, National-museum). From 1542 to 1543 he worked for Duke Albrecht V at the Stadtresidenz, Landshut; his ceiling decoration for the *Planetenzimmer* has survived, but his work in other rooms has either been re-painted (see no.125) or completely obliterated by re-building. It is also recorded that he made twenty-four designs for glass paintings for the Stadt-residenz.

None of his drawings is signed but a small, coherent group, characterised by elaborate architectural forms, which reveal the influence of Albrecht Altdorfer (q.v.), have been connected with his paintings for stylistic reasons.

BIBLIOGRAPHY: Thieme-Becker, xxviii, p.81 (for further litera-ture); E. Schilling, *Munich Jahrbuch*, v, 1954, pp.131ff.; Blankenagel; *Stadtresidenz Landshut*.

125 *Recto:* The Crossing of the Red Sea

Verso: Studies for a Resurrection of Christ, an Agony in the Garden, a (?) Last Supper, and an architectural scene with figures

Pen and brown ink with watercolour, the *verso* in brown ink alone.

23.4 × 66.4 cm

PROVENANCE: Sloane bequest, 1753

5218–205

LITERATURE: E. Schilling, *Munich Jahrbuch*, v, 1954, pp.139–40, pls.6–7; Blankenagel, pp.207ff.

Inscribed on the left-hand side of the *verso* in the artist's hand in brown ink, *ein trüber himmel und die Lanschafft auch trüb alles (?) rüsten hier muss (?) glelet oder liecht (?) vlüchtig darin/stand (?) forn hin bis (?)*; and on the study for the Agony in the Garden, *stgrau/rot/forn liecht/in der finster/stundt/des Hern/finster in himel und Lanschaft/stein (?) pliessen wird grau/einzig steinfarb*; and on the study for a Last Supper, *diese sind drei Fenster/(?) grün/(?)/(?)/rund gedacht*

On the *recto* is an impressive design for a dramatic biblical subject, in which nature and the miraculous deliverance of the Israelites from Pharaoh's host play a dominant role. Refinger's use of watercolour here is particularly effective in his rendering of a sense of atmosphere.

The drawing is evidently a preparatory study for a fresco of the same subject on a vault in the west arcade of the inner courtyard of the Stadtresidenz, at Landshut, where the artist worked from 1542 to 1543. As Schilling has pointed out the fresco is a reduced version of the composition as it appears in the present drawing. The autograph quality of this sheet, established by comparison with other drawings by Refinger, strongly supports the traditional attribution of the fresco to this artist, although Blankenagel considers the attribution uncertain. It has to be acknowledged that this painting, like the other frescoes in the west arcade, has been damaged and heavily re-painted. Judgement over the question of attribution would not be possible were it not for the existence of the present study, which makes Blankenagel's doubts seem somewhat academic.

Most of Refinger's known drawings possess elaborate architectural components and are usually executed in pen and ink alone. The rapid pen and ink sketches on the right-hand side of the *verso* of no.125 were made for four subjects unrelated to the *recto*. Their technique is closely comparable in its execution to a sketch on the *verso* of Refinger's *Scene from classical history: probably the Arrest of Helen*, in a private collection (E. Schilling, *Munich Jahrbuch*, v, 1954, p.135, repr.). The annotations on the *verso* of no.125 are also typical of Refinger's style and may be seen on other drawings, such as the *Christ and the Woman of Samaria*, in a private collection (Rowlands, *Private Collection*, p.49, repr.).

Hans Wertinger

1465/70 – Landshut 17 November 1533

Painter, glass-painter, designer of woodcuts and miniaturist. First recorded in a document of 18 August 1491, in which he acquired citizenship of Landshut and in which he is described as a painter, indicating that he must have had the status of master by this date. The Swabian characteristics of his work suggest that he trained in Augsburg.

Numerous documents record his commissions. From 1497 to 1499 he made works for the cathedral at Freising including an altarpiece of the *Legend of St Sigismund*, dated *1498* (Freising, cathedral sacristy) which reveals the influence of Mair von Landshut (q.v.). This was commissioned by Philipp, Bishop of Freising for whom other works by Wertinger are recorded in several commissions between 1515 and 1526. In 1503 and 1508 he made paintings for Friedrich the Wise of Saxony. In 1515–16, he made panel paintings, of which only those for the predella have survived, for the carved altarpiece by Hans Leinberger (active 1510–30) at Moosburg (former Stiftskirche). From 1515 onwards he produced numerous portraits, particularly of the Wittelsbach family, the Counts of the Pfalz and other members of the nobility, many of which are now in the Bayerisches Nationalmuseum, Munich. His portraits were much in demand, since many repetitions of them exist, probably executed in part by assistants. Examples of his portraiture at its best, are *Duke Wolfgang* of *c.*1526 (Vienna, Kunsthistorisches Museum), and the diptych of *Duke Wilhelm IV and his wife, Jacobaea von Baden*, dated *1526* (Munich, Alte Pinakothek). Other works include wall decorations at Trausnitz castle for Duke Ludwig X (destroyed) and a painting of *Alexander the Great and his doctor, Philippus*, dated *1517* (Prague, National Gallery) in which various members of the Landshut court are represented.

Woodcuts attributed to Wertinger date from *c.*1515 to 1520, when it seems he designed illustrations for books printed by Johann Weyssenburger in Landshut. Three drawings have been associated with these cuts of which

126

that at Constance (Wessenberg Gallery; T. Musper, *Munich Jahrbuch*, NF, xi, 1934, p.181, repr.) makes an interesting comparison with no.126; certainly it is from the same region of Germany and from the same period. The influence of the Renaissance, detectable in his later work by the decorative Italianate elements which appear in his portraits in the form of swags of fruit, was probably passed on to him through the prints of, among others, the Augsburg masters Hans Burgkmair (q.v.) and Jörg Breu the Younger (q.v.).

BIBLIOGRAPHY: Altdorfer, pp.165ff.; Thieme-Becker, xxxv, 1942, pp.425ff.; Ehret, *Wertinger* (for further literature).

126 St Bartholomew and a kneeling canon

Pen and brown ink with grey wash. 17.7 × 10.9cm

England, Private Collection

LITERATURE: Schilling, *Gesamm. Zeichn.* p.235, no.67, repr.; Rowlands, *Private Collection*, p.45, no.41, repr.

This drawing was most convincingly associated by Edmund Schilling with Hans Wertinger. The attribution finds further confirmation from a comparison with the pair of glass-paintings from the Charterhouse at Prüll near Regensburg. These are of Duke Albrecht IV of Bavaria, the founder of the monastery, with St John the Evangelist, and of Duke Wilhelm IV of Bavaria, son of Albrecht IV with St Bartholomew, the patron of the monastery (Munich, Bayerisches Nationalmuseum; *Bayerische Frömmigkeit*, p.55, nos.T.170/171 repr.). They are credibly assigned to the circle of Hans Wertinger by Elisabeth von Witzleben, and were evidently placed in windows either side of the high altar, and executed certainly after the death of Duke Albrecht in 1508, and most probably in time for the re-dedication of the new monastery church at Prüll, in 1513. It is not inconceivable, given the presence of the donor's patron saint in the present drawing, that it may be associated with the design of another glass-painting at Prüll; and it should probably be dated about 1510, a decade later than has been tentatively suggested previously. A remarkable fact about the two extant glass-paintings is that two well-nigh exact contemporaneous duplicates exist in the parish church at Tölz in Upper Bavaria.

13 The Danube School, XVI century

Albrecht Altdorfer

c.1482/85 – Regensburg 12 February 1538

Painter, draughtsman, architect, engraver, etcher, and designer of woodcuts. Probably the son and pupil of Ulrich Altdorfer, a 'Briefmaler' and miniaturist, who was active in Regensburg from 1478 to 1491. Described as a 'Maler von Amberg' (Upper Palatinate) when he acquired citizenship in Regensburg in 1505. Little is documented of his youthful career, although his earliest works, reveal the influence of Lucas Cranach the Elder (q.v.) and Albrecht Dürer (q.v.), and also a knowledge of the *St Wolfgang Altarpiece* by Michael Pacher (c.1435–98), indicating that he visited Salzburg then. He must have studied Italian engravings, a collection of which is recorded in his will, particularly those of Andrea Mantegna (1431–1506) and Jacopo de' Barbari (c.1450–1515/6).

The majority of his prints and drawings appear to have been made between 1506 and 1520. They reveal a knowledge of the work of Wolf Huber (q.v.) and a rapid development to artistic maturity. Among the surviving paintings, the most notable is a large altarpiece with scenes from the *Passion of Christ and the Life of St Sebastian*, made for the Augustine monastery at St Florian, near Linz, from c.1509 to 1516; sixteen panels have survived (St Florian, Augustiner-chorherrenstift, and Vienna, Kunsthistorisches Museum). Other important works are the signed *Landscape with Schloss Wörth*, of c.1520, one of the earliest examples of German landscapes painted as a subject in its own right (Munich, Alte Pinakothek), and the *Battle of Alexander* signed and dated *1529*, one of a series commissioned by Duke Wilhelm IV of Denmark (Munich, Alte Pinakothek).

He worked on collaborative ventures for Maximilian I, supplying some of the miniatures for the *Triumphal Procession*, of 1513–16 (Vienna, Albertina), drawings for the *Prayer Book* of 1515 (Besançon, Bibliothèque), and woodcuts for the *Triumphal Arch* in c.1515 and for the *Triumphal Procession* in c.1517–18. His thirty-six known etchings number among the earliest northern examples of this technique.

Altdorfer also pursued a political career in Regensburg. He became a member of the city council in 1517, and was offered the office of mayor in 1528; his refusal of this position may have been due to a preoccupation with the painting of the *Battle of Alexander*. He was also employed by the city as an architect. His long will testifies to his success and worldly prosperity.

BIBLIOGRAPHY: *Altdorfer*; Winzinger, *Altdorfer*; Linz, *Donauschule*, pp.35ff.; Yale, *Danube School*, pp.31ff.; Andersson, *Detroit*, pp.178ff.; Meissner, ii, 1986, pp.391ff. (for further literature); George R. Goldner and Lee Hendrix, *Burlington*, cxxix, no.1011, June 1987, pp.383ff.

127 *Recto:* A wildman carrying an uprooted tree

See colour plate section following p.200

Verso: Architectural studies

Pen and black ink, heightened with white bodycolour on reddish-brown prepared paper, the *verso* in pen and black ink.
21.4 × 14.6cm

PROVENANCE: A. von Lanna (sale, Stuttgart, H.G. Gutekunst, 1910, 6 May, lot 7, bt *Obach RM 1320*)

1910-6-11-1

LITERATURE: Winzinger, *Altdorfer*, pp.66ff., no.6, repr.; (for further literature); Oettinger, *Altdorfer-Studien*, pp.15–17, 37; F. Winzinger, *Vienna Jahrbuch*, xviii (xxii), 1961, pp.11ff., repr. (*verso*)

Inscribed by the artist in black ink, on a rock in the foreground, with his monogram and the date *1508*

The earliest of Altdorfer's drawings, those produced in the years 1506/07, were highly individual in character, but the figures in them were rather stiff in posture. By 1508, however, he had achieved a freedom of expression ideally suited to his subjects and their interpretation. The present drawing together with one from the same year, *St Nicholas rebuking the storm* in the Ashmolean Museum, Oxford (inv.no.P.268; Winzinger, *Altdorfer*, pl.5), are the first in which his recently found liberty of expression is apparent. The wildman's uncontrolled strength and the exuberant growth of the foliage are admirably captured

127v

through his sketchy but deft use of the pen. Similarly, in the Oxford drawing, the raging of the sea and the miraculous intervention are made quite credible through his dramatic 'shorthand', emphasised in the present drawing with a skilfully expansive use of white bodycolour. An even more lively woodland scene with a wildman and his family, executed *c*.1510, is in the Albertina, Vienna (inv.no.17548 Winzinger, *Altdorfer*, pl.24). The architectural and geometrical studies on the *verso* are amongst the earliest of their kind by Altdorfer. For, although it does not follow that drawings on the *verso* are necessarily by the same hand as that on the *recto*, in the present case there is no reason for thinking that they are not by him. They consist of two sketches of vaultings, one very freely drawn of a perspective construction and the other of what appears to be the same sort of geometric construction. Winzinger connects them with the vaulting in Altdorfer's etching, the *Interior of the Synagogue in Regensburg*, of 1519 (Bartsch, viii, pp.63f., no.63); however, this is no reason for assuming that there is an immediate connection. Altdorfer was employed as an architect and this interest is revealed in his paintings. Architectural drawings by him and his circle are among the finest of the period in south Germany (see Winzinger, *Altdorfer*, pls.107–12; P.Halm, *Munich Jahrbuch*, DF, ii, 1951, pp.127–78).

128 Saint Barbara

Pen and black ink, heightened with white bodycolour, on brown prepared paper. 12.6 × 9cm

PROVENANCE: Obach & Co

1909–1–9–12

LITERATURE: Obach & Co, *Old Master Drawings*, no.62; Becker, p.115, no.50

Becker regarded this drawing as being probably from Altdorfer's own hand. She dated it *c*.1517, and connected it on stylistic grounds with the *St Barbara* in Budapest (Szépmüvészeti Múzew Museum, inv.no.E17–35; Winzinger, *Altdorfer*, pl.62) while at the same time noting the disparity of the width of the pen strokes in each. In our view, however, the present drawing is closest in style to the *Martyrdom of St Sebastian*, signed and dated *1511* in Brunswick (Herzog Anton Ulrich-Museum; Winzinger *Altdorfer* pl.26), and the *Sacrifice of Isaac* of *c*.1510 in Vienna (Albertina, inv.no.3212; Winzinger, *Altdorfer*, pl.25). In both these drawings the economy in the use of white bodycolour, and the controlled delicate pen strokes are strong points of similarity to no.128. The present sheet is unaccountably not mentioned by Winzinger in his monograph.

128

129

129 St Christopher carrying the Christ Child

Pen and black ink, heightened with white bodycolour, on dark brown prepared paper. 27.2 × 15.5cm

PROVENANCE: presented by Granville Tyser, through N.A.-C.F., 1925

1925-5-9-1

LITERATURE: *N.A.-C.F. Report*, xxii, 1925, p.38, no.522, repr.; C. Dodgson, *Burlington*, xlviii, 1926, pp.140f., repr.; Winzinger, *Altdorfer*, p.77, no.38, repr. (for further literature); Oettinger, *Altdorfer-Studien*, pp.55ff.; Manchester, *German Art*, p.55, no.141

Inscribed by the artist in black ink in the upper right-hand corner, *1512*, with his monogram

Altdorfer has depicted the saint unusually from the rear, dramatising as well as heightening the forms with an exaggerated use of white bodycolour. 1512 was evidently the year when Altdorfer achieved a highly original fluency of expression that followers attempted to emulate without much success. To appreciate the extent of his development at this time, one has just to compare this drawing with that of *St Christopher* in Hamburg (Kunsthalle, inv.no.22887; Winzinger, *Altdorfer*, pl.22), done two years earlier.

Lucas Cranach the Elder

Kronach 1472 – Weimar 16 October 1553

Painter, engraver and designer of woodcuts. Son of the painter, Hans Maler (d. Kronach, 1527/8) with whom he probably made his first training. Lucas took his surname from his birthplace. The style of his early work indicates that he may have been active in his youth in Munich, and some of his prints and paintings of the early 1500s reveal the influence of Albrecht Dürer (q.v.). As a journeyman, he seems to have travelled up the Danube to Austria, and from 1501/2 to 1504/5 he worked in Vienna. During this period he painted the notable portraits of *Johannes Cuspinian and his wife, Anna*, in *c*.1502 (Winterthur, Museum am Römerholz) and of the principal of Vienna University, *Johann Stephan Reuss*, dated *1503* (Nuremberg, Germanisches Nationalmuseum). The exuberant style of his prints, drawings and paintings produced then, was evidently a source of inspiration for artists of the Danube School.

In 1505 he became court painter to Duke Friedrich the Wise of Saxony, and established his workshop at Wittenberg. He supplied decorations for various ducal residences, including many, now lost, for the Veste Coburg, where he worked intermittently from 1505 to 1509. As court painter, a position he held under successive Electors from 1505 to 1547 and from 1550 until his death, he developed an elegant style, verging on the mannered in his later years, which had a pervasive influence on sixteenth-century Saxon painting. In 1508, Duke Friedrich granted him a coat of arms and thereafter, Cranach used the principal charge, a winged serpent, as his signature: on earlier works with its

wings upraised, and after 1534 with its wings lowered. He also carried out commissions for the Emperor Maximilian I, including eight drawings for his *Prayer Book* of 1515 (Munich, Bayerisches Staatsbibliothek) a project to which Albrecht Dürer (q.v.), Hans Baldung (q.v.) and others also contributed.

In Wittenberg, Cranach was a town councillor from 1519 to 1545, and held the post of mayor several times between 1537/8–1543/4. In addition to running a large workshop, in which both his sons, Hans (*c*.1513–37), and Lucas the Younger (q.v.) worked, he owned several houses, an apothecary's shop and, from 1523 to 1525/6, with Christian Döring, a publishing firm which specialised in Reformation literature. He was a close friend of Martin Luther, for whom he illustrated the influential *Passional Christi und Antichristi* (1521) after the latter's excommunication; and he produced both painted and printed portraits of Luther, his wife and associates. He also worked for Luther's adversary, Cardinal Albrecht of Brandenburg, and other Catholics.

When Johann Friedrich temporarily lost his dukedom between 1547 and 1552, Cranach followed him into exile in Augsburg, where his portrait of *Charles V* was painted in *c*.1550, somewhat under the influence of Titian, who was in Augsburg in 1548 and 1550/1 (Eisenach, Wartburg-Stiftung). After Johann Friedrich's return to Saxony in 1552, he established his court in Weimar, where Cranach died.

BIBLIOGRAPHY: Thieme-Becker, viii, 1913, pp.55ff.; Rosenberg; Yale, *Danube School*, pp.26ff.; Schade, *Cranach* (archival references pp.410ff.); Basel, *Cranach* (for further literature); Friedländer-Rosenberg; Andersson, *Detroit*, pp.215ff.

130 Three boys playing

See colour plate section following p.200

Pen and black ink with grey-brown wash, heightened with white bodycolour on reddish-brown prepared paper. Outlines of the left-hand figure pricked for transfer. The drawing has been cut out, and was recently laid on to nineteenth-century paper, tinted brown. Drawing: 15.2 × 12.7cm; sheet: 21.7 × 17.9cm

PROVENANCE: acquired from an English private collection

1987-4-11-35

This can be attributed to the young Cranach on the basis of a stylistic comparison with the earliest of Cranach's drawings, the *Foolish Virgin* at Nuremberg (Germanisches Nationalmuseum, inv.no.H.z.56; Zink, pp.145f., no.116, repr.). The penwork and the use of bodycolour is the same in each, and the similarity of such details as the facial features and the hands makes it abundantly clear that the same artist has executed both. The attribution of the present drawing to Cranach is thus entirely dependent on its link with the Nuremberg sheet, and the degree of certainty of the latter's attribution to him. Bock, who first identified the *Foolish Virgin* as the work of Cranach, supported his attribution by associating it with the woodcut, dated *1502*, universally accepted as by Cranach, of *St Stephen, as the first Christian martyr, and as patron saint of Vienna and the diocese of Passau* (Hollstein, vi, p.66, no.89, repr.) in particular noting the similar representation of the eyes and drapery in each. The connection is now further strengthened by the general kinship, despite the difference of media and scale, between the putti playing the drum and the flute in this print, especially the former, and those in the newly discovered drawing.

The attribution of the *Foolish Virgin* to Cranach and its dating of *c.*1502 has been accepted in almost all subsequent scholarly discussion, with F.Thöne (Thöne, *Cranach*, pp.8–10, pl.24) dating it slightly earlier, *c.*1501, that is probably before Cranach is known to have arrived in Vienna. Only Otto Benesch has rejected this attribution. He considered the Nuremberg sheet to be by the earliest of Cranach's Viennese followers, the Master of the Legend Scenes who takes his name from a series of panel paintings with scenes from the legend of St Cosmas and St Damian, in the Österreichische Galerie, Vienna (see Baum, *Österreichische Galerie*, pp.171–2, nos.152–4, repr.). The Master of the Legend Scenes, like the Master of the Miracles of Mariazell whom Buchner and Benesch later mistakenly identified with him, is a minor figure of charming anecdote, whose work lacks the vigour and original expression that we find in Cranach's early works, such as the *Penitent St Jerome*, dated *1502* (Vienna, Kunsthistorisches Museum; inv.no.6739) and the *St Valentine and a kneeling donor*, of *c.*1502 (Vienna, Akademie der bildenden Künste, inv.no. 549). Cranach maintained the primitive exuberance of his draughtsmanship throughout his stay in Austria, as witnessed in the drawing of *St John the Baptist seated in a landscape* of *c.*1504 (Lille, Musée des Beaux Arts), although by that time, his early painted masterpiece, the *Flight into Egypt*, dated *1504* (Berlin-Dahlem, Gemäldegalerie, inv.no.564A) shows the first signs of that courtly refinement which was the secret of his success at the Saxon court.

See nos.139–43 for futher works by Cranach.

Wolfgang (Wolf) Huber

Feldkirch (?) c.1480/85 – Passau 3 June 1553

Painter, designer of woodcuts, architect, draughtsman. Little is known of his early life. An eighteenth-century copy of a contract dated *1515*, for the *St Anne Altarpiece* (dated *1521*; Bregenz, Landesmuseum) describes him as 'Master Wolfgang Huber from Feldkirch, now living in Passau', and indicates that he was running a sizeable workshop by this date. His early style, revealed in works such as the drawing of *Pyramus and Thisbe* of *c.*1503/5 (Budapest, Nationalgalerie) suggests that as a journeyman

he may have met Lucas Cranach the Elder (q.v.) in Vienna. Early in his career he must also have known the work of Albrecht Altdorfer (q.v.) with whom he was jointly the most influential artist of the Danube School.

He worked for Duke Ernst of Bavaria, whom he apparently accompanied in 1530 to Vienna where the Duke attended the funeral of Graf Niklas I von Salm. His drawing of the *View of Vienna after the Turkish Siege*, dated *1530* (Vienna, Albertina) and that of the *Battle of Pavia*, of *c.*1530 (Munich, Staatliche Graphische Sammlung), are connected with reliefs on the tomb of Graf Niklas I, which he was presumably commissioned to design by the latter's son, Graf Niklas II (Vienna, Dorotheenkirche). Huber was also employed as architect and painter by Niklas II on the Renaissance-style renovations made to his castle at Neuburg am Inn (1529–31); little of this work has survived. His position as court painter was confirmed in 1542 by Niklas II's successor, Graf Wolfgang I von Salm, who had recently been appointed Prince-bishop of Passau, and whose portrait as a donor appears in Huber's painting of the *Allegory of Redemption* of *c.*1550 (Vienna, Kunsthistorisches Museum).

Only about twenty-five of Huber's paintings are known to have survived; chiefly panels from altarpieces, and a few portraits including that of the humanist, *Jacob Ziegler*, made at some time between 1544 and 1549 during the latter's presence at the Passau court (Vienna, Kunsthistorisches Museum). Huber's art is well represented by his drawings of which approximately 150 are known. Most notable are his evocative landscape drawings, which are made in a fantastical style and sometimes represent specific locations along the Danube and in the east and Central Alps. His drawings were often copied, and were very influential; they are reflected in the work of Augustin Hirschvogel (q.v.), Hans Lautensack (*c.*1520–64/6) and others.

BIBLIOGRAPHY: Thieme-Becker xviii, 1925, pp.21f.; Weinberger, *Huber*; Passau, *Huber*; Linz, *Donauschule*, pp.110ff.; Yale, *Danube School*, pp.76ff.; Rose, *Huber*; Winzinger, *Huber* (for further literature); Hollstein, xva, 1986, pp.85ff.

131 The Last Judgement

Pen and black ink on orange tinted paper. 28.8 × 20cm

PROVENANCE: A. Rosenthal

1938-1-8-1 (Malcolm Add.171)

LITERATURE: A.E.Popham, *BMQ*, xii, 1938, pp.48f., repr.; Winzinger, *Huber*, i, pp.78f., no.13, ii, pl.13 (for further literature)

Inscribed by the artist in black ink, on the upper edge, *1510*

This is the earliest sketch for a complex religious composition to have survived, which although unsigned can be readily attributed to Huber through the distinctive character of the penwork, and the shorthand way he used for depicting figures in such rapidly conceived preliminary studies. Similar freely executed compositional sketches do

131

not occur again among his known drawings until 1525 when he produced the *Crucifixion* (Cambridge, Fitzwilliam Museum, inv.no.2076) and the *Lamentation* (Bautzen, Stadtmuseum; Winzinger, *Huber*, ii, pls.72 and 73). In the former in particular we find precisely the same method used as in the present drawing to represent the figures. A similar manner was used by Huber in the four more precisely wrought preparatory drawings of 1519/20 at Munich (Staatliche Graphische Sammlung, inv.nos. 1965 109–114;. Winzinger, *Huber*, ii, pls.143–6), for the *St Anne altarpiece* now at Bregenz (Landesmuseum).

132 Portrait of a young man

Pen and black ink. The upper left-hand corner has been made up and a worm-hole repaired in the lower right-hand corner. 14.4 × 11 cm

PROVENANCE: Dr W.H. Willshire, by whom bequeathed, 1899

London, Guildhall Library

LITERATURE: C. Dodgson, *Vasari Society*, iii, 1907/08, no.28, repr.; Weinberger, *Huber*, p.88, repr.; Winzinger, *Huber*, i, pp.120f., no.113, ii, pl.113 (for further literature)

Inscribed by the artist, in black ink, either side of the sitter, *H*, on the left, *P* on the right, and in the upper left-hand corner, *1517*

The *H* and *P* have been understood to be the monogram of a Master HP, identified as the painter from Passau, Hans Pruckendorfer (d.1518), a very minor figure; however, Weinberger and Dodgson rejected this, considering the letters could refer to the person portrayed. Winzinger's solution, which has the most to recommend it, is that they signify *H*(uber von) *P*(assau) or *P*(ataviensis). This is given abundant support from the penwork of the drawing, which matches in many calligraphic details that used by Huber in his *Crucifixion*, signed and dated *1517*, in Berlin-Dahlem (Kupferstichkabinett, inv.no.KDZ 4325; Winzinger, *Huber*, ii, pl.47). In addition to this strong stylistic kinship, the drawing of the eyes suggests those apparently exophthalmic eyes unique to the features of the participants in the religious paintings by Huber.

133 A hermit holding a crucifix

Pen and brown ink; the eyes and part of the beard reworked in black ink. 19.4 × 16 cm

PROVENANCE: Obach & Co; Campbell Dodgson bequest, 1949

1949-4-11-116

LITERATURE: *Altdorfer*, p.102, no.517; O. Benesch, *OMD*, xiv, 1939–40, pp.6off., repr. (reprinted in *Collected Writings*, pp.410f., repr.;) F. Winzinger, *Zeitschr. f. Kunstwiss.*, xii, 1958, pp.83f., n.28; F. Winzinger, *Zeitschr. f. Kunstwiss.*, xviii, 1964, pp.81ff., repr.; Winzinger, *Huber*, i, p.153, no.211, ii, pl.211 (for further literature)

Inscribed by the artist in black ink, in the upper left-hand corner, *1521*

In the catalogue of the 1938 Altdorfer exhibition, Baumeister ascribed this drawing to the Franconian school, even though its distinguished owner, Campbell Dodgson had long held it to be by Huber. Unquestionably, as Benesch (who supported Dodgson's view) pointed out, this drawing is by the same hand as that responsible for *Eight studies of men's heads* in Stockholm (Nationalmuseum, inv.no.40/1918; Bjurström, *German Drawings*, no.59, repr.), and it was likewise responsible for the *Portrait of a young man* in the Guildhall Library (see no.132). In all three drawings, the line is infected with an expressive quality, and the same curling linear patterns which describe the hair of the sitters is seen in tufts and clumps of grass in Huber's landscape drawings. Despite these important visual pointers, Winzinger, implying the verbal agreement of Dodgson, reattributed both this present drawing and the Stockholm sheet, to Georg Lemberger (q.v.) without any cogent support from documented works. He also included the *Head of a bearded man*, dated *1511* (Brunswick, Herzog Anton Ulrich-Museum) which had been published much earlier by Flechsig as Upper German, speculating, rather wildly, that this was Lemberger's earliest known work.

132

133

Not only can one relate the calligraphy in the present drawing to other pen drawings by Huber from the same period, for instance, the *St Sebastian* signed and dated *1520*, in Berlin-Dahlem (Kupferstichkabinett inv.no.17663/102 –1938; Winzinger, *Huber*, ii, pl.67) but also one can see the same hand at work in his chalk drawings, such as the *Heads and shoulders of two women, and head of an old man*, signed and dated *1522*, at Erlangen (Universitätsbibliothek, inv. no.IIE 48; Winzinger, *Huber*, ii, pl.126). The dates on both these drawings are characteristic of Huber's method of writing numerals, and are strikingly allied in type to those on the present sheet.

134 Head of a man wearing a fur hat

Black chalk with grey and brown wash, and grey and green bodycolour, heightened with white chalk and bodycolour (and possibly touches of oil paint) on red prepared paper. The drawing was executed on three pieces of paper, and has been cut out round the outlines and laid onto a sheet of light brown prepared paper. Traces of the former background could be the areas of grey and green bodycolour visible on the shoulders. Whole sheet: 21.4 × 17.2 cm

PROVENANCE: T.Hudson (L.2432); E.Bouverie (L.325); R.P. Roupell (L.2234 on *verso*; sale, Christie, 1887, 12 July, lot 885 as 1 by Dürer); A.von Lanna (L.2773; sale, Stuttgart, H.G.Gutekunst, 1910, 7 May, lot 311, bt *Obach RM 400*); presented by Max Rosenheim, 1910

1910–5–23–1

LITERATURE: Weinberger, *Huber*, p.125; Passau, *Huber*, p.13, under no.49; Kuhrmann, *Erlangen*, p.77 under no.65; Winzinger, *Huber*, i, pp.124f., no.125a (for further literature)

Inscribed along the lower edge, by a later hand in black ink, partly erased, *Pieter Breugel*; and on the *verso*, by a different hand in black ink, *Albert Durer*; and an illegible pencil inscription.

As in the case of no.135, the determination of the status of this drawing again highlights to what extent repetitions or variants of Huber's drawings are by the artist himself or copies made by followers. The present drawing is related to a version, dated *1522*, executed in charcoal or black chalk and heightened with white chalk, on brick-red tinted paper in Erlangen (Universitätsbibliothek, inv.no.B.818; Winzinger, *Huber*, ii, pl.125). The latter drawing belongs to a group of grotesque heads mostly signed with the artist's initials and dated *1522*, all of which are drawn in the same medium and free style as the drawing at Erlangen. Most scholars agree that because of its fresh spontaneous execution the Erlangen version is certainly an original by Huber himself. The stiffly drawn version at Dresden (Kupferstichkabinett, inv.no.C.2129) and the feeble one, dated *1546*, in Hamburg (Kunsthalle, inv.no.1975/23; Winzinger, *Huber*, i, p.125, nos.125b & c) can justifiably be classed as copies: the present drawing, which Winzinger also considered a copy, should not be so readily dismissed as such, as Winzinger to some extent concedes, when he refers to the sureness of technique in the 'authentic' part.

Although the cutting of the sheet round the outlines of the drawing has a disfiguring effect to the shape of the figure, there is no reason to suggest, as Winzinger does, that the drawing is too damaged for one to recognise Huber's hand. The present drawing is quite unlike the other versions of the grotesque heads in its medium and the rendering of the sitter's features. It is a true portrait, lacking any vestiges of the caricature present in the other grotesque heads. Compared with Huber's portrait drawings, in which the contours of the face are usually defined by a subtle use of delicate strokes in chalks of differing colours, the present drawing occupies an isolated middle point between their finesse and the vigour of the grotesque heads; its quality as well as the characteristic taste for rich colouring, surely supports the attribution to Huber. The superb execution of the eyes with the intense gaze common to so many of his figures confirms this.

135 View of Feldkirch

Pen and brown ink. Cut down on all sides. 31.3 × 21.3cm

PROVENANCE: Thibaudeau

1883-7-14-101

LITERATURE: Riggenbach, pp.5, 17, 56f., P. Halm, *Munich Jahrbuch*, NF, vii, 1930, p.88, no.25, repr.; Rose, *Huber*, p.7; Winzinger, *Huber*, i, pp.99f., no.71, ii, pl.71 (for further literature)

Inscribed by the artist in brown ink between the branches of the tree in the centre, *1.5.23*

This drawing was first recognised as being that of Huber's home town, Feldkirch, in the Vorarlberg, by Härtenberger, a citizen of Feldkirch in 1905 (see Riggenbach, p.5). The view is taken from the banks of the river Ill, looking west towards the Swiss peaks of the Blasenberg and the Ardetzerberg in the background, from approximately the position where a Jesuit college stands today.

Riggenbach and Halm conjectured that the drawing must have been based on an earlier record of the scene made by Huber, who lived in Passau, when he was supposedly in Feldkirch in 1521, the date on his *St Anne altarpiece*, for the church of St Nicholas in that town. Winzinger pointed out that this date is only on one of the panels of the altarpiece, which need not therefore have been necessarily completed in its entirety, or installed in the church by 1521 since it was probably made in Passau. He considered it likely that Huber installed the altarpiece in 1523 and took the opportunity while he was in Feldkirch to make the present drawing. As Rose pointed out, it is however, possible that Huber could have made drawings of his home town from memory, or based them on records made in Feldkirch at an earlier date.

Winzinger lists six copies of no.135, some of which have been thought to be produced by Huber at a later date, although Winzinger considers most of them to be workshop productions (Winzinger, *Huber*, i, pp.100ff., nos.71a–f).

135

136 Lakeland landscape with a town overlooking a bay, and a mountainous coastline in the far distance

See colour plate section following p.200

Pen and black ink with watercolour, and some strengthening in bodycolour. Both sheets trimmed on all sides. 20.8 × 31.3cm and 18.1 × 16.6cm

WM: (in right-hand sheet): Gothic P surmounted by a shield (close to Piccard, xvii, 49–51)

(a) Left-hand sheet:

PROVENANCE: A.P. Rudolph

1925-11-17-4

LITERATURE: Weinberger, *Huber*, p.188, repr.; P. Halm, *Munich Jahrbuch*, NF, vii, 1930, p.99, no.103, repr.; Passau, *Huber*, p.21, under no.82; Winzinger, *Huber*, i, pp.111f., no.93, ii, pl.93 (for further literature)

Inscribed by the artist in black ink on the upper edge, *1541*

(b) Right-hand sheet:

PROVENANCE: Obach & Co

134

137r

1909–1–9–14

LITERATURE: Obach & Co, *Old Master Drawings*, no.49; Weinberger, *Huber*, p.188, repr.; P.Halm, *Munich Jahrbuch*, NF, vii, 1930, p.100, no.104, repr.; Passau, *Huber*, p.21, under no.82; Winzinger, *Huber*, i, p.111, no.92, p.198, no.11, ii, pl.92 (for further literature)

Inscribed by the artist in black ink on the upper edge partly erased, *1541*; and by a later hand in brown ink on the *verso*, *A.Durer*

The two sheets which constitute no.136 arrived separately in the British Museum from left to right respectively, in 1925 and 1909. It has only recently been noticed that they belong together since the small landscape on the right is a continuation of the same view seen in the drawing on the left. There is a difference of a centimetre or so between the two drawings which can be explained by the fact that both sheets have been cut down.

137 *Recto:* A rocky landscape with a bridge in the foreground

Verso: Figure studies and a study of a hand

Pen and black ink with grey wash, the *verso* in red chalk. 21.4 × 33.3 cm

WM: high crown, surmounted by a cross and a star (of a type similar to Piccard, vii, 25–43)

PROVENANCE: Grote bequest, 1872

London, University College, G 1333

LITERATURE: K.T.Parker, *Belvedere*, no.40, 1925, pp.78f., pl.2; E.Buchner, *OMD*, ii, 1927, p.28; Weinberger, *Huber*, p.208, pl.127; P.Halm, *Munich Jahrbuch*, NF, vii, 1930, p.43, repr.; E.Poeschel, *Anz.* xxxv, 1933, pp.142ff., repr.; Manchester, *German Art*, pp.54ff., no.139; J.Rowlands, *MD*, viii, no.2, 1970, pp.170f., repr., *verso*; Winzinger, *Huber*, i, pp.118f., no.109, p.133, no.149, ii, pls.109 and 149 (for further literature); Geissler, *Deutsche Zeichner 1540–1640*, i, p.26, no.A26, repr.

Inscribed on the *recto* by the artist, in black ink, in the lower right-hand corner, *W.H.* (subsequently falsified to read HH); and in the sky in the middle of the drawing *1552*; and in a later hand in pencil on the upper edge, *94*; and on the *verso*, in brown ink in the upper right-hand corner, in a modern hand, *Hans Holbein*, and in the lower left-hand corner, *N.234*

166

The landscape, on the *recto*, is perhaps the finest dramatic extensive view of mountainous country by Huber. The evocative sweep of the valley floor with the mountainside billowing over it like a great wave suggests that this is an idealised portrayal, largely the creation of Huber's imagination. Despite these rather fantastic features, Poeschel attempted to prove that the drawing does represent a particular location at the mouth of the Prätigau valley in the Swiss Bündnerland with, on the left, the ruins of the castle of Fragstein and, beyond, under the overhanging cliff the 'Apernkapelle', the remains of which only disappeared at the beginning of this century; and on the right, the bridge with the old road to Chur. Several other landscape drawings like no.137, and the *Castle on the Danube* dated *1542* (Winzinger, *Huber*, ii, pl.95) have been identified with particular places; in the case of the latter, with Schloss Aggstein in the Wachau, near Melk, Austria.

The studies on the *verso* were first published by myself and associated with the *Study of a man holding a stick* (New York, Woodner collection; Winzinger, *Huber*, ii, pl.150) whose attribution to Huber was proposed by Schilling. Winzinger's association of the studies of the bending figure with that of St John in the painting, dated *1521*, the *Lamentation over the dead Christ* (Winzinger, *Huber*, ii, pl.287) in the church of St Nicholas, Feldkirch, is not close enough to be of significance. The profile head is, of course, dependent on Dürer's diagrammatic proportional studies of parts of the human body.

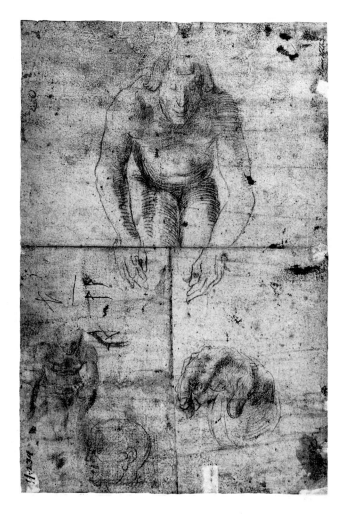

14 Saxony and Northern Germany, XVI century

Heinrich Aldegrever

Paderborn 1501/2 – Soest 1555/61

Engraver, painter and designer of woodcuts. His family name was Trippenmeker (clog-maker). He became a citizen of Soest in 1527, and was the most important artist active in sixteenth-century Westphalia, yet nothing is recorded of his training. Many of his figures reveal the influence of the Antwerp Mannerists, and he may have spent his *Wanderjahre* in the Netherlands; other sources for his work include, in particular, the prints of Albrecht Dürer (q.v.), the engravings of Lucas van Leyden (1494?–1533)and, for his ornamental prints, those of Zoan Andrea (active *c.*1475–1505).

Many of his engravings, made in the manner of the so-called 'Little Masters' (see Georg Pencz and Sebald Beham), were highly influential. His ornamental engravings, about one third of his total output of just under 300 known prints, were widely used by other artists and craftsmen well into the seventeenth century, and his figurative prints also reappear occasionally on glass-paintings, metal and stoneware. He may have practised as a goldsmith (Kreis Unna, *Aldegrever*, pp.46ff.) and in 1552 he is known to have cut silver seals for the Duke of Cleves.

Only two paintings are firmly attributed to him: the wings and predella of the *Marienaltar*, of *c.*1525/6 (Soest, Wiesenkirche) and the *Portrait of Graf Phillip III von Waldeck*, of 1537 (Schloss Arolsen). A number of his preparatory drawings for engravings have survived, of which the largest single collection is in the Rijksmuseum, Amsterdam.

BIBLIOGRAPHY: Zschelletzschky, *Aldegrever*; A.Shestack, *MD*, viii, 1970, pp.141ff.; Meissner, i, 1983, pp.928ff. (for further literature); Andersson, *Detroit*, pp.176f.; Münster, *Aldegrever*; Kreis Unna, *Aldegrever*.

138 Portrait of Jan van Leyden

See colour plate section following p.200

Black chalk, with red chalk on parts of the face. Outlines indented for transfer. The drawing has been cut out round the outline of the sitter and through the back of his head, and made up with modern paper. Drawing: 26.6 × 23.3cm; sheet: 27.5 × 23.3cm

PROVENANCE: S.Rogers (sale, Christie, 1856, 6 May, lot 881, as 'Head of elector of Saxony'); Marquis of Breadalbane (sale, Christie, 1886, 4 June, lot 157, bt *Thibaudeau £20* for BM)

1886–6–9–38

LITERATURE: Geisberg, *Aldegrever*, pp.26ff., pl.3; *Vasari Society*, iii, 1st series, 1907–8, no.31, repr.; Zschelletzschky, *Aldegrever*, p.93; A.Shestack, *MD*, viii, 1970, pp.144f., repr.; BM *Portrait Drawings*, p.8, no.10; Münster, *Wiedertäufer*, p.179, no.118, repr.; Münster, *Aldegrever*, p.42 under no.3, p.70, repr.

A detailed preparatory study in the reverse sense, for Aldegrever's engraving of Jan van Leyden, dated *1536* (Bartsch, viii, p.415, no.182). From what remains of it, the drawing corresponds closely with the print except for a few details: the most notable being the omission, in the drawing, of the sceptre which rests on the sitter's arm in the print. To accommodate the sceptre, the sitter's left hand has been moved forward, and the book that he holds is consequently seen at a more acute angle than in the drawing. Furthermore, the lettering on the scroll, which refers to Jan van Leyden's right, as King of the Anabaptists, to name all new-born infants in alphabetical order, is changed from ABC in the drawing to DEF in the print.

The majority of Aldegrever's known drawings were made in the medium of pen and ink. The handling of the present study may, however, be compared with the *Portrait of a man* possibly the Anabaptist Bernd Krechting, in Berlin-Dahlem (Kupferstichkabinett inv.no.KDZ 4242; Münster, *Wiedertäufer*, pp.179ff., no.119, repr.; Münster, *Aldegrever* p.46, no.5, repr.), made in the similar, although less elaborately treated, technique of black and coloured chalk.

Jan Bockelson, called Jan van Leyden (1509–36) was an illegitimate son of a village mayor from near Leyden, and a one time taylor's apprentice and amateur playwright. He became the leader of a group of Anabaptist refugees in Münster in March 1534. A heretical sect who denied infant baptism and practised the baptism of believers, the Anabaptists in Münster expelled all Lutherans and Catholics from the town, and established a form of theocracy, with Bockelson calling himself King. The town was besieged by Imperial troops and, after its capture in June 1535, Bockelson was imprisoned; he was put to death, together with two of his followers, Bernd Knipperdolling and Bernd Krechting, in January 1536. Their bodies were suspended in cages from the tower of St Lambert's church, where the cages may still be seen today.

Geisberg considered that Aldegrever, who had Lutheran sympathies but was probably not himself an Anabaptist, was commissioned by the Bishop of Münster, Franz von Waldeck, to make the engraved portrait of Bockelson. This presumably appeared shortly after the latter's death, and was made with a pendant engraving of Bernd Knipperdolling (dated *1536*, Bartsch, viii, p.416, no.183). It seems likely that no.138 was not itself drawn from life, but made after life-studies while Bockelson was in prison. Bockelson's emblem, an imperial orb pierced with two swords and surmounted by a cross, which was adopted by him for the arms of his kingdom, is seen in no.138 on the large chain which the sitter wears, and is also recorded in an anonymous pen and ink drawing in the British Museum (inv.no.1862-2–8–51) inscribed *Arma regis catabaptistarum . . .* and dated *1534* (Münster, *Wiedertäufer*, p.173, no.115, repr.). Three gold chains traditionally thought to have belonged to Bockelson, are known to be in two private collections in Germany (Münster, *Wiedertäufter*, pp.192ff., nos.129 & 130, repr.). They are not the same as the chains represented by Aldegrever, and it seems likely that the artist, who may have practised as a goldsmith, invented the design of these together with that of the crown and sceptre.

Lucas Cranach the Elder

(For biography, see before no.130)

139 Head of a peasant

See colour plate section following p.200

Brush drawing with black, grey, yellow and red wash, heightened with pink and white bodycolour, over slight traces of an underdrawing in black chalk. 23.6 × 16.7 cm

WM: oxhead (close to Briquet, 14875 and Piccard, xii, 793)

PROVENANCE: Sloane bequest, 1753

5218–19

LITERATURE: Ephrussi, pp.84f.; Lippmann, iii, p.5, no.227, repr.; C.Dodgson, *Dürer Society*, 3rd series, 1900, no.10, repr.; Conway, p.13, no.170; Pauli, p.10, no.196; Friedländer-Bock, p.55, pl.68; Parker, *German Schools*, p.31, under no.33; J.Rosenberg, *Prussian Jahrbuch*, lv, 1934, p.184; Girshausen, pp.43f., no.52; Panofsky, ii, p.116, no.1156; Rosenberg, p.28, no.71, repr.; Basel, *100 Master Drawings*, under no. 39; D.Koepplin, *Kunstchronik*, xxv, 1972, p.347; Basel, *Cranach*, ii, p.689, no.608 (for further literature)

Inscribed in faded grey wash by a later hand with a false Dürer monogram in the upper right-hand corner

Until recognised by Friedländer and Bock as by Cranach it was always assumed, no doubt partly because of the monogram, that this was by Dürer. Cranach's authorship was not questioned until the appearance of a similar drawing, said to have been found in an album from Wittenberg whose contents had been put together in 1590–3. This second drawing was acquired by the Kupferstichkabinett, Basel, in 1937 (inv.no.1937.21; see Basel, *Cranach*, ii, p.688, no.607, for full bibliographical details of this second version; Basel, *100 Master Drawings*, pl.39).

Opinions have been divided about the relative status of the drawings. Girshausen and Rosenberg considered the London drawing to be the original and that at Basel a copy of it. Others, like Landolt, Winzinger and Koepplin think the opposite is the case. Although the sitter in both

is clearly drawn according to the same pattern, the men represented in each were probably intended to be different persons. It is unlikely that they were meant to be the same person at different ages. Rosenberg has dated the present drawing about 1505/6, linking it in its matter-of-fact portrayal with the portrait-heads in Cranach's altarpiece of *St Catherine* in Dresden. One should note particularly the wizened old man on the right in the painting. Furthermore, the similarity of colouring makes Rosenberg's observations particularly credible. Koepplin's reservations about the rendering of the peasant's features in the London drawing, however, seem misplaced. He argues that the absence of a black spot on the sitter's forehead in the Basel drawing means that it could not be a copy of the London drawing. This greyish black mark is, in fact, oxidised white bodycolour which has recently responded to treatment.

Despite having had reservations previously about the London version, it seems to me now that these were mistaken, and that overall the London version is more impressive than that in Basel. For instance, the fur hat in the present drawing is executed with much more skill. The Basel version is altogether more blandly done, and the appearance is not enhanced by the way the colouring of the clothes and background has been added. It is claimed, according to the 'evidence' of the watermark of the Basel sheet, that the paper was not produced before 1519; however, it is not prudent to press such an indication too far, certainly not where the question of priority between these two versions is concerned. It would seem likely, in view of its lack of vigour and its vacuity, that the Basel drawing is a variant that was produced in Cranach's studio, based on the present drawing. Although the present drawing assuredly lacks the mastery achieved by Cranach in his later watercolours of still-life subjects such as the *Two dead bullfinches hanging from a nail* (formerly Dresden, Kupferstichkabinett, Rosenberg, pl.68), dated *1530*, it would be stylistically credible to place it alongside the lively and often vigorously executed paintings of the period 1505–10, even though in doing so one lacks any other comparable drawing of the same type surviving from those years.

140 Head of a man wearing a hat

Brush drawing in brown, grey, black and red wash, heightened with creamy white bodycolour, on light brown paper. 26.8 × 18.7cm

PROVENANCE: H.Wroot

1896–5–11–1

LITERATURE: Parker, *German Schools*, p.31, no.33, repr.; Girshausen, pp.69f., no.41; Rosenberg, p.28, no.72, repr.; H.Zimmerman, *Pantheon*, xx, 1962, p.9; BM *Portrait Drawings*, p.7, no.7

This was acquired as an anonymous German sixteenth-century drawing, and placed by Campbell Dodgson with the drawings by Lucas Cranach in 1921. In its frank

141

portrayal of the sitter's features, it goes well with Cranach's painted portraits of the period 1510–15, which is the approximate dating proposed by Girshausen and accepted by Rosenberg. They were both sceptical about the suggested identification of the sitter with the figure sometimes called Sixtus Oelhafen. The latter was the imperial councillor, who is seen looking over a parapet in the central panel of the Torgau Princes' *Altarpiece of the Holy Kindred* of 1509. To his left is a figure wearing a golden chain who has been dubiously identified as the Emperor Maximilian I. The painting is now in Frankfurt (Städelsches Kunstinstitut, inv.no.1398; Friedländer-Rosenberg, pl.18). A similarity of approach in the portrayal of features is more clearly discernible in the *Portrait of a man with a fur hat and collar* in Bremen (Kunsthalle, inv.no.160; Friedländer-Rosenberg,

pl.62). This is dated *1514* on a piece of vellum attached to the back of the panel, with the arms of the sitter, and those probably of his wife, of whom Cranach could well have painted a companion portrait which is not known to have survived. One may also note a parallel and even more marked affinity with the *Portrait of a man, thought to have been the mayor of Weissenfels,* dated *1515,* at Berlin-Dahlem (Gemäldegalerie, inv.no.618A; Friedländer-Rosenberg, pl.63), and the dignified portrayal of a man of somewhat similar features in a portrait drawing also in Berlin-Dahlem (Kupferstichkabinett, inv.no.4478; Rosenberg, pl.73).

142v

142r

141 The Crucifixion

Pen and brown ink with grey wash on brown paper. 28 × 20.8cm

PROVENANCE: The Rev. T.Kerrich (*Catalogue of the Kerrich Collection*, MS, p.24, 'Christ on Ye Cross between the Thieves a great many figures below M.L. . . . L.von Cranach/Drawn with a pen and wash with brown. Somebody has written 'Lucas van/Leyden' under it. Bt. in London since 1796'); the Rev. R.E.Kerrich, by whom bequeathed, 1872.

Cambridge, Fitzwilliam Museum, 2929

LITERATURE: C.Dodgson, *Vasari Society*, 1st series, iii, 1907/8, no.30, repr.; Girshausen, pp.18–20, 63, no.8; Rosenberg, pp.16f., no.8, repr.; Manchester, *German Art*, p.56, no.144; D.Koepplin, *Kunstchronik*, xxv, 1972, pp.345f.; Basel, *Cranach*, ii, p.484, no.332, repr.; *Fitzwilliam Drawings*, pp.32f.; no.52, repr. (for further literature)

Inscribed in black chalk, in the lower left-hand corner, *Lucas Van Leyden*

We may suppose that this drawing was produced in preparation for the painting at Copenhagen (Statens Museum for Kunst; Friedländer-Rosenberg, p.77, no.38B) as there are only very slight differences between the two. This painting belongs to the period 1512/14, when, as Friedländer and Rosenberg have pointed out, the growing participation of the studio makes the extent to which the artist himself contributed toward the execution of his paintings difficult to determine. Koepplin's proposed dating of the painting to *c*.1515 accords well with the style of the present drawing. There are no substantial grounds for associating it, as was formerly done by Girshausen and Rosenberg, with the artist's early works done in Vienna. Neither the *Crucifixion*, the painting in the Kunsthistorisches Museum, Vienna (inv.no.6965; Friedländer-Rosenberg, pl.1) to which Friedländer and Rosenberg give the very early date of *c*.1500, nor the two very rare woodcuts of the same subject (Hollstein, vi, pp.23f., nos.25 and 26, repr.) one of which is dated *1502*, have anything more in common than some general similarities which one would expect to find in the work of an artist as prolific as Cranach.

A damaged copy of no.141 is in Würzburg (Universitätssammlung; E.Baumeister and W.Boll, *Munich Jahrbuch*, xi, 1934–6, pp.36f., fig.16).

142 *Recto:* St Thomas with the spear

Verso: St Jacob as a pilgrim

Pen and brown ink with grey wash, the flesh touched with pink wash. 15.8 × 5.8cm

England, Private Collection

LITERATURE: Rosenberg, p.21, no.32, repr.; U.Steinmann, *Berlin Forsch. u. Berichte*, xi, 1968, p.85; Schade, *Cranach*, p.386, n.482; Schilling, *Gesamm. Zeichn.*, p.187, no.38, repr.; Rowlands, *Private Collection*, p.50, no.46, repr.

Inscribed by the artist with pen and brown ink, on the *recto*, *S.thamas* and on the *verso*, *S.jakob*

This is part of a finished design for the wing of an altarpiece, the rest of which is missing, produced by the artist to give the client a clear idea of how the composition would appear when completed, with the wings either open or closed. According to Steinmann this drawing was produced for the St Thomas altarpiece, formerly in the Stiftskirche, Halle, which was made between 1519/20, the date of a plan which described the decoration of the church, and 1525, the date of an inventory which lists the altarpiece as being in the south aisle (Steinmann, op.cit., p.72). There are, in addition, five further surviving designs by Cranach comparable in date with no.142, whose appearance accords with other altarpieces, few of which have survived (see Basel, *Cranach*, ii, p.449, no.288), listed in the Halle inventory. They are as follows: design for an altarpiece, with *Christ nailed to the Cross* (Weimar, Schlossmuseum; Rosenberg, pls.29 and 29a); design for an altarpiece with *Christ carrying the Cross* (Paris, Louvre, inv.no.18,863; Rosenberg, pls. 30 and 30a); design for an altarpiece with *Lamentation over the dead Christ* (Berlin-Dahlem, Kupferstichkabinett, inv.no.387; Rosenberg, pls. 31, 31a and 31b); designs for two altarpieces, one with *Christ before Caiaphas*, the other with the *Flagellation of Christ* (both at Leipzig, Museum der bildenden Künste, inv.nos.NJ13 and NJ14; Rosenberg, pls.36, 36a, 37 and 37a). Apart from this group by Cranach, few other finished designs for altarpieces by German artists from that period are known, although such drawings must have been done. There is, however, a fine one surviving by Kulmbach for an altarpiece, with carved figures, of the *Coronation of the Virgin* (no.100) which is both comparable in scale, and contemporaneous with the earliest of those by Cranach.

Attributed to Lucas Cranach the Elder

143 The meeting of the living and the three dead

Pen and black ink 12.7 × 20.2cm

WM: star (the upper part of an imperial orb)

PROVENANCE: Rev.W.H.Barnard (from an album, bound in black leather and stamped in gold on the cover, LVCAS TEEKENINGE 1637, which chiefly contained drawings by Lucas van Leyden)

1892-8-4-23

LITERATURE: S. Colvin, *Prussian Jahrbuch*, xiv, 1893, p.166; D.Koepplin, *Kunstchronik*, xxv, 1972, p.347; Basel, *Cranach*, ii, p.469, no.309, repr.

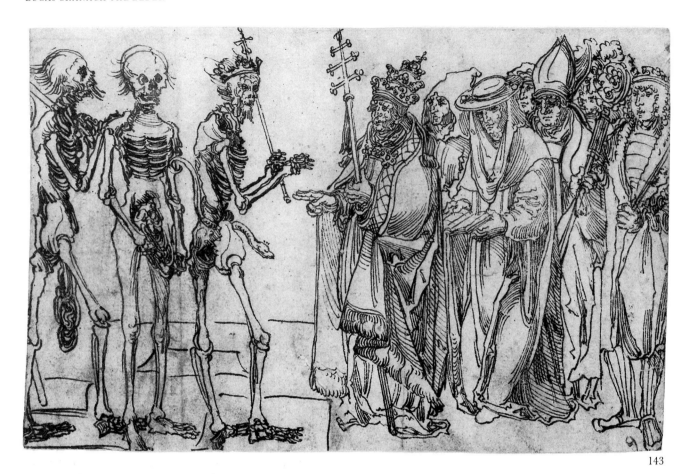

143

The subject of the drawing is a variant of the tale of the three Living (or Quick) and three Dead, a popular medieval legend in which three young kings out hunting meet three dead kings, who greet them, saying 'What you are, that we were, what we are, that you will be'. The earliest sources in Europe of this tale, apparently of oriental origin, are from Italy; representations of it are most abundant in late medieval Italy, where the tale was known from the twelfth century. In France, two poems entitled *Li Trois Mors et li Trois Vifs* were written in the thirteenth century by Baudouin de Condé and Nicolas de Marginal respectively, and were first illustrated *c.*1300 (see Raimond van Marle, *Iconographie de l'Art profane au Moyen Age et à la Renaissance – allégories et symboles*, The Hague, 1932, pp.383f.). By the end of the fifteenth century, the subject had become linked with the more powerful theme of the *Dance of Death*.

Colvin thought that the drawing was executed in the manner of Hans Burgkmair (q.v.), and that it was done by one of his followers as a projected design for a book illustration. The connection with book illustration is a credible idea, but does not lead one to Augsburg and the circle of Burgkmair. Falk's attribution of the drawing to Cranach, published by Koepplin, is much more convincing, especially if one compares it with some of the woodcuts in the *Wittenberger Heiligtumsbuch* of 1509 (Hollstein, vi, pp.72ff., no.96, repr.). Koepplin and Falk made a telling

comparison with the woodcut of St Wolfgang from this series (Basel, *Cranach*, ii, p.468, fig.256a), in which the crabbed features of the saint mirror those of the pope in the drawing to a remarkable extent. Their second comparison, that with the woodcut portrait of Erich von Braunschweig, Bishop of Paderborn, of 1513 (Hollstein, vi, p.103, no.126) is less apposite, as the facial characteristics, especially the shape of the mouth and jaw, are to be found fairly generally among Cranach's prints and drawings; however, the drawing's incisive penwork is a more pronounced link, and one which can be underlined by comparison with the vigorous drawing of *St Margaret* dated *1513*, at Dessau (Staatliche Galerie; Rosenberg, pl.20). Although this latter drawing is a repetition of the woodcut of the saint in the *Heiligtumsbuch* of 1509 with the addition of a landscape background, the spontaneity of its execution leaves little reason to doubt that it was executed by Cranach. One searches in vain however, for this type of penwork elsewhere among his surviving drawings, and as the basis on which the attribution of no.143 to Cranach is rather slender, albeit persuasive, it would be prudent for want of further evidence merely to classify it as attributed to the artist.

Lucas Cranach the Younger

Wittenberg 4 October 1515 – Weimar 25 January 1586

Painter, designer of woodcuts. Trained with his father, Lucas Cranach the Elder (q.v.) whose workshop he took over, and whose mark, the winged serpent, he adopted. He was mayor of Wittenberg in 1565. His earlier paintings are difficult to distinguish from those of his father, whose polished style he perpetuated, and those of his elder brother, Hans Cranach (after 1500–37). His woodcuts consist mainly of portraits, and of religious subjects of a Protestant nature.

BIBLIOGRAPHY: Dodgson, ii, pp.338ff.; Thieme-Becker, viii, 1913, p.58; Basel, *Cranach* (for further literature); Schade, *Cranach*; Geissler, *Deutsche Zeichner 1540–1640*, i, pp.15ff.

144

144 Calvary

Pen and black chalk with grey wash. 31.2 × 21 cm

PROVENANCE: bequeathed by F.W.Smith through the N.A.-C.F.

1923-1-13-24

LITERATURE: *N.A.-C.F. Report, 1922*, p.43, under no.403; Girshausen, p.87, no.132; Rosenberg, p.38, no.A.21, repr.

This can be connected with the late paintings of this subject by Lucas Cranach the Elder such as the *Crucifixion*, dated *1538*, at the Chicago Art Institute (inv.no.47.62; Friedländer-Rosenberg, pl.377). Technically, however, the drawing lacks the vitality of the father and could be by Lucas Cranach the Younger as Rosenberg has suggested. The composition has most in common with the altarpiece of the *Calvary* (Hanover, Schlosskirche and Niedersächsisches Landesmuseum). Despite Stuttman's attribution of this painting to Cranach the Elder (*Zeitschr. f. bild.Kunst.*, lxi, 1927/8, pp.341ff., repr.) its quality suggests that it is much more likely to be by the artist's son.

Georg Lemberger

Landshut c.1495 – probably Magdeburg c.1540

Painter and designer of woodcuts. Having absorbed the influence of the Danube School, he moved to Saxony where he became a citizen of Leipzig in 1523. Here he was employed to produce illustrations for the Leipzig and Wittenberg printers. As an adherent of the Reformation he was expelled from Leipzig in 1532, and settled in Magdeburg, where he is last recorded in 1537. His early work, the *Schmidburg Epitaph* of 1522 may be considered his most outstanding painting.

BIBLIOGRAPHY: Dodgson, ii, pp.353ff.; Thieme-Becker, xxiii, 1929, pp.21ff.; Hollstein, xxii, 1978, pp.11ff. (for further literature).

145 Portrait of a man wearing a hat

Black chalk. 18.6 × 20.5 cm

England, Private Collection

LITERATURE: E.Schilling, *Pantheon*, xxi, 1963, pp.206ff., repr.; F.Winzinger, *Zeitschr. f. Kunstwiss.*, xviii, 1964, pp.81f., repr.; Schilling, *Gesamm. Zeichn.*, p.55, no.20, repr.; Rowlands, *Private Collection*, p.52, no.48, repr.

Inscribed by the artist in black chalk on the right, *1526*

This drawing, and the black chalk drawing of a *Man with a walrus moustache*, dated *1525*, in the Schlossmuseum, Weimar, are clearly both by the same hand, which has been very convincingly identified by Schilling as that of Lemberger. He did this on the basis of a comparison with the heads of four saints in Lemberger's earliest known work,

145

the impressive woodcut that serves as the frontispiece to
the *Missale Pragense*, printed by Melchior Lotter at Leipzig
in November 1522 (E. Schilling, *Pantheon*, xxi, 1963, p.207,
repr.). Schilling's attribution can be further strengthened
by comparing these portrait drawings with the portrayal
of the male donors in the *Crucifixion with donors*, an epitaph-
painting of the Schmidburg family dated *1522*, formerly in
the Nikolaikirche, Leipzig, and now in the Museum der
bildenden Künste, Leipzig.

15 Augsburg, late XV and XVI centuries

Christoph Amberger

? Nuremberg c.1505 – Augsburg 1561/2

Painter and designer of medals, woodcuts and sculpture. He was probably a pupil of his father-in-law, Leonhard Beck (q.v.) in Augsburg, where he became a master in 1530 and where he was active throughout his life. He may have visited northern Italy between *c.*1525 and 1527. The most accomplished and productive side of his work consists of portraits, which often reveal the influence of Venetian painters, particularly Titian (*c.*1487/90–1576) who visited Augsburg in 1548 and 1550/1. Other influences on his work are the paintings of Hans Holbein the Elder (q.v.) and Hans Burgkmair (q.v.). His most important religious paintings are the high altarpiece of the *Virgin and Child with Sts Ulrich and Afra*, signed and dated *1554* (Augsburg Cathedral), for which there is a study in the British Museum (no.146); and the Steininger-Österreicher epitaph, *Christ with the wise and foolish Virgins*, signed and dated *1560*, which reveals mannerist tendencies. His designs for sculpture are exemplified by eight drawings (Dresden, Staatliche Kunstsammlungen, Kupferstichkabinett, and Vienna, Österreichische Nationalbibliothek) for bronze statues on the tomb of Emperor Maximilian I of *c.*1548 in the Hofkirche, Innsbruck. Amberger is the last important exponent of the Renaissance style in Augsburg.

BIBLIOGRAPHY: Thieme-Becker, i, 1907, pp.387f.; Dodgson, ii, pp.187f.; Geissler, *Deutsche Zeichner 1540–1640*, i, pp.4f.; Augsburg, *Umbruch*, ii, pp.97ff., 212ff.; Meissner, ii, 1986, pp.584ff. (for further literature).

146 Studies for the wings of an altarpiece with St Ulrich and St Afra

Pen and brown ink with grey wash. Cut irregularly, 30.3 × 20.9cm

WM: arms of Nuremberg (Briquet, 916)

PROVENANCE: W.Koller (sale, Vienna, A.Posonyi, 1872, 14 February and following days, lot 14); A.von Lanna (sale, Stuttgart, H.G.Gutekunst, 1910, 6 May, lot 10, bt *Obach 3850 RM*); H.Oppenheimer, by whom bequeathed to the British Museum, through the N.A.-C.F., 1933

1933–2–11–2

LITERATURE: Schönbrunner-Meder, x, no.1151, repr.; Parker, *German Schools*, p.32, no.40, repr.; Buchner, *Beiträge*, ii, p.136; A.E.Popham, *BMQ*, vii, no.4, 1933, p.106; Augsburg, *Holbein*, pp.161f., no.191, pl.197; U.Finke, *Berl. Mus.*, NF, xvii, 1967, Heft 2, p.51, repr., detail; K.Löcher, *Munich Jahrbuch*, xxx, 1979, pp.42ff., repr. (for further literature); Geissler, *Deutsche Zeichner*

1540–1640, i, pp.5f., no.A5, repr.; Augsburg, *Umbruch*, ii, pp.216f., no.594, repr.

This is a preparatory study by Amberger for the wings of his high altarpiece of Augsburg Cathedral (still there, but now in a chapel in the north choir aisle; K.Löcher, *Munich Jahrbuch*, xxx, 1979, p.45, repr.) executed in 1554 to replace the one of 1508/9 by Hans Holbein the Elder (q.v.), which had been destroyed by the iconoclasts in the *Bildersturm* of 1537. The chief purpose of Holbein's altarpiece was to serve not only as a focus of devotion, but also as a cover for the silver altar executed by Jörg Seld (*c.*1448–1527), that was only displayed on feast days and was destroyed with Holbein's altarpiece (A.Schröder, *Munich Jahrbuch*, NF, vii, 1930, pp.111–24). From Holbein's preparatory drawing (National Museum, Gdansk (Danzig), inv.no. KBR.7863; Augsburg, *Holbein*, pl.78) it is clear that Amberger was expected to follow the iconographic arrangement of the earlier altarpiece in his replacement. In the central section, the enthroned Virgin and Child are surrounded by kneeling angels who play musical instruments, with above, the crucified Christ between the Virgin and St John. Throughout the composition, Amberger has substituted a Renaissance architectural setting for Holbein's late Gothic pinnacles, arches and niches. The seven saints of the legend of St Afra, seen on the predella of Holbein's altarpiece, are changed by Amberger in his drawing to members of the Habsburg house: on the left, Maximilian I and Mary of Burgundy, and on the right, Charles V and Isabella of Portugal whose inclusion could be a reference to the two reigns in which the two altarpieces were commissioned; however, in his altarpiece as it was executed Amberger reverts to Holbein's iconography. The present drawing indicates that Amberger originally planned an altarpiece with movable wings, with the patron saints Ulrich and Afra seen on the outside when the altarpiece would have been closed, as is made clear by the single flying angel divided between the two wings. In the finished work, this plan is abandoned, and the single angel is altered to two angels; otherwise the painting mainly follows the preliminary study.

Mathias Gerung (*c.*1500–68/70) adapted Amberger's figures of the Virgin and Child with St Ulrich and St Afra as they appear in his painting for a woodcut, signed and dated *1555*, in the *Missale secundum ritum Augustensis ecclesie*, published by S. Mayer, at Dillingen in 1555 (Hollstein, x, p.56, no.74, repr.).

146

147r

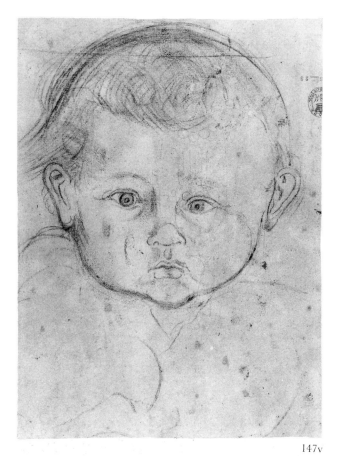

147v

Ulrich, Jakob or Michael Apt the Younger

Active in Augsburg 1510 – before 1553

Painters. Ulrich Apt the Elder (active 1481–1532) had three sons, Ulrich (active 1512–d. before 1533), Jakob (active 1510–18) and Michael (active in Augsburg 1520–7), are all known to have been painters, but about whom very little is recorded. Of three paintings, signed *Apt*, which are known to have survived, two may be given on a stylistic basis to Ulrich the Elder (*Adoration of the Magi*, in the Louvre, Paris; *Portrait of a man* in the Fürstlich Liechtensteinischen Gemäldegalerie, Vaduz) and the third, an altarpiece of the *Crucifixion* in Augsburg (Staatsgalerie) dated *1517* to a member of the younger generation.

BIBLIOGRAPHY: Thieme-Becker, i, 1907, p.35; Augsburg, *Altdeutsche Gemälde*, pp.13ff. (for further literature)

147 *Recto:* Portrait of a man wearing a hat
Verso: Head of a child

Charcoal. 31.3 × 22.2cm

WM: high crown (Piccard, xiii, 5)

PROVENANCE: Sloane bequest, 1753

5218–28

LITERATURE: Hausmann, *Naumann's Archiv*, p.36, no.28; Hausmann, p.107, no.28; Ephrussi, pp.81f.; F. Wickhoff, *Zeitschr. f. bild. Kunst*, xvii, 1882, p.218; W.v.Seidlitz, *Repertorium*, vi, 1883, p.205; *Vasari Society*, iv, 1st series, 1908–9, no.28, repr.; H. Rupé, in Buchner, *Beiträge*, ii, pp.202f., repr. *verso*; K.T. Parker, in Buchner, *Beiträge*, ii, p.220, nos.22 and 23, repr. *recto*; BM *Portrait Drawings*, p.8, no.9

Initially no.147 was assumed to be by Dürer (q.v.). Wickhoff was the first to recognise it as by Hans Burgkmair (q.v.), an attribution which has gained wide acceptance; however, the recent reassessments by Halm and Falk have prompted me to question this attribution. The tightly-knit strokes of charcoal and the distinctive way the features, especially the eyes, are drawn, are quite foreign to Burgkmair. The drawing may be connected with the sons of Ulrich Apt the Elder, in whose work one finds the characteristics present here, in particular the rather doleful expression that he imparts, perhaps not always intentionally, to the features of people in his altarpiece of the *Crucifixion*, mentioned in the biographical note. An apposite comparison may be found in those of the bystanders below the unrepentant robber in the right-hand wing of this altarpiece (the 'Rehlingeralter') in the Staatsgalerie, Augsburg (inv.nos.5349–51, 5373–74; Augsburg, *Altdeutsche Gemälde*, pls. 44–6; col.pl.vii), which is signed *Apt*, and dated *1517*. Fortunately, too, on the central panel of the same commission a small boy stands, whose features, although not rivalling in ugliness those of the younger child on the *verso* of the drawing, are certainly strong competition. The existence of a silverpoint portrait drawing based on the present one and dated *1520*, formerly in the collection of Walter Gay, Paris, and now in the Louvre (Paris, inv.no.R.F.29074) provides a *terminus ante quem* for the execution of no.147, most probably *c.*1515–20.

Georg Beck

Active in Augsburg 1490–1512/15

Miniaturist. Probably from Giengen an der Brenz, in the Swabian Alps, he became a citizen of Augsburg in 1490. Chiefly worked for the Benedictine Abbey of Sts Ulrich and Afra in Augsburg. Father of Leonhard Beck (q.v.).

BIBLIOGRAPHY: Thieme-Becker, iii, 1909, pp.137f.; Augsburg, *Holbein*, pp.175f.

148 Dedicatory frontispiece

See colour plate section following p.80

Bodycolour and gold-leaf on vellum. 38.5 × 28cm

PROVENANCE: Abbey of Sts Ulrich and Afra, Augsburg (according to Placidus Braun, *Notitia de Codd. Mss in Biblioteca Monasterii ad SS. Vdalricum et Afram Augustae extantibus*, iii, 1793, p.100, this sheet was then still in the *Psalterium*, to which it belonged; the choirbook is now in the Staatsbibliothek, Augsburg (Cod. in fol.49a), and the frontispiece separated from it was acquired by the Victoria and Albert Museum in 1892)

London, Victoria & Albert Museum, Ms.425 (D.86–1892)

LITERATURE: Bradley, *Introduction*, p.131, pl.8; BFAC, *Early German Art*, 1906, pp.119f., no.22; Steingräber, *Buchmalerei*, pp.21, 24, 49, n.30, 62, no.28, pl.12; Manchester, *German Art*, p.16, no.22, repr.; Augsburg, *Holbein*, p.175, no.235

The scribe of the choirbook, Leonhard Wagner, supported by his patron, St Jude, is seen in the foreground presenting the choirbook, to which no.148 was the frontispiece, to Johann von Giltlingen, abbot of Sts Ulrich and Afra, from 1482 to 1496. The patron saints of the Abbey are depicted seated in the background, whose arms (Kyburg, for St Ulrich; Jerusalem quartered with Lusignan for St Afra, who had been a princess of Cyprus), are introduced as part of the decoration of the late Gothic arch. Wagner states in his manuscript (folio 191 *verso*) that he began to write it at 10 in the morning on 7 April 1494 and completed the text at the same hour on the same day in 1495, in his forty-first year.

The evidence for Beck being responsible for the illumination comes from the Abbey's chronicler, Wilhelm Wittwer (1449–1512) (printed in Braun, op.cit., p.31) who states that of five psalters written by Wagner and Kramer, two were produced in 1495 with illuminations by Georg Beck and his son who, although not mentioned by name, was Leonhard Beck (q.v.). It is generally accepted that Georg only executed the frontispiece and that Leonhard was responsible for the remaining decorative illumination, that is forty-nine coloured initials, some of which are historiated, and border ornamentation.

Leonhard Beck

Augsburg c.1480 – Augsburg 1542

Painter, miniaturist and designer of woodcuts. Trained initially with his father Georg Beck (q.v.). He is documented in Frankfurt in 1501, where he was active as an assistant in the workshop of Hans Holbein the Elder (q.v.) and collaborated with the production of Holbein's Dominican altarpiece, of 1500/1 (Frankfurt, Städelsches Kunstinstitut). He became a master in the Augsburg guild in 1503. His numerous woodcuts, of which only three are signed, all reveal a characteristic style, and were made chiefly for Imperial commissions, such as *Der Weisskunig* (1514–16),

149

Theuerdank (1517) and the *Triumphal Procession of Maximilian* (1516–18). He was the father-in-law of Christoph Amberger (q.v.).

BIBLIOGRAPHY: Thieme-Becker, iii, 1909, pp.140f.; Dodgson, ii, pp.122ff.; Buchner, *Beiträge*, ii, pp.388ff.; Hollstein, ii, pp.163ff.; Augsburg, *Umbruch*, ii, pp.222f.

149 Portrait of a young man

Black and red chalk with yellow wash in the eyes, the cloak and background brushed with whitish bodycolour. 25 × 17.4cm

PROVENANCE: George Grote bequest, 1872

London, University College, G.146

LITERATURE: Hind, *Select List*, p.13, no.15; Düsseldorf, *UCL Drawings*, p.10, no.7, repr.

See no.150.

150 Portrait of a young man wearing a cap, seen from the front

See colour plate section following p.200

Black and red chalk, with pink, yellow and grey wash, and blue and grey bodycolour in the background and on the sitter's right shoulder. 24.8 × 16.9cm

PROVENANCE: George Grote bequest, 1872

London, University College, G.145

LITERATURE: Buchner, *Beiträge*, ii, p.403, repr.; Hind, *Select List*, p.13, no.14; R.A., 1953, p.55, no.215; Manchester, *German Art*, p.56, no.145; Düsseldorf, *UCL Drawings*, pp.9f., no.6

This drawing has been considered a self-portrait, despite lacking the steadfast gaze characteristic of such portraits, and was first attributed to Leonhard Beck by Buchner, together with its companion drawing (no.149).

Apart from the difference of medium, a comparison between these portrait drawings and Beck's painted portraits has not been a straightforward matter in the past, made difficult by a certain lack of agreement about the attribution of some of the latter to Beck; however, now that the development of Hans Holbein the Elder (q.v.) as a portrait painter is more fully understood, the boundary between his work and that of Beck is clearer. Amongst these paintings, the *Portrait of a young man with a ring* (Vienna, Kunsthistorisches Museum, inv.no.2182) and the *Portrait of Lukas or Hans Rem* dated *1505* (Augsburg, Städtische Kunstsammlungen, inv.no.11960; Augsburg, *Altdeutsche Gemälde*, pl.40) can be compared in a general way with these drawings. After due allowance has been made for the less formal, more intimate approach in the drawings, especially marked with the so-called self-portrait, they have so much more in common with Beck's paintings than the work of other Augsburg portraitists of the period for the attribution to Beck to be reasonably secure. The drawings do at least reveal an individual hand, quite distinct from the masterly freedom of Hans Holbein the Elder, or the rather mundane manner of Jörg Breu the Elder (q.v.).

Attributed to Leonhard Beck

151 St Catherine

Pen and black ink and grey wash, heightened with white bodycolour on light brown prepared paper; the sky in bright blue bodycolour. The sheet has a few holes and tears, and has been laid down. 25.3 × 15.6cm

PROVENANCE: not recorded

England, Private Collection

LITERATURE: Schilling, *Gesamm. Zeichn.*, p.39, no.12, repr.; Rowlands, *Private Collection*, p.36, no.33, repr.

151

Inscribed on the backing in an old hand, in pencil, *In der Manier des Ölbildes der Hl: Barbara von H.Holbein der Münchner Gallerie* (a reference to the full-length figure of this saint painted on a wing of the St Sebastian altarpiece of 1516 by Hans Holbein the Elder (q.v.) from St Salvator, Augsburg, now in the Alte Pinakothek, Munich, inv.no.669)

Despite this early comparison the stylistic link between no.151 and Holbein the Elder is, in fact, rather weak, although the drawing is certainly the work of an Augsburg master, and probably done in the early part of the sixteenth century. Schilling's tentative proposal that it may be by Leonhard Beck is given some credence if one places this drawing alongside Beck's woodcuts of female Hapsburg saints, especially those of *St Kunigunda* and *St Ursula* (Dodgson, ii, pp.136–7, nos.133 and 141).

Jörg Breu the Elder

Augsburg c.1475 – Augsburg May/October 1537

Painter and designer of woodcuts and glass paintings. In 1493 he was apprenticed to Ulrich Apt the Elder (active 1481–1532). As a journeyman, he was in Austria from 1498 to 1502, and produced the Aggsbach altarpiece, with *Scenes from the life of Christ*, signed and dated *1501*, parts of which are now in the Augustinerchorherrenstift, Herzogenburg, and in Nuremberg (Germanisches National-museum) as well as altarpieces at Zwettl (1500) and Melk (1502). These early altarpieces are important represen-tations of the Danube School style of painting. In 1502 he was a master in Augsburg where he came increasingly under the influence of Hans Burgkmair (q.v.). His first dated woodcut was made in 1504, and thereafter he pro-duced numerous book illustrations for the leading Augsburg publishers. He probably visited Italy in 1508 and 1514/15, and in 1522 he was in Baden and Strassburg. He contributed drawings to the *Prayer Book* of *Emperor Maximilian* (Besançon, Bibliothèque) of 1515, but the majority of his drawings are designs for glass-paintings.

BIBLIOGRAPHY: Thieme-Becker, iv, 1910, pp.594ff. (for further literature); Dodgson, ii, pp.108ff.; Buchner, *Beiträge*, ii, p.272ff.; W.Hugelshofer, ibid., pp.384ff.; Hollstein, iv, pp.157ff.; Linz, *Donauschule*, pp.27f.; Augsburg, *Umbruch*, i, pp.116ff., ii, pp.112ff., 224ff.; Andersson, *Detroit*, pp.82f.

152 The Virgin and Child seated by a table

Pen and black ink. 15.9 × 13.6cm

WM: small bear (close to Briquet, 12270)

PROVENANCE: formerly mounted in a copy of *Kellermaisterey. Gründtlicher Bericht . . .*, Augsburg, 1536

England, Private Collection

LITERATURE: Schilling, *Gesamm. Zeichn.*, p.37, no.11, repr.; Rowlands, *Private Collection*, p.34, no.30, repr.

Inscribed on the upper edge in an early hand, in black ink, *preu*

This is an early drawing by Breu, which, from a comparison of the representations of the Virgin and Child in his altar-piece at Aggsbach can be established as contemporaneous with it. The panels of the *Birth of Christ* and the *Circumcision* of the latter, are signed with Breu's monogram, and in-scribed, *JORGPREW VON AV[GSBURG] 1501*.

The types of the Virgin and Child, particularly in the *Birth of Christ*, are unquestionably by the artist who was responsible for the present drawing; the features of the Virgin in each are markedly similar and the modelling of the Child's body confirms the association. The altarpiece was commissioned for the Carthusian Church at Aggsbach, and was the chief work executed by Breu from his time in a workshop in Krems between 1498 and 1502. Since 1816 most of the painted panels of the altarpiece have been in

152

Herzogenburg, and two panels with the *Flight into Egypt* and the *Crucifixion* have been at Nuremberg since 1927 (Germanisches Nationalmuseum, inv.nos.1153 and 1152). Nothing is known, however, about its carved sculpture. The only other known drawing which would date from the beginning of Breu's career when he was in Austria, is the *St Christopher* now at Budapest (Szépmüvészeti Múzeum, inv.no.289), but the attribution of this sheet to Breu is admittedly much less secure.

This work is one of the earliest masterpieces of the artistic movement that arose in Vienna and the Danube valley, now known as the Danube School (see nos.127–37).

153 Book-plate of the family of Tänzl von Trazberg

See colour plate section following p.200

Brush drawing in bodycolour, heightened with gold. 31.6 × 22cm

PROVENANCE: Library of Kloster Wilten, near Innsbruck (the volume is stamped *Bibliotheca Wiltin* on the title-page and elsewhere)

British Library, Department of Printed Books, c.35.k.11

LITERATURE: K.T.Parker, *OMD*, xxix, 1933, pp.13f., pl.15

Inscribed by the artist on the scroll in grey bodycolour, *1518*

Painted book-plates are reasonably common in sixteenth-century German printed books, but one of this fine quality is quite exceptional. It is mounted in the front-end of a copy of the *Brixen Missal* which is illustrated with woodcuts by the Master DS (active 1503–15) and was printed at Basel by Jacob von Pforzheim, and published in August 1511. Campbell Dodgson identified the dexter coat-of-arms as that of the family of Tänzl von Trazberg, which has been located by Rietstap (*Armorial Général*, Gouda [1884–7], tome ii, 2nd edition, p.883) in Bavaria and Siebmacher (*Grosses und allgemeines Wappenbuch . . .*, xxii, pt.ii, 1, Neustadt an der Aisch, 1971 [modern reprint], p.60), in the Tyrol. Given the use of the missal and its provenance, the Tyrol is probably the more likely of the two; however, the sinister arms need to be identified to discover more about the branch of the family concerned.

After considering the inviting claims of Leonhard Beck (q.v.), whom we know trained and worked as an illuminator, Parker came down firmly in favour of an attribution of the book-plate to Jörg Breu. He made a compelling comparison between the appearance of nude children in Breu's paintings, particularly that of the Christ child in the *Adoration of the Magi*, also of 1518 in the Schlossmuseum, Koblenz (Buchner, *Beiträge*, ii, pl.240) and that of the child in the present drawing, which is so close as to settle the matter unquestionably.

154 Ulysses and Telemachus slaying the suitors

Pen and black ink. Diameter: 24.4cm

PROVENANCE: A.von Lanna (sale, Stuttgart, H.G.Gutekunst, 1910, 6 May, lot 120, bt *Artaria, 1600 RM*); anon. collector (sale,

Berlin, P.Graupe, 1929, 17 April, lot 57); H.A.Strölin, Lausanne; Campbell Dodgson bequest, 1949

1949–4–11–109

LITERATURE: Schönbrunner-Meder, xi, no.1286, repr.; H.Röttinger; Thieme-Becker, iv, 1910, p.595

This was probably produced for one of a series of glass roundels on the theme of famous women of antiquity. Others in the series, if this suggestion is right, could have included the *Cleopatra* at Stuttgart (Staatsgalerie, Graphische Sammlung, inv.no.7; Gernsheim, no.83922), and *Lucretia*, dated *1522*, in Berlin-Dahlem (Kupferstichkabinett, inv. no.4406; Gernsheim, no.56941). Their dimensions and the consistent styles of the designs support this proposal.

Jörg Breu the Younger
Augsburg soon after 1510 – Augsburg 1547

Painter, miniaturist and designer of woodcuts, glass-paintings and goldsmiths' work. Son and pupil of Jörg Breu the Elder (q.v.), whose workshop he took over. He travelled in Italy, in particular to Venice, as a journeyman and in 1534 was a master in Augsburg. He was much employed as a wall-painter, and worked in this capacity in 1536–7 for the Pfalzgraf Ottheinrich, at Schloss Neuburg and Grünau. His designs for woodcuts, which were often made on a large scale and printed from numerous blocks, continue a formula established in Augsburg by Hans Burgkmair (q.v.) and Breu's father.

BIBLIOGRAPHY: Thieme-Becker, iv, 1910, pp.596f.; Hollstein, iv, pp.185ff.; Geissler, *Deutsche Zeichner 1540–1640*, i, p.10 (for further literature); Augsburg, *Umbruch*, ii, pp.230f.

155 *Joannis Tirolli Antiquitates*

See colour plate section following p.200

Ms volume, containing 220 folios with approx. 200 illustrations, 4 of which are double folio size on vellum. Pen and brown and black ink, with watercolour, bodycolour and gold. Many sheets made up. Folio, approx. 49.4 × 34.6cm

WM: shield with star and anchor surmounted by the Augsburg arms, a fir-cone (Briquet 2125; Briquet's source was the *Baumeisterbuch*, 1536–40, Augsburg, Stadtarchiv)

PROVENANCE: probably not in England before the end of the sixteenth century; S.Stebbing (see Hearne, op.cit.); T.Jett FRS (sale, C.Bateman, 1731, 11 May, pp.8ff., bt in at £200); Henry Temple, Lord Viscount Palmerston, by whom given to Sir R.Ellys (according to his inscription inside the front cover); returned by Lady Ellys following her husband's death to Lord Viscount Palmerston, by whom presented to the College, 26 April 1750

Eton College Library, signature BL.1(1)

LITERATURE: Hearne, *Remarks and Collections*, viii, 1907, p.9; James, pp.33ff., nos.92 to 95, MS92; C.Dodgson, *Munich Jahrbuch*,

154

NF, 1934/5, xi, Heft 2, pp.191ff., repr.; R.Birley, *The Eton College Collections: One Hundred Books*, Eton, 1970, p.8, no.16.

This volume, the first of four, contains a history with richly illuminated illustrations. It was a private commission from Jakob Hörporth, one of the two mayors of Augsburg, for presentation to Henry VIII. The reason for this sumptuous gift is not known, but it would appear that it did not reach the King of England, whose arms are incorrectly emblazoned within. It was possibly part of a misguided and futile plan to enlist Henry VIII's support for the Protestant cause.

The author of the work is Johann Tirol, the architect, who became responsible for the public buildings and works in Augsburg from 1541. Whilst the three other volumes have woodcut outlines of arms, mostly emblazoned in colours of the kingdoms of Europe and the German nobility, the first volume contains miniatures by Jörg Breu the Younger, which constitutes his best work, and is certainly an outstanding production of its kind from Augsburg from the second quarter of the sixteenth century. The most impressive illuminations are those executed on two folded sheets of vellum; the first of which, folio 40, represents the *Triumph of L. Tarquinius Priscus over the Etruscans*, dated on a standard, *1541*. The second of these, folio 42, which is exhibited here, is on a similar folded sheet of vellum (approx. 49.4 × 66.5cm), and is executed in pen and black ink with watercolour, and heightened with gold leaf. The sheet is divided equally between two subjects, on the left, the *Battle of Regillus*; on the right, *Scenes from the life of Lucretia*, with above, Sextus' attack on her, and below, her death and funeral, with the citizens swearing to expel the kings from Rome. In many of the scenes the events in the history of ancient Rome are pictured as though they were taking place in Augsburg in the 1540s. Such reflections of local patriotism are similarly found in the designs of Jörg Breu the Elder (q.v.), the artist's father.

Hans Burgkmair

Augsburg 1473 – Augsburg 1531

Painter, etcher and designer of woodcuts. He received his first training with his father Thoman Burgkmair (q.v.) and, from 1488 to 1490, was apprenticed to Martin Schongauer (q.v.) in Colmar. In 1491 he was designing woodcuts for the publisher, Erhard Ratdolt, and continued throughout his life to produce designs for the leading Augsburg presses. He became a master in 1498. He first made contact with Emperor Maximilian, his chief patron, particularly between 1508 and 1519, at the Diet of Augsburg in 1500. The imperial commissions include drawings for the *Prayer Book of Maximilian* of 1515 (Besançon, Bibliothèque) to which Albrecht Dürer (q.v.), Hans Baldung (q.v.) and other leading artists also contributed; and designs for the emperor's major printed projects, *Der Weisskunig* (1514–16), *Der Theuerdank* (1517) and the *Triumphal Procession* (1516–18).

His contribution to printmaking includes playing a seminal rôle, between 1508 and 1512, in the development of the chiaroscuro woodcut. He also received important commissions for paintings, of which notable examples include the portrait of the Strassburg preacher, *Johannes Geiler von Kaysersberg* (see under no.21), signed and dated *1490* (Augsburg, Staatsgalerie); the altarpieces of *St John the Baptist*, signed and dated *1518*, and the *Crucifixion*, signed and dated *1519* (both divided between Augsburg, Staatsgalerie, and Munich, Alte Pinakothek); and *Esther and Ahasuerus*, signed and dated *1528* (Munich, Alte Pinakothek).

Together with Hans Holbein the Elder (q.v.) Burgkmair was the most important artist of the early sixteenth century in Augsburg. He is known to have spent at least part of 1507 in Italy, and was influential in the introduction of Renaissance forms into Augsburg, whose art at this period reflected the new Italian style more noticeably than any other German city.

BIBLIOGRAPHY: Thieme-Becker, v, 1911, pp.252ff.; Hollstein, v, pp.27ff.; P.Halm, *Munich Jahrbuch*, DF, xiii, 1962, pp.75ff.; Falk, *Burgkmair* (for further literature); *Hans Burgkmair: das graphische Werk*, exhib.cat. Augsburg, Städtische Kunstsammlungen, 19 May–29 July 1973, edited by I.Hausberger and R.Biedermann; *Hans Burgkmair 1473–1531 Holzschnitte Zeichnungen Holzstöcke*, exhib. cat. East Berlin, Bode Museum, 1974, edited by R.Kroll and W.Schade; Augsburg, *Umbruch*, i, pp.141f., 235ff.

156 A decapitated head

Charcoal, heightened on the face with white bodycolour. 19.9 × 25.6cm

WM: high crown with a cross

PROVENANCE: E.Rodrigues (sale, Amsterdam, F.Muller, 1921, 12 July, lot 16, bt *Colnaghi 720 guilders* for BM)

1921–10–12–1

LITERATURE: H.Rupé, in Buchner, *Beiträge*, ii, pp.203f., pl.147; Falk, *Burgkmair*, pp.84, 111, n.538

Inscribed by the artist, in charcoal, in the upper left-hand corner, *1522 HB*; and by a later hand, in brown ink, in the upper right-hand corner, *Hans Burgmair*

Falk, following Rupé's opinion, sees this as a highly naturalistic record of an execution, rather than an imaginative study for a painting of the decapitation of St John the Baptist. Whatever one's views, undoubtedly this is Burgkmair's most spirited sketch, and is admirably suited to the macabre subject.

156

157 The Visitation

Pen and brown ink with grey wash. 21.7 × 19.3cm

WM: high crown (close to Piccard, xii,5.)

PROVENANCE: E. Peart; Sir T. Lawrence; probably F. Abbot (sale, Christie, 1929, 11 February, lot 4, bt *Colnaghi* £10.10s for the BM)

1929–4–16–2

LITERATURE: C.Dodgson, *BMQ*, iv, 1929–30, p.10, repr.; E. Schilling, *Wallraf Jahrbuch*, NF, ii/iii, 1933–4, pp.266, 271, repr.; E.Halm, *Munich Jahrbuch*, DF, xiii, 1962, pp.106, 161, repr.; Falk, *Burgkmair*, pp.74, 108, n.472; T.Falk, *Pantheon*, xxxi, 1973, pp.22ff., repr.

Inscribed by the artist in black ink on the right-hand base of the column on the right of the drawing, *H.B*; and on the *verso* in an early hand, in black chalk, *H.burckmair*.

Until it was acquired by the Department it was thought to be by Hans Baldung. It had always been assumed that this drawing, together with that of the *Death of the Virgin* in Frankfurt (Städelsches Kunstinstitut, inv.no.st.G.1027; Schilling op.cit., p.267, repr.) with which it is readily associated, were the remnants of a series of Marian subjects executed about 1520 for missing paintings. They were, in fact, as Falk made clear, intended as designs, not for paintings but for the carved reliefs of wings for a large altarpiece. The relief of the *Death of the Virgin* is in the Museo di Palazzo Venezia, Rome, and that of *The Visitation* appeared at a sale in the Dorotheum, Vienna (no.550, December 1960, lot 474; T.Falk, *Pantheon*, loc.cit., p.23, pl.2). A third relief, for which no preparatory drawing has so far come to light, the *Meeting of Joachim and Anne at the Golden Gate*, is in the Staatliche Museen, Berlin-Dahlem. This is similar in style and would seem to be by the same hand as the other two reliefs after Burgkmair, but Falk entertained serious doubts as to whether they belonged together, owing to the disparity in dimensions. All three are more or less the same width, but the Berlin piece is

157

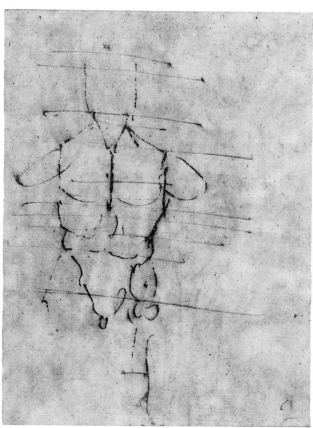

158(a)v

taller than the others by about 20cm. Falk also considers the possibility that the reliefs might have originally formed part of the documented, but mostly lost altarpiece, signed and dated *1522*, by Burgkmair and Sebastian Loscher, the Augsburg sculptor (1482/3–1551), for the high altar in the parish church at Rauris im Pinzgau, near Salzburg. There are also objections to this, according to Falk: the high altar was most probably not dedicated to the Virgin Mary since the church's patrons are St Jacob and St Martin, and the reliefs do not harmonise with our current view of Loscher's work in the early 1520s. No other attribution is offered as a possible alternative; however, they are strongly dependent on the decorative features of the Fugger Chapel in the St Annakirche, Augsburg, the first significant Renaissance work produced north of the Alps, partly designed by Dürer and chiefly inspired by him. This could mean a sculptor of the first wave of the Renaissance in south Germany was responsible for carving them.

158(a) *Recto:* Standing black youth dressed in a feather skirt, cape, and headdress and holding a club and shield

See colour plate section following p.200

Verso: Sketch of a man

Pen and black ink, with brown, black and grey wash, the *verso* in brown ink. 23.5 × 16cm

PROVENANCE: Sloane bequest, 1753

5218–128

LITERATURE: Hausmann, *Naumann's Archiv*, p.39, no.128; Hausmann, p.110, no.104; P.Halm, *Munich Jahrbuch*, D.F. xiii, 1962, pp.125ff., 161, repr.; H.Honour, *The New Golden Land: European Images of America from the Discoveries to the Present Time*, London, 1975, p.14, repr.; *European Vision of America*, pp.4, 16, n.11; C.Feest, *American Indian Workshop Newsletter*, xix, Vienna, 1984, p.11.

See no.158(b).

(b) Standing black youth dressed in a feather skirt, cape and headdress and holding an axe with a shrunken human head on the end

See colour plate section following p.200

Pen and black ink, with grey, brown and green wash. 24 × 16.1cm

PROVENANCE: Sloane bequest, 1753

5218–129

LITERATURE: Hausmann, *Naumann's Archive*, p.39, no.129; Hausmann, p.110, no.105; P.Halm, *Munich Jahrbuch*, DF, xiii, 1962, pp.125ff., 161, repr.; *European Vision of America*, pp.4, 16, n.11

Together with no.158(a), this drawing reflects the lively interest in the New World which was prevalent during the sixteenth century. They were first recognised as the work of Burgkmair by Halm, having previously been classified as anonymous sixteenth-century German drawings. Hans Burgkmair, like Albrecht Dürer (q.v.) who made a fairly accurate drawing of an American Indian of the Tupinamba tribe, in the pages of the *Prayer Book of Maximilian*, dated *1515* (Munich, Staatsbibliothek, fol.41r.; Strauss, iii, p.1537, repr.), was known to be fascinated by the exotic. The description of the first voyage made by German merchants in 1505–6 to the Portuguese Indies in India, written by Balthasar Springer, was illustrated with woodcuts designed by Burgkmair in 1508 (later accounts by Springer, with different woodcuts, were published in 1509 and 1511) which clearly demonstrate his creative abilities in dealing with representatives of African and Asiatic races (Dodgson, ii, pp.71f., no.11; Hollstein, v, p.132, nos.731–6, repr.). This interest is further seen in his designs of 1516–18 for the woodcuts which represent Asiatic types in the 'people of Calicut' from the *Triumph of Maximilian* (Dodgson, ii, p.100, nos.165 and 166; Hollstein, v, p.121, repr.). These latter prints reveal a mixture of American Indian and oriental motifs, since it was not established until 1522, after the globe had been circumnavigated, that the West Indies formed part of a continent separate to that of Asia (see William C.Sturtevant, in *First Images of America*, edited by F.Chiappelli, Berkeley/Los Angeles, i, 1976, pp.417ff.). The treatment of perspective and musculature seen in Burgkmair's figures in the *Triumph* is, as Halm pointed out, closely comparable with that of the figures in nos.158(a) and (b).

It would appear that the apparel of the figures in nos. 158(a) and (b) is composite in nature. The dress and accoutrements are quite probably based on actual objects which may well come from different places, but the artist has either applied his own imagination or relied on someone else's recollection in the manner of dress, and has used a negroid type to serve as a model for an American Indian. The shield in no.158(a) is, according to Christian Feest, of Mexican origin, which would date the drawings to after 1519, when the European discovery of Mexico by Cortés was made, and is apparently very similar to a circular turquoise mosaic shield now in the Museum für Völkerkunde, Vienna (Karl A.Nowotny, *Mexikanische Kostbarkeiten aus Kunstkammern der Renaissance*, Vienna, 1960, no.2, pl.5). From sixteenth-century European inventories it is known that such shields had coloured feather-work suspended from their edges. The club held by the shield-bearer may also be Mexican. The feather-work is considered to be mainly South American, and has been compared with known objects and published material (e.g. British Museum, Department of Ethnography, inv.no.1954 wam.5.896; *Handbook of South American Indians*, edited by J.H.Steward, Washington, 1946–8, iii, pl.123) although it is possible that some of it may also be Mexican. The headdresses, with halo-type crowns, are seen here worn by the models

back to front. The axe in no.158(b) appears to be of Amazonian origin (e.g. The British Museum, Department of Ethnography, inv.no.1938–3–7–3). Shrunken heads, or 'Tsantsa', one of which has been drawn stuck on the end of the axe in no.158(b), were produced by the Jivaro Indians of Ecuador, but usually worn attached to a cord round the neck (see W.H.Bollaert, *The Intellectual Observer: review of Natural History*, i, London, 1862, pp.134ff.; and *Transactions of the Ethnological Society of London*, ii, London, 1863, pp.112ff.).

Thoman Burgkmair
Augsburg 1444 – Augsburg 1523

Painter. In 1460 he was apprenticed to the miniaturist and printer, Hans Baemler (*c*.1435–1504). In 1471 he wrote the first account to be made of painters who worked at that time in Augsburg. His single documented work, which has a contemporary inscription on the reverse, is a portrait of the Franciscan, *Johannes Capistranus* (Prague, National Gallery). Other works considered to be by him include the altarpiece with *Scenes from the life of Christ*, in Augsburg (Staatsgalerie); part of a series of portraits of bishops in Augsburg Cathedral, on which Peter Kaltenhofer (died *c*.1490) also worked; and the portraits of *Jakob Fugger* and *Sibylla Arzet* (private collection). He was the father and teacher of Hans Burgkmair (q.v.).

BIBLIOGRAPHY: Thieme-Becker, v, 1911, p.258; Falk, *Burgkmair*, p.87, n.22 (for further literature).

159 St Francis of Assisi with the stigmata

Pen and black ink over black chalk. The upper right-hand corner of the sheet has been burnt. 21 × 18.1 cm

WM: three mounds surmounted by a cross (probably Briquet, 11810)

PROVENANCE: Count F. Sternberg-Manderscheid (sale, Dresden, Frenzel and Sieber, 1845, 10 November, lot 597); Freiherr R. von Liphart (L.1758; sale, Leipzig, Boerner, 1898, 24 April, lot 873); F. Ritter von Hauslab; the Fürstlich Liechtenstein'sche Galerie.

England, Private Collection

LITERATURE: Augsburg, *Holbein*, pp.153ff., no.169, repr.; Schilling, *Gesamm. Zeichn.*, p.21, no.4, repr.; Rowlands, *Private Collection*, p.31, no.26, repr.

This was first attributed by Schilling to Thoman Burgkmair on strong stylistic grounds from the clear links he perceived between it and a series of paintings (now destroyed), from St Stefan, Augsburg, with scenes from the life of St Benedict. The saint's head in these is very similar to that of St Francis in this drawing, and the series was credibly attributed to this artist by Buchner, who dated it *c*.1490 (Buchner, *Beiträge*, ii, pp.66ff., repr.). It is possible, as Schilling suggested, that the drawing is an unfinished sketch for a painting rather than a copy made to record one of his pictures.

Hans Holbein the Elder

Augsburg c.1460/65 – Basel? or Isenheim? 1524

Painter, designer of woodcuts, glass paintings, goldsmiths' work and sculpture. Little is known of his early years, part of which he probably spent in Ulm and the Upper Rhineland. As a journeyman, he travelled at least as far as Cologne, where he would have seen the 'Columba' altarpiece of Rogier van der Weyden (1399/1400–64), and possibly also to the Netherlands, since the art of this region was an important influence on his style. He was active in Augsburg by 1490, the date on his painted wings of the altarpiece of *St Afra* (Basel, Kunstmuseum) which probably originated from the Benedictine church of Sts Ulrich and Afra in Augsburg. In 1493 he was a citizen of Ulm, but returned to Augsburg the following year where he lived until 1515, after which he is recorded in Isenheim and Lucerne.

Holbein was one of the foremost artists of his generation. He controlled a large workshop, which handled prestigious commissions not only in and around Augsburg, but also further afield in Alsace and Frankfurt-am-Main. His most important works were large elaborate late Gothic altarpieces, on which sculptors such as Michel Erhart (active 1469–1522) and Gregor Erhart (active 1494–1540) also worked, and which are characterised by his distinctive, luminous colouring. Notable examples of these include the 'Weingartner' altarpiece, of *Scenes from the life of the Virgin*, signed and dated *1493* (Augsburg Cathedral); a wing from the 'Kaisheimer' high altarpiece, with the *Passion of Christ* on the outside, and *Scenes from the life of the Virgin* on the inside, signed and dated *1502* (Munich, Alte Pinakothek); and the altarpiece of *St Catherine*, dated *1512* (Augsburg, Staatsgalerie). Today, he is best known as a draughtsman. His numerous silverpoint portrait-drawings (many in Berlin-Dahlem, Kupferstichkabinett; Basel, Kunstmuseum; Copenhagen, Statens Museum for Kunst), are mostly of citizens of Augsburg, in which the characteristics of the sitters are vividly portrayed with a masterly technique, only rivalled and eventually surpassed by his son Hans Holbein the Younger (q.v.).

BIBLIOGRAPHY: Thieme-Becker, xvii, 1924, pp.333ff.; Stange, viii, pp.57ff.; Basel, *Holbein* (for further literature, pp.39ff.); Augsburg, *Holbein*; Bushart, *Holbein*.

160 St Margaret and St Dorothy

See colour plate section following p.200

Pen and black ink with grey wash, heightened with white bodycolour, on light brown prepared paper. 21 × 15.3 cm

WM: upper half of an oxhead surmounted by a cross (like Piccard, v,357).

PROVENANCE: Rev. Canon A. F. Sutton (sale, Christie, 1926, 12 February, lot 8, bt with one other, *Colnaghi*)

1926-7-13-8

LITERATURE: C. Dodgson, *OMD*, no.4, 1927, pp.56f., pl.66; Augsburg, *Holbein*, p.103, no.69, pl.68; *Israhel van Meckenham*, p.59, repr.; T. Falk, *Zeitschr. f. Kunstwiss.*, xxx, 1976, pp.7ff., pl.1; Falk, *Basel*, p.87 under no.190, p.88 under no.192

A particularly fine example, in excellent condition, of Holbein's early drawing style. The drawing displays the artist's characteristically delicate touch and is comparable in quality and technique to his drawing of St Peter and St Paul, inscribed *H*, in Berlin-Dahlem (Kupferstichkabinett, KDZ.12238; Augsburg, *Holbein*, pl.69).

No.160 must have been made at some time before 1496, since, as originally observed by Falk, it is connected with figures on the wing of an altarpiece executed in that year for the Abbot's chapel in the Abbey of Sts Ulrich and Afra in Augsburg, by Gumpolt Giltlinger (d.1522), a follower of Holbein (*Zeitschr. f. Kunstwiss.*, xxx, 1976, pp.4ff., pl.2). The wing is the only part of the altarpiece to have survived and is much overpainted; its outer side shows St Catherine, St Barbara, St Margaret and St Dorothy. The designs of the latter two saints are clearly inspired by Holbein's drawing. The essential appearance of the figures in no.160 has been recorded with some variations of detail, such as the shape of St Dorothy's basket, and the position of her head which is in a more frontal position in the painting.

Another drawing related to the altarpiece represents *St Catherine and St Barbara* and was sold at the Sutton sale in the same lot as the present drawing (formerly Koenigs Collection, Haarlem; T.Falk, *Zeitschr. f. Kunstwiss.*, xxx, 1976, pp.8ff., repr.). It is similar in technique but not by the same hand as no.160. Schilling attributed it to Thoman Burgkmair (*OMD*, no.31, 1933, p.48f. repr.) with reference to a portable altarpiece, now in the Augsburg Staatsgalerie; but the positions of the figures seem to relate more closely to those of St Catherine and St Barbara in Giltlinger's altarpiece and Falk's suggestion that the sheet may be by the latter artist is not implausible.

In the Kupferstichkabinett in Basel there are two copies of the present sheet (St Dorothy, U.VII34; St Margaret, shown without the attributes, U.VII20) and five further drawings of inferior quality produced in Holbein's workshop, which also display standing female figures close in appearance to those on Giltlinger's altarpiece. To what extent, if at all, Giltlinger made use of these workshop drawings is difficult to say; their significance lies more in the fact that they record designs, of which some are lost, made by Holbein himself.

161 *Recto:* Head of a young man
Verso: St Sebastian

Metalpoint on white prepared paper. 13.1 × 9.6cm

PROVENANCE: A.Grahl (L.1199; sale, Sotheby, 1885, 27 April, lot 118, bt *Thibaudeau £61*)

1885-5-9-1612

LITERATURE: *Vasari Society*, 1905/6, nos.15, 16, repr.; Lieb-Stange, p.90, no.154, pl.232 (*recto*); Augsburg, *Holbein*, p.108, no.81, pl.84 (*recto*), pp.47, 101, no.64, p.204 under no.276, pl.105 (*verso*); Manchester, *German Art*, p.30, no.68; P.Strieder, *Kunstchronik*, v, 1965, Heft 11, p.297, pl.2 (*verso*); Falk, *Basel*, p.91, under no.207 (*verso*)

Inscribed on the *recto* in the upper left-hand corner, in pencil, *62*; and on the *verso* in the upper right-hand corner, in pencil, *69*

On the *verso* is a design for a silver statuette of St Sebastian of 1497, now in the Wernher collection at Luton Hoo (see no.162). It was made, evidently by a goldsmith from Augsburg, for the Abbot Georg Kastner (died 1509) of the Cistercian monastery at Kaisheim where Holbein was later to paint the high altarpiece (dated *1502*; now Munich, Alte Pinakothek, inv.no.721/736). The pose of the saint is closely followed by the goldsmith in the statuette, although there are some differences in the tree to which the figure is tied, especially in the branch to which his right arm is bound. The ornamental reliquary sockel of the statuette, which is not seen in the drawing is thoroughly characteristic of the high-class work of the period. The general design for the sockel which was provided separately could have been done by Holbein, but probably was supplied from the goldsmith's workshop; however the details of its decoration, the statuettes and the relief of the *Virgin of Pity* were made most probably after Holbein's designs. In the latter we find an anticipation of the *Virgin of Pity* in the

161r

161v

glass-painting of 1502 in a window in the mortuary chapel in the cathedral at Eichstätt, for which Holbein executed the design.

The drawing on the *recto*, the *Head of a young man* is an early portrait drawing made by Holbein at some time between 1495 and 1500. Other comparable examples from this period are to be found in Bamberg (Staatliche Bibliothek, Graph. 1A6, 1A7, 1A10), Vienna (Albertina, inv.no. 7825), and elsewhere (see Lieb-Stange, nos.150–9, pls.227–36). The St Sebastian on the *verso* is not mentioned in Lieb-Stange and has by some in the past been mistakenly considered a workshop production (see Manchester, *German Art*, loc.cit.), despite its fine quality and the fact that it clearly is by the same hand as the drawing on the *recto*, which is unquestionably by Holbein the Elder. In Basel, there is a study for a statuette of St Sebastian tied to a tree, drawn in pen and ink with wash, by a member of Holbein's workshop, which may possibly record an alternative design for the Luton Hoo statuette (Kupferstichkabinett, inv.no.U.V.11.9). Amongst other examples of

workshop drawings which provide further evidence of connections between Holbein and the goldsmith trade, is the design for a bishop's crozier in Vienna (Österreichisches Museum für angewandte Kunst, inv.no.K.I.619). Holbein himself is known to have collaborated with the goldsmith Jörg Seld (c.1448–1527), in Augsburg (see under no.146; Augsburg, *Holbein*, pp.49, 106 under no.77), of whom he made a portrait drawing in 1497 (Bayonne, inv.no.1532).

Augsburg goldsmith

Late 15th century

162 St Sebastian

Silver, partly gilt cast, embossed, and engraved; pearls, rubies and sapphires on sockel. Some pinnacles missing. The six-sided sockel, which encloses a relic of the saint behind a crystal pane is decorated with statuettes of Saints Catherine, George, Wolfgang and probably Boniface, and a relief of the Virgin of Pity. Overall height: 50 cm; height of sockel: 15.2cm.

PROVENANCE: Kaisheim Abbey; Soltykoff collection (according to 1912 inventory of Wernher collection); Sir Julius Wernher

Luton Hoo, The Wernher collection, c3/507/679

LITERATURE: J.Knebel, *Die Chronik des Klosters Kaisheim*, edited by F.Hüttner, Tübingen, 1902, p.368; BFAC, *Early German Art* (illustrated edition), 1906, pp.115f., no.8, pl.xliv; Manchester, *German Art*, p.27, no.59, repr.; Augsburg, *Holbein*, pp.203f., no.276, pl.273 (for further literature)

Engraved on the cover-plate of the reliquary, ORA PRONOBIS. S. SEBASTIANE./VT MEREAMVR. PESTEM [illegible, as carved next to the saint's foot] ESI.TRANSIRE. ET./PROMISSIO[N]EM. XPI. OBTINERE./ILLVD CLENODIVM. PROCVRATVM. EST./PER ABBATEM. GEORGIVM. SECVNDVM. MONASTERY. CESARE. SVBREGE. MAXIMI°. ET GEORIO [sic] DVCE/·BAVARIE BROTVNC. DE. FENSORE., followed by a five-petalled flower, possibly the maker's mark. The date *1497* is engraved above the fifth line of the inscription.

This object was recorded, together with a reliquary silver statuette of St Christopher of 1493, also now at Luton Hoo, as a gift of Abbot Georg Kastner (died 1509) to his community, the Cistercian Abbey at Kaisheim, near Donauwörth, north of Augsburg.

See no.161.

162

163r

163v

163 *Recto:* The death of Lucretia
Verso: An alternative design for the death of Lucretia

The *recto* in pen and black ink with grey, brown and blue wash; the *verso* in pen and black ink with grey wash, heightened with white bodycolour, on yellow prepared paper. Diameter: 10.6cm.

PROVENANCE: W.B. Tiffin

1853-10-8-12

LITERATURE: K.T. Parker, *OMD*, no.31, 1933, p.50, pls.50, 51

The drawings were thought by Parker to be the work of Thoman Burgkmair, on the basis of a stylistic comparison with some of the paintings attributed to this artist by Buchner (Buchner, *Beiträge*, ii, pp.65-92). But very few drawings by him are known (see no.159) and an attribution to Holbein would appear more appropriate since the form and technique of no.163 are compatible with that of pen-drawings clearly assignable to Holbein's hand. A comparable example is the design for an altarpiece in the Museo Civico, Pavia (Lieb-Stange, p.51, no.80, repr.) which is drawn on a similar scale, in pen and ink with coloured wash.

The purpose for which no.163 was made is not known. The composition and arrangement of the figures on both *recto* and *verso* of the sheet are reminiscent of Holbein's *Scenes from the life of St Paul* (the so-called 'Basilikatafel San Paolo fuori le mura'; Augsburg, Staatliche Gemäldegalerie, inv.5332/34; Lieb-Stange, pl.88) of 1503-5, and the drawings may accordingly be dated *c.*1500-5.

Two early copies of the *recto* are known: in Berlin-Dahlem (Kupferstichkabinett, inv.no.KDZ.1928, pen and black ink with grey wash, 16.9cm diameter); and formerly in the Winckler collection (sale catalogue, F.A.C Prestel, Frankfurt-am-Main, 1920, 10-16 Nov, lot 1899, as by *Albert Glockenden*, repr.).

164 Virgin and Child with a donor

Pen and black ink with grey wash and gold leaf. 30.1 × 12.3cm

Private Collection

LITERATURE: Manchester, *German Art*, p.31, no.70; Augsburg, *Holbein*, p.118, no.108, repr.

Inscribed by the artist, in black ink on the sockel, *1508*

This is evidently a design for a silver or silver-gilt statuette, first attributed by Grossman very credibly to Hans Holbein the Elder. A piece executed from the drawing is not known. As Bushart pointed out, similar renderings of the subject are the early painting by Holbein, of the *Virgin with a donor* in a Swiss private collection (Augsburg, *Holbein*, pl.5), as well as a drawing at Weimar, the *Virgin as Queen of Heaven* (Schlossmuseum; Lieb-Stange, pl.132).

For another design for goldsmith's work by Hans Holbein the Elder, see no.161 *verso*.

165 Portrait of Sigmund Holbein

Metalpoint with black ink and red chalk, heightened with white bodycolour, on white prepared paper. The sheet appears to have been cut down along the upper, right and left edges. 12.9 × 9.6cm

PROVENANCE: Joachim von Sandrart; F. Fagel (sale, T. Philipe, 1801, 29 May, lot 84, bt with one other, *?Philipe 12s*); Sir T. Lawrence (L.2445); S. Woodburn (sale, Christie, 1860, 4 June,

165

164

lot 510, bt with two others, *Herman £1–15–0*); Sir J.C. Robinson (L.1443); Malcolm

1895–9–15–987

LITERATURE: JCR, pp.185f., no.531; Woltmann, ii, p.84, no.235; Sandrart, *Teutsche Academie*, pp.98f.; Schilling, *Holbein*, p.14, no.3, repr.; Lieb-Stange, p.102, no.228, pl.306; Augsburg, *Holbein*, pp.112f., no.92, pl.93; BM *Portrait Drawings*, pp.7f., no.8; J. Heringa, *Ned. Kunst. Jaarb.*, xxxii, 1981, pp.80, 93, fig.17

Inscribed by the artist along the upper edge, in metalpoint, *1512/Sigmund holbain maler hans [?s]//pruder des alten*; and on the *verso*, in brown ink, when in the collection of the Fagel family, *Portrait van den Schilder Sigismundus Holbein, Broed[er]//van Hans Holbein d'Oude./609.* (see no.191 for inscription in the same hand)

This portrait of the artist's younger brother, Sigmund Holbein (q.v.) is undoubtedly much finer and freer in its execution than a second, autograph version of the drawing in Berlin-Dahlem (Kupferstichkabinett, inv.no.2508, inscribed by another hand, *Sigmund Halbein maler*; Lieb-Stange, p.101, no.227, fig.305; see also Berlin, *Dürer und seine Zeit*, p.87, no.101; Basel, *Holbein*, pp.88f., no.34).

When Joachim von Sandrart (1606–88), the well-known artist, collector and biographer possessed the drawing, after which he designed an engraving, he assumed it to be by Hans Holbein the Younger. It was first attributed correctly to this artist's father by Woltmann. According to Schilling, *hans pruder des alten* was added at a later date;

but the inscription does appear to be all in the artist's hand.

The present drawing is the only fully documented portrait of Sigmund Holbein. A later copy, made according to an inscription on the *verso* from the version in Berlin, is in Düsseldorf (inv.no.FP 9757). Other important drawings by Hans Holbein the Elder which record the appearance of his family are the portrait of his sons, Ambrosius and Hans in Berlin-Dahlem (inv.no.2507; Lieb-Stange, p.103, no.237, fig.315); and the self-portrait at Chantilly (Musée Condé), also from Sandrart's collection (Lieb-Stange, p.112, no.293, fig.370).

Sigmund Holbein

Active Frankfurt-am-Main 1501 – Bern 1540

Painter. Brother and assistant of Hans Holbein the Elder (q.v.) who made a portrait-drawing of him (no.165). Little is known of his life, and his work has proved difficult to define within the artistic *milieu* of Holbein the Elder's workshop. In 1501 he worked with Hans on the Dominican altarpiece in Frankfurt-am-Main, and was in Augsburg from 1504, where in 1517 he took out a law-suit against his brother (Rowlands, *Holbein*, p.24, n.38). His later years were spent in Bern. His will names his nephew, Hans Holbein the Younger (q.v.) as his heir. Attempts have been made to identify him with the Master of the Nuremberg Apostles (see no.167), a Swabian painter active during the late fifteenth and early sixteenth centuries.

BIBLIOGRAPHY: Thieme-Becker, xvii, 1924, pp.375ff., xxxviii, 1950, p.22; Basel, *Holbein* (for further literature, p.42)

166 Studies of four heads

Pen and black ink with grey wash, heightened with white body-colour on reddish-brown prepared paper. 27.5 × 17.8cm

PROVENANCE: George Grote bequest, 1872

London, University College, G.1223

LITERATURE: Hind, *Select List*, p.9, no.1; E.Buchner, *OMD*, iv, 1929, pp.69ff., repr.; Thieme-Becker, xxxvii, 1950, p.22; Stange, viii, p.77; Beutler & Thiem, *Holbein*, pp.83f.; Augsburg, *Holbein*, pp.159f., no.186, pl.187; Düsseldorf, *UCL Drawings*, p.12, no.13, repr.

Inscribed by the artist on the *recto* in black ink, as though from the mouth of the lower left-hand head, *vach qui/destruis demp/lum* (Matthew, xxvii, 40); and by a contemporary hand, probably that of the artist, in black ink, on the *verso*, *hensly/brosy*

The heads on this sheet are not preliminary studies for a painting, but records executed for use by the workshop. According to Hind, Parker first recorded the relationship between the style of this drawing and that of a predella painting of the *Mocking of Christ* in a private collection by the Master of the Nuremberg Martyrdoms of the Apostles,

with whom Sigmund Holbein has been identified. The studies also show a strong affinity with painted heads in the altarpiece by this master from which he takes his name, the majority of which were formerly in the Germanisches Nationalmuseum, Nuremberg (Stange, viii, pl.168). Apart from the stylistic link with Hans Holbein the Elder (q.v.) in whose studio Sigmund worked, the Christian names on the *verso*, which are shortened intimate forms of Hans and Ambrosius, surely refer to Sigmund Holbein's nephews.

167 Judas bargaining with the High Priest, with two prophets above and two below

Pen and black ink with black and grey wash, and red chalk. 30.4 × 20.5cm

PROVENANCE: G. Nebehay; Campbell Dodgson bequest, 1949

1949-4-11-100

LITERATURE: W. Hugelshofer, *OMD*, viii, 1934, p.5; *Old Master Drawings from the Collection of Mr C.R.Rudolf*, Arts Council exhib. cat., London, 1962, pp.29f., no.155; E.von Borries, *Baden-Württemberg Jahrbuch*, xvii, 1980, pp.216–18

Another drawing in the same medium by the same hand and of a similar type, of *David and Nathan*, is in the Kunsthalle, Karlsruhe (inv.no.1979–7). This also at one time belonged to Campbell Dodgson, who had acquired it from the Earl of Sussex. He exchanged it with Colnaghi in 1946. These two drawings, together with that of *Christ expelling the money-changers from the temple*, in Darmstadt (Hessisches Landesmuseum, inv.no.AE 319; Basel, *Holbein*, pl.111), have been attributed to Sigmund Holbein on the basis of a speculative identification of this artist with the Master of the Nuremberg Apostles, so named after a series of paintings formerly in the Germanisches Nationalmuseum, Nuremberg; two further paintings from the series are in the Catholic Pfarrkirche, Rödelheim. The decorative elements in the Karlsruhe drawing, especially the *putti*, are close to those in a design for a heraldic glass-painting in the Fogg Museum, Cambridge, Mass. (inv.no.1932.376). This drawing, with the spurious inscription, *1519 HH*, was regarded by Ganz as a contemporary copy recording a lost drawing by Hans Holbein the Younger (q.v.) of the period 1519–21 (Ganz, pp.98f., no.c.55). which had also been worked over by a later hand. This drawing is now claimed to be by Hans Holbein the Younger himself (*Old Master Drawings. Selections from the Charles A. Loeser Bequest*, Fogg Art Museum, Cambridge, edited by K.Oberhuber, 1979, p.100, no.44, repr.). Ganz later attributed the work in brown ink and wash to Holbein but gave that in black ink and coloured wash to another hand, a view shared by A.Mongan and P.Sachs (*Drawings in the Fogg Museum of Art*, Cambridge, 1940, i, pp.195f., no.387, repr.). Even so, the design both in invention and execution is so far below the resources of Hans Holbein the Younger in this field as to make the attribution quite untenable.

166

167

Daniel Hopfer

Kaufbeuren c.1470 – Augsburg 1536

Painter, etcher and designer of woodcuts. Son of the painter Bartholomäus Hopfer (born probably 1431). He became a citizen of Augsburg in 1493, and he is recorded as a master in the same year. His first profession as an armourer probably accounts for his presence in Augsburg, the main residence of the Emperor Maximilian and the leading centre for the manufacture of arms and armour. He was one of the earliest artists to adapt etching on iron to printmaking, and as such may have influenced other early practitioners of the technique, Hans Burgkmair (q.v.), Albrecht Dürer (q.v.) and Urs Graf (q.v.). His two sons Hieronymus (*c.*1500–63?) and Lambert (active *c.*1525–50) continued the family reputation as etchers.

In 1524 the Emperor Charles V conferred on Hopfer a coat-of-arms for his 'true accomplishments in the service of the Emperor and Empire'. He was an active supporter of the Reformation.

BIBLIOGRAPHY: Thieme-Becker, xvii, 1924, pp.474ff.; R.A.Vogler, *The Hopfers of Augsburg. Sixteenth-century etchers*, exhib.cat., Los Angeles, UCLA Dickson Art Center, 14 Nov.–11 Dec. 1966; Augsburg, *Umbruch*, ii, pp.246ff.; Hollstein, xv, 1986, pp.33ff. (for further literature)

168 Justice

Pen and black ink. Cut along upper and lower edges. 21.5 × 14.1 cm

PROVENANCE: C.D.Ginsburg (sale, Sotheby, 1915, 20 July, part of lot 20, bt *Parsons £5.5s.*); Campbell Dodgson bequest, 1949

1949-4-11-115

LITERATURE: W.Wegner, *Zeitschr. f. Kunstgesch.*, xx, 1957, pp.253f., repr.; Augsburg, *Umbruch*, ii, pp.247f., no.628, repr.

Inscribed by the artist in black ink on the cornice of the arch, MDXXIX, with the artist's monogram on the base of the right-hand column, and partly cut off on the lower edge, *JUSTITIA*

It is not easy to decide the purpose for which Hopfer drew this design, and it cannot be likened at all with any of his etchings. Given the prominence of the emblem of Augsburg, the pine-cone, and the elaborate architectural setting seen from below, we may consider whether it was produced as a preliminary study for a civic wall-decoration. Even though Hopfer is not known himself to have painted murals, it could have been drawn for use by another artist.

Of the figure of Justice herself, the influence of the Venetian artist, Jacopo de' Barbari (*c.*1440/50–1515) who worked north of the Alps and made a marked impression on several German artists, is unmistakable, both in the features and the pose, and in the dress. There is a striking similarity between Justice and Jacopo's painting, of *St Catherine*, for example, in Dresden (L.Servolini, *Jacopo de' Barbari*, Padua, 1944, pp.121–2, pl.xxiii). The crane, which holds a stone in its foot, seen to the left of the figure of Justice, is a symbol of vigilance.

Monogrammist IZ (probably Wilhalm Ziegler)

Draughtsman, whose name comes from the mark, ⚹ on a charcoal drawing of a young boy dated *1520* in Berlin-Dahlem (Kupferstichkabinett) and formerly present on a similar drawing in the British Museum (no.169). Meder considered the artist to be a master from Regensburg, but Baum's more recent identification with the painter Wilhalm Ziegler is generally considered to be the most acceptable proposition (Thieme-Becker). Ziegler was born *c.*1480 in Creglingen. He was apprenticed to Hans Burgkmair (q.v.) in Augsburg in 1502, and from 1507 was a citizen of Rothenburg ober der Tauber. From 1522 to 1531 he lived in Freiburg im Üchtland, and then again in Rothenburg until 1535. According to Baum, a number of Ziegler's paintings are signed with a mark similar to that seen on the Berlin drawing, including one of two large panels from an altarpiece, *St Louis of Toulouse* (Rottenburg am Neckar, Diözesanmuseum), which is also inscribed by the artist, *Wilhalm Ziegler hat das [ ]. .*; the companion panel of *St Louis of France* bears the monogram of Thomas Schmid of Schaffhausen (*c.*1490–1551/9). The mark also appears on a wing of the altarpiece with *Scenes from the life of St Wolfgang*, made *c.*1514, in the church of St Wolfgang, Rothenburg.

Baum also proposed that Ziegler's late works should be identified with those of the artist known as the Master of Messkirch (active *c.*1530–43?), so-called after his major work, the altarpiece of the *Adoration of the Magi*, formerly in the Stadtkirche, Messkirch. This identification should be rejected on stylistic grounds, even though there are some general similarities between the Monogrammist and this Master.

BIBLIOGRAPHY: J.Meder, *Mitt. Kunst*, no.3, 1908, pp.38ff.; J.Baum, *Zeitschr. f. schweiz. Arch.*, iv, 1942, pp.47ff.; J.Baum, *Zeitschr. f. schweiz. Arch.*, v, 1943, pp.21ff.; Thieme-Becker, xxxvi, 1947, pp.484ff. (for further literature) and xxxvii, 1950, p.426.

169 Portrait of a young man

Charcoal. 30.3 × 18.8 cm

WM: imperial orb

PROVENANCE: Sir A.Fountaine (sale, Christie, 1884, 10 July, lot 847, as 'The Master Z' signed with monogram and dated *1520*); R.von Liphart (sale, Leipzig, Boerner, 1898, 26 April and following days, lot 592); E.Rodrigues (L.897; sale, Amsterdam, F.Muller, 1921, 12 July, lot 17, bt *Wendland 1150 guilders*); R.von Hirsch (sale, Sotheby, 1978, 20 June, lot 15); Y.Tan Bunzl

1983-1-27-1

LITERATURE: J.Meder, *Mitt. Kunst*, no.3, 1908, pp.38ff., repr.; *Société de Reproduction des Dessins de Maîtres*, Paris, 1ère Année, 1909, no.1, repr.; Swarzenski & Schilling, *Privatbesitz.*, pp.xif., no.13, repr.; Thieme-Becker, xxxvi, 1947, p.485, xxxvii, 1950, p.426; J.Baum, *Meister und Werke spätmittelalterlicher Kunst in Ober-*

168

169

deutschland und der Schweiz, Lindau, 1957, p.104, pl.29; Berlin, *Dürer und seine Zeit*, p.97, under no.122; Winzinger, *Huber*, i, p.156, no.224, repr.

Inscribed by the artist in charcoal to the left and right of the sitter's head *15...20*.

According to the Fountaine Collection sale catalogue, the drawing was formerly also inscribed with the artist's monogram or mark; there are signs of an erasion visible to the right of the sitter's head and not, as Schilling suggested, on either side of it, which indicate the former location of this mark. It would seem that the erasion was made when the drawing was in the von Liphart collection, and the fact that there is no mention of the mark in the Liphart sale catalogue seems to confirm this. The mark was evidently the same as that on a similar drawing of the head of a boy in charcoal, ⚒ dated *1520*, in Berlin-Dahlem (Kupferstichkabinett, inv.no.kdz. 17689; Berlin, *Dürer und seine Zeit*, pl.120) which, as Meder first established, is by the same hand as the present drawing. The loss of the mark prompted a variety of solutions to the question of authorship. The commonest attribution was formerly to Hans Burgkmair (q.v.), a not unreasonable proposal, considering Ziegler was a pupil of his.

According to the label formerly on the back of the old mount, which dates from the period when the drawing was in the von Hirsch collection, it was then attributed at first tentatively to Wolf Huber (q.v.) and later merely called 'South German Master' on the advice of Schilling. Von Hirsch himself recorded in his notes that a copy of the drawing appeared on the market in Paris in 1956.

Hans Schäufelein

Nuremberg or Augsburg c.1480 – Nördlingen 1538/40

Painter and designer of woodcuts and glass-paintings. Said to be of Swabian origin, Schäufelein's earliest works show the strong influence of Albrecht Dürer (q.v.) in whose studio he worked from *c.*1503. His earliest known woodcuts include illustrations for Ulrich Pinder's *Der Beschlossen Gart des Rosenkranz Maria* (1505) and *Speculum passionis* (1507). After Dürer left Nuremberg for Italy in 1505, Schäufelein was instructed to paint the altarpiece for Ober St Veit (Vienna, Diözesanmuseum) after Dürer's design, for which five of Dürer's drawings have survived (Winkler, *Dürer*, ii, pls.319–23). His earliest dated painting is the *Crucifixion* of 1508 (Nuremberg, Germanisches Nationalmuseum). He probably worked with Hans Holbein the Elder (q.v.) in Augsburg during this period (see Augsburg, *Holbein*, p.138) and was also influenced by the youthful works of Jörg Breu the Elder (q.v.) and Lucas Cranach (q.v.). In 1509/10 he was in the Tyrol where he painted the wings of a carved altarpiece in Niederlana, near Meran. From 1510 to 1515 he was active in Augsburg, where he designed numerous woodcuts for the local printers. In 1513 he

painted the high altarpiece for the Benedictine abbey at Auhausen (see no.173(a) and (b)).

In 1515 he settled in Nördlingen where he was granted citizenship. Between 1515 and *c.*1522 his career was particularly productive; works include the *History of Judith* of 1515 painted in the Nördlingen Town Hall, *Christ on the Mount of Olives*, dated *1516* (Munich, Alte Pinakothek), the memorial panel to Emmeran Wager (Nördlingen, Town Hall), the *Ecce Homo*, dated *1517* (Schleissheim, Staatsgalerie) and his most important painting, the *Ziegler altarpiece*, dated 1521 (Nördlingen, Georgskirche). He also produced a number of portraits (Warsaw, National Museum; Washington, National Gallery of Art, and elsewhere) and many woodcuts, which include contributions to Maximilian's *Weisskunig* (1514–16), *Theuerdank* (1517) and *Triumphal Procession* (1516–18). His illuminations in a prayer book for Count Oettingen were made in 1537/38 (Berlin-Dahlem, Kupferstichkabinett). His last dated work, the *Adoration of the Lamb*, of *1538*, originally formed part of an altarpiece of the *Coronation of the Virgin* (Berlin-Dahlem, Gemäldegalerie).

About ninety drawings, mostly from the first fifteen years of Schäufelein's activity, are known to have survived, of which there is a good collection in the British Museum.

BIBLIOGRAPHY: Dodgson, ii, pp.3ff.; Thieme-Becker, xxix, 1935, pp.557ff. (for further literature); Winkler, K&S; E. Schilling, *Zeitschr. f. Kunstwiss.*, ix, 3/4, 1955, pp.151ff.; *Meister um Dürer*, pp.167ff.; Oldenbourg, *Schäufelein*; Austin, *Nuremberg*, pp.139ff.

170 The Last Supper

Pen and black and brown ink. 15.5 × 22cm

PROVENANCE: R.M.Taylor

1892-8-4-22

LITERATURE: BM *Guide*, 1928, p.36, no.315; Schilling, *Nürnberger Handz.*, p.32, no.37, repr.; Winkler, K&S, p.150, no.42, repr.; Rowlands, *Dürer*, p.58, no.357

Inscribed by the artist in black ink, in the lower right-hand corner *Daman die Muschlan auf den Huot band*, with below the artist's monogram and a little shovel (Schäufelein) and, in the lower left-hand corner, *1509*. The examples of Schäufelein's handwriting (for two of them, see Winkler, K&S, pp.167f.) in a manuscript volume of 1531 (R.Weigel, *Kunstlagerkatalog*, xxiv, Abtheilung, Leipzig, 1852, no.19224) in the Kunstgewerbe Museum in Vienna, are of a similar character to the calligraphy of the inscription on the present drawing. As Winkler points out, the inscription can be interpreted in various ways, but the most likely is that it refers to the conch-shell of St James, which was worn in the hats of pilgrims who visited the saint's shrine at Santiago da Compostella. Perhaps the drawing was executed on St James's Day (25 July) 1509

No.170 is a useful indicator of Schäufelein's development as a draughtsman, in that it is the only dated drawing of his own design executed before 1510. The drawing at

PLATE XVII

Leonhard Beck: *Portrait of a young man wearing a cap* (no.150)

PLATE XVIII

Albrecht Altdorfer:
*A wildman carrying an
uprooted tree*
(no.127 recto)

Wolfgang Huber: *Lakeland
landscape* (no.136)

PLATE XIX

The Master of
Mühldorf:
The Virgin of Altötting
(no.124)

Peter Vischer the
Younger:
Bath-house scene
(no.111)

PLATE XX

Heinrich Aldegrever: *Portrait of Jan van Leyden* (no.138)

PLATE XXI

Lucas Cranach the Elder: *Head of a peasant* (no.139)

PLATE XXII

Jörg Breu the Elder:
*Book-plate of the family
of Tänzl von Trazberg*
(no.153)

Lucas Cranach the
Elder:
Three boys playing
(no.130)

PLATE XXIII

Hans Burgkmair: *Standing black youth holding a club and shield* (no.158a recto)

Hans Burgkmair: *Standing black youth holding an axe with a shrunken human head* (no.158b)

PLATE XXIV

Jörg Breu the Younger: *Joannis Tirolli Antiquitates* (no.155)

PLATE XXV

PLATE XXVI

Hans Holbein the Elder: *St Margaret and St Dorothy* (no.160)

(*Facing page*) Nicolaus Manuel Deutsch: *The Virgin and Child
enthroned* (no.180)

PLATE XXVII

PLATE XXVIII

PLATE XXIX

Ambrosius Holbein: *Portrait of a young man* (no.187)

(*Facing page*) Hans Baldung: *Head of an old man with a heavy beard* (no.114)

PLATE XXX

Hans Holbein: *Portrait of a lady, thought to be Anne Boleyn* (no.203)

PLATE XXXI

Hans Holbein: *Design for a chimney-piece* (no.210)

PLATE XXXII

Hans Holbein: *A wildman brandishing an uprooted tree trunk* (no.195)

170

Erlangen, of a *Woman and child*, signed and dated *1507* (Universitätsbibliothek, inv.no.B.730) is a copy of a drawing dated *1502* by Albrecht Dürer (q.v.) now in the Ashmolean Museum, Oxford (inv.no.P.286; Winkler, *Dürer*, i, pl.186). This is the earliest surviving version of a *Last Supper* by Schäufelein, and the only one which is a drawing. He followed it with the woodcut (Dodgson, ii, p.20, no.43) from the series of the Life of Christ, and other sacred subjects of similar dimensions and style, first recognised as a group by Campbell Dodgson (*Mitt. Kunst*, 1905, Heft 1, p.4). A *Virgin and Child with St Anne* (Dodgson, ii, p.24, no.54), and *St Roch and St Sebastian* (Dodgson, ii, p.24, no.53), which Dodgson assigned to this series are both signed with the monogram and shovel, and dated *1510*. The figures of Christ and the Apostles in the woodcut of the *Last Supper*, mentioned above, are close to those in the drawing, but the arrangement of the figures is altered, and the composition deepened by the addition of an architectural background. In 1511 Schäufelein made a signed and dated painting of the *Last Supper* (East Berlin, Bode Museum, inv.no.560). In this, the simple room with an arch has been retained, and the arrangement of figures is more akin to the present drawing in having less depth to

its composition. Later, Schäufelein did another painting of the *Last Supper*, now on the right-hand altar in the church of Sts Peter and Paul in Dollnstein, Kreis Eichstätt, Bavaria, in which he arranged the group around a table which is rather longer than that in the drawing. Josef Dettenthaler (*Das Münster*, xxiv, Munich, 1971, pp.411–3) links it with the painting of an *Epitaph for Jörg Prigel*, who died in 1521, in the Reichsstadt Museum, Nördlingen, and the *Man of Sorrows* in the same museum, of 1522. It is difficult to fit Schäufelein's undated later paintings, as opposed to his drawings, chronologically into his final phase, as, after his establishment in Nördlingen in 1515, they appear to vary remarkably little in style, although there is, as time goes on, a general decline and increased lack of vitality in his paintings. However, there is nothing against dating the Dollnstein painting to the 1520s. Dettenthaler suggests that Schäufelein at this time was working solely on commissions in and around Nördlingen, and that originally it would have come from that district.

It is interesting to note a link between Schäufelein and an artist trained in Prague, a Master Hanuš, probably Hanuš (Hans) Efeldar or Elfeder, who became a master there in 1515. Hans painted in that same year a predella with the *Last Supper* (J. Pešina, *Acta Hist. Art.*, xx, 1979, pp.66–8) for the Jakobskirche at Kutná Hora (Kuttenberg) which is so closely modelled on Schäufelein's work at that time that one must assume that Hans had first-hand knowledge of it.

171 Four scenes from the life of knights and landsknechts with, in the centre, a crowned head of a woman on a shield

Pen and black and brown ink over black chalk, the head of the woman in black chalk. Diameter: 26.7cm

PROVENANCE: Sloane bequest, 1753

5218–122

LITERATURE: BM *Guide*, 1928, p.36, no.317; Winkler, K&S, pp.129, 151, under no.43, 168; E. Schilling, *Zeitschr. f. Kunstwiss.*, ix, 1955, pp.156–7, 173, 175–6, 178, no.11, repr.

The glass-painting for which Schäufelein produced this design was formerly in the Schlossmuseum, Berlin, but was destroyed with the rest of the painted-glass collection in 1945 (Schilling, op.cit., p.174, pl.24). The window, dated *1510*, was in the main carried out in accordance with the design, except for the crowned female bust in the shield at the centre, which was replaced with the arms of the German Empire with the double-headed eagle.

This glass-painting had two companion quatrefoil windows with heraldic shields at their centres, also in the Schlossmuseum, one of *Four scenes from the life of St John the Baptist with the arms of the bishopric of Augsburg*, and the other of *Four Labours of Hercules*. The design for the former, in the Uffizi, Florence (Winkler, K&S, pl.43), has in the centre of the shield, a putto holding a standard and another playing two small kettle-drums. A further design of the same format, signed with the artist's monogram and emblem, a small shovel, of *Scenes from the Life of St Andrew*, (Schilling, op.cit., p.157, pl.8), was formerly in the collection of G. Schwarting, Delmenhorst, near Bremen, and is now in the Pierpont Morgan Library, New York; a preliminary sketch for the left-hand scene is in the Bibliothèque National, Paris (inv.no.B.13 rés.; Schilling, op.cit., p.158, pl.9).

With the exclusion of the last drawing all these designs were completed for presentation to the patron so that he could see how the finished work would appear (see no.86). The only other design of this kind by Schäufelein known to us is the finished composition study for the central panel of the high altarpiece at Auhausen (nos.173(a) *recto* and 173(b)).

172 Pope Honorius II presenting the rule to the Premonstratensian Order

Pen and black and brown ink. 28.7 × 25.9cm

PROVENANCE: S. Sheikévitch (sale, Amsterdam, F. Muller, 1908, 18 June, lot 536); Obach & Co

1909–1–9–17

LITERATURE: Obach & Co, *Old Master Drawings*, no.53; C. Dodgson, *Vasari Society*, vi, 1910–11, no.28, repr.; BM *Guide*, 1928, p.36, no.316; Winkler, K&S, pp.127, 149, no.41, repr.; Rowlands, *Dürer*, p.58, no.358

Inscribed by a later hand, in brown ink on the lower edge, *albert Durer* and, further to the right, a fake Dürer monogram

This drawing, of exceptionally fine quality, is likely to be a preparatory study for the composition of a wall-painting, probably made during Schäufelein's most fruitful period from 1510 to 1515 when he was at Augsburg. The painting may well have been commissioned by either the priory at Roth, near Memmingen, or that at Ursberg near Krumbach, both in the diocese of Augsburg. Both these priories go back to the earliest years of the Order, being founded in 1126 and in 1126–8 respectively. St Norbert, the founder of the Premonstratensian Order, had established himself at Prémontré in 1121, and the Order was approved by Pope Honorius II in 1126.

173(a) *Recto:* Coronation of the Virgin
Verso: Drolleries

Pen and black ink, with watercolour, the *verso* in black ink. 34.1 × 27.1cm

PROVENANCE: Sloane bequest, 1753

5218–189

LITERATURE: Waagen, *Treasures*, p.233, no.189; Parker, *German Schools*, p.29, no.26, repr.; BM *Guide*, 1928, p.37, no.320; Winkler, K&S, pp.130, 154, no.55, repr.; G. Lill, *Pantheon*, 1942, pp.95ff.; E. Schilling, *Zeitschr. f. Kunstwiss.*, ix, 1955, p.160

The drolleries on the *verso* of the sheet are unlike any other drawing by Schäufelein, but this would not preclude them being by him.

See no.173(b).

171

172

173(a)r

173b

(b) Christ appearing to the Virgin with, kneeling on the left, the donor, Abbot Georg Truchsess von Wetzhausen, and on the right, a Pope, probably Innocent II

Pen and black ink with leadpoint. 8 × 22.2 cm

PROVENANCE: Sloane bequest, 1753

5218–140

LITERATURE: Winkler, K&S, p.168; E. Schilling, *Zeitschr. f. Kunstwiss.*, ix, 1955, pp.160f., 178f., no.13, repr.

No. 173(a) *recto*, and no.173(b), are respectively the finished composition study, or 'modello', for the central panel, and the preparatory drawing for the predella of Schäufelein's largest altarpiece, the *Coronation of the Virgin*, in the former Benedictine abbey church at Auhausen an der Wörnitz, near Nördlingen, which is signed and dated *1513* on a tablet in the central predella panel. Standing among the saints on the inner side of the lower left-hand wing, the artist portrayed himself holding a tablet with his monogram and a shovel (Schäufelein), accompanied by his assistant, Sebastian Dayg (active 1508–54). Now placed upon the high altar, the altarpiece was originally located under the romanesque triumphal arch at the entrance to the choir, the central feature of a building scheme commissioned by the last abbot, Georg Truchsess von Wetzhausen (1465–1552), which included two aisle chapels, also of 1513; a new choir in 1519, with roof-bosses which display the arms of the abbot and his family's arms, the arms of Jerusalem to commemorate the abbot's pilgrimage, and those of the abbey's secular protector Markgraf von Brandenburg-Ansbach; and new choir stalls in 1520, by Melchior Schabert of Donauwörth. Although the general arrangement of the various groups in the drawings remains similarly placed in the final painting, the scale of the figures in the painting has been sufficiently reduced to accommodate a greatly increased angelic host, a choir of angels surrounding the Holy Dove, the emblems of the four evangelists at the four corners of the central Coronation group and, below, the Holy Lamb with a Flag, upon the Book with seven seals.

The donor himself (for details of his career, see W.H. von Schmelzing and Wernstein, *Prussian Jahrbuch*, lvii, 1936, pp.23f.; K. Gröber & A. Horn, *Die Kunstdenkmäler von Schwaben, I Bezirksamt, Nördlingen*, Munich, 1938, pp.47ff.) has been moved from the left of the drawing in the central predella panel to a more prominent position in the lower right-hand corner of the main panel, kneeling immediately below the twelve apostles. This move necessitated the redesigning of the central predella panel with three equally divided, more upright scenes, bounded by pillars, which show from the left: the kneeling Pope, probably Innocent II, who granted the Abbey privileges in 1136 with, in the background, a distant view of the Abbey church and buildings and, in the foreground, the tablet, dated *1513*; in the centre the same subject as in the drawing but represented in a narrower field; and, on the right, the *Resurrection of Christ*, which links thematically with the subjects on the predella wings, of the *Risen Christ with St Thomas and St Peter*, and *Christ harrowing Hell*. This last panel appears to be largely the work of Schäufelein's assistant, Sebastian Dayg, whose portrait, mentioned above, is an acknowledgement of the extent of Dayg's participation in the work. Schäufelein also used Dayg as an assistant when he was completing the altarpiece with *Scenes from the Life of the Virgin and St Peter*, in the village church at Weitlingen, near Auhausen.

A replica of the *Coronation of the Virgin*, signed and dated by Schäufelein *1538*, now much cut-down, is in Berlin-Dahlem (Gemäldegalerie, inv.no.1903; W.H. von Schmelzing and Wernstein, *Prussian Jahrbuch*, lvii, 1936, pp.22ff., repr.).

174

175 Adoration of the Magi

Pen and black ink, heightened with white bodycolour, on green prepared paper. 22.1 × 18cm

PROVENANCE: Sloane bequest, 1753

5218–123

LITERATURE: BM *Guide*, 1901, p.16, no.A73; BM *Guide*, 1928, p.37, no.321; Winkler, K&S, pp.164f., under no.A 8; E.Schilling, *Zeitschr.f. Kunstwiss.*, ix, 1955, pp.168, 179, no.16, repr.

Inscribed by the artist in black ink on the roofbeam, *1522*.

After the attribution to Albrecht Dürer (q.v.) was discarded, this was thought to be by Hans Springinklee (q.v.) until shortly before the 1928 Dürer exhibition, when it was re-attributed to Schäufelein.

This drawing is unusual among Schäufelein's work in that it appears to be a record of a composition rather than a preparatory study for one. This evidently prompted Winkler to reject it when discussing a less good version, also dated *1522*, formerly in the Lahmann collection (now Kupferstichkabinet, Dresden) which he described as a copy after a lost drawing by Schäufelein. Schilling, when he published the Lahmann collection, considered it superior to the London version, a view which he subsequently reversed when he judged the present drawing to be by Schäufelein. Parker had first proposed this attribution in the 1928 Dürer exhibition, on the basis of a comparison of the composition with that of an earlier painting by Schäufelein at Innsbruck (see E.Buchner, *Festschrift Max J.Friedländer*,

174 A landsknecht with his head turned to look behind him

Pen and black ink. 20.6 × 15.9cm

PROVENANCE: H.Belward (sale, Christie, 1856, 5 July, part of lot 53).

1856–7–12–998

LITERATURE: Dodgson, ii, p.19, under no.36; Winkler, K&S, p.168; E.Schilling, *Zeitschr.f. Kunstwiss.*, ix, 1955, pp.155, 169, 178, no.12, repr.

This drawing was acquired as by Baldung (q.v.); however, it is clearly dateable early in Schäufelein's career, *c.*1507/8, and is closely allied to a woodcut of a landsknecht (Bartsch, vii, p.266, no.99) as noted by Dodgson. Winkler did not include this drawing in his corpus, as he was unable to examine it in the original because of the Second World War. Schilling accepted the attribution and compared the landsknecht's stocky build with the similar physique of the soldier in the drawing formerly in the Liechtenstein collection (Winkler, K&S, pl.53) – a drawing, however, whose execution is more assured than the present drawing, and is thus probably later in date; Winkler assigned it to *c.*1510–*c.*1515.

175

Leipzig, 1927, pp.50–2). Prior to that the drawing had been attributed to Springinklee. A comparison of composition and types confirms that this drawing records an otherwise unknown version of the subject by Schäufelein. Closely similar variants of this subject abound in his *oeuvre* among the prints as well as the paintings. A good example of the latter is the early painting of about 1506/7 at Stuttgart (Staatsgalerie, inv.no.58). Although the penwork in the present drawing is somewhat mechanical in execution when one compares it with that of many of his other drawings, we nevertheless may reasonably attribute it to Schäufelein's hand if we assume the drawing's function to be that of a record kept by Schäufelein for possible future use. An early pedestrian copy, with a heavy-handed use of white bodycolour, is in the Uffizi, Florence (inv.no.2290F).

Hans Weiditz

Active in Augsburg and Strassburg c.1500–36

Painter, designer of woodcuts, and glass-paintings. He first trained in Strassburg in *c.*1515, and in 1518 was a journeyman with Hans Burgkmair (q.v.) in Augsburg. He returned to Strassburg in 1522/23. Only two of his woodcuts are signed; but, since his identification with the artist formerly known as the Petrarch Master, so called after the famous woodcuts to Petrarch's *Von der Artzney bayder Glück* (Augsburg, 1532), his work has been more clearly defined. Amongst his numerous woodcuts, another important work is a design for the large view of Augsburg, dated *1521*, which was printed from eight blocks, and is the first German panorama of its kind.

Little is known of his activity as a painter, and the few drawings which have survived are primarily designs for glass-paintings, a field in which he exercised a considerable influence in Strassburg.

BIBLIOGRAPHY: Dodgson, ii, pp.139ff.; Thieme-Becker, xxxv, 1942, pp.269ff.; Andersson, *Detroit*, pp.158ff.

176 The Wheel of Fortune

Pen and black ink, with yellow, red, blue, green and grey wash. 20.6 × 15.7cm

PROVENANCE: Count F.Sternberg-Manderscheid (sale, Dresden, Frenzel and Sieber, 1845, 10 November, lot 287 as 'Aldegrever'); Friedrich August II of Saxony (L.971); P & D Colnaghi

England, Private Collection

LITERATURE: M. Lossnitzer, *Archiv. f. Kunstgesch.*, iii, 1913, pl.34; E. Buchner, in *Festschrift Heinrich Wölfflin*, Munich, 1924, pp.221ff.; Th. Musper, *OMD*, viii, 1933, p.31; Halm, *Deutsche Zeichn.*, p.44, no.96, repr.; Schilling, *Gesamm. Zeichn.*, p.67, no.26, repr.; Rowlands, *Private Collection*, p.39, no.34, repr.

Inscribed by the artist in pen and black ink on the scroll above the wheel, *Als Midt der Zeydt* in the 'course of time', and in the lower left-hand corner, *1519*, above a false Dürer monogram

This drawing is undoubtedly connected with three differing woodcuts of the *Wheel of Fortune* which Weiditz made for a German edition of Petrarch's *Von den Artzney bayder Glück*, published by Heynrich Steyner, in Augsburg, 1532. This drawing was most probably executed about the same time as Weiditz was working on the designs for the woodcuts, works as rich in imaginative fire as they are brilliant in technique, which were evidently completed in 1520, as the last of them bears that date.

The representation of the changes of fortune by a wheel, the rotation of which symbolises the rise and fall of men, especially of kings, has a long history. It first appeared *c.*1100 in manuscripts of Boethius, but perhaps the most notable earlier medieval example, is the drawing of *c.*1175/90, *Fortune turning the Wheel of Fortune* in the *Hortus deliciarum*, of Herrad von Landsberg (formerly Strassburg City Library). The subject occurs in various media throughout the Middle Ages and into the Renaissance. The fifteenth century sees the introduction, as an occasional feature representing the arbitrary nature of Fortune, either Fortune blindfold, or the hand of God in the clouds, as in the present drawing (see *Lexikon der christ. Ikonog.*, iii, 1971, cols.492–4). In the woodcut of the same subject of *c.*1534, by Georg Pencz (q.v.), both motifs are shown: the hand of God protrudes from a cloud and controls with a rein a blindfold figure of Fortune who turns the wheel (Landau, *Pencz*, p.167, no.146, repr.).

177 Design for a seal of Cardinal Matthäus Lang von Wellenburg

Pen and brown ink with grey wash, heightened with white bodycolour, some of which has oxidised, on brownish pink prepared paper. 14.2 × 8.8cm

PROVENANCE: Sloane bequest, 1753

5218–107

LITERATURE: Th.Musper, *OMD*, viii, 1933, pp.30–1, pl.34

Inscribed by a later hand in brown ink with a false Dürer monogram at the upper point of the seal

This design was executed for Matthäus Lang (1468–1540), the leading diplomat and chief counsellor of the Emperor Maximilian, only after 24 September 1519, for on the following day he was consecrated archbishop in the Cathedral at Salzburg, the earliest occasion when he had the right to quarter his arms with those of the see of Salzburg, as displayed on the drawing. The seal itself, however, was only for use outside the archdiocese, because the figure of the angel holding the cross-staff refers to Lang's cardinalate with the titular church of S. Angeli in foro piscium in Rome. He had been appointed cardinal *in petto* by Pope Julius II on 10 March 1511, and his creation as cardinal deacon followed on 24 November 1512; in 1514, as Bishop of Gurk, he was elected to the Chapter of Salzburg Cathedral as coadjutor of the ruling Archbishop

176

Leonhard van Keutschaeh, with the right to be his follower.

Although the drawing has remained in the collection under the broad classification of 'South German School XVI century', Musper's attribution to the Petrarch Master, who is now generally accepted as Hans Weiditz, ought to be given further consideration. The Augsburg publishers, Dr Sigismund Grimm and Marx Wirsung, became important employers of the Petrarch Master in the year before Lang became Archbishop of Salzburg. The cardinal's patronage was recognised by them, through the inclusion of woodcuts of his arms quartered with those of Salzburg, as in the drawing. It appeared together with the arms of Wirsung, on the title-page of the German translation of the Spanish tragedy, *Celestine*, published at Augsburg on 20 December 1520. This support from Lang had been given a month earlier, a spectacular acknowledgement, with the inclusion of the publisher's dedication to him of a large woodcut similarly designed by the Master, of Lang's arms again quartered with Salzburg in Ludwig Senfl's *Liber selectorum cantionum . . .*, the first German printed anthology of motets. This colour print is only to be found in copies in the libraries at Stuttgart, and Porrentruy, and on a loose sheet in the British Museum (Dodgson, ii, 181.137).

There are also stylistic grounds for attributing the seal-design to the Petrarch Master. The comparison suggested by Musper, between the angel in the drawing and the woodcut of St Michael, evidently from the years 1519/20 (Musper, *Petrarkameister*, p.50, no.428) is, however, less compelling than one with the figures of the Evangelists, within the niches of the architectural frame of the woodcut of 1521, *The Virgin standing on the Crescent Moon* (Friedländer, *Weiditz*, pp.2, 13). The similarity of the stance of the figure and the features are particularly marked in the case of St John.

177

210

16 Swiss School, XVI century

Anonymous artist

Early sixteenth century

178 *Recto:* A bear holding a skep on his back with a leaf-shaped shield suspended from his neck

Verso: Head of a bearded man in profile to the left

Pen and black ink, the *verso* in brown ink. 12.5 × 9.8cm

PROVENANCE: François Des Marais (from an album inscribed, *Dessins origin^x/des plus fameux/Peintres, Rassemblez/Par M. Des Marais:/1729*; sale, Nouveau Drouot, Paris, Hubert de Blanc, 1984, 2 March, lot 139)

1984–6–9–1

LITERATURE: Yvonne Tan Bunzl, *Old Master Drawings*, London, 1984, no.3, repr. (as Swiss School early sixteenth century)

Inscribed on the *verso* in a (?) sixteenth-century hand, in brown ink, *Hannes* [?] *je ny Kotomeneray ma . d.* The drawing on the *verso* is probably by a seventeenth-century French hand

This is a study for a charming ornamental feature, characteristic of the taste favoured in the late gothic period for such naturalistic conceits. The idea of the supporter of a heraldic shield, shaped like a large leaf, being a bear carrying a skep full of bees and honey-comb is just the type of amusing device that appealed to the cultivated in Northern Europe during this period. As the bear as an emblem was particularly common with the rising power and expansion of the Swiss Confederacy, at the end of the fifteenth century, and the beginning of the following one, it is quite natural to think that this drawing should be of Swiss origin. For not only is the bear the emblem of the canton and city of Bern, but also it was often used to support the arms of the Swiss cantons, as well as being the device of a leading watermark of Swiss paper during this period.

While considering the possibility of it being by an Augsburg artist (see, for instance, the bears that occur in some woodcut initials by Hans Weiditz (q.v.) (Musper, *Petrarkameister*, p.9, repr.), it seems perhaps more likely that the draughtsman was active in Basel or possibly of upper Rhineland origin. So far no particular artist suggests himself as a thoroughly convincing candidate. While it is possible to note a certain superficial link with Urs Graf (q.v.), the spirit of its conception, as well as the calmer, less vigorous penwork rules out his authorship entirely. But it is quite likely to be the work of a contemporary from the same region and probably from the second decade of the sixteenth century. One may recall Graf's use of figures of crouching bears who hold shields in his woodcut, *The Imperial Arms and Arms of the Cantons of the Swiss Confederacy*, published in 1514 (Hollstein, xi, p.153, no.318, repr.). It is not impossible that the bear in the present drawing may have been intended as a single element in a much larger ornamental scheme as, for instance, a frieze of different animals supporting a series of shields.

Nicolaus Manuel Deutsch

Bern 1484 – Bern 1530

Painter, poet and politician. Grandfather came from Chieri, near Turin (family name originally Aleman or Alemans). His early works suggest that he may have been apprenticed to a glass-painter. He served as a mercenary soldier in Italy, on various campaigns from 1516 to 1522

178r

(wounded at Bicocca, 1522). From 1510 until his death he was a member of Bern City Council. From 1523 to 1528 he was a provincial government official in Erlach, but was recalled in 1528 to Bern, where he was highly regarded as a diplomat, to assist with the secularisation of churches and convents. He produced a number of plays and satirical writings against the Catholic Church, and spent his last years in government service and in promoting the cause of the Reformation.

First recorded as a painter in 1513, but he did not work as one for much more than twelve years. His earliest dated painting, a panel of *St Eligius* of 1515, is part of a diptych showing scenes from the life of St Anne, and is now in the Kunstmuseum, Bern, where much of his work is preserved. Other important paintings, including the *Beheading of St John the Baptist* (*c.*1517) and the *Judgement of Paris* (1517/18) as well as many of his drawings, are in the Kunstmuseum, Basel. His famous wall-painting, the *Dance of Death* (*c.*1516–19), executed for the Dominicans in Bern, was destroyed, after numerous restorations, in 1660, but its appearance is known from copies by Alfred Kauw (1649) and others. His work reveals the influence of Albrecht Dürer (q.v.), Hans Baldung (q.v.), Urs Graf (q.v.) and Lucas Cranach the Elder (q.v.). Some ninety drawings survive, executed *c.*1507–29. These include the *Schreibbuechlein*, two pattern books which were made for studio use.

BIBLIOGRAPHY: Thieme-Becker, ix, 1913, pp.175ff.; Bern, *Deutsch* (for further literature).

179 A man tied to a cross

Pen and black ink. 27.4 × 20.1 cm

WM: bear

PROVENANCE: P.Vischer-Burckhardt (sale, Paris, Delbergue-Cormant, 1852, 4 May, lot 52), E.Rodrigues (sale, Amsterdam, F.Muller, 1921, 12 July, lot 23, bt *Colnaghi, 1100 guilders* for BM)

1921–10–12–3

LITERATURE: Stumm, p.88, no.13; L.Stumm, *Schweizer Künstlermappen*, i, Bern, 1928, no.13, & p.19, pl.54; Parker, *German Schools*, p.34, no.54, repr.; Manchester, *German Art*, p.62, no.163; Bern, *Deutsch*, pp.321f., no.157, repr. (for further literature)

Inscribed by the artist in black ink, on a stone at the man's feet, with his initials and emblem, an unsheathed dagger

As von Tavel has noted, the drawing represents neither a saint nor a Christian martyr, but one foolish enough, in Deutsch's view, to come under the dominance of women, a perennial theme for the satirist of the period. It can hardly be doubted that the drawing also is intended as a mocking, irreverent reference to the Cross of Christ, which may well seem surprising to us given the fact that the artist was a zealous reformer. This is not, however, an isolated case of such profanity in Swiss art of the period. A further example is Urs Graf's mock *Place of Martyrdom*, known only from a later copy by the monogrammist H.R., dated

1547 (Basel, Kupferstichkabinett, inv.no.U.VI.23). A supposedly grief-struck female kneels at the right, hands raised in horror, but she does nothing to save the three nude men, who are admittedly surrounded by decapitated heads and hacked-off limbs hanging from the trees. They are otherwise uninjured but howl an appeal to us. One must recognise that both these drawings were unlikely to have been more than personal statements by either artist, although Deutsch's approach is much less blatant or coarse than Graf's. This is borne out by the prolonged obscurity of the present drawing's true subject. The message of other drawings by Deutsch, like the *Cuckold* (Basel, Kupferstichkabinett, inv.no.U.X.20; Bern, *Deutsch*, pl.99) are clearer and are stylistically akin to his chalk drawings of the Foolish Virgins (Basel, Kupferstichkabinett, inv.nos.U.X.22–6; Bern, *Deutsch*, pls.101–6) placed by von Tavel *c.*1513/14, slightly earlier than the *Cuckold*, which he dates *c.*1514. This latter dating he bases on the supposed dependence of the drawing on Urs Graf's companion drawings of 1514 of a semi-nude man and a nude woman (Basel, Kupferstichkabinett, inv.nos.U.X.54 and U.X.60) each of whom holds a rope. While there is a clear iconographic link between these drawings and Deutsch's, one should hesitate in using such a connection for dating purposes.

The chronology of Deutsch's drawings is not easy to disentangle; there are, however, a number of general pointers in the present case. The background, in both its fantasy and

179

brilliant execution, is strangely reminiscent of the *Promontory with a mine* (Basel, Kupferstichkabinett, inv.no.U.X.19; Bern, *Deutsch*, pl.112) and of the outside of the left-hand wing of a St Anne altarpiece, *St Eligius in his workshop*, dated *1515* (Bern, Kunstmuseum, inv.no.2020b; Bern, *Deutsch*, pl.19). Von Tavel thereby dates no.179 before 1515, not very securely, it seems to me. On credible stylistic grounds, Hugelshofer considered the present drawing contemporaneous with the altarpiece with the *Martyrdom of the Ten Thousand* (Bern, Kunstmuseum, inv.no.1131; Bern, *Deutsch*, pl.20) which can be dated on documentary evidence, 1516/17. Given these indications an approximate dating *c.*1515–17 would appear likely.

180 The Virgin and Child enthroned

See colour plate section following p.200

Pen and brown ink with brown and grey wash, and blue body-colour over traces of black chalk. Some outlines indented. 42.1 × 30.4cm

PROVENANCE: J.E.Wyss; G.Fairholme (from an album, inscribed on the title-page by G.Fairholme, *This collection of old drawings of Swiss and German artists of the 16th and 17th centuries was purchased from Monsr J.E.Wyss, heraldic painter at Bern, in 1829*)

1899-1-20-26

LITERATURE: Stumm, p.96, no.114; Bern, *Deutsch*, p.379, no.213, p.409, under no.253, pl.136

Inscribed by the artist along the lower edge, in dark grey wash, with his monogram, a dagger, and the date *1520*; and on the Virgin's dress, in black chalk, *bla[u]*; and by a different, later hand, underneath the figure of the Virgin, in black chalk, *Niclaus Manuel Deutch/Bern*

The drawing is a design for a glass-painting, presumably commissioned by the Company of Merchants in Bern. The balance, seen in the centre of the lower border, was made an official emblem of the Company in 1540, and very probably appeared in connection with it before this date. The head of the oriental, seen here in the lower right-hand corner, appears as a more developed emblem on the Company's heraldic shield in a seventeenth-century glass painting in Pfistern (see *Berner Taschenbuch auf des Jahr 1862*, edited by Ludwig Lauterburg, Bern, 1862, frontispiece).

The statuesque form of the Madonna seen in the drawing, together with the round-backed throne and the indication of an apse, suggest a North Italian influence. This could have come from paintings and prints which Deutsch may have seen during his campaigns in Italy. A further influence apparent in the drawing is that of Urs Graf (q.v.), rather than, as has been suggested, Holbein the Younger (q.v.). The simplified forms, the flat appearance of the decorative border round the Madonna and Child which seems in particular to be inspired by book illustrations, and the striated nimbus are all very similar to those seen in Graf's work (Hollstein, xi, 1977, nos.290, 292, repr.).

181 Christ and the woman taken in adultery

Pen and brown ink with grey wash. 34.2 × 30.9cm

PROVENANCE: Francis Douce bequest, 1834

Oxford, Ashmolean Museum, P.330

LITERATURE: Stumm, p.97, no.124, repr.; Parker, *Ashmolean*, p.144, no.330, repr.; Bern, *Deutsch*, pp.458f., no. 292, repr. (for further literature); Lloyd, *Ashmolean Drawings*, p.12, no.9, repr.

Inscribed by the artist in brown ink on the pillar on the left, with his monogram, the date, *1527* and his emblem, a dagger in its sheath. Above centre, the cartouche is inscribed by another hand, with the biblical quotation relating to the scene below, *Wer under üch an [ohne] sund ist, der/werff den Ersten Stein vff sy/* and *Johani ann̄ viij Cap* (the text is taken from Luther's translation of 1522)

The drawing is a design for a glass-painting, to which it closely corresponds, made by an anonymous Bernese glass-painter, now at Bad Schinznach (Bern, *Deutsch*, pl.169). The subject of no.181, together with that of the Expulsion of the money-changers from the Temple, was a potent vehicle for conveying the moral stance of the reformers against the hypocrisy, as they saw it, of the ecclesiastical establishment and its corrupt basis of power within the Church. As one would expect, Lucas Cranach (q.v.) and his school, in addition to Manuel Deutsch, produced paintings and drawings of such subjects. It is possible, but by no means certain, that a wall-painting of this subject may have been contemplated for inclusion in the final phase (*c.*1530) of Holbein's decoration of the council chamber of the Basel town hall (see Rowlands, *Holbein*, p.221, no.L.6 II(c)).

It would appear at first sight from copies of Manuel Deutsch's *Dance of Death* (destroyed), formerly in the Dominican priory at Bern of 1516/17–1519/20, that the composition of *Christ and the woman taken in adultery*, on the side of the papal litter in the scene of the Pope and the cardinal, would precede the present design to which it corresponds; but it is more likely that this scene was added during a subsequent repainting, and that no.181 was used as the basis for it. The artist's concentration on the central action, to the exclusion of any interest in feeling for depth of the stage on which the biblical drama is portrayed, and the attention to detail betray this design as thoroughly characteristic of Deutsch's later works, especially of other glass-painting designs such as the *King Josiah destroying the idols*, also of 1527 (Basel, Kunstmuseum, inv.no.U.I.77; Bern, *Deutsch*, pl.166).

A copy of the design is in the Graphische Sammlung der Eidgenössischen Technischen Hochschule, Zürich (inv.no. GKS 1906,23:19(448); Bern, *Deutsch*, p.461, no.294). Another copy, from the collection of Hans Jörg Wannewetsch was sold at auction in Bern in 1959 (Gutekunst & Klipstein, catalogue 94, 5 June, lot 179); while a further copy, possibly a fake, according to von Tavel, is in the Ecole des Beaux-Arts, Paris (Masson collection, inv.no.140).

181

182

Hans Franck

Active in Basel 1505–22

Painter and designer of woodcuts. He was a contemporary of Urs Graf (q.v.) whom he accompanied on numerous mercenary campaigns, including the battle of Novara in 1515. He worked in Basel chiefly as a wall-painter, and seems to have specialised in the type of decoration of buildings later used by Hans Holbein the Younger (q.v.) during his years in Basel. Schmid and others have identified him with the Monogrammist HF (active 1516–22 in Basel) whose woodcuts and drawings reveal an inventive personality, and are akin to the manner of Graf.

BIBLIOGRAPHY: H.A.Schmid, *Prussian Jahrbuch*, xix, 1898, pp.64ff.; Thieme-Becker, xii, 1916, pp.345f.; Basel, *100 Master Drawings*, under nos.55 and 56.

182 Soldiers storming a fortress

Pen and black ink. 7 × 25.2cm

PROVENANCE: Sir J.C.Robinson; Malcolm 1895-9-15-968.

LITERATURE: JCR p.173, no.515

This drawing entered the Museum with the tentative attribution to Albrecht Altdorfer (q.v.) under whom it was placed when in the Malcolm collection. Subsequently Meder suggested that it might be by F.Brun, by which he presumably meant the designer and engraver, Franz Brun (active *c*.1559–96), while E.Bock proposed the Basel master, Hans Franck. Of these two opinions, both noted in the annotated Departmental copy of the Malcolm catalogue, Bock's view is much more persuasive. Indeed, a comparison with two particular drawings by Franck, signed with his monogram, the *Five mercenaries* of 1516 in Berlin-Dahlem (inv.no.4058) and the *Judgement of Paris* of 1518 in Basel (inv.no.U.IX.26b) makes such an attribution very plausible (cf. H.A.Schmid, *Prussian Jahrbuch*, xix, 1898, pp.73–4, nos.1, 5).

Urs Graf

Solothurn c.1485–?Basel 1529/30 (by 16 March 1530)

Goldsmith, draughtsman, designer of glass-paintings, woodcuts, engravings and etchings, die-and block-cutter and painter. Probably trained with his father Hug Graf, a goldsmith in Solothurn. A woodcut dated *1503*, one from a Passion series printed in Strassburg by Knoblouch in 1506, is his earliest known work. He was recorded in Basel in 1507, and in Zürich the same year, apprenticed to the goldsmith Lienhardt Triblin. In Basel he designed book illustrations for Adam Petri and Johannes Amerbach in 1509; and in 1511 was the assistant of the glass-painter, Hans Heinrich Wolleb. In 1512 he entered the guild of goldsmiths and money-changers and became a citizen of Basel. He participated in mercenary expeditions to Burgundy and Italy in 1510, 1513, 1515, 1521–2. He was frequently in trouble with the authorities in Basel over a variety of offences, including libellous behaviour, involvement in brawls and beating his wife. In 1518 he fled to Solothurn to evade punishment for having crippled a stranger in an attack; here he joined the goldsmiths' guild and did not return to Basel until the town council appointed him die-cutter to the mint in 1519, an office which he held until 1523. Examples of his coins are to be found in the Historisches Museum, Basel.

Graf's most important work as a goldsmith, a reliquary head of *St Bernard* with scenes from the life of the saint, was commissioned in 1519 by the monastery of St Urban (canton of Lucerne); eight plates from it are known (Zürich, Schweizerisches Landesmuseum, and on deposit at the British Museum). The only known signed glass-painting by Graf is a fragment in the Schweizerisches Landesmuseum, Zürich. Only two extant paintings are ascribed to him, *St George and the Dragon* and *Allegory of War*, both in the Kunstmuseum, Basel, where the majority of his approximately two hundred known drawings are also located. The chief influences on his early graphic work were those of Schongauer (q.v.), Dürer (q.v.), and Baldung (q.v.). Unusually for this period of German art, it appears that a remarkably high proportion of his drawings were executed as ends in themselves; made in a lively, calligraphic style,

the subjects were often inspired by his life as a soldier, and frequently display a satirical, even brutal, humour, particularly against women. Throughout his career, he was much in demand as a book illustrator, and worked for printers in Strassburg, Paris and Basel. Perhaps his most remarkable prints are the white-line cuts of the Standard Bearers of the Swiss Confederacy (Hollstein, xi, 1977, nos.29–44). He is credited with producing the earliest dated etching in 1513 (Hollstein, xi, 1977, no.9). His last known work, a drawing dated *1529*, is in Basel (Andersson, *Graf*, fig.41).

BIBLIOGRAPHY: Thieme-Becker, xiv, 1921, pp.486ff.; Major & Gradman, *Graf*; Andersson, *Graf* (for further literature); Andersson, *Ausgew. Zeichn. Graf.*

183 Daniel in the lions' den, fed by the prophet Habakkuk

Pen and black and brown ink. The sheet, which has been extensively damaged particularly round the edges and over the lower part, has an arched top and has been backed. 29.7 × 21.5cm

PROVENANCE: C. von Ludwigburg; H.R. Lando (L.1658); Webb family, of Newstead Abbey, Notts. (according to the late owner); Sir Herbert Chermside of Pepper Arden Hall, Yorks; R. Gatty; presented by the N.A.-C.F.

1952-4-5-8

LITERATURE: N.A.-C.F. *Report*, 1952, p.20, under no.1658

Inscribed on a piece of paper formerly attached to the top of the drawing and the old backing, in brown ink, by a later hand, possibly after the drawing had been damaged, *[Is]arael. Van M[eckenam]*; and in the lower right-hand corner, in pencil, in a later hand, *10*. The artist would have undoubtedly inscribed this drawing with his monogram. Due to the extensive damage at the bottom of the sheet, only his device, a borax box, is now visible. This formed a regular part of his signature until *c*.1512.

Inscribed by H.R. Lando, in brown ink, on the *verso*, *Christoph von Ludwigburg nach mit R H Lando* [initial letters linked] *1605 Jar*

This drawing, which is clearly a design for a glass-painting, can be dated early in the artist's career. Both the vigorous shading with the emphatic use of parallel pen-lines and the naivety of the facial expression can be found in other important drawings which evidently also come from the beginning of his career, such as the *Man wearing a cap* in the collection of the Graf Waldburg-Wolfegg (inv. no.25) and the *Half-length portrait of a young man with a pocket-sundial*, formerly in the collection of Robert von Hirsch, and now in the Basel Kunstmuseum (inv.no.1978.91; Major & Gradman, *Graf*, pl.2). The latter was dated by Parker *c*.1508, and it is likely that the present drawing was also executed about the same time, possibly in Graf's birthplace Solothurn. The mark on the shield would seem to support this location, since it appears to have belonged to a member of the Zurschnitten family of Solothurn. A similar mark was used on the bookplate preserved in the Zentralbibliothek, Zürich, as the arms of Elsbeth Zursch-

nitten, wife of Urs Wielstein of Solothurn, town councillor from 1543. Elsbeth was probably the sister of Wilhelm Zurschnitten who, besides being a town councillor in 1518, was a member of the innkeepers' guild in Solothurn. The coat of arms on the present sheet would have belonged to an older member of the family, who may also have been an innkeeper, since the subject of the drawing appears to be suitably sympathetic with their trade. It comes from an apocryphal text, *Bel and the Dragon*, attributed to the book of Daniel in certain Greek manuscripts. Having killed a dragon, Daniel is cast into a den with seven lions, and by the miraculous intervention of an angel, the prophet Habakkuk, is transported to Babylon from Judaea in order to feed him, and so he is freed. In the middle ages, the subject appears as a prefiguring of the Resurrection of Christ in cycles of glass-paintings, and in the *Biblia Pauperum*.

184 A mercenary soldier and a monster

Pen and black ink. Cut along edges. 20.7 × 15.5cm

PROVENANCE: Francis Douce bequest, 1834

Oxford, Ashmolean Museum, P.296

LITERATURE: H. Koegler, *Anz.*, NF, xxiii, 1920, p.219, no.22A; K.T. Parker, *Zwanzig Federzeichnungen von Urs Graf*, Zürich, 1922, pl.13; Parker, *German Schools*, p.33, no.51, repr.; Parker, *Ashmolean*, p. 130, no.296, repr.; Lloyd, *Ashmolean Drawings*, p.14, no.11, repr.

Inscribed by the artist in black ink on the lower edge, *1518*

One can see from the clipping of the date that this drawing has been cut along the lower edge, and it could well be cut on the other sides also, since the artist's monogram (which Graf habitually included, often with some additional decorative function) is curiously absent. There is, however, no mistaking Graf's authorship of this drawing, which is evidently one of his satires directed against the landsknechts, the German mercenary soldiers who were, as rivals in plunder and pillage, greatly hated by their Swiss equivalents, the *Reisläufer* (see F. Bächtiger, *Jahrbuch des Bernischen Historischen Museums*, Bern, li/lii, 1971/72, pp.205–70). Even though the identity of this mercenary as a landsknecht is less obvious than usual, there being no cross of St Andrew decorating his dress, or mocking tag on his sword or on a scroll, certainly his drooping beard and, less obviously, his ill-fitting cloak and large sword mark him down as a German enemy since these are a mocking reference to the social inferiority, as the Swiss saw it, of the landsknechts to their own mercenaries. If there were any lingering doubt as at whom Graf was aiming his derisive pen, the fiendish monster which accompanies the man clinches the matter. The coarse, brutal landsknecht cannot hide his gallows-bird character under a cloak; the croaking monster in any case broadcasts the mercenary's brutality which will take him in the end to perdition.

In the annotated copy of Parker's catalogue in the Ashmolean Print Room, the monster in the drawing is

184

associated with E. Wind's brief note on 'Homo Platonis' (see *Warburg Journal*, i, 1938/39, p.261). In this article the amusement of humanists and Renaissance artists at Diogenes's comparison of a plucked rooster with Plato's definition of a man as a 'feather-less biped', is recorded, and used to explain the presence of the unfortunate bird in the woodcut of Diogenes by Ugo da Carpi (*c*.1450–after 1525). This, however, was not quite the world in which Graf was at home. His satire and humour were directed very pointedly at subjects of personal hate or fear, such as the wiles of women, landsknechts, and the uncertainties of fortune.

185 The bearer of the 'Julius' banner of the canton Zug

Pen and black ink. 27 × 18cm

WM: bear (close to Briquet, 12267)

PROVENANCE: Sir Harry Wilson KCMG

1912–7–9–1

LITERATURE: C. Dodgson, *Vasari Society*, viii, 1912–13, no.30, repr.; K. T. Parker, *Anz.* NF, xxiii, 1921, p.211, no.18; Hugelshofer, *Schweizer Handz.*, p.32, no.30, repr.

Inscribed by the artist, in black ink, on the lower edge, with his monogram, of which the left branch of the V is formed by a dagger, and dated *1521*

This sheet may have formed, together with two surviving drawings of banner-bearers of the Swiss cantons, part of a series of the cantons of the Swiss Confederacy, produced in the same year, 1521, as his series of white-line woodcuts of the same subject (Hollstein, xi, 1977, pp.55ff., nos.29–44, repr.). The other two drawings, are the *Banner-bearer of the canton Glarus*, in the Liechtenstein collection, Vaduz (Parker, op. cit., p.217, no.4) and the *Banner-bearer of the canton Unterwalden*, dated *1521*, in the Graphische Sammlung

185

der Eidgenössischen Technischen Hochschule, Zürich (Parker, op. cit., p.217, no.4).

As Dodgson pointed out, the banners which appear in these series show religious images, or scenes from the Passion, in their upper corners, which were bestowed in 1512 on the Swiss cantons by Pope Julius II, in recognition of the services rendered in defeating the forces of the French king and especially for the taking of Pavia. Zug had received an earlier privilege, in 1509, from Pope Julius to place an image of the Pietà on their banner. This canton, together with a number of others, who had already been using religious emblems, received in 1512 some sort of augmentation to it, usually the addition of an extra figure or figures to their subject. In Zug's case sorrowing women and disciples were added. The appearance of all these embroidered banners, including those with the arms of the Papacy and the Pope which had been presented earlier, are to be found represented on a large anonymous woodcut of 1512 (S. Vögelin, *Die Holzschneidekunst in Zürich im sechszehnten Jahrhundert*, Zürich, 1881–2, p.52, n.15, p.66). This print, as Dodgson plausibly suggested, was evidently the source for all subsequent pictorial representations of the 'Julius' banners, and some, although not that of Zug, survive to this day; however, with the coming of the Reformation, understandably only the Catholic cantons retained the use of the papal banners.

For some unexplained reason, the gesticulating bannerbearer in the present drawing wears an engagement crown.

186

Hans Leu the Younger

(For biography see before 91(b))

186 The baptism of Christ

Brush drawing in black ink with grey wash over traces of black chalk. 31.6 × 24.4 cm

WM: bunch of grapes

PROVENANCE: J.E.Wyss; G.Fairholme (see no.180)

1899–1–20–28

LITERATURE: BM *Guide*, 1901, p.18, no.A.81; L.Stumm, *Anz. NF*, xi, no.3, 1909, pp.248ff., pl.ix

Inscribed by the artist, in the centre foreground, in black ink, with his monogram, and in the centre of the upper edge of the sheet, *1514*. There are traces of an old inscription, now illegible, in black chalk along the lower edge of the sheet

This design for a glass-painting is likely to have been executed shortly after Leu had returned to his native city, Zürich. Although the use of the brush has rather blunted the individuality of the line, a common feature in drawings of this kind, there is no mistaking Leu's particular way of representing the features of Christ and St John the Baptist. Such details in his drawings are readily recognisable as Leu always worked according to the same formula throughout his career, after his return to Switzerland. For instance, there is a close kinship between the Christ in the present drawing and his representation of the figure in *Christ and doubting Thomas*, also a design for a glass-painting, signed and dated *1514*, in Copenhagen (Royal Museum, inv.no.T.U.97/2).

17 Holbein in Basel

Ambrosius Holbein

Augsburg probably 1494 – Basel(?) 1519(?)

Painter and designer of woodcuts and engravings. The elder son of Hans Holbein the Elder (q.v.) and brother of Hans Holbein the Younger (q.v.) with whom he is portrayed in his father's drawing *Ambrosius and Hans Holbein*, dated *1511*, in Berlin-Dahlem (Kupferstichkabinett). In 1515 he is recorded in Basel, after passing through Stein-am-Rhein where he worked on the wall-paintings of the monastery of Saint George. In 1517 he was admitted to the painter's guild in Basel, where in the following year he became a citizen. His small *oeuvre* has unfortunately, through circumstance, been partly confused with his brother's early work, but he has always been considered a portrait painter and draughtsman of considerable sensitivity.

BIBLIOGRAPHY: Thieme-Becker, xvii, 1924, pp.327ff.; Basel, *Holbein* (for further literature pp.42f.).

187 Portrait of a young man

See colour plate section following p.200

Brush drawing in grey and black wash, the face touched with red chalk and features finished in pen and brown ink, and the background painted with red opaque pigment. 14.8 × 12.2cm

PROVENANCE: T.Kerrich (1748–1828), and thence by descent; presented by the N.A.-C.F., with the aid of contributions from Sir Otto Beit, and C.S.Gulbenkian.

1926-4-10-1

LITERATURE: C.Dodgson, *BMQ*, i, 1926, pp.35f.; C.Dodgson, *Vasari Society*, vii, 2nd series, 1926, no.10, repr.; Hugelshofer, *Schweizer Handz.* p.39, no.55, repr.; Winkler, K&S, p.163, no.A.1, repr.

Inscribed by a later hand, in black ink, in the lower left-hand corner, *Hans Holbin*

This was first published by Dodgson, who attributed it without hesitation to Hans Holbein the Younger. He places it at the beginning of the artist's career, even though, as he readily admits, there exist no similarly executed drawings from that period with which it can be compared. He discounted the possibility of it being by Ambrosius on the grounds that he was not capable of such fine work; however, both Parker and Hugelshofer disagreed with this, the latter asserting Ambrosius's authorship by comparing it with his *Portrait of a young man* in silver-point, signed with his monogram and dated, *1517* in Basel (Kunstmuseum,

inv.no.1662.207a). There is no doubt that the shortness of Ambrosius's career and the small number of surviving works have made it difficult to attribute this drawing to him, but it is worth considering, in this connection, the painted portrait of *Johannes Zimmermann*, dated *1520* (Rowlands, *Holbein*, pl.212) now in the Germanisches Nationalmuseum, Nuremberg (inv.no.1195) which is almost certainly the last important work by Ambrosius that has come down to us. Close examination of the painting suggests that in fact it was completed by another artist after Ambrosius's death. There is such a close affinity between the present drawing and this portrait in the manner in which the sitters have been depicted that it seems highly probable that the present drawing is a late work by Ambrosius.

Hans Holbein the Younger

Augsburg 1497/8 – London 1543

Painter, draughtsman and designer of woodcuts and metalcuts, glass-paintings, metalwork, jewellery etc. Son of Hans Holbein the Elder (q.v.), and younger brother of Ambrosius Holbein (q.v.), he received his initial training from his father. He arrived in Basel as a journeyman at the end of 1515 and found his first employment together with Ambrosius working for the circle of humanists and their printers. The brothers collaborated in decorating a sign board for the teacher, Myconius, each painting a side. The main commission of 1516 was the double portrait of the mayor of Basel, Jacob Meyer, and his wife (Basel, Kunstmuseum) whose subsequent patronage was of key significance. At some point between 1517 and the summer of 1519 Hans assisted his father in decorating with murals both the inside and the outside of the new town house in Lucerne of Jacob von Hertenstein, a rich merchant of that city. At this point in his career it has been thought that Holbein could have visited northern Italy. In the autumn of 1519 he was admitted to the painters' guild in Basel, becoming a citizen in the following summer. Then there began a very fruitful period with one important commission after another, including the famous *Dead Christ* of 1521/2 (Basel, Kunstmuseum), the decorations of the Haus 'zum Tanz', now destroyed and, most prestigious of all, the first and principal stage of decorating in 1521/2 the council chamber of the newly rebuilt town hall with murals, now largely destroyed. Against a background of social and religious strife in Basel in 1524 Holbein visited France doubtless in the hope of royal patronage, and on his return produced two masterpieces, his *Passion Altarpiece* (Basel, Kunstmuseum) and the *Meyer Madonna* (Darmstadt, Prinz von Hessen und bei Rhein) which was commissioned in 1526, or slightly earlier, and only fully completed in 1528.

With an introduction from Erasmus, of whom he had done his first portrait in 1523 (the Earl of Radnor), to Sir Thomas More he left Basel for England at the end of August 1526 and stayed for two years before returning to Basel. Through More Holbein was introduced to court circles and painted his famous group portrait of Sir Thomas and his family (now destroyed, but its appearance is recorded in a drawing by Holbein sent to Erasmus, now in Basel, Kunstmuseum).

Holbein spent the next four years in Basel chiefly completing the town hall decorations for the city fathers, and painting perhaps his most moving work, the *Portrait of his wife and his two elder children* (Basel, Kunstmuseum), who were to be left behind when he returned to settle in England in 1532. Then began a period when, although his chief clients were Hanseatic merchants, he was endeavouring to win royal attention and a post as a court painter, which it is likely was achieved through the support of Anne Boleyn, but when precisely is unknown. The chief commission executed for Henry VIII was the mural painting glorifying the Tudor dynasty in the Whitehall Palace (destroyed in the fire of 1698; part of Holbein's cartoon for it survives, see no.213). The mural was to be the source of a group of full-length portraits of Henry VIII by followers of Holbein. Throughout this whole period he was producing a succession of magnificent portraits of which perhaps the most accomplished are the so-called '*Ambassadors*' of 1533 and the *Portrait of Christina of Denmark* of 1538 (both in the National Gallery, London). After the production of his *Portrait of Anne of Cleves* (Paris, Louvre), produced for the prospective and soon to be disappointed bridegroom, Henry VIII, the signs are that Holbein fell from the heights of royal favour, never to regain them. His final image of the King was that ordered by the Company of Barber Surgeons, *Henry VIII granting a charter to the Barber-Surgeons* (London, Barber-Surgeons), showing a degree of studio work. He was, however, still a royal servant on his death in November 1543.

BIBLIOGRAPHY: Thieme-Becker, xvii, 1924, pp.335ff.; Woltmann; Chamberlain; Ganz; Parker; Basel, *Holbein* (for extensive bibliography); Rowlands, *Holbein*.

188 Coat-of-arms, probably of a Lucerne family, with St George as a supporter

Pen and brush in black ink with watercolour. Much cut down on all sides. 40.6 × 29.5cm

PROVENANCE: Sloane bequest, 1753

5218–197

LITERATURE: BM *Guide*, 1901, p.18, no.A.84; Ganz, p.43, no.185, repr.

Ganz noted that the *Wappenbuch* of Rennwart Zysat of 1581 recorded the arms of the now extinct family of Rood, as a green toad on gold, but with a springing hunting hound, rather than as seen here, a white crane with an open beak. Conceivably the arms represented here are of another branch of the same family. This is Holbein's earliest known heraldic design complete with crest and mantle, for a glass-painting. It can be dated to within the period 1517 to 1519, during which time he is known to have been employed in various commissions in Lucerne, chiefly collaborating with his father in the decoration of the Von Hertenstein town-house. No.188 is close in treatment to his design for a glass-painting of *Three farmers with the arms of the Lucerne painter, Sebastian Holdermeyer*, dated *1518* (Basel, Kunstmuseum, inv.no.1823.138; Ganz, p.43, no.183, repr.). The figures in this drawing possess a similar stocky build as the present St George, who also has himself unusually rustic features.

189 A halbardier supporting the arms of Graf Christoph zu Eberstein

Pen and black ink with black and grey wash, lightly tinted with red watercolour on the heraldic roses, parts of the feather and mantling, and red chalk within the arms. Many areas of repair, especially along the upper edge. 33.5 × 29.3cm

PROVENANCE: Sir William Stirling-Maxwell, Bt; Sir Archibald Stirling of Keir; Lt.-Col. W.J.Stirling of Keir (sale, Sotheby, 1946, 26 June, lot 128); presented anonymously, with a contribution from the Blakiston Fund, 1946

Oxford, Ashmolean Museum, P.299*

LITERATURE: Hugelshofer, *Schweizer Handz.*, p.40, no.59, repr.; Ganz, p.46, no.192, repr.; H.A. Schmid, *Zeitschr. f. Kunstgesch*, x, 1941/2, p.267; Basel, *Holbein*, p.222, no.201 (for further literature)

Inscribed by an early hand, in black ink on the tablet, *Cristoff graff zů ebersteÿn 1522*

Despite the date on the inscription, which Ganz accepted as accurate, if not from the artist's own hand, the style of the draughtsmanship suggests that it belongs with designs for glass paintings produced by Holbein in 1519 in Lucerne, before he returned to Basel, a view put forward by Schmid. I see no reason for disregarding the evidence of the inscription entirely, even though the style of the design links it very convincingly with no.188. It could be of course that the completion of the commission was delayed for some reason, and the design not delivered until 1522.

Criftoff graf zü eberftÿn .

189

190 The Adoration of the Christ Child, with, in the background, the Annunciation to the shepherds

Pen and black ink and grey wash, heightened with yellow ochre and oxidised white bodycolour. 16.9 × 11.2cm

PROVENANCE: Sir T. Lawrence (L.2445); J.B. Murray

Oxford, Ashmolean Museum, P.297*

LITERATURE: C. Dodgson, *OMD*, xiii, 1938–9, p.29, repr.; *Ashmolean Museum Annual Report*, Oxford, 1938, p.34; H.A. Schmid, *Zeitschr. f. Kunstgesch.*, x, 1941/2, pp.288f., repr.; Schmid, *Holbein*, i, pp.118, 245, repr.; Schilling, *Holbein*, pp.17f., no.25, repr.; Basel, *Holbein*, p.240, no.242, repr.; Manchester, *German Art*, p.58, no.150

Usually this drawing has been dated *c.*1520, or soon after, and connected with the left-hand wing, the *Adoration of the Shepherds*, of the Oberried altarpiece in the Münster, Freiburg-im-Breisgau (Rowlands, *Holbein*, pls.11 and 12) whose date, although uncertain, may be said to be *c.*1520/21. The scale of the figures in the drawing, and its composition, suggest, however, that it was probably produced as a first idea for a devotional panel painting, which was either never executed, or must be presumed lost, and which would have been comparable with the wings of the diptych,

190

Christ as the Man of Sorrows and the *Virgin as the 'Mater dolorosa'* (Basel, Kunstmuseum, inv.no.317; Rowlands, *Holbein*, pls.9 and 10) of 1519 or 1520. Grossman's idea that it might be as early in date as the lost *Nativity* of the altarpiece formerly in the Augustinian Church, Lucerne, supposedly of 1518, is too speculative, since its date is uncertain, and the appearance of the panel with this subject is quite unknown, only that of the *Lamentation* being recorded in copies (see Rowlands, *Holbein*, pp.218ff., no.L.2). Similarly, Schmid's proposed link with the metalcut of the *Annunciation to the Shepherds*, for one of the illustrations in the *Hortulus Animae*, executed *c.*1522 almost entirely by Jacob Faber and the Master CV, although unpublished until 1545, has no more than a general connection (Basel, *Holbein*, pp.306ff., no.382, repr.).

191 Mining

Pen and brown ink with grey wash. Diameter: 22.5cm

PROVENANCE: F. Fagel (sale, T. Philipe, 1801, 27 May, lot 58, bt with another drawing of the same subject (see below) *Hey £1-3s*); Daniells

LITERATURE: E. His, *Prussian Jahrbuch*, xv, 1894, pp.207ff., repr.; BM *Guide*, 1895, p.58, no.290; LB, ii, pp.329f., no.14; Chamberlain, i, p.80, repr.; Ganz, p.56, no.255, repr.; Braunfels, pp.28, 58, repr.

Inscribed on the *verso* by a later hand (possibly a member of the Fagel family) in black ink, *Affbeelding van het Bergwerken in Zwitserland.*

A list in the Fagel archives, made in 1717, of the drawings in the collection, describes two sheets acquired in Italy, which may be a reference to the present drawing together with the other one mentioned in the Fagel sale catalogue, as *La minière de Bâle, deux feuilles* (information kindly supplied by Dr J. Heringa, Rijksarchiv in de Provincie Drenthe, Assen, Holland). The second sheet may otherwise refer to the copy of no.191, now in the École des Beaux-Arts, Paris (Masson collection, no.91) of which, however, only the upper two-thirds survives. It is executed in the same medium as the original, but is in poor condition. Another copy, made in the same medium but rather weak in execution, which dates possibly from the late sixteenth century and has some of its upper rim missing, is in the Kunstmuseum, Basel (inv.no.1960.44).

According to Édouard His, who considered it a design for a glass-painting, this drawing could be attributed to Holbein on largely historical grounds. This view was rejected by Ganz, because he considered its composition too loosely arranged for Holbein, and he regarded it instead to be a sketch for goldsmith's work of some unspecified kind. Furthermore Ganz was not impressed by the drawing's quality, although he does place it within the artist's second English period, 1534–43. He thought that its original state had been severely weakened by the process of taking an offset, and its character obscured by later overworking in brown ink.

191

Although it is likely that it has faded through over-exposure at some point in its history, its condition is, in general, very sound for a sixteenth-century drawing. Nor does one share Ganz's view that the brown ink pen-work is a later addition, since it is, unquestionably, an integral part of the design. The line is characteristic of Holbein's early work, most probably soon after 1520. A comparison between the line of the pen in the *Adoration of the Christ-child* (no.190) with that in the present drawing provides striking stylistic evidence to support this. Chamberlain also saw it as an early work, although on the assumption that it was to be associated with Holbein's supposed journey across the Alps to Italy before he settled in Basel as a member of the guild in 1519.

It does not follow that the composition was based on studies after the life drawn by Holbein at a mine. It is much more likely to be a composition constructed from the works of others, since there must have been a considerable number of such scenes from which to choose, judging from what has survived. Already in the latter part of the fifteenth century important manuscripts produced in mining regions were decorated with scenes of mining. Notable examples of such manuscripts are two graduals of Kutná Hora, formerly Kuttenberg, in Bohemia, a prosperous silver-mining town in the fifteenth century with a majority German population. The earlier one dates from 1471, and was executed in the Prague workshop of Valentin Noh, and the later one is dated *c*.1490. Both have full-page scenes of mining. While clearly these illustrations would not have been known to Holbein, it is not unlikely that Holbein did not have other similar scenes from sources close to hand on which he could have based his design. Despite Ganz's doubts, it is quite likely to have been intended for a glass-

painting. The patron involved would probably have been a Basel citizen with mining interests.

Holbein's design was evidently well-known in Basel in the sixteenth century, as we find that Hieronymus Vischer (1564–1631) based one of his mining scenes upon it in the *Münz- und Mineralienbuch* (Basel, Universitätsbibliothek) that he decorated with illuminations for Andreas Ryff of Basel in 1594. Ryff had acquired through his wife a stake in the silver mines at Giromagny near Belfort, at the southern extremity of the Vosges mountains not far from Basel.

192 Two angels supporting a shield surmounted by a mitre and crozier

Pen and black ink with grey wash, and traces of black chalk on the shield. 37.5 × 29.5 cm

WM: the Basel staff, of which only the lower part is visible

PROVENANCE: Sir P. Lely (L.1753 twice); J. Richardson senior (L.2184); G. Le Hunte 1842, Artramont, Co. Wexford, and thence by descent to the Misses M.H.L.E. and M.D. Le Hunte (sale, Sotheby, 1955, 9 June, lot 40, bt *Professor Bodkin £3,400*, for the Institute)

Birmingham, Barber Institute of Fine Arts

LITERATURE: Basel, *Holbein*, p.237, no.236; Manchester, *German Art*, pp.58f., no.152; *Barber Institute Handbook*, p.38; *Barber Institute Drawings*, no.6, repr.; Washington, *Albertina*, p.199, under no.18, with an incorrect repr.

Inscribed by a later hand, in brown ink, below the shield, *H Holbein* (the 'H's are linked)

This design for a glass-painting is thoroughly characteristic of Holbein's first years as a master in the guild at Basel. It was done *c*.1520, as first proposed by Reinhardt, a period when Holbein was much employed to produce such drawings in which the new Renaissance vocabulary was introduced with a clarity in lighting and balance of composition, for which he is unrivalled. A companion drawing also from the collection of the Misses Le Hunte, and since 1955 in the Albertina, Vienna (inv.no.31705), is likewise a design of superb quality with two angels supporting a shield. Both designs could have been made for the same client, and would have been for private use. Holbein's designs for glass-paintings established a long tradition in the decoration of Swiss houses. In the present case, it would appear that they were for the rooms of a newly appointed bishop or abbot, whose cathedral, or abbey, to judge from the decoration on the mitre which the angel has unveiled, could have been dedicated to the Virgin Mary. The quartered arms on the shield are hardly legible; in the third quarter one can make out a faintly drawn arrow placed diagonally pointing upwards, but in the fourth quarter there is only the outline, just visible through the help of an infra-red spectrometer, of what may be the head of a bird.

193

194

193 Ecce Homo

Offset of drawing in pen and black ink, retouched by the artist himself with the point of the brush in black ink. 39.3 × 29.4 cm

PROVENANCE: as no.194

1846–9–18–3

LITERATURE: Sandrart, *Teutsche Academie*, pp.102, 333; Waagen, *Treasures*, i, p.236; Woltmann, i, pp.172f., ii, pp.56, 133, no.179; LB, ii, p.327, no.3; Basel, *Holbein*, p.261, under no.290

See no.194.

194 Christ carrying the Cross

Offset of a drawing in pen and black ink, retouched by the artist himself with the point of the brush in black ink. In important areas of the composition it was later retouched and altered by Rubens in pen and brown ink and wash, heightened with grey and white bodycolour with some outlines in pen and black ink. 37.6 × 27.8 cm

PROVENANCE: Sir P.P. Rubens; J. von Sandrart; G.F. Fagel (sale, T. Philipe, 1801, 29 May, lot 93, bt *Ottley £27.6s.*); W.Y. Ottley (sale, T. Philipe, 1814, 11 June, lot 670); Sir T. Lawrence (L.2445); P & D Colnaghi

1846–9–18–5

LITERATURE: Sandrart, *Teutsche Academie*, pp.102, 333; Waagen, *Treasures*, i, p.236; Woltmann, i, pp.172f., ii, pp.56, 133, no.181; LB, ii, p.328, no.5; Chamberlain, i, pp.156f., ii, p.327; Basel, *Holbein*, p.262, under no.292; M. Jaffé, *MD*, iii, 1965, p.34, n.6

This drawing and no.193 are two of the seven offsets taken from the series, of which ten survive, of designs for glass-paintings of the Passion at Basel (Ganz, pp.39ff. nos.169–78 repr.). They were evidently skilfully retouched with the brush by Holbein. Sandrart, to whom the group of offsets belonged, all of which are now in the British Museum, was evidently unaware of the existence of the drawings at Basel, and that his own drawings were, in fact, offsets.

There has been a difference of opinion among scholars about the possible dating of this series. Schmid placed the whole series between 1528 and 1530, while Ganz, who divided the drawings into three groups, considered them datable *c.*1523/24; the first is the latest date into which they could be placed and the second the earliest. As, however, they are such fine mature compositions in which Holbein depicts the Passion with such inventiveness – with the occasional telling references to Dürer – and nobility of feeling, a date close to his masterly painting, the *Passion Altarpiece* in the Kunstmuseum, Basel (inv.no.315; Rowlands, *Holbein*, pls.38–46) executed, after his visit to France in 1524, in Basel in 1525/26 is highly plausible. It is perhaps worth noting too that the decorative framework of these designs was used again in a glass-painting in the town hall Rheinfelden, dated *1532*.

No.194 was reworked substantially by Rubens when it was in his collection (for a discussion of this aspect of the history of the offset and Rubens's transformation of it into a Counter-Reformation image, see Rowlands, *Rubens*, p.55, no.48).

195 A wildman brandishing an uprooted tree trunk

See colour plate section following p.200

Pen and black ink with grey, brown and blue wash. 32.1 × 21.5cm

PROVENANCE: G.F.Fagel (sale, T.Philipe, 1801, 29 May, lot 91, bt *Philipe £3*); Malcolm

1895-9-15-992

LITERATURE: Woltmann, i, p.163, ii, p.139, no.209; JCR, pp.179f., no.536;* BM *Guide*, 1895, p.57, no.288; LB, ii, p.329, no.13; Chamberlain, i, p.147; Ganz, p.48, no.200, repr.; E. Major, *Zeitschr. f. schweiz. Arch.*, viii, 1946, pp.116ff.; Basel, *Holbein*, p.271, under no.313; Dreyer, *Berlin*, p.17, under no.9

The wildman is often represented as a supporter of arms, especially in South Germany and Switzerland. In the present drawing, which is a design for a glass-painting, the wildman is not, however, shown as a supporter but, as Major pointed out, probably represented in his capacity as *Ehrenzeichen* (honorary emblem) of the *Ehrengesellschaft* 'Zur Hären'. The members of this civic society were originally hunters and fishermen of Kleinbasel, but later included in addition, members of the aristocracy (see *Basler Stadtgeschichte*, ii, Basel, 1981, p.30; U.Barth, *Zünftiges Basel*, Basel, 1986, p.20). As a symbol of the society, a wildman holding an uprooted tree was painted over the entrance-gate of the *Ehrengesellschafthaus* 'Zur Hären'. The appearance of this painting is recorded in a watercolour by J.J.Neustück of 1856 (Staatsarchiv, Basel; E.Major, op.cit., pl.35). The wildman also appears in an annual festival, in which men appropriately dressed to personify various *Ehrenzeichen* parade through the city, each performing a special dance. This event, which still takes place every January, was described as an old custom in 1597, by Andreas Ryff in his *Der Stadt Basel Regiment und Ordnung* (edited by R.Wackernagel, *Beiträge zur vaterländischen Geschichte, Historischen Gesellschaft*, Basel, xiii, 1893, p.12). In his dance, the wildman twirls around, and with an uprooted fir tree pushes back the crowds, and this, as Major has plausibly proposed, is the action that Holbein suggests in this drawing, which would presumably have been made for a glass-painting in the *Gesellschafthaus* 'Zur Hären' in Kleinbasel. Major's idea that Bonifacius Amerbach recommended Holbein for the work is certainly possible, although we do not know when Amerbach became a member of this civic society, only that he was one. The mature, polished style of execution of no.195 makes it seem likely that Holbein made this design soon after his

return from his first visit to England, in the summer of 1528. The glass-painting itself is lost, although it may have been the one in the possession of the Basel dealer, Johann Heinrich Speyr der Ältere in 1841, described as, 'Vitrau [*sic*] peint. Armoirie de la société de la Hären au petit Bâle, un homme sauvage' (*Catalog und Verzeichnis der Kunst-Gegenstände und Eigenthum des Antiquar J.H.v.Speyr Aelter*, MS catalogue, Basel, Universitäts-Bibliothek, inv.no.H.IV 81c, p.17, no.235).

Sandrart possessed a drawing of a wildman, which he attributed to Hans Holbein the Younger (*Teutsche Academie*, p.333, and n.1514). It is uncertain whether this could have been the present drawing, or a version presumed to be an early drawn copy, now in Berlin-Dahlem (Kupferstichkabinett, inv.no.KdZ 3091; Dreyer, *Berlin*, pl.15), or another one now untraced. It may be, as Peter Dreyer has suggested, that the copy, which very closely follows the present drawing in its details, could have been executed in the artist's studio; certainly the pen-work in the Berlin version lacks something of the vigour of no.195. It is doubtful, however, that if the British Museum version were not known, the drawing in Berlin would not have been accepted as an original. Such a change of opinion occurred with the glass-painting design of St Kunigunda at Basel (Kupferstichkabinett, inv.no.1662.156; Basel, *Holbein*, p.270, no.312) which was considered to be by Holbein until the version, also of *c.*1528, now in Berlin-Dahlem (Kupferstichkabinett, inv.no.7028; Basel, *Holbein*, p.270, no.311) was recognised to be the original.

18 Holbein in England

196 St Andrew carrying the Cross

Pen and black ink, heightened with white bodycolour on brown
prepared paper. 20.3 × 10.5 cm

PROVENANCE: Sir T. Lawrence (L.2445); S. Woodburn (sale,
Christie, 1860, 4 June, lot 34, bt with 16 others, *Thorp 18s.*);
Phillips-Fenwick; presented anonymously, 1946

1946–7–13–128

LITERATURE: Popham, *Fenwick*, p.231, no.1

Inscribed by the artist in white bodycolour on the bottom of the
cross, *1527*

This drawing belongs to an incomplete series of drawings
of the *Apostles*, which was published by Hugelshofer (*OMD*,
iv, June 1929, pp.1ff.), the present drawing being unknown
to him. Four, those of Sts Bartholomew, James the Great,
Mathias and James the Less were then with Julius Böhler,
Lucerne; two, Sts Peter and John belonged to Franz
Koenigs, Haarlem, and one of St Thomas, is now in a
Dutch private collection and is on loan to the Boymans-van
Beuningen Museum, Rotterdam. They are approximately
20 × 10 cm in size, executed in the same medium and technique as the present drawing and like it, five of them are
dated *1527*. Although none is signed, there seems to be no
reason, because of their striking quality and character, why
they should not be accepted as works of Holbein's first
English period, even though as such they are an isolated
example of religious work from that point in his career. In
any event, they can be clearly associated with the religious
masterpiece of Holbein's maturity, executed in Basel shortly
before his first departure for England, the *Passion Altarpiece*
(Basel, Kunstmuseum, inv.no.315; Rowlands, *Holbein*,
pls.38–46). There are so many telling comparisons to be
made between details in this magnificent work and the
series of *Apostles* that there can be no doubt about the
drawings' attribution to Holbein. Similarly the drawings
provide, if any additional stylistic grounds were needed,
further support for the dating of the *Passion Altarpiece* in
the late 1520s, rather than *c.*1520 as proposed by Ganz.

Part of another, not very well preserved, series of pen
drawings of the Apostles, executed on greyish-brown prepared paper, somewhat smaller in size, has survived at
Lille (Musée Wicar, inv.nos.924–31), and was attributed
to Hans Holbein the Younger by T. Muchall-Viebrook
(*Munich Jahrbuch*, NF, viii, 1931, pp.156–71). Some of
these drawings, eight in number, are signed with the
monogram, *HH* and dated *1518*. Schmid and Reinhardt
(Basel, *Holbein*, pp.225f., no.209; H. Reinhardt, *La Revue
du Louvre et des Musée de France*, no.415, 1961, pp.177–83)
have supported Muchall-Viebrook's attribution, pointing

196

to stylistic traits which they considered reflected Holbein's reaction to the work of Baldung (q.v.) and Grünewald (q.v.). Although somewhat lacking the finesse of the brush work in the *Seated Virgin with Child* (Leipzig, Museum der bildenden Künste, inv.no.N1.25) signed with the monogram *HH* and dated *1519*, it is not unreasonable to see the series as the exuberant work of a young impressionable artist still feeling his way. While not wholeheartedly accepting their attribution to Holbein, Ganz's rejection of them may perhaps have stemmed from Muchall-Viebrook's too broadly based and uncritical comparison with accepted works, which does not carry conviction, and his rejection of the later series to which the present drawing belongs.

197 Two views of the same lady wearing an English hood

Brush drawing in black ink, tinted with pink and grey wash, on off-white paper. 15.9 × 11 cm

PROVENANCE: Sir T. Lawrence (L.2445); Sir J. C. Robinson; Malcolm

1895–9–15–991

LITERATURE: Woltmann, ii, p.139, no.210; JCR, p.179, no.535;

LB, ii, p.329, no.11; Chamberlain, i, pp.356f.; Ganz, p.35, no.150), repr.; White, p.558, no.2; Roberts, *Holbein*, p.60 under no.13, repr.

Inscribed by a later hand in brown ink in the upper and lower right-hand corners respectively, HHB linked together as a monogram, and similarly linked together, HH.

The details of costume and headdress which the artist has noted in these two studies bear a close resemblance to the dress worn by Lady Guildford in Holbein's portrait of her, dated *1527* (Missouri, St Louis Art Museum; Rowlands, *Holbein*, pl.54). The English hood is of the same type and worn with the two tails hanging loose down the back. While his female sitters continued to be painted in the English hood as late as Jane Seymour's portrait of 1536 (Vienna, Kunsthistorisches Museum, inv.no.881; Rowlands, *Holbein*, pl.99), by the mid-1530s it became fashionable for the sides and tails of the hood to be turned up, as one finds is the case with the majority of female sitters wearing the English hood in Holbein's portrait drawings of his second English period. In style these studies, evidently rapidly drawn, differ markedly from the group of drawings that Holbein had done earlier, according to Ganz before 1520, but more probably by 1524, of women in different Basel costumes, executed in stiff poses with sharp outlines and very finished in detail. Because of the clear link Ganz saw with the *Portrait of Lady Guildford*, he dated the present drawing to 1527/28; even so 1532/33 is also not impossible. Another costume study of a woman, evidently a citizen's wife, completely worked up with watercolour was also executed in England (Oxford, Ashmolean Museum; Parker, *Ashmolean*, pl.lviii).

198 A woman seated on a settle with four children

Pen and black ink, with grey and black wash over traces of an underdrawing in black chalk. 13.4 × 16.9 cm

PROVENANCE: R. Cosway (sale, Stanley, 1822, 16 February, probably part of lot 437, one of 'Three washed drawings, by Holbein'); E. V. Utterson (L.909; sale, Sotheby, 1852, 30 April, lot 277, bt with one other, *Tiffin* for BM)

1852–5–19–1

LITERATURE: Metz, *Imitations*, 1798, repr.; Waagen, *Treasures Suppl.*, p.36; Woltmann, ii, p.134, no.189; S. Colvin, BM *Guide*, 1895, p.58. no.291; LB ii, p.328, no.8; C. Dodgson, *Vasari Society*, i, 1905/6, no.18, repr.; Chamberlain, ii, pp.226f., repr.; Ganz, p.22, no.100, repr.; White, p.558, no.1

Inscribed by a later hand, probably eighteenth-century, along the lower edge in brown ink, *exaltate Cedrus. H. Holbein* (probably a reference to Ecclesiasticus (Vulgate), xxiv, 17 'Quasi cedrus')

Various attempts have been made, none of them plausible, to identify the sitters in this drawing. According to Dodgson, following an idea of Peartree, the dress and features of the woman are said to clearly resemble those of the *Portrait of*

197

198

an unknown woman at Windsor (The Royal Library, inv.no. 12217; Parker, pl.9), whom Wornum first suggested might be Mother Jak, the nurse of Edward VI. Parker rightly rejected this identification on grounds of chronology and style. The connection between the woman in the Windsor drawing and the woman here is much too tenuous, and in any case there is a large difference in scale between the two drawings.

There are also strong objections to the identification of the two boys as the ill-fated Henry and Charles Brandon, the 2nd and 3rd Dukes of Suffolk, of whom Holbein did two miniatures (The Royal Collection, Windsor Castle; Rowlands, *Holbein*, col.pls.28 and 29) one of which, that of Henry Brandon, shows the figure in a similar pose to the boy seated on the bench. But as Chamberlain pointed out, the two younger children in the drawing stood in the way of this because the boys' father had no other children by his fourth marriage. Those children from earlier marriages would have been too old for one of them to be the standing little girl. Judging the drawing on purely stylistic grounds, it may be reasonably placed at the commencement of the artist's second stay in England, probably in the years when Holbein was working intensively for the merchants of the German Steelyard in Blackfriars. The character of the penwork is particularly close to a preliminary drawing for one of the two allegorical paintings of *c.*1532–3 that he executed for the Merchants' Hall, the *Triumph of*

Riches, now in Paris (Louvre, inv.no.18694; Ganz, p.28, no.120, repr.). The wash is used less effectively than in the present drawing, where the areas of shade and shadow model the figures so well that it seems very likely the group was drawn from the life, to give the client an idea of how they might appear in a painting. But this either was not executed or has not survived. However, there is a small painting it is worth recalling, a *Portrait of a woman* now at Detroit (Institute of Arts, inv.no.77.81.; Rowlands, *Holbein*, pl.89) most probably of about the same date, in which the sitter is wearing a similar coif and is seated on a linen-fold backed bench. Dodgson pointed this out when he published the portrait (*Burlington*, liii, 1928, p.105). Ganz, on the flimsy pretext that the sitter did not appear to him to be English, proceeded to conclude that because she is wearing fine rings she was most probably the wife of Hans of Antwerp, the goldsmith with whom Holbein was closely associated.

An etching was made after the drawing, when it was in the possession of Richard Cosway, and published by Conrad Metz in 1798. A drawing whose description, 'Holbein – A Mother and Children – *Indian Ink*', suggests that it might have been a copy of the present sheet, appeared in Samuel Woodburn's sale at Christie's in 1854 (19 June, lot 621, bt with lot 622, *Prout 16s*) and also, in his later sale at Christie's in 1860, as 'A Nurse, with Four Children – *Indian Ink*' (12 June, lot 1243, bt *Seymour £1-1s*).

231

199

199 Portrait of George Nevill, third Baron of Bergavenny (?1459–1535)

Black and coloured chalk, partly stumped, with yellow wash on the jewel in the cap, on pink prepared paper; outlines of the face reinforced with pen and black ink, and the eyes touched with white bodycolour. 27.3 × 24.1 cm

PROVENANCE: originally part of the 'Great Booke' (first recorded in the 1590 inventory of Lord Lumley, this contained portrait drawings by Holbein, chiefly of members of Henry VIII's court, the majority of which are now in the Royal Library, Windsor Castle; for details of the early history, see Parker, pp.8ff.); Earl of Pembroke. (This sheet is probably the only tangible witness of the fact that the 'Great Booke' (see also nos.202 and 203) was for a period in the hands of the Earls of Pembroke. The then Lord Chamberlain, Lord Pembroke, evidently received the 'Booke' from Charles I in exchange for his painting by Raphael, *St George and the Dragon* (now Washington, National Gallery of Art) between 1627 and 1630. The present drawing would have been detached from the 'Booke' in the brief interval before the Earl of Pembroke gave it to his brother-in-law Thomas Howard, the Earl of Arundel, and it has remained at Wilton House ever since. By 1675 the 'Booke' was again in the Royal Collection)

Wilton House, Salisbury, Wiltshire, the Earl of Pembroke and Montgomery

LITERATURE: Wornum, *Holbein*, p.287; Woltmann, i, p.376, ii, p.155, no.263; *Tudor Exhibition*, 1890, p.277, no.1414; BFAC, 1909, p.104, no.70; Campbell Dodgson, *Vasari Society*, part v, 1909/10, no.28, repr.; Chamberlain, ii, pp.62, 222, 248, 255; Ganz, p.10, no.37, repr.; Parker, pp.12, 23f.; RA, 1950–1, p.49, no.90; Rowlands, *Holbein*, p.150 under no.M2, p.232 under no.R.20

Inscribed by a later hand with pen and brown ink in the lower left-hand corner, *LORD CROMWELL*, and in the lower right-hand corner, *HOLBEIN*

The sitter was only correctly identified in 1909 at the BFAC exhibition, as the above inscription prompted writers in the last century, despite the disparity in likeness with painted portraits, to declare this drawing as a portrait of Sir Thomas Cromwell, later Earl of Essex.

This drawing and that of Lady Audley in the Royal Library, Windsor Castle (inv.no.12191) are the only ones surviving which were to be used as the basis for miniatures by Holbein himself (see Rowlands, *Holbein*, pp.150–1, M.2 and M.9). The miniature which corresponds to no.199 is in the collection of the Duke of Buccleuch (Rowlands, *Holbein*, pl.127).

200 Three Biblical studies within an architectural frame: Lot and his daughters; the drunkenness of Noah; Judith and Holofernes

Brush drawing in black ink, heightened with white bodycolour, on grey prepared paper. 7.7 × 14.8cm

PROVENANCE: T. Kerrich (1748–1828); thence by descent in his family, from whom obtained and presented by the N.A.-C.F. with the aid of contributions from Sir Otto Beit and C.S. Gulbenkian, 1926

1926–4–10–2

LITERATURE: C. Dodgson, *BMQ*, i, 1926, p.36, repr.; N.A.-C.F. *Report*, 1926, no.5326

Although ignored by Ganz who does not include it in his *catalogue raisonné* of the drawings, Dodgson is surely right in advocating the attribution to Holbein. The most clearly comparable work is the painted decoration executed in *grisaille* on the inside of the cover of the box intended to hold Holbein's *Portrait of Philipp Melanchthon*, in the Landes-

200

museum, Hanover (inv.no.PAM.798; Rowlands, *Holbein*, col.pl.31). Ganz dated this portrait *c*.1530, mainly on the strength of a supposed visit of Melanchthon to Freiburg-im-Breisgau, to where Holbein would have travelled from Basel to make the portrait. Apart from the problem of the distances involved, the style of the painting, in any case, speaks strongly against this, and in favour of a date of *c*.1535/36, and there is nothing about the decoration of the cover to contradict this either, which, contrary to Ganz's opinion, belongs unmistakably to Holbein's last stay in Basel.

201 Portrait of an unknown gentleman

Red, black and yellow chalk, heightened with white chalk, on pink prepared paper; reinforced with metalpoint on eyes, eyebrows, nose, mouth and ears. Upper corners made up. Surface much rubbed, horizontal crease across centre. Whole sheet: 36.2 × 26.8cm.

PROVENANCE: Padre Sebastiano Resta (according to *Dyce Collection*); Nicholas Lanier? (L. *Suppl.* 2908, in black); The Rev. Alexander Dyce, by whom bequeathed to the Victoria and Albert Museum, 1869

Victoria and Albert Museum, London, Dyce 363

LITERATURE: *Dyce Collection*, pp.17,56; VAM, *Technique & Purpose*, p.21, no.45

201

Inscribed on the old backing in a modern hand, in pencil, *Holbein*

Despite disfigurements caused by rubbing, especially of the sitter's fur coat, and the crease across the middle of the sheet, the quality of execution of the facial features is quite consistent with Holbein's portraiture of the mid-1530s. The delicate use of white heightening and the precise outlines of the eyebrows, eyes, nose and mouth all point inevitably to the conclusion that the drawing is the work of Holbein himself and not that of a follower.

202 Portrait of an English woman

Black and red chalk, with touches of white bodycolour, principally on the eyes, tip of the nose, cheeks, around the mouth and on the close fitting cap, the outlines of facial features with the point of the brush in black ink, on pink prepared paper. Signs of surface damage and small holes in the lower part of the drawing. The outline of the sitter has been silhouetted, and the sheet laid down. 27.6 × 19.1cm

PROVENANCE: Probably from the 'Great Booke' (see no.199; although clearly its silhouetting means that rather more than 'cutting along the upper outlines', mentioned by Parker in this connection, has befallen it); J.Richardson senior (L.2183; sale, Lock, 1746, 4 February, probably part of lot 48, bt with two others, *Knapton £10.10s*); ? G.Knapton until 1806; the 1st Duke of Sutherland; Lord Ronald Sutherland Gower, from whom acquired by G.Salting, November 1905; Salting bequest, 1910

1910-2-12-105

LITERATURE: C.Dodgson, *Vasari Society*, part 1, 1905–6, no.31, repr.; BFAC, *Early English Portraiture*, 1909, p.105, no.72; Chamberlain, i, p.309, pl.79, ii, pp.248, 252; Ganz, p.21, no.93, repr.; Parker, p.24; Schmid, *Holbein*, ii, pp.278, 365, 389, iii, p.33, no.95, repr.; RA, 1950–1, pp.53f., no.103; Manchester, *German Art*, p.57, no.149, repr.; White, p.558, no.3; BM *Portrait Drawings*, p.19, no.52

Formerly some have tried to identify the sitter with Margaret Roper, Sir Thomas More's favourite daughter. There is little similarity between her appearance either in Holbein's group portrait of the *Family of Sir Thomas More* (formerly at Kremsier Castle) the appearance of which is recorded in a drawing by Holbein at Basel (Kunstmuseum, inv.no.1662.31) and in a painting by Rowland Lockey (Nostell Priory; see Rowlands, *Holbein*, pls.188–90); or in his later miniature of 1536 (New York, The Metropolitan Museum of Art, inv.no.50.69.2; Rowlands, *Holbein*, pl.128). It is likely that the present drawing, with its characteristic soft pink ground was executed during Holbein's second English period.

202

203 Portrait of a lady, thought to be Anne Boleyn

See colour plate section following p.200

Black chalk, partly stumped, and red chalk; facial features, part of the cap and top of the bodice reinforced with the point of the brush in black ink, and with yellow wash on the gable of the cap, on pale pink prepared paper. Some retouching by a later hand in black chalk on the left shoulder, and in black and yellow chalk on the right shoulder. The corners have been cut diagonally. 32.1 × 23.5 cm

WM: lower part of an imperial eagle (a variant of Briquet, 1457; see Roberts, op.cit.)

PROVENANCE: originally in the 'Great Booke' of portrait drawings by Holbein, chiefly of members of Henry VIII's court, the majority of which are in the Royal Library, Windsor Castle (see no.199); Thomas Howard, Earl of Arundel; J. Richardson senior; Henry Newport, the 3rd Earl of Bradford; thence by descent to the 6th Earl of Bradford; purchased with the aid of the N.A.-C.F., 1975

1975-6-21-22

LITERATURE: Ganz, p.11, no.39, repr.; Parker, pp.24, 53, under no.63; RA, 1950-1, p.53, no.102; Manchester, *European Art*, p.97, no.323; J. Rowlands, BM *Yearbook*, ii, 1977, pp.231ff., repr.; Brown, p.536, under no.1539; J. Rowlands and D.R. Starkey, *Burlington*, cxxv, 1983, pp.88ff.; E.W. Ives, *Anne Boleyn*, Oxford, 1986, pp.52-6; Roberts, *Holbein*, p.142

Inscribed by a seventeenth-century hand, in brown ink, to the left of the sitter, *Anna Bullen de collata/Fuit Londini 19 May 1536*

The idea that this drawing is a portrait of Queen Anne Boleyn can be traced no further than 1649, the date of an etching made by Wenceslaus Hollar (Pennington, p.229, no.1342) after the present sheet in 1649 when it was in the collection of the Earl of Arundel. The print is inscribed *ANNA BVLLEN REGINA ANGLIÆ/HENRICI VIIIui Vxor 2da Elizabeth Regine/Mater, fuit decollata, Londini 19 May Ao 1536*, but it is not clear whether the inscription on it was taken from the drawing, or *vice versa*. Subsequent painted and engraved representations of Anne Boleyn were based on this image. Early portraits of the Queen are scarce and the work of hack image-makers (e.g. National Portrait Gallery, inv. no.668). Her coronation medal has survived only in a single worn lead impression (British Museum, Department of Coins and Medals, inv.no.M1 vol.1, p.34, no.22).

Although imperfectly preserved, this drawing is of high quality and equal to the best of those at Windsor. It was undoubtedly executed during Holbein's second stay in England, when he had abandoned the practice of drawing portraits in coloured chalks on unprimed paper on a relatively large scale, in favour of working on paper prepared with a flesh colour, on a smaller scale.

There is a copy of the present drawing in the Ashmolean Museum, Oxford, drawn in black lead on vellum. This was formerly ascribed to George Vertue, but has been attributed by Brown to Jonathan Richardson senior (1665-1745), a former owner of no.203. It is accompanied by a curious account written by the younger Richardson

of how his father lent the original, which was never returned, to the then Earl of Bradford.

As proposed by myself and Starkey, the portrait drawing at Windsor with the inscription *Anna Bollein Queen* (Parker, p.53, no.63, repr.) has much about it to recommend its reinstatement as the Queen's portrait. Its rejection by Ives in his brilliant historical study is based on a mistaken disregard of the widely varying value of the different supposed likenesses of the Queen; for it is not wise to rely too readily on inferior Elizabethan portraits to form a basis for establishing her appearance. Again, although possibly of Anne Boleyn, we cannot be sure that the minute portrait of the lady in a French hood with the portrait of Queen Elizabeth I set in the English locket ring, now at Chequers, is necessarily of her. It is in any case a small, not finely defined representation of the lady's features (VAM, *Court Jewels*, p.60, no.37, repr., p.26). The circumstantial grounds in favour of the Windsor drawing are really very compelling, and one cannot necessarily cast aside Sir John Cheke's authority for the identification merely because of the confusion over a sitter in the Windsor series being called by him in error 'Mother Iak', Amy Jackson, Edward VI's nurse, whom he did know, with another sitter, Margaret Giggs, foster daughter of Sir Thomas More, whom he almost certainly did not know (Parker, p.37, no.8, repr.). Furthermore, the majority of misinterpretations of the inscriptions cannot usually be laid at Cheke's door. They were probably obvious to members of the Tudor court.

204 Design for a dagger

Brush drawing in black ink. 45.5 × 12.6 cm

PROVENANCE: Earl of Wicklow

1874-8-8-33

LITERATURE: Woltmann, ii, p.137, no.200; His, pl.xxix, LB ii, p.331, no.19; Chamberlain, ii, p.277; Ganz, p.75, no.443, repr., Birmingham, *Jewellery*, p.99, no.442

This type of dagger, known as a baselard, appears from the fourteenth century onwards (cf. Claude Blair, *European & American Arms c.1100-1850*, New York, London 1962, p.13). Given its rich ornamentation and the setting of jewellery, the weapon would obviously have been intended for ceremonial purposes only, and almost certainly made, presumably in either gold or silver, for King Henry VIII himself. Apart from the evident skill lavished upon the design, the production of a variant design for the hilt (Basel, Kunstmuseum, inv.no.1662.16597; Ganz, p.75, no.444, repr.) is further evidence of the importance attached to the commission for what is perhaps the most luxurious weapon of the sixteenth century.

205 Design of a cup for Jane Seymour

Pen and point of the brush and black ink on white paper, yellowed with age and surface dirt. There are a few spots of yellow paint scattered over the sheet. The paper was folded down the centre of the drawing by the artist to make an offset; the right-hand side of the design, where it mirrors the left, has been produced by this technique. The drawing has been cut out around the subject and laid down on to brown paper. Where the right-hand tip of the rim of the cup joins its cover, the sheet has been made up. Drawing: 37.5 × 14.3cm; sheet: 44.6 × 23.8cm

PROVENANCE: Sir T. Lawrence (L.2445); W. Beckford; Smith 1848-11-25-9

LITERATURE: Woltmann, ii, p.143 under no.222; LB, ii, p.311, no.18; L. Cust, *Burlington*, viii, 1905-6, p.359; Chamberlain, ii, pp.113, 274; Ganz, p.50, no.207, repr,; Parker, *Ashmolean*, p.134,

204

205

under no.299; Collins, p.279, under no.47; White, p.570, no.186; Lloyd, *Ashmolean Drawings*, p.14, under no.12

Inscribed by the artist with the brush in black ink on the lid, *BOUND TO OBEY AND [SERVE]*, and on the foot, *BOUND TO OBEY*

This is a preliminary design for a cup given by Henry VIII to Jane Seymour, decorated with the King's and Queen's initials intertwined with love knots, and the Queen's motto. The pose of the upper right-hand putto obtained by the offset has been changed by the artist, and certain other alterations appear, such as to the left-hand head seen in relief on the middle section of the cup, and to the pipe blown by the left-hand siren. There is no particular reason for accepting Ganz's proposal that these changes were the work of a later hand and, in any case, they are incorporated in a modified form in Holbein's final design for the cup at Oxford (Ashmolean Museum; Parker, *Ashmolean*, pl.lix). The composition of the latter clearly follows that of no.205, although the design is shown in a much more detailed form to which light washes of grey and pink have been added, as well as being heightened with gold. Also the Queen's motto, seen twice on the present sheet, appears there thrice. The precision with which Holbein has made the Ashmolean drawing, seen, for instance, in the way he has modelled the recessed areas of the cup with the grey wash, indicate that this is the most complete form of the design, which would have been shown to the King for his approval, and then used by the goldsmith.

The designs for Queen Jane Seymour's cup can be dated between her marriage to the King on 30 May 1536 and her death on 24 October at Hampton Court in the following year, twelve days after she had given birth to prince Edward, later Edward VI. As in the designs for this cup, Henry had ordered their intertwined initials to be incorporated with the Queen's motto in the decorations just completed in the banqueting hall, and at the entrance to the chapel, at Hampton Court.

It has been conjectured by Cust that the cup was made by the goldsmith John of Antwerp who was active in London, and of whom Holbein painted a portrait in 1532 (Windsor Castle; Rowlands, *Holbein*, pl.68). A cup, whose description answers that of the present designs, is listed in the inventory of 1574 of royal plate, 'Item oone faire standing Cup of golde garnisshed about the Couer with eleuen table Diamoundes and two pointed Diamoundes about the Cup Seventene table Diamoundes and thre pearles pendaunt vpon the Cup with this worde bounde to obeye and serue and H and J knitte together in the toppe of the Couer the Quenis Armes and Quene Janes Armes holdone by two boyes vnder a Crowne Imperiall poiz lxv ox. dim.' (see Collins). In an inventory of the royal collection made on the accession of Charles I in 1625, a description of the cup indicates that by then it had only one pendant pearl (quoted by Chamberlain). The cup was subsequently taken to Holland by the Duke of Buckingham in October 1629 to be pawned, only to be redeemed shortly after, melted down, and the gold sold to the Bank of Amsterdam.

206 Four designs for pendant jewels

(a) Design for a cruciform pendant

Pen and black ink. 6.8 × 5 cm

PROVENANCE: Sloane bequest, 1753

5308–50

LITERATURE: Woltmann, ii, p.136, no.199, 50; His pl.xliii, 10, L.B., ii, p.334, no.27a; Chamberlain, ii, p.27a, pl.48.8; Ganz, p.72, no.418, repr.; White, p.561, no.53; Birmingham, *Jewellery*, p.101, no.444,1; VAM, *Court Jewels*, pp.118f., no.G10,2a

There is no surviving cross of English origin from the 1530s comparable with this finely executed design, which has Renaissance floriated decoration. Contrary to Yvonne Hackenbroch's suggestion (Hackenbroch, p.271), there are no grounds for supposing that the cross worn by the sitter in the *Portrait of Sir Thomas More* – a painting after Holbein, probably from the mid to late sixteenth century at Knole, Sevenoaks, Kent (S. Morison & N. Barker, *The Likeness of Thomas More: an Iconographical Survey of Three Centuries*, London, 1963, fig.6) – is necessarily based on a design by Holbein, any more than one might consider that the cross worn by Sir Bryan Tuke in Holbein's portrait of him (Washington DC, National Gallery of Art, inv.no.65; Rowlands, *Holbein*, pl.102) was necessarily designed by the artist. A cruciform pendant with a figure of the crucified Christ which, according to tradition, belonged to Sir Thomas More, is now at Stonyhurst College, Lancashire (Birmingham, *Jewellery*, p.74, no.283c; Hackenbroch, p.271, repr.), which likewise cannot be associated with Holbein.

(b) Design for a pendant set with four emeralds and a single suspended pearl

Pen and black ink with green, yellow, and grey wash. 8.6 × 5.5 cm

PROVENANCE: Sloane bequest, 1753

5308–37

LITERATURE: Reid, pl.13; Woltmann, ii, p.136, no.199, 37 (incorrectly described); His, pl.xliii, 1; LB, ii, p.334, no.27d; Chamberlain, ii, p.279, pl.48, 4; Ganz, p.63, no.313, repr.; White, p.560, no.40; Birmingham, *Jewellery*, p.101, no.444, IV; VAM, *Court Jewels*, pp.118f., no.G10, 2d

206b   206c   206d

(c) Design for a pendant in the form of a monogram RE, set with various stones and three suspended pearls

Pen and black ink with watercolour. 8.4 × 4.1 cm

PROVENANCE: Sloane bequest, 1753

5308–117

LITERATURE: Reid, pl.13; His, pl.xliii, 3; LB, ii, pp.334f., no.27e; Chamberlain, ii, p.279f., pl.48,7; J.Evans, *English Jewllery from the Fifth Century AD to 1800*, London, 1921, pl.xvi, 4; Ganz, p.65, no.328, repr.; O.Pächt, *Burlington*, lxxxiv, 1944, p.137, repr.; White, p.566, no.119; Birmingham, *Jewellery*, p.101, no.444, V; VAM, *Court Jewels*, pp.118f., no.G10, 2e, repr.

This drawing and no.206(d), are designs in the form of monograms ornamented in the same floriated manner, and were most probably drawn as a pair. If so this would indicate that, like no.206(d), the present drawing was executed during Queen Jane Seymour's brief marriage to Henry VIII. The type of letter used for these two pieces was not, however, first devised then, as we find lettering like it in a manuscript in the Bodleian Library, Oxford (Ms Bodley 504) of Nicolaus Kratzer's short astronomical treatise, *Canones Horoptri*, datable 1528/9, which was intended as a New Year's gift for the King. The initial E on folio 1 *recto* is so like that in the present drawing that Pächt was prompted to attribute the decorative lettering to Holbein. It was also in 1528 that the artist painted Kratzer's portrait (Paris, Louvre, inv.no.1343; Rowlands, *Holbein*, col.pl.19) whom Holbein had known at least since May the previous year, and possibly since he had first arrived in England, and who was to remain a lifelong friend.

For another jewellery in which the initials are joined with a lovers' knot, see no.209 II (g).

(d) Design for a pendant in the form of a monogram HI, set with an emerald and three suspended pearls

Pen and brown ink with watercolour. 7.2 × 4.8cm

PROVENANCE: Sloane bequest, 1753

5308–116

LITERATURE: Reid, pl.13; His, pl.xliii, 2; LB, ii, p.335, no.27f; Chamberlain, ii, p.280, pl.48b; Ganz, p.64, no.326, repr.; White, p.566, no.118; Birmingham, *Jewellery*, p.101, no.444, VI; VAM, *Court Jewels*, pp.118f., no.G.10, 2f

It can hardly be doubted that this design was intended for a pendant to be made for Queen Jane Seymour, between the time of her marriage to Henry VIII on 30 May 1536 and her death on 24 October 1537 (see also no.206(c), evidently as a companion to the present drawing). Although such a jewel was not in the inventory made after the Queen's death (see *Letters and Papers. Foreign and Domestic, of the reign of Henry VIII*, edited by J.Gairdner, London, xii, pt.2, 1891, p.340, no.973), this does reveal that the Queen possessed a pomander, whose design incorporated the Queen's and King's initials (listed as 'It[em] Greate pomander of golde with hand and cro[w]ne' (British Library, Royal Ms 7 C.XVI, fol.16)).

239

207a

207b

207c

207d

207 (a) Design for a metalwork book-cover

Pen and black ink with black, grey, and yellow wash 7.9 × 5.9 cm

PROVENANCE: Sloane bequest, 1753

5308–8

LITERATURE: Reid, pl.8; R.Marsham, *Archaeologia*, xliv, pt.ii, 1873, p.259; Woltmann, i, p.440, ii, p.134 under no.191; His, pl.xliv, 1; LB, ii, p.337, no.31a; Chamberlain, ii, p.280; Ganz, p.71, no.405, repr.; White, p.558, no.11; BM, *Jewellery*, pp.173, 175, no.287b, repr.

(b) Design for a metalwork book-cover

Pen and black ink with black, grey and yellow wash. 8.1 × 6 cm

PROVENANCE: Sloane bequest, 1753

5308–10

LITERATURE: Reid, pl.8; R.Marsham, *Archaeologia*, xliv, pt.ii, 1873, p.259, n.a; Woltmann, ii, p.134, under no.191; His, pl.xliv, 2; LB ii, p.337, no.31b; Chamberlain, ii, p.280; Ganz, p.71, no.404, repr.; White, p.558, no.13; BM *Jewellery*, pp.173, 175f., no.287a.

These two designs, no.207(a) and (b), were drawn, possibly as alternatives, for the use of a goldsmith in making covers for girdle prayer books, which were in vogue in the sixteenth century. As Tait indicated, the designs were probably executed in black enamel on gold, as for instance on the girdle-book in the British Museum (Department of Medieval & Later Antiquities, inv.no.94.7–29.1; BM *Jewellery*, col. pl.24). Within the intricate arabesque patterns on each, the initials of the intended recipients, evidently the husband as well as the wife, who would carry the girdle book, are placed in varying order and position. On no.207(a), they are arranged in the upper half, *TWI*, and in the lower, *IWT*; on no.207(b), in the centre are *TIW*, while in the upper corners are *TW*, and in the lower, *WT*.

Chamberlain proposed that these designs were probably intended for the poet, Sir Thomas Wyatt (1503–42); however, Marsham suggested that the initials might either stand for Thomas Wyatt Junior (beheaded, 1554), or for Thomas and Jane Wyatt, Sir Thomas Wyatt the younger having married Jane Hawste in 1537. Of these two suggestions, the latter has more to recommend it, in that such a girdle-book was meant to be carried by a woman; if this is the case, it is not impossible that the designs were produced at about the time of their marriage. This association is given support by the clear kinship between the details of the pattern on no.207(a), and that on the metal cover of a prayer book belonging to the descendants of the Wyatt family, whose whereabouts cannot at present be ascertained; however, in Marsham's publication of the book (R.Marsham, op.cit., p.262, repr.) the cover is reproduced the same size as the original, and is sufficiently clear for one to be able to see how very similar its design is to Holbein's. Indeed, this cover, which lacks any initials, has in my view, been based either directly on no.207(a), or on a derivation from it.

(c) Design for the end of a jewellery casket

Pen and black ink with black and yellow wash. 11.5 × 7.9 cm

PROVENANCE: Sloane bequest, 1753

5308–1

LITERATURE: Reid, pl.8; His, pl.xliv, 3; LB, ii, p.337, no.31c; Chamberlain, ii, p.280; Ganz, p.71, under no.403; White, p.558, no.4

(d) Design for the end of a jewellery casket

Pen and black ink with black and yellow wash. 11.3 × 7.9 cm

PROVENANCE: Sloane bequest, 1753

5308–5

LITERATURE: Reid, pl.8; His, pl.xliv, 4; LB, ii, p.337, no.31d; Chamberlain, ii, p.280; Ganz, p.71, no.403, repr.; White, p.558, no.8

No.207(c) and (d) are alternative designs for a casket with elaborate arabesque ornament, and may perhaps be linked through scale, technique and medium, with the foregoing designs for metalwork book-covers, no.207(a) and (b); like them, they may have been executed for the Wyatt family.

208 *Designs for personal adornments: pendants, medallions, etc.*

(a) Design for a seal of Charles Brandon, Duke of Suffolk

Pen and black ink with grey wash. Cut diagonally. 4.7 × 4.7 cm

PROVENANCE: Sloane bequest, 1753

5908–44

LITERATURE: Reid, pl.4; Woltmann, i, p.439, ii, p.136, no.199, 44; His, pl.xl, 1; LB, ii, pp.335f., no.29a; Chamberlain, ii, p.280, pl.50,4; Ganz, p.69, no.387, repr.; White, p.561, no.47

Inscribed by the artist in black ink around the outer edge, *CAROLVS. DVX. SVFFYCIE. PRO. HONORE. SVO. RICHEMOND*, and on the garter, *HONY. SOYT. QVI. MAL. Y. PENSE*.

The reference in the inscription to 'the Honour of Richmond' enables us to date the drawing with reasonable accuracy. From the Inventory of Exchequer, Augmentation Office (Public Record Office, E.318, no.1076; the document was discovered by Miss Margaret Condon) we learn that the 1st Duke of Suffolk (d.1545) received by exchange in the twenty-ninth year of Henry VIII's reign (i.e. 22 April 1537–21 April 1538) and amongst grants of Crown Lands chiefly in Lincolnshire, the office of feodary of the

208b   208c   208g

Honour of Richmond. All these lands were then called 'Richmondlands' as they had been formerly in the possession of the late Duke of Richmond and Somerset, Henry Fitzroy, an illegitimate son of the King, who had died on 22 July 1536. It is highly likely that this design was ordered from Holbein by the Duke of Suffolk on gaining the office of feodary, most probably when the grant was made, or shortly afterwards. An impression of this seal has not been traced, despite extensive enquiries.

(b) Design for a medallion with a device: a hand issuing from a cloud resting on a closed book

Pen and black ink with grey wash. Cut octagonally. 5.5 × 5.5 cm

PROVENANCE: Sloane bequest, 1753

5308–22

LITERATURE: Waagen, *Treasures*, i, p.203; Reid, pl.4; Woltmann, i, p.439, ii, p.136, no.199, 22; His, pl.xl, 2; LB, ii, p.336, no.29b; Chamberlain, ii, pp.284–5, pl.50, 7; Ganz, p.69, no.338, repr.; White, p.559, no.25

Inscribed by the artist in black ink in the cartouche, SERVAR' VOGLIO/QVEL CHE HO/GVIRATO (I desire to observe that which I have sworn).

See no.208(c).

(c) Design for a medallion with a device: a hand issuing from a cloud resting on a closed book

Pen and black ink with brown wash. Diameter: 5.5 cm

PROVENANCE: Sloane bequest, 1753

5308–34

LITERATURE: Waagen, *Treasures*, i, p.203; Reid, pl.4; Woltmann, as above; His, pl.xl, 3; LB, ii, p.336, no.29c; Chamberlain, ii, pp.284–5; Ganz, p.69, no.389, repr.; White, p.560, no.37

Inscribed by the artist in black ink on the cartouche with the same motto in Italian as no.208(b).

No.208(c) is an alternative design for the preceding, described, probably mistakenly, by Ganz as for a seal. It may be assumed that the book on which the oath is taken is the Bible, and the hillock on which it is placed doubtless symbolises steadfastness.

(d) Shield with the charge of the arms of Holbein

Pen and black ink with blue wash. 2.1 × 2.1 cm

PROVENANCE: Sloane bequest, 1753

5308–154

LITERATURE: Reid, pl.4; His, pl.xl, 4; LB, ii, p.336, no.29d; Ganz, p.70, no.395, repr.; White, p.568, no.158

See no.208(e) for a discussion of the different designs with the artist's arms.

(e) The arms of Hans Holbein

Pen and black ink, touched with gold and blue wash. Diameter: 4.3 cm

PROVENANCE: Sloane bequest, 1753

5308–42

LITERATURE: Reid, pl.4; Woltmann, ii, p.136, no.199, 42; His, pl.xl, 5; LB, ii, p.336, no.29e; Chamberlain, ii, pp.284, pl.50, 6; Ganz, p.70, no.394, repr.; White, p.561, no.45

No.208(d) and 208(f) of the artist's arms in an ornamental shield were clearly drawn as alternative designs for some kind of personal adornment, probably an enamelled brooch. Holbein's arms are also recorded on a panel painting, formerly in the Himmelszunft (the artists' guild) at Basel, and now in the Historisches Museum there. It is inscribed *Hans Holbein de Maller* (Ganz, *Holbein*, p.xl).

No.208(e) is a full heraldic representation of Holbein's

arms with crest, helm and mantling. There are important differences between Holbein's arms as recorded in the Guild-painting and as recorded by the artist himself in this group of drawings, whose attribution to Holbein is in no doubt. For instance, Holbein represents the bull's head in silver while it is black in the painting. The field is blue in two of the drawings and gold in the painting. Of the two sources, we should give preference to the artist's own design rather than the painting, which is in any case undistinguished and more than likely not even early sixteenth century in date.

(f) Shield with the charge of the arms of Holbein

Pen and black ink. Diameter: 2cm

PROVENANCE: Sloane bequest, 1753

5308–164

LITERATURE: Reid, pl.4; His, pl.xl, 6; LB, ii, p.336, no.29f; Chamberlain, ii, p.284; Ganz, p.70, no.393, repr.; White, p.569, no.168

See no.208(e).

(g) Design for a medallion set with a single central stone (perhaps with the death of Pyramus)

Illustrated on p.242.

Pen and black ink with grey wash. Diameter: 5.4cm

PROVENANCE: Sloane bequest, 1753

5308–28

LITERATURE: Reid, pl.4; Woltmann, i, p.439, ii, p.136, no.199, 28; His, pl.xl, 7; LB, ii, p.336, no.28g; Chamberlain, ii, p.284, pl.50,9; Ganz, pp.59f., no.280, repr.; White, p.560, no.31

A boy is depicted lying under a fountain, from which jets of water pour over him. It is interesting to note that 'a Broche of thistory of Piramys & Tysbe wt a fayr table

Diamond in it' is listed in the inventory of the jewels belonging to the Lady Mary, daughter of King Henry VIII, 1542–6 (see F.Madden, *Privy Purse expenses of the Princess Mary, daughter of King Henry VIII*, London, 1831).

(h) Design for a circular pendant, probably with the death of Queen Dido

Pen and black ink with grey wash, and touched with yellow wash heightened with white bodycolour (oxidised). 5.3 × 4.2cm

PROVENANCE: Sloane bequest, 1753

5308–15

LITERATURE: Waagen, *Treasures*, i, p.203; Reid, pl.4; Woltmann, i, p.439, ii, p.136, no.199, 15; His, pl.xl, 8; LB, ii, p.336, no.29h; Chamberlain, ii, p.284; Ganz, p.61, no.291, repr.; White, p.559, no.18

The pendant is set with a central stone which, as it is placed in the midst of the flame rising from the pyre, was evidently a ruby.

(i) Design for a medallion with a pair of compasses, serpents, dolphins and cornucopias

Pen and black ink with black wash. 4.9 × 5.1cm

PROVENANCE: Sloane bequest, 1753

5308–40

LITERATURE: Reid, pl.4; His, pl.xl, 9; LB, ii, p.336, no.29i; Chamberlain, ii, pp.286ff., pl.50,8; White, p.561, no.43

Inscribed by the artist in black ink on an entwined ribbon, *PRVDENTEMENT ET PAR COMPAS INCONTINENT VIENDRAS* 'You would come at once [or unchaste], prudently and by calculation'. Such double meanings were readily understood by and appealed to the courtiers of Henry's court. Anne Boleyn was, of course, fluent in French, but from what one knows it is unlikely that this device would have found favour with her, although when she fell from grace she was accused of gross impropriety of behaviour.

208h

208i

208k

(k) Design for a medallion with, at the centre, the Annunciation, surrounded by a border of marigolds

Illustrated on p.243

Pen and black ink with green and yellow washes. Diameter: 5.9cm

PROVENANCE: Sloane bequest, 1753

5308–19

LITERATURE: Reid, pl.4; Woltmann, i, pp.438–9, ii, p.136, no.199,19; His, pl.xl, 10; LB, ii, p.336, no.29k; Chamberlain, ii, p.284; Ganz, p.58, no.265, repr.; White, p.559, no.22

Inscribed by the artist in black ink in the frame of the Annunciation, *ORIGO MVNDI MELIORIS* 'the origin of a better world'. The subject has probably been effaced by an iconoclast.

(1) Design for a medallion with, at the centre, the Holy Trinity, surrounded by a border of red roses

Pen and black ink with green and red washes. Diameter: 5.8cm

PROVENANCE: Sloane bequest, 1753

5308–13

LITERATURE: Reid, pl.4; Woltmann, i, p.439, ii, p.136, no.199, 13; His, pl.xl, 11; LB, ii, p.336, no.29l; Chamberlain, ii, p.284, pl.50,5; Ganz, p.57, no.264, repr.; White, p.559, no.16

Inscribed by the artist in black ink in the frame of the Holy Trinity, *TRINITATIS GLORIA SATIABIMVR* 'We will be filled with the glory of the Trinity'.

This is either a design for the reverse of or an alternative for no.208(k).

2081

209 Cyphers, and jewellery formed with cyphers

I CYPHERS OF ROMAN LETTERS

(a) The letters, AHNLIO

Pen and black ink. 2.4 × 4cm

PROVENANCE: Sloane bequest, 1753

5308–119

LITERATURE: Reid, pl.12; Woltmann, ii, p.135, under no.199; His, pl.xxxix, 10; LB, ii, p.344, no.38q; Ganz, p.65, no.340, repr.; White, p.566, no.121

(b) The letters, THEOSYBLA

Pen and black ink. Diameter: 4.3cm

PROVENANCE: Sloane bequest, 1753

5308–110

LITERATURE: Woltmann, as above; LB, ii, p.341, no.38e; Ganz, p.65, no.341, repr.; White, p.565, no.112

(c) The letters, CTPNAESO

Pen and black ink. 2.3 × 3.5cm

PROVENANCE: Sloane bequest, 1753

5308–120

LITERATURE: Reid, pl.12; Woltmann, as above; His, pl.xxxix, 4; LB, ii, p.341, no.38k; Ganz, p.65, no.333, repr.; White, p.566, no.122

(d) The letters, LONHVAYGIM

Pen and black ink with a background of black wash. Diameter: 3.6cm

PROVENANCE: Sloane bequest, 1753

5308–108

LITERATURE: Woltmann, as above; His, pl.xxxix, 3; LB, ii, p.344, no.38i; Ganz, p.66, no.344, repr.; White, p.565, no.110

(e) The letters, MTHFNRADOGV

Pen and black ink.
4.5 × 4.5 cm

PROVENANCE: Sloane
bequest, 1753

5308–113

LITERATURE: Woltmann,
as above; His, pl.xxxix, 2;
LB, ii, p.341, no.38h;
Ganz, p.65, no.338, repr.;
White, p.566, no.115

(f) The letters, ATLHENRSIGH

Pen and black ink with a background
of black wash. Diameter: 2.8cm

PROVENANCE: Sloane bequest, 1753

5308–9

LITERATURE: Woltmann, as above; His, pl.xxxix, 1 (incorrectly
reproduced); LB, ii, p.341, no.38g; Ganz, p.66, no.343, repr.;
White, p.558, no.12

(g) The letters, TWES

Pen and black ink. 2 × 3.1 cm

PROVENANCE: Sloane bequest, 1753

5308–38

LITERATURE: Reid, pl.12; Woltmann, as above; His, pl.xxxix,
12; LB, ii, p.342, no.38s; Ganz, p.65, no.342, repr.; White,
pp.560f., no.41

Jewellery with a cypher of Roman letters

(h) Pendant with four pearls and the letters, HNAVGRSYD

Pen and black ink. 3.2 × 3 cm

PROVENANCE: Sloane bequest, 1753

5308–14

LITERATURE: Reid, pl.12; Woltmann, as above; His, pl.xxxix,
7; LB, ii, p.341, no.38n; Ganz, p.15, no.331, repr.; White, p.559,
no.17

Cypher with Roman letters of minimal floriation

(i) The letters, ENLRAOD

Pen and black ink. 1.8 × 2.8cm

PROVENANCE: Sloane bequest, 1753

5308–4

LITERATURE: Woltmann, as above; LB, ii, p.341, no.38f; Ganz,
p.65, no.339, repr.; White, p.558, no.7

II CYPHERS WITH FLORIATED INTERLACED LETTERS

(a) The letters, ABCE

Pen and black ink. 2.1 × 2.6cm

PROVENANCE: Sloane bequest, 1753

5308–7

LITERATURE: Woltmann, as above; LB,
ii, p.341, no.38c; Ganz, p.65, no.336,
repr.; White, p.558, no.10

(b) The letters, ABCE

Pen and black ink. 2.2 × 2.8cm

PROVENANCE: Sloane bequest, 1753

5308–6

LITERATURE: Woltmann, as above; LB,
ii, p.341, no.38a; Ganz, p.65, no.334,
repr.; White, p.558, no.9

(c) The letters, ABCE

Pen and black ink. 2 × 2.7cm

PROVENANCE: Sloane bequest, 1753

5303–3

LITERATURE: Woltmann, as above; LB,
ii, p.341, no.38d; Ganz, p.65, no.337,
repr.; White, p.558, no.6

(d) The letters, HISA

Pen and black ink with light brown wash.
Sheet cut octagonally 2.4 × 2.4cm

PROVENANCE: Sloane bequest, 1753

5308–11

LITERATURE: Woltmann, as above; LB, ii, p.341, no.38b; Ganz,
p.65, no.335, repr.; White, p.559, no.14

This combination of letters differently arranged occurs
carved twice on the choir stalls of King's College Chapel,
Cambridge, in addition to the repetitions of the *HR* [Hen-
ricus Rex] and *RA* [Regina Anna], both on the stalls and
the screen. It is not, however, likely, and the existence of

this design supports this, that Macquoid is correct in his grim interpretation of the letters as standing for 'Henry Rex. Anne.Jane Seymour' (see P.Macquoid *A History of English Furniture*, i, *the Age of Oak, 1500–1660*, London, 1904, p.27). The probable solution to the cypher would be H [Henry] I [perhaps, *Indispute* or *Inimitable*] S[*Serviteur*] A [*Anne*].

(e) The letters, SEHINPK

Pen and black ink. 2.2 × 2.9 cm

PROVENANCE: Sloane bequest, 1753

5308–36

LITERATURE: Reid, pl.12; Woltmann, as above; His, pl.xxxix, 6; LB, ii, p.341, no.38m; Ganz, p.65, no.332, repr.; White, p.560, no.39

Jewellery with floriated letters

(f) Oval pendant with leaf ornament, set with ten stones, and formed with the cypher, AVRNTEKCIS

Pen and black ink. 5.7 × 6.9 cm

PROVENANCE: Sloane bequest, 1753

5308–114

LITERATURE: Reid, pl.12; Woltmann, as above; His, pl.xxxix, 8; LB, ii, p.341, no.38o; Ganz, p.64, no.325, repr.; White, p.561, no.116

(g) The letters, R and E linked with a lovers' knot

Pen and black ink. Three pendant pearls were added by another hand, perhaps the jeweller's, in brown ink. 5.4 × 4.2 cm

PROVENANCE: Sloane bequest, 1753

5308–46

LITERATURE: Reid, pl.12; His, pl.xxxix, 5; LB, ii, p.341, no.38l; Ganz, p.64, no.327, repr.; White, p.561, no.49

Such trinkets were intended as private tokens of affection. So it is not surprising that often we cannot be sure for whom they were made.

(h) Pendant with a single central stone and the monogram of floriated letters, HA

Pen and black ink with grey and touches of light yellow washes. 4.8 × 4.5 cm

PROVENANCE: Sloane bequest, 1753

5308–115

LITERATURE: Reid, pl.12; His, pl.xxxix, 11; LB, ii, p.342, no.38r; Ganz, p.65, no.329, repr.; White, p.566, no.117; Rowlands, *Holbein*, p.88

(i) A small shield with the monogram AH joined with a lover's knot; a side view of the same shield

Pen and black ink. 3.1 × 3.1 cm

PROVENANCE: Sloane bequest, 1753

5308–79

LITERATURE: Reid, pl.12; Woltmann, as above; His, pl.xxxix, 9; LB, ii, p.341, no.38p; Ganz, p.73, no.424, repr.; White, p.563, no.82; Rowlands, *Holbein*, p.88

This, and the preceding design no.209II(h), were clearly produced in connection with Henry VIII and Anne Boleyn's courtship and subsequent marriage, when the King lavished a prodigious quantity of jewellery on Anne.

The foregoing drawings by Holbein, nos.209I and 209II are the only surviving designs for letters, and they were produced by the artist at the English court in connection with his work for jewellers. The use of such lettering in such elaborate and complicated cyphers must mean that

209II(f)

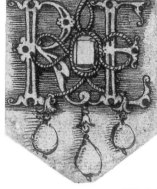

209II(g)

209II(h)

they were devised to transmit a message that would be understood by a small inner circle of intimates or just two lovers. They could have also been invented to provide a tantalising game, following the still-surviving codes of courtly love. So we should not be surprised that their import remains unknown today, except in the few instances explained above. The intricately interlaced and conjoined Roman letters, although distorted by elongation and interweaving to form a cypher, nevertheless follow in their characteristics the noble examples familiar to Holbein from the founts used by the workshop of Froben in Basel and Christoph Froschauer in Zürich, for whom he provided designs for title-pages, decorated initial letters, printer's marks and other features. None of his designs for such work survive, however. Holbein's painted portraits with their inscriptions in distinguished Roman capital letters demonstrate the importance that he attached to fine lettering. It is worth comparing his use of cypher, for secret messages, with the method propounded for the making of cyphers, through interleaved lettering, by Geofrey Tory, the French bookseller and printer in his book on the proper proportion of Roman letters, *Champleury*, Paris, 1526. It inevitably owed a good deal to Dürer's discourse and designs for Roman letters in his *Underweysung der Messung* just published in the previous year, but that did not prevent Tory from being rather patronising about his German colleague. Tory in the construction of his cyphers used neither elongation nor an additive system. Instead he treated each letter as a solid body as though carved in wood or metal. His interleaving involves one letter slotting through a cut in another letter, a method used only occasionally by Holbein in his letters in no.209. This device means that the linking of the number of letters that Holbein was required to join would not have been possible, according to Tory, who warned against cyphers of more than a few letters. Holbein, however, in 209II(e) made use of Tory's method and has interleaved six letters in solid black reasonably successfully so as to disprove the rule about only linking a few letters. He then repeats the usage in two other cyphers of only a few letters each, 209I(g) and 209II(b). Although based on his knowledge of the Roman capitals used in Basel books with leaf-like decoration, the floriated letters drawn here by Holbein are peculiar to him and do not occur elsewhere in his work. The formation of these specially devised letters is basically Roman, to which have been added decorative elements of a late Gothic kind, such as floriated serifs and leaf curves, variants of which may be found in initials in English and French printed books of the period (see, in a rather exaggerated form, the initials of Wynkyn de Worde's printer's mark, cf. *Erasmus*, the Houghton Library, Cambridge, Mass., p.27, pl.iv), and in the lettering on English architectural, especially sepulchral, projects (see the letters forming the name of John Islip (d.1532) on the chantry-chapel of the last Abbot c.1530 in Westminster Abbey, which must have been known to Holbein).

210 Design for a chimney-piece

See colour plate section following p.200

Pen and black ink, with grey, blue and red wash. 53.9 × 42.7cm

PROVENANCE: Earl of Arundel; J.Richardson senior (L.2184); T.Hudson (L.2432; sale Longfords, 1779, 25 March, lot 59, bt *Walpole £4.4s*); H.Walpole (sale, Strawberry Hill, 1842, 17 May, lot 64, bt *Dommes £33-12s*); Graves

1854-7-8-1

LITERATURE: M.L.Cox, *Burlington*, xix, 1911, p.283, col.1; H.Peacham, *Compleat Gentleman*, 1622 & 1634, modern edition, Oxford, 1906, p.128; *The Works of Horatio Walpole, Earl of Orford*, edited by R.Berry, ii, London, 1798, p.460; Waagen, *Treasures Suppl.*, pp.37f.; Reid, pl.1; Woltmann, ii, p.135, no.197; His, pls.xlviii, xlix, 1; BM *Guide*, 1895, p.58, no.291*; LB, ii, p.330, no.16; L.A.Shuffrey, *The English Fireplace*, London, 1912, pp.82ff.; Chamberlain, ii, pp.269f.; Ganz, p.30, no.123, repr.; Schmid, *Holbein*, ii, pp.343, 400, 408ff., 425, iii, p.38, no.141, repr. detail; J.Summerson, *Architecture in Britain 1530–1830*, Harmondsworth, 1955, p.333, n.7; White, p.570, no.188; M.Biddle, *Journal of the British Archaeological Association*, 3rd series, xxix, London, 1966, pp.112–13; S.Béguin, *La Revue du Louvre et des Musées de France*, xx, Paris, 1970, no.1, p.10, repr.; C.Wainwright, *Burlington*, cxiii, 1971, p.258, repr.; NPG, *More*, pp.50f, no.74, repr.; Colvin, *King's Works*, iv, part ii, 1982, p.25

This is almost certainly the design seen by Henry Peacham, which he claimed 'Henry had bespoke for his new built pallace at Bridewell'. The building, which was to be Henry's principal London residence for a few years, was almost complete when the Emperor Charles V stayed there in June 1522. It is mentioned in a letter of 6 June, written by Gasparo Contarini to the Venetian *Signoria*, where he describes the entry of Henry VIII with the Emperor into the city of London and refers to, 'Uno palazo fornito novamente' where they lodged after visiting the Cathedral (St Mark's Library, Venice, Contarini's Original Letter Book, no.167; see R.Brown, *Calendar of Slate Papers. Venetian, etc.*, iii, 1520–6, London, 1869, p.236, no.466). This was undoubtedly a reference to Bridewell, which Henry later abandoned in favour of Whitehall (formerly York House) of which he took possession after the fall of Wolsey in 1530. As Holbein did not arrive in England for the first time before the late summer of 1526, the design must clearly be unconnected with Bridewell; however, from the lavish heraldic details of the design we know that it was intended for a royal building.

As Summerson noted, this drawing is the only certain evidence we have of Holbein's architectural work in England. Even so, there have been recent attempts, admittedly not at all convincing, to reattribute it to Nicholas Bellin of Modena (c.1490–1569), by Biddle and then Béguin. The former, however, who not surprisingly saw some French influence in aspects of the design, went too far in considering this grounds for doubting Holbein's authorship. Sylvie Béguin assembled a small group of architectural studies, including no.210, and followed Otto Kurz's initial suggestion (*Burlington*, lxxxii/iii, 1943, p.81) of an attribution to Bellin.

Contrary to her intention, her article convinces one that this drawing cannot be by Bellin, whose generally accepted work shows the strong influence of the Fontainebleau school, especially that of his master, Francesco Primaticcio (1504–70). The present drawing, by contrast, has none of these reflections, but stylistically may be placed towards the end of Holbein's career, *c*.1537–43.

If the design was employed in the production of a chimney-piece, then one can certainly see it as the predecessor of the work of later decades, of which the grand chimney-piece at Loseley of 1562–8 is a fine example. This could have been copied or adapted from such work at Nonsuch Palace, given the known connection between the two buildings in the person of Sir Thomas Cawarden (see J. Dent, *The Quest for Nonsuch*, 1962, pp.42–53).

211 Design for a clock-salt, comprised of an hour-glass, a sun-dial, and a compass for which there is a separate study on the left

Pen and black ink with grey wash, and red wash on the compass. The sheet has been cut down on all sides. 41 × 21.3cm

PROVENANCE: P. J. Mariette (L.1852; sale, Paris, F. Basan, 1775, 15 November and following days, lot 943); H. Walpole (sale, Strawberry Hill, G. Robins, 1842, 17 May, lot 72, bt *Graves £6-16s.-8d.*)

1850-7-13-14

LITERATURE: W. H. Smyth, *Archaeologia*, xxxiii, 1849, pp.15f.; J. Burtt, *Archaeological Journal*, xviii, 1861, p.137; Waagen, *Treasures Suppl.*, p.37; Wornum, *Holbein*, pp.358f.; Reid, pl.3; Woltmann, i, p.444, ii, p.134, no.193; His, pl.47; BM *Guide*, 1895, p.58, no.289; LB, ii, pp.330f., no.17; Chamberlain, ii, pp.276, 286, pl.43; C. Dodgson, *Burlington*, lviii, 1931, pp.226ff.; Ganz, pp.52f., no.220, repr.; O. Pächt, *Burlington*, lxxxiv, 1944, pp.134f., repr. detail; Collins, p.101, repr.; White, p.570, no.187; J. F. Hayward, *Connoisseur*, clxii, 1966, pp.90ff., repr.; Paris, *Mariette*, pp.117f., no.180, repr. (for further literature); Hayward, *Virtuoso Goldsmiths*, p.342, pl.47; *Exhibition of Thirty Old Master Drawings of the Northern Schools*, London, Baskett and Day, 2–26 April 1974, under nos.3 and 4

Inscribed by a contemporary hand in brown ink, on the left-hand door of the clock, *coniunctis/sive novi/lunium pro/20 Annis* and, to the right of the clock, *compassu/superiarus* and, below, *oppō scu*... By a comparison with various manuscripts, Pächt has recognised the handwriting of Nicolaus Kratzer, the Royal Astronomer and Horologer, on Holbein's 'record' drawing of his group portrait of the *Family of Sir Thomas More* (Basel, Kunstmuseum, Kupferstichkabinett, inv.no.1662.31; Rowlands, *Holbein*, pl.188) and on the present drawing in the inscriptions given above. Also inscribed, by another early hand, in brown ink, in the lower left-hand corner, *[S]trena facta pro anthony/deny camerario regis quod/in initio novi anni 1544/regi dedit*; and by a later hand, in brown ink, in the lower right-hand corner, an old collection number, *46*

This design, one of the last of Holbein's works, was, as the above inscription tells us, made for a clock presented by Sir Anthony Denny to Henry VIII on New Year's Day, 1544 (1545 new style) shortly after the artist's death.

211

Denny, gentleman of the Bedchamber, was one of the select initiates who were permitted to 'forge' the royal signature, and was knighted in the September of the same year that the king received this gift from him. Henry VIII had a passion for clocks, on which he spent in three years over £100 (see N. H. Nicolas, *The Privy Purse Expences of King Henry the Eighth from November 1529 to December 1532*, London, 1827, pp.310f.).

The clock consists of an hour-glass within a case on a pedestal, supported on legs with two satyrs. Above the hour-glass stand two putti, each pointing to a metal arc which serves as a sun-dial, their fingers indicating the hour. An alternative design (Ganz, p.53, no.221, repr.) for these putti is also in the British Museum (no.212(a)).

In their liveliness they are reminiscent of the putti on the top of the sketch for a decorative frame at Basel, Kunstmuseum, Kupferstichkabinett, inv.no.1662. 165, 95; Ganz, p.53, no.222, repr.), also from the second English period. Resting on the heads of the putti is a mechanical clock, surmounted with a crown. On its face is a sun with a fiery pointer. To the left of the clock is the compass which no doubt was fitted with the head of the hour-glass case. It seems likely that the sundial top with the two putti either lifted off or was hinged.

There exists an old copy of the present drawing, without the compass and inscriptions, and a copy of a now lost, alternative design, with which the drawing for the putti (no.212) is also connected. These copies, which were formerly the property of Mrs Alfred Noyes, and were exhibited by Baskett and Day in 1974, were dated by Dodgson to 1578/90, on the strength of the watermark of the paper of the copy of the lost design (Dodgson. op.cit., p.227, pls.A and B). This is of the letter 'M' surmounted by a star within a shield, similar to Briquet, 8391 (Lucca, 1578–9; Ferrara, 1580; Fabriano, 1596). Dodgson rightly was not prepared to attribute these copies to Federico Zuccaro (1542/3–1609) as there is nothing about them to associate them stylistically with this artist; they are quite unlike his copies after Holbein's Steelyard Triumphs, which were made when Zuccaro was in London between March 1574 and August 1575, and are now in Berlin-Dahlem (Kupferstichkabinett, inv.nos.HDZ 12886–7). These copies could, in fact, be earlier in date than Dodgson proposed, as a variant of the watermark – Briquet, 8390, not referred to by Dodgson – occurs in Florentine paper of 1529. It is not possible to be sure as to whether an early, or, as Dodgson proposed, a later dating is the more likely. The most we can be certain of is that they were produced in the sixteenth century and that the original of the alternative design, although evidently rejected by Denny, was initially considered worth preserving. There are no particular grounds for supporting Dodgson's suggestion that the copyist was a Flemish draughtsman.

212 (a) Two putti for the sun-dial on the Denny clock-salt

Pen and black and brown ink and grey wash. 8.3 × 6.7 cm

PROVENANCE: Sloane bequest, 1753

5308–86

LITERATURE: Waagen, *Treasures*, i, p.204; Wornum, *Holbein*, p.358; Woltmann, ii, p.135, no.194; His, pl.xlvi, 1; LB; ii, p.332, no.22 a; Chamberlain, ii, p.276; Ganz, p.53, no.221, repr.; White, p.564, no.88

(b) Terminal figures of satyrs supporting a base

Pen and black ink with grey wash, somewhat smudged. Outlines partly silhouetted. 7.5 × 3.8 cm

PROVENANCE: Sloane bequest, 1753

5308–49

LITERATURE: Woltmann, ii, p.135, under no.199; His, pl.xlvi, 2; LB, ii, p.332, no.22 b; Ganz, pp.51f., no.215, repr.; White, p.561, no.52

212a

212b

212c

212d

212e

212f

(c) A nude woman seated on a globe

Pen and black ink with grey wash. Silhouetted around the outlines. 7.6 × 4.3 cm

PROVENANCE: Sloane bequest, 1753

5308–72

LITERATURE: Woltmann, as above; His, pl.xlvi, 3; LB, ii, p.332,
no.22 c; Ganz, p.54, no.238, repr.; White, p.563, no.75

(d) Design for a foliated ornament with a satyr's head

Pen and black ink with grey wash. 3.1 × 3.5 cm

PROVENANCE: Sloane bequest, 1753

5308–12

LITERATURE: Woltmann, as above; His, pl.xlvi, 4; LB, ii, p.332,
no.22 d; Ganz, p.73, no.428, repr.; White, p.559, no.15

(e) A nude woman reclining against a globe

Pen and black ink with grey wash. Silhouetted around the outlines. 5.1 × 4.5 cm

PROVENANCE: Sloane bequest, 1753

5308–73

LITERATURE: Woltmann, as above; His, pl.xlvi, 5; LB, ii, p.332,
no.22 e; Ganz, p.54, no.239, repr.; White, p.563, no.76.

(f) Stem of a cup

Pen and black ink with black and grey wash, and with some
traces of a free underdrawing in black chalk. Cut out irregularly.
10.7 × 12.6 cm

PROVENANCE: Sloane bequest, 1753

5308–124

LITERATURE: Woltmann, as above; His, pl.xlvi, 6; LB, ii, p.332,
no.22 f; Ganz, p.51, no.214, repr.; White, p.566, no.26

No.212(a) is a vigorous preliminary sketch for the putti
on the crown of the clock-salt ordered by Sir Anthony
Denny, for which Holbein's final drawing survives (no.211),
as well as two drawn copies, one of which records Holbein's
initial design in which the principal difference is that the
putti are represented with wings, each with one arm raised
to grasp the central pillar or dial, as in no.212(a). The

213

remaining studies (no.212(b)–(f)) are all designs for details of different pieces of metalwork, produced during the artist's second English period (1534–43). No.212(b), (c), and (e) are drawings for parts of the base of large ornamental dishes: (b) includes a diagram showing how the herms are to be screwed to the sockel; (c) and (e) are decorative features for the feet of a metalwork vessel. Further studies for similar figures intended to decorate dishes or other vessels are also in the British Museum (Ganz, p.54, nos.232–7, repr.). No.212(f) is a finely conceived stem of a cup in the new Renaissance style of metalwork similar to the designs for a fruit-dish in Basel (Ganz, p.51, no.212, repr.).

213 Henry VII and Henry VIII

Brush and black ink, with purple, brown, grey and black wash, drawn on cut-out sheets, laid down and mounted on canvas. 257.8 × 137.1 cm

PROVENANCE: John, 1st Lord Lumley; Earls of Scarborough; 2nd Duke of Devonshire by 1727 (seen by William Cole at Hardwick Hall in 1775, and later appears hanging in the Long Gallery there in a watercolour by David Cox, of c.1839; at Chatsworth from c.1912); accepted by the Treasury in lieu of death duties, and given to the National Portrait Gallery, 1958

London, National Portrait Gallery, 4027

LITERATURE: Woltmann, i, p.418, repr., ii, pp.129–30, no,167; BFAC, 1909, pp.88f., no.40; Chamberlain, ii, pp.97ff., 351; L. Cust, *Walpole Society*, vi, 1917–18, p.21, no.4; G. Vertue, *Walpole Society*, xx, 1931–2, p.36; Ganz, pp.29f., no.122, repr.; R. Strong, *National Portrait Gallery: Tudor and Jacobean Portraits*, London, 1969, pp.153ff., repr.; G. Vertue, *Walpole Society*, xxx, 1951–2, p.72; NPG, *More*, p.48, no.71, repr.; Rowlands, *Holbein*, pp.225f., no.L.14b, pl.195 (for further literature)

This is the only known cartoon by Holbein. It was executed for part of the left-hand side of the Whitehall Mural, which was completed in 1537, and is the only piece surviving by the artist's own hand of his most important commission for Henry VIII. From the cartoon and painted copies of the mural, we know that it depicted Henry VII and Elizabeth of York, and Henry VIII and Jane Seymour, the mother of the heir, Prince Edward, standing in a grand setting either side of an altar, on which verses, whose message is essential to the meaning of the painting, proclaim the power and continuance of the Tudor dynasty, and its triumph over the Papacy and Henry VIII's protection of the new religion. Until destroyed in the Whitehall Palace fire in 1698, this wall-painting was one of the sights of London seen by important visitors, such as the Moravian nobleman, Waldstein, in 1600 (see *The Diary of Baron Waldstein*, edited by G. W. Groos, London, 1981, p.57) and originally would have been seen by all who were granted an audience with the King prior to entering the royal presence. After a change to the function of the room, it became known as the 'Privy Chamber' Mural. Its overall dimensions can be estimated as approximately 270 × 360 cm.

The head of King Henry VIII, which has been drawn on its own sheet within the cartoon, is derived from the painted portrait now in the Thyssen collection, Lugano (inv.no.197; Rowlands, *Holbein*, col.pl.25) the only portrait of Henry VIII to have survived by Holbein's own hand. But we know from the copies and the other portraits based on the Whitehall Mural that in the finished work, unlike the cartoon, the King's face is shown in a frontal position. It is thus very likely that he may have sat afresh for Holbein after the cartoon was completed. But there is no reason to think that the drawing of the King's head, in a frontal position, in Munich (Staatliche Graphische Sammlung, inv.no.12,785) could be the study in question, since it appears to be the work of a studio assistant made after the mural for future use. It is interesting to note that the inscription on the *verso* of this sheet, *Hanns Swarttung*, may conceivably refer to the name of the assistant in question. (Ganz, p.79, no.c.1 repr.; Woodward, no.1, repr.

The figure here of Henry VIII, standing with his legs astride, is the abiding image of him. But it will not be readily appreciated that this impressive effect results from a calculated falsification of the proportions of the King's body. From his armour we know that Henry was 6ft 3in tall. The distance from his knees to the ground was a quarter the length of his entire body, whereas Holbein makes this proportion a third of his body. Holbein's majestic figure was, however, perpetuated in the mind by his followers, who used the Whitehall portrait of the monarch as the model for a succession of full-length portraits. Of these, one of the finest, and probably one of the earliest, is that formerly at East Knoyle, Wiltshire, and now in the Walker Art Gallery, Liverpool; others are at Belvoir Castle and Petworth. Another important derivative is that by Hans Eworth, dated *1567*, in Trinity College, Cambridge. Of the three-quarter or half-length portraits based on the Whitehall Mural, the finest is the three-quarter length in the Galleria Nazionale, Rome (Rowlands, *Holbein*, pl.199) which, from its inscription, would seem to have been painted in 1539/40 before the King's marriage to Anne of Cleves. Ganz at one time thought it an original by Holbein, only ultimately rejecting this idea because of a certain weakness in the rendering of some of the detail. The likelihood is that it is a very good studio work.

Bibliography

Works referred to in abbreviated form

Acta Hist. Art.: Acta Historiae Artium. Academiae Scientiarum Hungaricae. Budapest, 1954–.

Add. Manuscripts: Catalogue of Additions to the Manuscripts in the British Museum, 1846–7. London, 1864.

Albertina Catalogue: Beschreibender Katalog der Handzeichnungen in der graphischen Sammlung Albertina. Edited by Alfred Stix. Vols.iv and v: *Die Zeichnungen der deutschen Schulen bis zum Beginn des Klassizismus.* Hans Tietze, E.Tietze-Konrat, Otto Benesch and Karl Garzarolli-Thurnlackh. Vienna, 1933.

Albertina, *Dürer:* Walter Koschatzky and Alice Strobl, *Die Dürerzeichnungen der Albertina zum 500 Geburtstag.* Exhib. cat., Vienna, Albertina, 12 Oct.–19 Dec., 1971.

Altdorfer: Albrecht Altdorfer und sein Kreis: Gedächtnisausstellung zum 400. Todesjahr Altdorfers. Amtlicher Katalog, Munich, 1938. Engelbert Baumeister *et al.*

Andersson, *Ausgew. Zeichn. Graf.:* Christiane D. Andersson, *Dirnen-Krieger-Narren. Ausgewählte Zeichnungen von Urs Graf.* Basel, 1978.

Andersson, *Detroit:* Christiane D. Andersson and Charles Talbot, *From a Mighty Fortress. Prints, Drawings and Books in the Age of Luther 1483–1546.* Exhib. cat., Detroit Institute of Arts, 3 Oct.–22 Nov. 1981; Ottawa, National Gallery of Canada, 4 Dec. 1981–31 Jan. 1982; Kunstsammlungen der Veste Coburg, 18 July–5 Aug. 1982.

Andersson, *Graf.:* Christiane D. Andersson, *Popular Lore and Imagery in the Drawings of Urs Graf (c.1485–1529).* Doctoral dissertation, Stanford University, 1977.

Anz. and Zeitschr. f. schweiz. Arch.: Anzeiger für schweizerische Altertumskunde, Indicateur d'antiquités suisses. Zürich, 1869–98. Neue Folge, 1899–1937. Continued as: *Zeitschrift für schweizerische Archaeologie und Kunstgeschichte.* Zürich, 1939–.

Anz. Germ. Nat.: Anzeiger des Germanischen Nationalmuseums. Leipzig and Nuremberg, 1884–.

Anzelewsky: Fedja Anzelewsky, *Dürer. His Art and Life.* London, 1980.

Anzelewsky, *Dürer:* Fedja Anzelewsky, *Albrecht Dürer. Das malerische Werk.* Berlin, 1971.

Archaeologia: Archaeologia. London, 1770–.

Archaeological Journal: The Archaeological Journal. London, 1845–.

Archiv f. Kunstgesch.: Archiv für Kunstgeschichte. Leipzig, 1913–14.

Art Quarterly: The Art Quarterly. Detroit, 1938–79.

Augsburg, *Altdeutsche Gemälde: Staatsgalerie Augsburg, Städtische Kunstsammlungen.* Vol.I, *Altdeutsche Gemälde Katalog.* Edited by Gisela Goldberg. 2nd edition. Munich, 1978.

Augsburg, *Holbein: Hans Holbein der Ältere und die Kunst der Spätgotik.* Exhib. cat., Augsburg, Rathaus, 21 Aug.–7 Nov., 1965. Edited by Bruno Bushart *et al.*

Augsburg, *Umbruch: Welt im Umbruch. Augsburg zwischen Renaissance und Barok.* Exhib. cat., Augsburg, Rathaus, 28 June–28 Sept. 1980. Edited by Rolf Biedermann *et al.* 2 vols.

Austin, *Nuremberg:* Jeffrey Chipps Smith, *Nuremberg. A Renaissance City, 1500–1618.* Exhib. cat., Austin, Archer M. Huntington Art Gallery, University of Texas, 1983.

Baden-Württemberg Jahrbuch: Jahrbuch der Staatlichen Kunstsammlungen in Baden-Württemberg. Munich, 1964–.

Barber Institute Drawings: Hamish Miles and Paul Spencer-Longhurst, *Master Drawings in the Barber Institute.* Exhib. cat., London, Morton Morris, 20 Nov.–12 Dec. 1986.

Barber Institute Handbook: The University of Birmingham. Handbook of the Barber Institute of Fine Arts. With a List of the Collection. 2nd edition. Birmingham, 1983.

Bartsch: Adam Bartsch, *Le Peintre Graveur.* Vienna 1803–21. 21 vols.

Basel, *Baldung:* Paul H. Boerlin, Tilman Falk, Richard W. Gassen and Dieter Koepplin, *Hans Baldung Grien im Kunstmuseum Basel.* Basel, 1978.

Basel, *Cranach:* Dieter Koepplin and Tilman Falk, *Lukas Cranach. Gemälde Zeichnungen Druckgraphik.* Exhib. cat., Basel, Kunstmuseum, 15 June–7 Sept., 1974. 2 vols. (vol.2 published in 1976).

Basel, *Holbein: Die Malerfamilie Holbein in Basel.* Exhib. cat., Basel, Kunstmuseum, 4 June–25 Sept., 1960. Edited by Erwin Treu *et al.*

Basel, *100 Master Drawings:* Hanspeter Landolt, *100 Master Drawings of the 15th and 16th Centuries from the Basel Print Room.* Basel, 1972.

Baum, *Österreichische Galerie:* Elfriede Baum, *Katalog des Museums Mittelalterlicher Österreichischer Kunst. Unteres Belvedere, Wien.* Vienna and Munich, 1971.

Baum, *Schongauer:* Julius Baum, *Martin Schongauer.* Vienna, 1948.

Bayerische Frömmigkeit: Hugo Schnell, *Bayerische Frömmigkeit: Kult und Kunst in 14 Jahrhunderten.* Munich and Zürich, 1965.

Becker: Hanna L. Becker, *Die Handzeichnungen Albrecht Altdorfers.* Munich, 1938.

Becksmann, *Baden & Pfalz:* Rüdiger Becksmann, *Corpus Vitrearum Medii Aevi. Die Mittelalterlichen Glasmalereien in Baden und der Pfalz, ohne Freiburg-im-Breisgau,* II. Berlin, 1979.

Behling, *Grünewald:* Lottlisa Behling, *Die Handzeichnungen des Mathis Gothart Nithart genannt Grünewald.* Weimar, 1955.

Bell: C.F.Bell, *Drawings by the Old Masters in the Library of Christ Church, Oxford.* Oxford, 1914.

Bellm, *Skizzenbuch:* Richard Bellm, *Wolgemuts Skizzenbuch im Berliner Kupferstichkabinett. Ein Beitrag zur Erforschung des graphischen Werkes von Michael Wolgemut und Wilhelm Pleydenwurff.* Strassburg, 1959.

Belvedere: Belvedere. Illustrierte Zeitschrift für Kunstsammler. Vienna, 1922–39.

Benesch, *Collected Writings:* Otto Benesch, *Collected Writings.* Vol.iii, *German and Austrian Art of the 15th and 16th Centuries.* Edited by Eva Benesch. London and New York, 1972.

Benesch, *Oesterr. Handz.:* Otto Benesch, *Oesterreichische Handzeichnungen des XV. und XVI. Jahrhunderts. Die Meisterzeichnung.* Vol.v. Freiburg-im-Breisgau and London, 1936.

Berlin, *Dürer und seine Zeit:* Fedja Anzelewsky, *Dürer und seine Zeit. Meisterzeichnungen aus dem Berliner Kupferstichkabinett.* Exhib. cat., Berlin-Dahlem, Kupferstichkabinett, 25 Nov. 1967–31 March, 1968 (English edition circulated by the Smithsonian Institution, 1965–6).

Berlin Forsch. u. Berichte: Staatliche Museen zu Berlin. Forschungen und Berichte. Kunsthistorisches Beiträge. East Berlin, 1957.

Berlin Jahrbuch: Das Jahrbuch der Berliner Museen. Berlin, 1959–.

Berl. Mus.: Amtliche Berichte aus den königlichen Kunstsammlungen. Berlin, 1907–19. Vols.29–40. Continued as, *Berliner Museen: Berichte aus den preussischen Kunstsammlungen.* 1920–43. Vols.41–64. Neue Folge, 1951–.

Bern, *Deutsch: Niklaus Manuel Deutsch: Maler Dichter Staatsmann.* Exhib. cat., Bern, Kunstmuseum, 22 Sept.–2 Dec., 1979. Edited by Cäsar Menz and Hugo Wagner.

Bernhard, *Schongauer: Martin Schongauer und sein Kreis, Druckgraphik Handzeichnungen.* Edited by Marianne Bernhard. Munich, 1980.

Beutler & Thiem, *Holbein:* Christian Beutler and Gunther Thiem, *Hans Holbein der Ältere. Die spätgotische Altar- und Glasmalerei.* Augsburg, 1960.

BFAC: Burlington Fine Arts Club, London: Exhibitions with printed catalogues, 1870–1939.

Birmingham, *Jewellery: Exhibition of Gemstones and Jewellery.* Birmingham City Museum and Art Gallery, 17 Feb.–16 March, 1960.

Bjurström, *German Drawings: Drawings in Swedish Public Collections 1.* Per Bjurström, *German Drawings.* Nationalmuseum, Stockholm, 1972.

Blankenagel: Gabriele Blankenagel, *Studien zu Ludwig Refinger.* Inaugural-Dissertation des Ludwig-Maximilians-Universität zu München. Munich, 1973.

BM, *Animals in Art: Animals in Art.* Edited by Jessica Rawson. Published in connection with the exhibition, 'Animals in Art', The British Museum, Dec. 1977–Feb., 1978. London, 1977.

BM *Guide*, 1895: Sidney Colvin, *British Museum. Guide to an exhibition of Drawings and Engravings by the Old Masters, principally from the Malcolm Collection.* London, 1895.

BM *Guide*, 1901: *British Museum. Guide to an exhibition of Drawings and Sketches by Old Masters, principally acquired between 1895 and 1901.* London, 1901.

BM *Guide*, 1928: Campbell Dodgson and K.T.Parker, *British Museum. Guide to the Woodcuts, Drawings, and Engravings of Albrecht Dürer in the Department of Prints and Drawings exhibited in commemoration of the fourth centenary of the artist's death on April 6th, 1528.* London, 1928.

BM, *Jewellery: Jewellery through 7000 Years.* Exhib. cat., London, The British Museum, 1976. Edited by Hugh Tait.

BM, *Portrait Drawings: Portrait Drawings XV–XX centuries.* Exhib. cat., London, The British Museum, Department of Prints and Drawings, 2 Aug.–31 Dec., 1974.

BM *Yearbook: The British Museum Yearbook.* London, 1976–80. 4 vols.

BMQ: The British Museum Quarterly. London, 1926–73.

Bock, *Berlin:* Staatliche Museen zu Berlin, *Die Zeichnungen alter Meister im Kupferstichkabinett.* Edited by Max J. Friedländer. Elfried Bock, *Die Deutschen Meister. Beschreibendes Verzeichnis sämtlicher Zeichnungen mit 193 Lichtdrucktafeln.* Berlin, 1921. 2 vols.

Bock, *Erlangen:* Elfried Bock, *Die Zeichnungen in der Universitätsbibliothek Erlangen.* Frankfurt-am-Main, 1929. 2 vols.

Bock, *Grünewald:* Franz Bock, *Die Werke des Mathias Grünewald.* Strassburg, 1904.

Bradley, *Introduction:* J.W.Bradley, *Historical Introduction to the Collection of Illuminated Letters and Borders in the National Art Library, Victoria and Albert Museum.* London, 1901.

Braunfels: Wolfgang Braunfels, *Industrielle Erzbergbau und Eisenhütten in der Frühzeit europäischen Malerei 1500 bis 1850 im Gemälde.* Düsseldorf, 1957.

Briquet: C.M.Briquet, *Les Filigranes. Dictionnaire historique des marques du papier dès leur apparition vers 1282 jusqu'en 1600.* Paris, 1907. 4 vols.

Brown: David Blayney Brown, *Ashmolean Museum Oxford. Catalogue of the Collection of Drawings.* Vol.iv. *The Earlier British Drawings.* Oxford, 1982.

Bruck: R.Bruck, *Das Skizzenbuch von Albrecht Dürer in der Königl. Öffentl. Bibliothek zu Dresden.* Strassburg, 1905.

Buchner, *Beiträge: Beiträge zur Geschichte der deutschen Kunst.* Edited by E.Buchner and K.Feuchtmayr. Augsburg, 1924, 1928. 2 vols.

Budapest Jahrbuch: Az Országos Magyar Szépmüvészeti Múzeum Évkönyvei. Jahrbücher des Museums der bildenden Künste in Budapest. Budapest, 1918–41. Vols.i–x.

Burlington: The Burlington Magazine. London, 1902–.

Bushart, *Holbein:* Bruno Bushart, *Hans Holbein der Ältere.* Augsburg, 1987.

Butts-Mende: Barbara Butts and Matthias Mende, *Hans Süss von Kulmbach: Das Graphische Werk.* Nördlingen (in course of publication).

Byam Shaw: James Byam Shaw, *Drawings by Old Masters at Christ Church, Oxford.* Oxford, 1976. 2 vols.

Chamberlain: Arthur B. Chamberlain, *Hans Holbein the Younger.* London, 1913. 2 vols.

Clarke, *Rhinoceros:* T.H.Clarke, *The Rhinoceros from Dürer to Stubbs 1515–1799.* London, 1986.

Cologne, *Spätgotik: Herbst des Mittelalters. Spätgotik in Köln und am Niederrhein.* Exhib. cat., Cologne, Kunsthalle, 20 June–27 Sept., 1970. Edited by Gert von der Osten and Heribert Meurer.

Collins: Arthur Jefferies Collins, *Jewels and Plate of Queen Elizabeth I: The Inventory of 1574.* Edited from Harley MS.1650 and Stowe MS.555 in the British Museum. London, 1955.

Colvin, *King's Works: The History of the King's Works.* Edited by Howard Colvin. Vol.iv, part ii. London, 1982.

Connoisseur: The Connoisseur. A magazine for collectors. London, 1901–.

Conway: Sir W.M.Conway, *The Art of Albrecht Dürer (1471–1528).* Exhib. cat., Liverpool, Walker Art Gallery, 16 April–11 June, 1910.

Deichsler: *Heinrich Deichsler's Chronik 1488–1506,* in *Die Chroniken der deutschen Städte vom 14. bis ins. 16 Jahrhundert,* vol.ii, *Nürnberg.* Leipzig, 1874.

Demonts, *Louvre:* L.Demonts, *Inventaire Général des Dessins des Écoles du Nord. Écoles Allemande et Suisse.* Paris, 1937/8. 2 vols.

Denison and Mules, *Pierpont Morgan Drawings: European Drawings 1375–1825.* Compiled by Cara B. Denison and Helen B. Mules with the assistance of Jane V. Shoaf. New York, Oxford and Toronto, 1981.

Dodgson: Campbell Dodgson, *Catalogue of Early German and Flemish woodcuts preserved in the Department of Prints and Drawings in the British Museum.* London, vol.1, 1903; vol.2, 1911.

Dodgson, *Dürer Engr.:* Campbell Dodgson, *The Masters of Engraving and Etching. Albrecht Dürer.* London and Boston, 1926.

Dreyer, *Berlin: Ex Bibliotheca Regia Berolinensi. Zeichnungen aus dem ältesten Sammlungsbestand des Berliner Kupferstichkabinetts.* Exhib. cat., Berlin-Dahlem, Kupferstichkabinett, 1982. Edited by Peter Dreyer.

Dublin Master Drawings: Raymond Keaveney, *Master European Drawings from the Collection of the National Gallery of Ireland.* Exhib. cat., organised by the Smithsonian Institution Traveling Exhibition Service, 1983.

Dürer aux Pays-Bas: Fedja Anzelewesky *et al, Albert Dürer aux Pays-Bas: son voyage (1520–1521), son influence.* Exhib. cat., Brussels, Palais des Beaux-Arts, 1 Oct.–27 Nov., 1977.

Dürer Society: The Dürer Society. With introductory notes by Campbell Dodgson, Gustav Pauli and S.Montagu Peatree. London, 1898–1908 and 1911. 12 vols.

Düsseldorf, *UCL Drawings: Aus dem University College London. Handzeichnungen alter Meister.* Exhib. cat., Düsseldorf, Kunstmuseum, 17 March–30 April, 1967. Edited by L.D.Ettlinger and K.Myers.

Dyce Collection: Dyce Collection. A Catalogue of the Paintings, Miniatures, Drawings, Engravings etc. bequeathed by the Reverend Alexander Dyce. London, 1874.

Ehret, *Wertinger:* Gloria Ehret, *Hans Wertinger. Ein Landshuter Maler an der Wende der Spätgotik zur Renaissance.* Munich, 1976.

Ephrussi: Charles Ephrussi, *Albrecht Dürer et ses dessins*. Paris, 1882.

Erler, *Leipzig*: *Die Matrikel der Universität Leipzig*. Edited by Georg Erler. Vol.i, *Die Immatrikulationen von 1409–1559*. Leipzig, 1895.

European Vision of America: Hugh Honour, *The European Vision of America*. Exhib. cat., Washington, National Gallery of Art, 7 Dec. 1975–15 Feb. 1976; The Cleveland Museum of Art, 28 April–8 Aug. 1976; Paris, Grand Palais, 17 Sept. 1976–3 Jan. 1977.

Falk, *Basel*: *Katalog der Zeichnungen des 15. und 16. Jahrhunderts im Kupferstichkabinett Basel*. Edited by Tilman Falk. Vol.i, *Das 15 Jahrhunderts, Hans Holbein der Ältere und Jörg Schweiger, die Basler Goldschmiederisse*. Basel and Stuttgart, 1979.

Falk, *Burgkmair*: Tilman Falk, *Hans Burgkmair. Studien zu Leben und Werk des Augsburger Malers*. Munich, 1968.

Fehring-Ress, *Nuremberg*: Günther P. Fehring and Anton Ress, *Die Stadt Nürnberg*. 2nd edition, edited by Wilhelm Schwemmer. Munich, 1977.

Festschrift O. Pächt: *Kunsthistorisches Forschungen Otto Pächt zu seinem 70. Geburtstag*. Salzburg, 1972.

Festschrift Winkler: *Festschrift Friedrich Winkler*. Edited by Hans Möhle. Berlin, 1959.

Flechsig, *Dürer*: Eduard Flechsig, *Albrecht Dürer. Sein Leben und seine künstlerische Entwicklung*. Berlin, 1928, 1931. 2 vols.

Flechsig, *Schongauer*: Eduard Flechsig, *Martin Schongauer*. Strassburg, 1951.

Fogg Bulletin: *Bulletin of the Fogg Art Museum*. Harvard University, Cambridge. Mass., 1931–.

Fitzwilliam Drawings: Malcolm Cormack and Duncan Robinson, *European Drawings from the Fitzwilliam*. Exhib. cat., organised and circulated by the International Exhibitions Foundation, USA, 1976–7.

Friedländer-Bock: *Handzeichnungen deutscher Meister des 15. und 16. Jahrhunderts*. Edited by Max J. Friedländer and E. Bock. Berlin (n.d.).

Friedländer-Rosenberg: Max J. Friedländer and Jakob Rosenberg, *The Paintings of Lucas Cranach*. London, 1978. (Revised edition of *Die Gemälde von Lucas Cranach*, Berlin, 1932.)

Friedländer, *Weiditz*: Max J. Friedländer, *Holzschnitte von Hans Weiditz*. Berlin, 1922.

Fritz, *Gestochene Bilder*: Johann Michael Fritz, *Gestochene Bilder. Gravierungen auf deutschen Goldschmiede- arbeiten des Spätgotik*. Beihefte der Bonner Jahrbücher, Vol.xx. Cologne and Graz, 1966.

Gantner, *Witz*: Joseph Gantner, *Konrad Witz*. Vienna, 1943, 2nd edition.

Ganz: Paul Ganz, *Die Handzeichnungen Hans Holbein d. J. Kritischer Katalog*. Berlin, 1912–37. Illustrations issued first in 40 parts. Text volume, 1937.

Ganz, *Holbein*: *Hans Holbein d. J. Des Meisters Gemälde*. Edited by Paul Ganz. Stuttgart and Leipzig, 1912.

Gazette: *Gazette des Beaux-Arts*. Paris, 1859–.

Geisberg, *Aldegrever*: Max Geisberg, *Die Münsterischen Wiedertäufer und Aldegrever*. Strassburg, 1907.

Geissler, *Deutsche Zeichner 1540–1640*: Heinrich Geissler, *Zeichnung in Deutschland. Deutsche Zeichner 1540–1640*. Exhib. cat., Stuttgart, Graphische Sammlung, 1 Dec. 1979–17 Feb. 1980. 2 vols.

Gernsheim: Walter Gernsheim, *Corpus Photographicum*. Photographs of drawings in public and private collections. Over 33,000 issued. In progress.

Gesamm. Aufsätze: *Gesammelte Aufsätze zur Kulturgeschichte Spaniens*. Münster, 1928–.

Girshausen: T. L. Girshausen, *Die Handzeichnungen Lucas Cranachs d.Ä.* Dissertation. Frankfurt-am-Main, 1936 (published 1937).

Goris & Marlier: *Albrecht Dürer. Diary of his Journey to the Netherlands 1520–21. Accompanied by the silverpoint sketchbook and paintings and drawings made during his journey*. With an introduction by J-A. Goris and G. Marlier. London, 1971. (English edition).

Graph. Künste: *Die Graphischen Künste*. Vienna, 1879–1933. Neue Folge, 1936–43.

Hackenbroch: Yvonne Hackenbroch, *Renaissance Jewellery*. Munich and New York, 1979.

Haendcke: Berthold Haendcke, *Die Chronologie der Landschaften Albrecht Dürers*, in: *Studien zur deutschen Kunstgeschichte*, Vol.xix. Strassburg, 1899.

Hafnia: *Hafnia. Copenhagen papers in the History of Art*. Copenhagen, 1970–.

Halm, *Deutsche Zeichn.*: Peter Halm, *Deutsche Zeichnungen 1400–1900*. Exhib. cat., Munich, Staatliche Graphische Sammlung, Haus der Kunst, July–Nov., 1956.

Haskell & Penny: Francis Haskell and Nicholas Penny, *Taste and the Antique. The Lure of Classical Sculpture. 1500–1900*. New Haven and London, 1981.

Hausberger: Isolde Hausberger, *Der Meister von Mühldorf, der Maler Wilhelm Pätzsold*. Mühldorf-am-Inn, 1973.

Hausmann: B. Hausmann, *Albrecht Dürer's Kupferstiche, Radierungen, Holzschnitte und Zeichnungen*. Hanover, 1861.

Hausmann, *Naumann's Archiv*: B. Hausmann, 'Die Werke Albrecht Dürers im Print-room des British Museum in London. In *Archiv für die Zeichnenden Künste*, edited by Dr Robert Naumann, iv, Leipzig, 1858, pp. 27–44.

Hayward, *Virtuoso Goldsmiths*: J. F. Hayward, *Virtuoso Goldsmiths and the Triumph of Mannerism 1540–1620*. London, 1976.

Hearne, *Remarks and Collections*: *Remarks and Collections of Thomas Hearne*. Edited by C. E. Doble, D. W. Rannie, H. E. Salter. Oxford, 1885–1921. 11 vols.

Heller: Joseph Heller, *Das Leben und die Werke Albrecht Dürer's*. Bamberg, 1827. Vol.2. (Vol.1 was not published).

Henkel-Schöne: *Emblemata. Handbuch zur Sinnbildkunst des XVI. and XVII. Jahrhunderts*. Edited by Arthur Henkel and Albrecht Schöne. Stuttgart, 1967.

Hind, *Early Italian Engraving*: Arthur M. Hind, *Early Italian Engraving. A critical catalogue with complete reproduction of all the prints described*. London, 1938, 1948. 7 vols.

Hind, *Introduction*: Arthur M. Hind, *An Introduction to the History of Woodcut*. London, 1935. 2 vols.

Hind, *Select List*: Arthur M. Hind, *Select List of Prints and Drawings in University College, London*. London, 1930.

His: Édouard His, *Dessins d'Ornements de Hans Holbein*. Paris, 1866.

Hollstein: F. W. H. Hollstein, *German Engravings, Etchings, and Woodcuts, c.1400–1700*. Amsterdam, 1954–.

Hugelshofer, *Schweizer Handz*: Walter Hugelshofer, *Schweizer Handzeichnungen des XV. and XVI. Jahrhunderts. Die Meisterzeichnung*. Vol.i. Freiburg-im-Breisgau and London, 1928.

Israhel van Meckenem: *Israhel van Meckenem und der deutsche Kupferstich des 15. Jahrhunderts*. Exhib. cat., Bocholt, Kunsthaus der Stadt Bocholt, May–June, 1972. Edited by Elisabeth Bröker.

James: Montague Rhodes James, *A descriptive catalogue of the manuscripts in the Library of Eton College*. Cambridge, 1895.

JCR: J. C. Robinson, *Descriptive Catalogue of Drawings by the Old Masters forming the collection of John Malcolm of Poltalloch, Esq.* London, 1876. 2nd edition.

Karlsruhe, *Altdeutsche Zeichn.*: *Altdeutsche Zeichnungen aus der Staatlichen Kunsthalle Karlsruhe.* Edited by Kurt Martin. Baden-Baden, 1955.

Karlsruhe, *Alte Meister*: *Staatliche Kunsthalle Karlsruhe. Katalog alte Meister bis 1800.* Edited by Jan Lauts. Karlsruhe, 1966.

Karlsruhe, *Baldung*: *Hans Baldung Grien.* Exhib. cat., Karlsruhe, Staatliche Kunsthalle, 4 July–27 Sept., 1959. Edited by Jan Lauts. 2nd edition.

Knappe, *Bamberger Fenster*: Karl-Adolf Knappe, *Albrecht Dürer und das Bamberger Fenster in St Sebald in Nürnberg.* Nuremberg, 1961.

Kniga i Grafika: *Kniga i Grafika.* Volume of articles published on the occasion of the 80th birthday of A.A. Sidorov. Compiled by E.V. Vengerova-Ziling. Moscow, 1972.

Koch: Carl Koch, *Die Zeichnungen Hans Baldung Griens.* Berlin, 1941.

Koepf, *Planrisse*: Hans Koepf, *Die gotischen Planrisse der Ulmer Sammlungen.* Ulm, 1977.

Kohlhaussen: Heinrich Kohlhaussen, *Nürnberger Goldschmiedekunst des Mittelalters und der Dürerzeit, 1240 bis 1540.* Berlin, 1968.

Koreny, *Tier- und Pflanzenstudien*: Fritz Koreny, *Albrecht Dürer und die Tier- und Pflanzenstudien der Renaissance.* Exhib. cat., Vienna, Albertina, 18 April–30 June, 1985.

Koschatzky: Walter Koschatzky, *Albrecht Dürer. Die Landschaftsaquarelle.* Vienna and Munich, 1971.

Kreis Unna, *Aldegrever*: Karl Bernd Heppe, *Heinrich Aldegrever. Die Kleinmeister und das Kunsthandwerk der Renaissance.* Exhib. cat., Kreis Unna, Ev. Stadtkirche Unna, 30 Sept.–2 Nov., 1986.

Kuhrmann, *Erlangen*: Dieter Kuhrmann, *Altdeutsche Zeichnungen aus der Universitätsbibliothek Erlangen.* Exhib. cat., Munich, Staatliche Graphische Sammlung, 7 June–28 July, 1974.

Kunstchronik: *Kunstchronik.* Munich, 1948–.

Kunstgesch. Anz.: *Kunstgeschichtliche Anzeigen: Beiblatt der 'Mitteilungen des Instituts für österreichische Geschichtsforschung'.* Innsbruck, 1904–7, 1909–13.

Kunstmuseets Aarsskrift: *Kunstmuseets Aarsskrift.* Copenhagen, 1914–.

Kurth: Willy Kurth, *The Complete Woodcuts of Albrecht Dürer.* London, 1927. (Paperback edition first printed 1963.)

L. and L. *Suppl.*: Frits Lugt, *Les marques de collections de dessins et d'estampes.* Amsterdam, 1921; *Supplément.* The Hague, 1956.

Landau, *Pencz*: *Catalogo completo dell'opera grafica di Georg Pencz.* Edited by David Landau. Milan, 1978.

LB: Lawrence Binyon, *Catalogue of Drawings by British Artists and Artists of Foreign Origin working in Great Britain, preserved in the Department of Prints and Drawings in the British Museum.* London, 1898–1907. 4 vols.

Lehrs: Max Lehrs, *Geschichte und kritischer Katalog des deutschen, niederlandischen und französischen Kupferstichs im XV Jahrhunderts.* Vienna, 1908–34. 9 vols.

Lexikon der christ. Ikonog.: *Lexikon der christlichen Ikonographie.* Edited by Engelbert Kirschbaum *et al.* Rome, 1968–76. 8 vols.

Lieb–Stange: Norbert Lieb and Alfred Stange, *Hans Holbein der Ältere.* Munich, 1960.

Linz, *Donauschule*: *Der Kunst der Donauschule 1490–1540, Malerei Graphik Plastik Architektur.* Exhib. cat., Stift St. Florian and Schlossmuseum, Linz, 14 May–17 Oct., 1965. Edited by Fritz Dworschak *et al.*

Lippmann: Friedrich Lippmann *et al.*, *Zeichnungen von Albrecht Dürer in Nachbildungen.* Berlin, 1883–1929. 7 vols.

Lloyd, *Ashmolean Drawings*: Christopher Lloyd, *Dürer to Cézanne: Northern European Drawings from the Ashmolean Museum.* Exhib. cat., New Brunswick, The Jane Vorhees Zimmerli Art Museum, 12 Sept.–24 Oct., 1982; Cleveland, The Cleveland Museum of Art, 16 Nov. 1982–2 Jan. 1983.

Lugt, *Bibl. Nat.*: Frits Lugt and J. Vallery Radot, *Bibliothèque Nationale Cabinet des Estampes. Inventaire général des dessins des écoles du nord.* Paris, 1936.

Lutze & Wiegand: *Kataloge des Germanischen Nationalmuseums zu Nürnberg. Die Gemälde des 13–16. Jahrhunderts.* Edited by Eberhard Lutze and Eberhard Wiegand. Nuremberg, 1936.

Manchester, *European Art*: F.G. Grossmann, *Between Renaissance and Baroque. European Art 1520–1600.* Exhib. cat., Manchester, City Art Gallery, 10 March–6 April, 1965.

Manchester, *German Art*: F.G. Grossman, *German Art 1400–1800 from collections in Great Britain.* Exhib. cat., Manchester, City Art Gallery, 24 Oct.–10 Dec., 1961.

Mann, *Arms and Armour*: Sir James Mann, *Wallace Collection Catalogues. European Arms and Armour. Text with historical notes and illustrations.* Vol.ii, *Arms.* London, 1962.

Mayor Collection: *A Brief Chronological Description of a Collection of Original Drawings and Sketches by the most celebrated Masters, formed by and belonging to Mr Mayor.* London, 1871. 2nd edition, London, 1874.

Mayor Collection 1875: *A Brief Chronological Description of a Collection of Original Drawings and Sketches by the Old Masters, formed by the late Mr William Mayor.* London, 1875.

Major & Gradman, *Graf*: Emil Major and Erwin Gradman, *Urs Graf.* Basel, 1946.

MD: *Master Drawings.* New York, 1963–.

Meder, *Dürer*: Joseph Meder, *Dürer-Katalog. Ein Handbuch über Albrecht Dürers Stiche, Radierungen, Holzschnitte, deren Zustände, Ausgaben und Wasserzeichen.* Vienna, 1932.

Meissner: *Allgemeines Künstler-Lexikon. Die bildenden Künstler aller Zeiten und Völker.* Edited by Günter Meissner. Leipzig, 1983–.

Meister um Dürer: *Meister um Albrecht Dürer.* Exhib. cat., Nuremberg, Germanisches Nationalmuseum. 4 July–17 Sept., 1961. Edited by Peter Strieder *et al.*

Meller, *Vischer*: Simon Meller, *Peter Vischer der Ältere und seine Werkstatt.* Leipzig, 1925.

Mende, *Baldung*: Matthias Mende, *Hans Baldung Grien. Das Graphische Werk. Vollständiger Bildkatalog der Einzelholzschitte, Buchillustrationen und Kupferstiche.* Unterschneidheim, 1978.

Mende, *Dürer-Bibliographie*: Matthias Mende, *Dürer-Bibliographie zur fünfhundertsten Wiederkehr des Geburtstages von Albrecht Dürer.* Wiesbaden, 1971.

Metz, *Imitations*: C.M. Metz, *Imitations of Ancient and Modern Drawings from the Restoration of the Arts in Italy to the Present Time,* 1st edition 1789, 2nd edition 1798.

Mitt. Kunst: *Mitteilungen der Gesellschaft für vervielfältigende Kunst. Beilage der 'Graphischen Künste'.* Vienna, 1901–33.

Mitt. Nuremberg: *Mittelungen des Vereins für Geschichte der Stadt Nürnberg.* Nuremberg, 1879–.

Monatshefte: *Monatshefte für Kunstwissenschaft.* Leipzig, 1908–22.

Müller: Theodor Müller, *Sculpture in the Netherlands, Germany, France and Spain 1400–1500.* Harmondsworth, 1966.

Münster, *Aldegrever*: *Heinrich Aldegrever und die Bildnisse der Wiedertäufer.* Exhib. cat., Münster, Westfalisches Landesmuseum für Kunst und Kulturgeschichte, 5 May–17 June, 1985. Edited by Jochen Luckhardt *et al.*

Münster, *Wiedertäufer*: *Die Wiedertäufer in Münster.* Exhib. cat., Münster, Stadtmuseum, 1 Oct. 1982–30 Jan. 1983. Edited by Hans Galen.

Munich, *Dürer:* Dieter Kuhrmann, *Dürer und seine Zeit. Zeichnungen und Aquarelle aus den Sammlungen Biblioteca Ambrosiana Mailand, Bayerische Staatsbibliothek Graphische Sammlung München.* Exhib. cat., Munich, Staatliche Graphische Sammlung, 14 Nov. 1967–14 Jan. 1968.

Munich, *Gemälde Köln:* Bayerische Staatsgemäldesammlungen. *Alte Pinakothek München. Altdeutsche Gemälde Köln und Nordwestdeutschland. Vollständiger Katalog.* Edited by Gisela Goldberg und Gisela Scheffler. Munich, 1972. 2 vols.

Munich Jahrbuch: Münchner Jahrbuch der bildenden Kunst. Munich i–xiii: 1906–23; Neue Folge i–xiii, 1924–39; 3rd series i, 1950–.

Musper, *Petrarkameister:* Theodor Musper, *Die Holzschnitte des Petrarkameisters. Ein kritisches Verzeichnis mit Einleitung und 28 Abbildungen.* Munich, 1927.

N.A-C.F. Report: The National Art-Collections Fund Annual Reports. London, 1903–.

Nagler, *Monogr.:* G.K.Nagler, *Die Monogrammisten.* Munich, 1858–79. 5 vols.

Ned. Kunst. Jaarb.: Nederlands(ch) Kunsthistorisch Jaarboek. The Hague, 1947–. Bussum, vol.5, 1954–. Haarlem, vol.27, 1976–.

Neudörfer, *Nachrichten:* Des Johann Neudörfer Schreib- und Rechenmeisters zu Nürnberg Nachrichten von Künstlern und Werkleuten daselbst aus dem Jahre 1547 nebst der Fortsetzung des Andreas Gulden nach den Handschriften und mit Anmerkungen. Edited by Dr G.W.K.Lochner. Vienna, 1875.

NPG, *More:* J.B.Trapp and H.S.Herbrüggen, 'The King's Good Servant, Sir Thomas More 1477/8–1535'. Exhib. cat., London, National Portrait Gallery, 25 Nov. 1977–12 March 1978.

Nuremberg, *Dürer,* 1928: Dr Fries, *Albrecht Dürer Austellung im Germanischen Museum.* Nuremberg, April–Sept., 1928.

Nuremberg, *Dürer,* 1971: *1471 Albrecht Dürer 1971.* Exhib. cat., Nuremberg, Germanisches Nationalmuseum, 21 May–1 Aug., 1971. Edited by Leonie von Wilckens.

Nuremberg, *Gothic & Renaissance: Gothic and Renaissance Art in Nuremberg 1300–1550.* Exhib. cat., New York, The Metropolitan Museum of Art, 8 April–22 June, 1986; Nuremberg, Germanisches Nationalmuseum, 24 July–28 Sept., 1986. Rainer Kahsnitz, William D. Wixom *et al.*

Obach & Co., *Old Master Drawings: Catalogue of Drawings by Old Masters.* Exhibited by Messrs. Obach & Co. in their Galleries, 168 New Bond Street. Nov.–Dec., 1908.

Oberrheinische Kunst: Oberrheinische Kunst. Freiburg-im-Breisgau, 1925–.

Oettinger, *Altdorfer-Studien:* Karl Oettinger, *Altdorfer-Studien.* Nuremberg, 1959.

Oettinger–Knappe: Karl Oettinger and Karl-Adolf Knappe, *Hans Baldung Grien und Albrecht Dürer in Nürnberg.* Nuremberg, 1963.

Oettinger, *Tübingen:* Karl Oettinger, *Hans von Tübingen und seine Schule.* Berlin, 1938.

Oldenbourg, *Hortulus Animae:* M. Consuelo Oldenbourg, *Hortulus animae [1494]–1523. Bibliographie und Illustration.* Hamburg, 1973.

Oldenbourg, *Schäufelein:* M. Consuelo Oldenbourg, *Die Buchholzschnitte des Hans Schäufelein. Ein bibliographisches Verzeichnis ihrer Verwendungen.* Baden-Baden and Strassburg, 1964.

OMD: Old Master Drawings. A Quarterly Magazine for Students and Collectors. Vols.i–xiv. London, 1926–40.

Osten, *Baldung:* Gert von der Osten, *Hans Baldung Grien, Gemälde und Dokumente.* Berlin, 1983.

Otto, *Strigel:* Gertrud Otto, *Bernhard Strigel.* Munich and Berlin, 1964.

Panofsky: Erwin Panofsky, *Albrecht Dürer.* London and Princeton, 2nd revised edition, 1945. 2 vols.

Pantheon: Pantheon Monatsschrifte für Freunde und Sammler. Munich, 1928–August 1939; 1960–.

Paris, *École des Beaux-Arts:* Emmanuelle Brugerolles, *Renaissance et Maniérisme dans les Écoles du Nord. Dessins des collections de l'École des Beaux-Arts.* Exhib. cat., Paris, École nationale supérieure des Beaux-Arts. 16 Oct.–16 Dec., 1985; Hamburg Kunsthalle, 16 May–29 June, 1986.

Paris, *Mariette:* Roseline Bacou *et al*, *Le Cabinet d'un Grand Amateur P-J. Mariette 1694–1774. Dessins du XVe siècle au XVIIIe siècle.* Exhib. cat., Paris, Musée du Louvre, 1967.

Parker: Karl T. Parker, *The Drawings of Hans Holbein in the Collection of His Majesty the King at Windsor Castle.* Oxford and London, 1945. 2nd edition, Johnson reprint, with an appendix to the catalogue by Susan Foister, London and New York, 1983.

Parker, *Alsatian Drawings:* Karl T. Parker, *Alsatian Drawings of the XV and XVI century. Die Meisterzeichnung.* Vol.ii. London and Freiburg-im-Breisgau, 1928.

Parker, *Ashmolean:* Karl T. Parker, *Catalogue of the collection of Drawings in the Ashmolean Museum.* Vol.I *Netherlandish, German, French and Spanish Schools.* Oxford, 1938.

Parker, *German Schools:* Karl T. Parker, *Drawings of the Early German Schools.* London, 1926.

Passau, *Huber: Wolf Huber Gedächtnisausstellung zum 400 Todesjahr.* Exhib. cat., Passau, 14 Aug.–6 Sept., 1953. Edited by Karl Busch and Peter Halm.

Pauli: Gustav Pauli, *Die Kunst Albrecht Dürers. Seine Werke in Originalen und Reproduktionen geordnet nach der Zeitfolge ihrer Entstehung.* Exhib. cat., Bremen, Kunsthalle, Oct., 1911.

Pennington: Richard Pennington, *A descriptive catalogue of the etched work of Wenceslaus Hollar 1607–1677.* Cambridge, 1982.

Pérignon, *Description:* A.N.Pérignon, *Description des Objets d'Arts qui composent le Cabinet de feu M. Le Baron V.Denon, Tableaux Dessins et Miniatures.* Paris, 1826.

Piccard: *Die Wasserzeichenkartei Piccard im Hauptstaatsarchiv Stuttgart.* Edited by Gerhard Piccard. Stuttgart, 1961–.

Pictures for Scotland: Colin Thompson, *Pictures for Scotland. The National Gallery of Scotland and its collection: a study of the changing attitude to painting since the 1820s.* Edinburgh, 1972.

Popham, *Fenwick:* A.E.Popham, *Catalogue of Drawings in the Collection formed by Sir Thomas Phillipps, Bart. F.R.S. now in the possession of his grandson, T.Fitzroy Phillipps Fenwick of Thirlestaine House, Cheltenham.* Privately printed, 1935.

Print Quarterly: Print Quarterly. London, 1984–.

Prussian Jahrbuch: Jahrbuch der Königlich Preussischen Kunstsammlungen. Berlin, 1880–1943 (from 1919 *Königlich* is omitted). 64 vols.

R.A. 1950–51: Ellis K.Waterhouse *et al*, *Catalogue of the Exhibition of Works by Holbein & other Masters of the 16th and 17th century.* Exhib. cat., London, Royal Academy of Arts, 9 Dec., 1950–7 March, 1951.

R.A. 1953: *Drawings by Old Masters.* Exhib. cat., London, Royal Academy, 13 Aug.–25 Oct., 1953.

R.A. *British Portraits: British Portraits.* Exhib. cat., London, Royal Academy of Arts. Winter Exhibition, 1956–7.

Rauch: Christian Rauch, *Die Trauts.* Strassburg, 1907.

Regensburger Buchmalerei: Regensburger Buchmalerei. Von frühkarolingischer Zeit bis zum Ausgang des Mittelalters. Exhib. cat., Regensburg, 16 May–9 Aug., 1987. Edited by Florentine Mütherich and Karl Dachs.

Reid: G.W.Reid, *Designs for Goldsmiths, Jewellers etc. by Hans Holbein. Twenty Photographs from the Original Drawings in the British Museum.* London, 1869.

Repertorium: *Repertorium für Kunstwissenschaft.* Berlin, 1876–1931.

Rettich, *Strigel:* Edeltraud Rettich, *Bernhard Strigel Herkunft und Entfaltung seines Stils.* Doctoral dissertation, Albert-Ludwigs-Universität, Freiburg-im-Breisgau, 1965.

Riggenbach: Rudolf Riggenbach, *Der Maler und Zeichner Wolfgang Huber (ca.1490–nach 1542).* Doctoral dissertation, Basel, 1907.

Roberts, *Holbein:* Jane Roberts, *Drawings by Holbein from the court of Henry VIII. Fifty drawings from the Collection of Her Majesty Queen Elizabeth II, Windsor Castle.* Exhib. cat., Houston, The Museum of Fine Arts, 17 May–16 Aug., 1987.

Röttinger, *Doppelgänger:* Heinrich Röttinger, *Dürers Doppelgänger.* Strassburg, 1926.

Rose, *Huber:* Patricia Rose, *Wolf Huber Studies: aspects of Renaissance thought and practice in Danube School Painting.* New York and London, 1977.

Rosenberg: Jakob Rosenberg, *Die Zeichnungen Lucas Cranachs d.Ä.* Berlin, 1960.

Rosenberg, *Schongauer:* *Martin Schongauer Handzeichnungen.* Edited by Jakob Rosenberg. Munich, 1923.

Rotterdam, *Erasmus:* *Erasmus en zijn tijd.* Exhib. cat., Rotterdam, Museum Boymans-van Beuningen, 3 Oct.–23 Nov., 1969. 2 vols.

Rowlands, *Dürer:* John Rowlands, *The Graphic Work of Albrecht Dürer. An Exhibition of Drawings and Prints in Commemoration of the Quincentenary of his Birth.* Exhib. cat., London, The British Museum, 1971.

Rowlands, *Holbein:* John Rowlands, *Holbein. The paintings of Hans Holbein the Younger. Complete edition.* Oxford, 1985.

Rowlands, *Private Collection:* John Rowlands, *German Drawings from a private collection.* Exhib. cat., London, The British Museum, 9 Feb.–29 April, 1984; Washington, National Gallery of Art, 27 May–8 July, 1984; Nuremberg, Germanisches Nationalmuseum, 2 Aug.–23 Sept., 1984.

Rowlands, *Rubens:* John Rowlands, *Rubens Drawings and Sketches.* Exhib. cat., London, The British Museum, 1977.

Rücker, *Weltchronik:* Elisabeth Rücker, *Die Schedelsche Weltchronik. Das grösste Buchunternehmen der Dürer-Zeit. Mit einen Katalog der Städteansichten.* Munich, 1973.

Ruhmer, *Grünewald:* Eberhard Ruhmer, *Grünewald Drawings. Complete Edition.* London, 1970.

Rupprich: *Dürer. Schriftlicher Nachlass.* Edited by Hans Rupprich. Berlin, 1956, 1966 and 1969. 3 vols.

Sandrart, *Teutsche Academie:* *Joachim von Sandrarts Academie der Bau-Bild und Mahlerey-Künste von 1675. Leben der berühmten Maler, Bildhauer und Baumeister.* Edited by A.R.Peltzer. Munich, 1925.

Schade, *Cranach:* Werner Schade, *Die Malerfamilie Cranach.* Dresden, 1974.

Schallaburg, *Polen:* *Polen im Zeitalter der Jagiellonen 1386–1572.* Exhib. cat., Schloss Schallaburg, 8 May–2 Nov., 1986. Edited by Franciszek Stolot *et al.*

Schilling, *Gesamm. Zeichn.:* *Die von Edmund Schilling gesammelten Zeichnungen.* Edited by Rosi Schilling. Private publication, 1982.

Schilling, *Holbein:* Edmund Schilling, *Drawings by the Holbein Family.* New York and Basel, 1955.

Schilling, *Nürnberger Handz.:* Edmund Schilling, *Nürnberger Handzeichnungen des XV. und XVI. Jahrhunderts. Die Meisterzeichnung.* Vol.iii. Freiburg-im-Breisgau and London, 1929.

Schilling, *Sketchbook:* *Albrecht Dürer: Sketchbook of the Journey to the Netherlands (1520–21).* Edited by Edmund Schilling. 2nd revised edition. London, 1968.

Schmid, *Grünewald:* *Die Gemälde und Zeichnungen von Matthias Grünewald.* Edited by Heinrich Alfred Schmid. Strassburg, 1911. 2 vols.

Schmid, *Holbein:* Heinrich Alfred Schmid, *Hans Holbein der Jüngere: sein Aufstieg zur Meisterschaft und sein englischer Stil.* Basel, 1945, 1948. 3 vols.

Schmidt: *Handzeichnungen alter Meister im Königlichen Kupferstichkabinett zu München.* Edited by Dr W.Schmidt, Munich, 1884–1900. 9 vols.

Schneider, *Schweizerdolch:* Hugo Schneider, *Der Schweizerdolch. Waffen- und Kulturgeschichtliche Entwicklung mit vollständiger Dokumentation der bekannten Originale und Kopien.* Zürich, 1977.

Schoenberger, *Grünewald:* *The drawings of Mathius Gothart Nithart called Gruenewald.* Edited by Guido Schoenberger. New York, 1948.

Schönbrunner–Meder: *Handzeichnungen alter Meister aus der Albertina und anderen Sammlungen.* Edited by J.Schönbrunner, i–x, and J.Meder, xi–xii. Vienna, 1896–1908. 12 vols.

Schubert, *Mair von Landshut:* Franz Schubert, *Mair von Landshut. Ein niederbayerischer Stecher und Maler des ausgehenden XV Jahrhunderts.* Dresden, 1930.

Stadler, *Kulmbach:* Franz Stadler, *Hans von Kulmbach.* Vienna, 1936.

Stadtresidenz Landshut: *Stadtresidenz Landshut. Stadt und Kreis-Museum. Amtlicher Führer.* Edited by Hans Thoma *et al.* Munich, 1985.

Städel-Jahrbuch: *Städel-Jahrbuch.* Frankfurt-am-Main, 1921–.

Stafski, *Vischer:* Heinz Stafski, *Der Jüngere Peter Vischer.* Nuremberg, 1962.

Stange: Alfred Stange, *Deutsche Malerei der Gotik.* Berlin and Munich, 1934–61. 11 vols.

Stange, *Tafelbilder:* Alfred Stange, *Die deutschen Tafelbilder vor Dürer.* Munich, 1967, 1970, 1978. 3 vols.

Steingräber, *Buchmalerei:* Erich Steingräber, *Die kirchliche Buchmalerei Augsburgs um 1500.* Augsburg and Basel, 1956.

Strauss: Walter L. Strauss, *The Complete Drawings of Albrecht Dürer.* New York, 1974. 6 vols.

Studien f. K.Bauch: *Kunstgeschichtliche Studien für Kurt Bauch zur 70. Geburtstag von seinen Schülern.* Edited by Margrit Lisner and Rüdiger Becksmann. Munich and Berlin, 1967.

Stumm: Lucie Stumm, *Niklaus Manuel Deutsch von Bern. Als bildender Künstler.* Bern, 1925.

Swarzenski & Schilling, *Privatbesitz:* Edmund Schilling, *Handzeichnungen alter Meister aus deutschem Privatbesitz.* Edited by Georg Swarzenski. Frankfurt-am-Main, 1924.

Térey: G. von Térey, *Die Handzeichnungen des Hans Baldung genannt Grien.* Strassburg, 1894–96. 3 vols.

Thausing: Moriz Thausing, *Albrecht Dürer. His Life and Works.* Edited by Fred A. Eaton. London, 1882. 2 vols.

Thieme–Becker: *Allgemeines Lexikon der bildenden Künstler von der Antike bis zur Gegenwart.* Edited by Ulrich Thieme and Felix Becker. Leipzig 1907–50. 37 vols.

Thöne, *Cranach:* Friedrich Thöne, *Lucas Cranach d.Ä. Meisterzeichnungen.* Burg bei Magdeburg, 1939.

Tietze: Hans Tietze and Erika Tietze-Conrat, *Kritisches Verzeichnis der Werke Albrecht Dürers.* Vol.1, *Der junge Dürer.* Augsburg, 1928; vol.2, *Der reife Dürer,* Erster Halbband, Basel and Leipzig, 1937; vol.3, Zweiter Halbband, Basel and Leipzig, 1938. The addition of an A or W refers respectively to the catalogue of *Ausgeschiedene Arbeiten* (unacceptable works) and *Werkstattarbeiten* (studio works).

Tudor Exhibition, 1890: *Exhibition of the Royal House of Tudor.* London, New Gallery, 1890.

Umění: *Umění. Sborník pro českou výtvarnou práci.* Prague, 1918–.

VAM, *Court Jewels: Princely Magnificence. Court Jewels of the Renaissance.* Exhib. cat., London, The Victoria and Albert Museum, 15 Oct. 1980–1 Feb. 1981. Edited by Anna Somers Cocks.

VAM, *Technique & Purpose:* Susan Lambert, *Drawing. Technique and Purpose.* Exhib. cat., London, The Victoria and Albert Museum, 28 Jan.–26 April, 1981.

Vasari Society: The Vasari Society for the Reproduction of Drawings by Old Masters. Parts i–ix, London, 1905–15; 2nd series, part i–xvi, London, 1920–35.

Veth & Muller: J. Veth and S. Muller, *Albrecht Dürers Niederländische Reise.* Berlin and Utrecht, 1918. 2 vols.

Vienna, L'Art Européen vers 1400: L'Art Européen vers 1400. Exhib. cat., organised by the Council of Europe, Vienna, Kunsthistorisches Museum, 7 May–31 July, 1962.

Vienna Jahrbuch: Jahrbuch der Kunsthistorischen Sammlungen des allerhöchsten Kaiserhauses. Vienna, 1883–1918. *Jahrbuch der Kunsthistorischen Sammlungen in Wien.* Vienna, 1919–.

Waagen, *Treasures* and Waagen, *Treasures Suppl.:* Dr Waagen, *Treasures of Art in Great Britain.* London, 1854. 3 vols. *Galleries and Cabinets of Art in Great Britain, forming a supplemental volume to the Treasures of Art.* London, 1857.

Wallraf Jahrbuch: Wallraf-Richartz Jahrbuch. Cologne from 1924. 1925–7 published in Leipzig. Neue Folge, 1930–.

Walpole Society: The Walpole Society. Oxford, 1912–.

Warburg Journal: Journal of the Warburg Institute. London, 1937–9. *Journal of the Warburg and Courtauld Institutes.* London, 1940–.

Washington, *Albertina: Old Master Drawings from the Albertina.* Exhib. cat., circulated by the International Exhibitions Foundation, Washington D.C., National Gallery of Art, 28 Oct. 1984–13 Jan. 1985; New York, The Pierpont Morgan Library, 8 March–26 May, 1985. Edited by Ilse Goffitzer.

Weihrauch: *Bayerisches Nationalmuseum München. Kataloge.* Vol. xiii, 5. *Die Bildwerke in Bronze und in anderen Metallen.* Edited by Hans R. Weihrauch. Munich, 1956.

Weinberger, *Huber:* Martin Weinberger, *Wolfgang Huber.* Leipzig, 1935.

Weisbach, *Junge Dürer:* Werner Weisbach, *Der Junge Dürer: Drei Studien.* Leipzig, 1906.

White: Edward Croft-Murray & Paul Hulton, *Catalogue of British Drawings.* Vol. i: *XVI and XVII centuries. Supplemented by a list of foreign artists' drawings connected with Great Britain,* by Christopher White. London, 1960. 2 vols.

Wilson, *Nuremberg Chronicle:* Adrian Wilson, *The Making of the Nuremberg Chronicle.* Amsterdam, 1976.

Winkler, *Dürer:* Friedrich Winkler, *Die Zeichnungen Albrecht Dürer.* Berlin, 1936–9. 4 vols.

Winkler, K&S: Friedrich Winkler, *Die Zeichnungen Hans Süss von Kulmbachs und Hans Leonhard Schäufeleins.* Berlin, 1942.

Winkler, *Kulmbach:* Friedrich Winkler, *Hans von Kulmbach. Leben und Werk eines fränkischen Künstlers der Dürerzeit.* Kulmbach, 1959.

Winkler, *Leben:* Friedrich Winkler, *Albrecht Dürer: Leben und Werk.* Berlin, 1957.

Winzinger, *Altdorfer:* Franz Winzinger, *Albrecht Altdorfer Zeichnungen. Gesamtausgabe.* Munich, 1952.

Winzinger, *Huber:* Franz Winzinger, *Wolf Huber: das Gesamtwerk.* Munich, 1979. 2 vols.

Winzinger, *Schongauer:* Franz Winzinger, *Die Zeichnungen Martin Schongauers.* Berlin, 1962.

Wölfflin, *Handz.:* Heinrich Wölfflin, *Albrecht Dürer Handzeichnungen.* Munich, 1914.

Woermann, *Dresden: Handzeichnungen alter Meister in Königlichen Kupferstichkabinett zu Dresden.* Edited by Karl Woermann. Munich, 1896–8. 10 vols.

Woltmann: Alfred Woltmann, *Holbein und seine Zeit. Des Künstlers Familie, Leben und Schaffen.* Leipzig, 1874, 1876. 2 vols. 2nd revised edition.

Woodward: John Woodward, *Tudor and Stuart Drawings.* London, 1951.

Wornum, *Holbein:* Ralph Nicholson Wornum, *Some Account of the Life and Works of Hans Holbein, Painter, of Augsburg.* London, 1867.

Woodner Coll. 1987: *Master Drawings. The Woodner Collection.* Exhib. cat., London, Royal Academy of Art, 1987. Edited by Jane Shoaf Turner.

Yale, *Baldung: Hans Baldung Grien. Prints and Drawings.* Exhib. cat., Washington, D.C., National Gallery of Art, 25 Jan.–5 April, 1981; New Haven, Yale University Art Gallery, 23 April–14 June, 1981. Edited by James H. Marrow and Alan Shestack.

Yale, *Danube School: Prints and Drawings of the Danube School.* Exhib. cat., New Haven, Yale University Art Gallery, 9 Oct.–16 Nov. 1969; St Louis, City Art Museum, 11 Dec. 1969–25 Jan. 1970; Philadelphia, Museum of Art, 10 Feb.–24 March, 1970. Edited by Alan Shestack and Charles Talbot.

Zeitschr. f. bild. Kunst: Zeitschrift für bildende Kunst. Leipzig, 1869–1932.

Zeitschr. f. christ. Kunst: Zeitschrift für christliche Kunst. Düsseldorf, 1888–1921.

Zeitschr. f. Kunstgesch.: Zeitschrift für Kunstgeschichte. Neue Folge von Repertorium für Kunstwissenschaft, Zeitschrift für bildende Kunst, Jahrbuch für Kunstwissenschaft. Berlin and Leipzig, 1932–.

Zeitschr. f. Kunstwiss.: Zeitschrift des Deutschen Vereins für Kunstwissenschaft. Berlin, 1934–40; 1943; 1947– (from 1947–62 known as *Zeitschrift für Kunstwissenschaft;* from 1963 – original title resumed).

Zeitschr. f. schweiz. Arch.: See: *Anz.*

Zeitschr. Oberrheins: Zeitschrift für die Geschichte des Oberrheins. Karlsruhe 1850–85. Freiburg-im-Breisgau, neue Folge, 1886; Karlsruhe, 1893–.

Zink: *Kataloge des Germanischen Nationalmuseums. Die deutschen Handzeichnungen.* Vol. i. *Die Handzeichnungen bis zur Mitte des 16. Jahrhunderts.* Edited by Fritz Zink. Nuremberg, 1968.

Zschelletzschky, *Aldegrever:* Herbert Zschelletzschky, *Das graphische Werk Heinrich Aldegrevers. Ein Beitrag zu seinem Stil im Rahmen der deutschen Stilentwicklung.* Strassburg, 1933.

Zschelletzschky: Herbert Zschelletzschky, *Die drei gottlosen Maler von Nürnberg: Sebald Beham, Barthel Beham und Georg Pencz, historische Grundlagen und ikonologische Probleme ihrer Graphik zu Reformations- und Bauernkriegszeit.* Leipzig, 1975.

Index of Artists